Models and Methods in Social Network Analysis

Models and Methods in Social Network Analysis presents the most important developments in quantitative models and methods for analyzing social network data that have appeared during the 1990s. Intended as a complement to Wasserman and Faust's *Social Network Analysis: Methods and Applications*, it is a collection of original articles by leading methodologists reviewing recent advances in their particular areas of network methods. Reviewed are advances in network measurement, network sampling, the analysis of centrality, positional analysis or blockmodeling, the analysis of diffusion through networks, the analysis of affiliation or "two-mode" networks, the theory of random graphs, dependence graphs, exponential families of random graphs, the analysis of longitudinal network data, graphic techniques for exploring network data, and software for the analysis of social networks.

Peter J. Carrington is Professor of Sociology at the University of Waterloo and Editor of the *Canadian Journal of Criminology and Criminal Justice*. His main teaching and research interests are in the criminal and juvenile justice systems, social networks, and research methods and statistics. He has published articles in the *Canadian Journal of Criminology and Criminal Justice, American Journal of Psychiatry, Journal of Mathematical Sociology*, and *Social Networks*. He is currently doing research on police discretion, criminal and delinquent careers and networks, and the impact of the Youth Criminal Justice Act on the youth justice system in Canada.

John Scott is Professor of Sociology at the University of Essex. An active member of the British Sociological Association, he served as its president from 2001 until 2003. He has written more than fifteen books, including *Corporate Business and Capitalist Classes* (1997), *Social Network Analysis* (1991 and 2000), *Sociological Theory* (1995), and *Power* (2001). With James Fulcher, he is the author of the leading introductory textbook *Sociology* (1999 and 2003). He is a member of the Editorial Board of the *British Journal of Sociology* and is an Academician of the Academy of Learned Societies in the Social Sciences.

Stanley Wasserman is Rudy Professor of Sociology, Psychology, and Statistics at Indiana University. He has done research on methodology for social networks for thirty years. He has co-authored with Katherine Faust *Social Network Analysis: Methods and Applications*, published in 1994 in this series by Cambridge University Press, and has co-edited with Joseph Galaskiewicz *Social Network Analysis: Research in the Social and Behavioral Sciences* (1994). His work is recognized by statisticians, as well as social and behavioral scientists, worldwide. He is currently Book Review Editor of *Chance* and an Associate Editor of the *Journal of the American Statistical Association* and *Psychometrika*. He has also been a very active consultant and is currently Chief Scientist of Visible Path, an organizational network software firm.

Mark Granovetter, General editor

The series *Structural Analysis in the Social Sciences* presents approaches that explain social behavior and institutions by reference to relations among such concrete entities as persons and organizations. This contrasts with at least four other popular strategies: (a) reductionist attempts to explain by a focus on individuals alone; (b) explanations stressing the causal primacy of such abstract concepts as ideas, values, mental harmonies, and cognitive maps (thus, "structuralism" on the Continent should be distinguished from structural analysis in the present sense); (c) technological and material determination; and (d) explanation using "variables" as the main analytic concepts (as in the "structural equation" models that dominated much of the sociology of the 1970s), where structure is that connecting variables rather that actual social entities.

   The social network approach is an important example of the strategy of structural analysis; the series also draws on social science theory and research that is not framed explicitly in network terms, but stresses the importance of relations rather than the atomization of reduction or the determination of ideas, technology, or material conditions. Although the structural perspective has become extremely popular and influential in all the social sciences, it does not have a coherent identity, and no series yet pulls together such work under a single rubric. By bringing the achievements of structurally oriented scholars to a wider public, this series hopes to encourage the use of this very fruitful approach.

Other books in the series:

Continued after the Index

Models and Methods in Social Network Analysis

Edited by

PETER J. CARRINGTON
University of Waterloo

JOHN SCOTT
University of Essex

STANLEY WASSERMAN
Indiana University

CAMBRIDGE UNIVERSITY PRESS
Cambridge, New York, Melbourne, Madrid, Cape Town, Singapore, São Paulo

Cambridge University Press
32 Avenue of the Americas, New York, NY 10013-2473, USA

www.cambridge.org
Information on this title: www.cambridge.org/9780521809597

First published 2005
Reprinted 2006 (twice), 2007

Printed in the United States of America

A catalog record for this publication is available from the British Library.

Library of Congress Cataloguing in Publication Data

Models and methods in social network analysis / edited by Peter J. Carrington, John Scott,
and Stanley Wasserman.
p. cm. – (Structural analysis in the social sciences)
Includes bibliographical references and index.
ISBN 0-521-80959-2 – ISBN 0-521-60097-9 (pb.)
1. Social networks – Mathematical models.   2. Social networks – Research – Methodology.
I. Carrington, Peter J., 1946–   II. Scott, John.   III. Wasserman, Stanley.   IV. Series.
HM741.M63   2005
302.3 – dc22   200405188

ISBN   978-0-521-80959-7 hardback
ISBN   978-0-521-60097-2 paperback

Contents

Acknowledgments

The editors want to thank Mary Child and Ed Parsons of Cambridge University Press and Mark Granovetter, the general editor of the series, for their support and patience during the long genesis of this volume. We are also grateful to Anthony Matarazzo, who prepared the index, and who created and maintained the Web site that served as a virtual workplace and meeting place for everyone who contributed to the book.

We are, of course, very grateful to our contributors. Their expertise and hard work have made this an easy project for us. Thanks go to all of them.

Preparation of the book was supported by Social Sciences and Humanities Research Council of Canada Standard Research Grants No. 410-2000-0361 and 410-2004-2136 and U.S. Office of Naval Research Grant No. N00014-02-1-0877.

We dedicate this volume to social network analysts everywhere, in the hope that they will find these chapters useful in their research.

Contributors

Vladimir Batagelj is a professor of discrete and computational mathematics at the University of Ljubljana and is chair of the Department of Theoretical Computer Science at IMFM, Ljubljana. He is a member of the editorial boards of *Informatica* and the *Journal of Social Structure*. He was visiting professor at the University of Pittsburgh in 1990/1991 and at University of Konstanz (Germany) in 2002. His main research interests are in graph theory, algorithms on graphs and networks, combinatorial optimization, data analysis, and applications of information technology in education. He is co-author (with Andrej Mrvar) of Pajek, a program for analysis and visualization of large networks.

Steve P. Borgatti is Associate Professor of Organization Studies at Boston College. His research interests include social networks, cultural domain analysis, and organizational learning. He is co-author of the UCINET software package and a past President of INSNA, the professional association for social network researchers.

Peter J. Carrington is Professor of Sociology at the University of Waterloo and Editor of the *Canadian Journal of Criminology and Criminal Justice*. His main teaching and research interests are in the criminal and juvenile justice systems, social networks, and research methods and statistics. He has published articles in the *Canadian Journal of Criminology and Criminal Justice, American Journal of Psychiatry, Journal of Mathematical Sociology*, and *Social Networks*. He is currently doing research on police discretion, criminal and delinquent careers and networks, and the impact of the Youth Criminal Justice Act on the youth justice system in Canada.

Patrick Doreian is a professor of sociology and statistics at the University of Pittsburgh, where he also chairs the Department of Sociology. He edits the *Journal of Mathematical Sociology* and is a member of the editorial board of *Social Networks*. His research and teaching interests include social networks, social movements, and mathematical sociology.

Marijtje A. J. van Duijn is an assistant professor in the Department of Sociology of the University of Groningen. Her research interests are in applied statistics and statistical methods for discrete and/or longitudinal data, including multilevel modeling and social network analysis. She teaches courses on multivariate statistical methods and on item response theory.

Martin Everett has a masters degree in mathematics and a doctorate in social networks from Oxford University. He has been active in social network research for more than

25 years. During a sabbatical at the University of California, Irvine, in 1987, he teamed up with Stephen Borgatti, and they have collaborated ever since. Currently he is a Provost at the University of Westminster, London.

Katherine Faust is Associate Professor in the Sociology Department at the University of California, Irvine, and is affiliated with the Institute for Mathematical Behavioral Sciences at UCI. She is co-author (with Stanley Wasserman) of *Social Network Analysis: Methods and Applications* and numerous articles on social network analysis. Her current research focuses on methods for comparing global structural properties among diverse social networks; the relationship between social networks and demographic processes; and spatial aspects of social networks.

Anuška Ferligoj is a professor of statistics at the University of Ljubljana and is dean of the Faculty of Social Sciences. She has been editor of the series *Metodoloski zvezki* since 1987 and is a member of the editorial boards of the *Journal of Mathematical Sociology*, the *Journal of Classification*, *Social Networks*, and *Statistics in Transition*. She was a Fulbright Scholar in 1990 and Visiting Professor at the University of Pittsburgh. She was awarded the title of Ambassador of Science of the Republic of Slovenia in 1997. Her interests include multivariate analysis (constrained and multicriteria clustering), social networks (measurement quality and blockmodeling), and survey methodology (reliability and validity of measurement).

Ove Frank was professor of statistics at Lund University, Sweden, 1974–1984, and at Stockholm University from 1984, where he recently became emeritus. He is one of the pioneers in network sampling and has published papers on network methodology, snowball sampling, Markov graphs, clustering, and information theory. Jointly with David Strauss he introduced Markov graphs in 1986 and explained how sufficient network statistics can be deduced from explicit assumptions about the dependencies in a network.

Linton C. Freeman is a research professor in the Department of Sociology and in the Institute for Mathematical Behavioral Sciences at the University of California, Irvine. He began working in social network analysis in 1958 when he directed a structural study of community decision making in Syracuse New York. Freeman was an early computer user and taught information and/or computer science at Syracuse and at the universities of Hawaii and Pittsburgh. In 1978 he founded the journal *Social Networks*. Beginning in the 1950s, and continuing to the present time, one of his continuing areas of interest has been the graphical display of network structure.

Mark Huisman is an assistant professor in the Department of Psychology of the University of Groningen. He teaches courses on statistics and multivariate statistical methods. His current research interests focus on statistical modeling of social networks, methods for nonresponse and missing data, and software for statistical data analysis.

Laura M. Koehly is an assistant professor in the Department of Psychology at Texas A&M University. She completed her Ph.D. in quantitative psychology at the University of Illinois–Urbana/Champaign, after which she completed postdoctoral training at the

University of Texas M.D. Anderson Cancer Center. Her methodological research interests focus on the development of stochastic models for three-way social network data and ego-centered network data. Her substantive research focuses on the application of social network methods in the health domain, specifically in the areas of hereditary cancers. She has recently developed a research program in organizational psychology that focuses on socialization processes within organizational settings, consensus and accuracy in perceptions of social structure, and the evolution of leadership within teams.

Peter V. Marsden is Professor of Sociology at Harvard University. His academic interests include social organization, social networks, and social science methodology. With James A. Davis and Tom W. Smith, Marsden is a co-Principal Investigator of the General Social Survey and has been a lead investigator for three National Organizations Studies conducted between 1991 and 2003.

Philippa Pattison is a professor in the Department of Psychology at the University of Melbourne. Her current research is focused on the development of dynamic network-based models for social processes and on applications of these models to a diverse range of phenomena, including mental health, organizational design, the emergence of markets, and disease transmission.

Garry Robins teaches quantitative methods in the Department of Psychology at the University of Melbourne, Australia. His research is centered on methodologies for social network analysis, particularly on exponential random graph (p^*) models. He has a wide range of collaborations arising from empirical research related to social networks.

John Scott is Professor of Sociology at the University of Essex. An active member of the British Sociological Association, he served as its president from 2001 until 2003. He has written more than fifteen books, including *Corporate Business and Capitalist Classes* (1997), *Social Network Analysis* (1991 and 2000), *Sociological Theory* (1995), and *Power* (2001). With James Fulcher, he is the author of the leading introductory textbook *Sociology* (1999 and 2003). He is a member of the Editorial Board of the *British Journal of Sociology* and is an Academician of the Academy of Learned Societies in the Social Sciences

Tom A. B. Snijders is professor of Methodology and Statistics in the Department of Sociology of the University of Groningen, The Netherlands, and Scientific Director of the Research and Graduate School ICS (Interuniversity Center for Social Science Theory and Methodology). His main research interests are social network analysis and multilevel analysis.

Thomas W. Valente is an associate professor in the Department of Preventive Medicine, Keck School of Medicine, and Director of the Master of Public Health Program at the University of Southern California. He is author of *Evaluating Health Promotion Programs* (2002, Oxford University Press); *Network Models of the Diffusion of Innovations* (1995, Hampton Press); and numerous articles on social network analysis, health communication, and mathematical models of the diffusion of innovations.

Stanley Wasserman is Rudy Professor of Sociology, Psychology, and Statistics at Indiana University. He has done research on methodology for social networks for 30 years. He has co-authored with Katherine Faust *Social Network Analysis: Methods and Applications*, published in 1994 in this series by Cambridge University Press, and has co-edited with Joseph Galaskiewicz *Social Network Analysis: Research in Social and Behavioral Sciences* (1994). He has also been a very active consultant and is currently Chief Scientist of Visible Path, an organizational network research firm.

1

Introduction

Stanley Wasserman, John Scott, and Peter J. Carrington

Interest in social network analysis has grown massively in recent years. This growth has been matched by an increasing sophistication in the technical tools available to users. *Models and Methods in Social Network Analysis (MMSNA)* presents the most important of those developments in quantitative models and methods for analyzing social network data that have appeared during the 1990s. It is a collection of original chapters by leading methodologists, commissioned by the three editors to review recent advances in their particular areas of network methods.

As is well-known, social network analysis has been used since the mid-1930s to advance research in the social and behavioral sciences, but progressed slowly and linearly, until the end of the century. Sociometry (sociograms, sociomatrices), graph theory, dyads, triads, subgroups, and blockmodels – reflecting substantive concerns such as reciprocity, structural balance, transitivity, clusterability, and structural equivalence – all made their appearances and were quickly adopted by the relatively small number of "network analysts." It was easy to trace the evolution of network theories and ideas from professors to students, from one generation to the next. The field of network analysis was even analyzed as a network (see, for example, Mullins 1973, as well as analyses by Burt in 1978, and Hummon and Carley in 1993). Many users eventually became analysts, and some even methodologists. A conference of methodologists, held at Dartmouth College in the mid-1970s, consisted of about thirty researchers (see Holland and Leinhardt 1979) and really did constitute a "who's who" of the field – an auspicious, but rather small gathering. Developments at this time were also summarized in such volumes as the methodological collection edited by Linton Freeman and his colleagues (1989), which presented a collection of papers given at a conference in Laguna Beach, California, in the early 1980s, and the collection edited by Barry Wellman and the late Stephen Berkowitz (2003 [1988]). Much of this early research has been brought together in a recent compilation, together with some later contributions (Scott 2002).

However, something occurred in about 1990. It is not completely clear to us what caused it. Interest in social networks and use of the wide-ranging collection of social network methodology began to grow at a much more rapid (maybe even increasing) rate. There was a realization in much of behavioral science that the "social contexts" of actions matter. Epidemiologists realized that epidemics do not progress uniformly through populations (which are almost never homogeneous). The slightly controversial view that sex research had to consider sexual networks, even if such networks are just dyads, took hold. Organizational studies were recognized as being at the heart of management research (roughly one-third of the presentations at the Academy of Management annual meetings now have a network perspective). Physicists latched onto the web and metabolic systems, developing applications of the paradigm that a few social and behavioral scientists had been working on for many, many years. This came as a surprise to many of these physicists, and some of them did not even seem to be aware of the earlier work – although their maniacal focus on the small world problem (Watts 1999, 2003; Buchanan 2002) has made most of their research rather routine and unimaginative (see Barabasi, 2002, for a lower-level overview). Researchers in the telecommunications industry have started to look at individual telephone networks to detect user fraud. In addition, there is the media attention given to terrorist networks, spawning a number of methodologists to dabble in the area – see *Connections* 24(3) (2001): a special issue on terrorist networks, as well as the proceedings from a recent conference (Breiger, Carley, and Pattison 2003) on this topic. Perhaps the ultimate occurred more recently when *Business 2.0* (November 2003) named social network applications the "Hottest New Technology of 2003." All in all, an incredible diversity of new applications for what is now a rather established paradigm.

Sales of network analysis textbooks have increased: an almost unheard-of occurrence for academic texts (whose sales tend to hit zero several years after publication). It has been 10 years since the publication of the leading text in the area – *Social Network Analysis: Methods and Applications* (Wasserman and Faust 1994) – and almost 15 years since work on it began. It is remarkable not only that is it still in print, but also that increasing numbers of people are buying it, maybe even looking at parts of it. Yet, much has happened in social network analysis since the mid-1990s. Some general introductory texts have since appeared (Degenne and Forsé 1999; Scott 2000), but clearly, there is a need for an update to the methodological material discussed in Wasserman and Faust's standard reference.

Consequently, we intend *MMSNA* to be a sequel to *Social Network Analysis: Methods and Applications*. Although our view of the *important* research during the 1990s is somewhat subjective, we do believe (as do our contributors) that we have covered the field with *MMSNA*, including chapters on all the topics in the quantitative analysis of social networks in which sufficient important work has been recently published. The presentations of methodological advances found in these pages are illustrated with substantive applications, reflecting the belief that it is usually problems arising from empirical research that motivate methodological innovation. The contributions review only already published work: they avoid reference to work that is still "in progress."

Currently, no volume completely reviews the state of the art in social network analysis, nor does any volume present the most recent developments in the field. *MMSNA* is a complement, a supplement, not a competitor, to Wasserman and Faust (1994). We expect that anyone who has trained in network methods using Wasserman and Faust or who uses it as a reference will want to update his or her knowledge of network methods with the material found herein. As mentioned, the range of topics in this volume is somewhat selective, so its coverage of the entire field of network methods is not nearly as comprehensive as that of Wasserman and Faust. Nevertheless, the individually authored chapters of *MMSNA* are more in-depth, definitely more up-to-date, and more advanced in places than presentations in that book.

We turn now to the individual chapters in *MMNSA*. Peter Marsden's "Recent Developments in Network Measurement" is a significant scene-setting chapter for this whole volume. He explores the central issues in the measurement of social relations that underpin the other techniques examined in the book. His particular concern is not with measuring network structures themselves, but in the acquisition of relevant and reliable data. To this end, he looks specifically at the design of network studies and the collection of source data on social relations.

Marsden's starting point is the recognition that whole network and egocentric approaches can be complementary viewpoints on the same data. Whole network studies are concerned with the structural properties of networks at the global level, whereas egocentric studies focus on the network as it appears from the standpoint of those situated at particular locations within it. Despite this complementarity, however, issues of sampling and data selection mean that it is rarely possible to move with any ease from the "structure" to the "agent," or vice versa. Marsden examines, in particular, the implications of the identification of network boundaries on the basis of positional, event-based, and relational measures, showing how recent developments have moved beyond the conventional, and often inadequate, approaches to boundary setting.

Data collection for network analysis, in whatever kind of study, has most typically involved survey and questionnaire methods, and Marsden reviews the work of recent authors on the specific response formats for collecting factual and judgmental data on social relations. He considers in particular depth the problems of recall and recognition in egocentric approaches, especially with the use of name-generator methods, and he gives focused attention to studies that aim to collect data on subjective images and perceptions of networks rather than merely reporting actual connections. A key issue in both types of research is the meaning given to the relations by the actors – most particularly, the meaning of such apparently obvious terms as "friend." Marsden shows that a number of issues in this area are significantly related to the position that the respondent occupies in the network on which he or she is reporting. The chapter concludes with some briefer remarks on archival and observational methods where the researcher has less direct control (if any at all) over the nature of the raw data.

Marsden's remarks on the sampling problem are further considered in Ove Frank's chapter, "Network Sampling and Model Fitting." Frank has been the leading contributor to work on network sampling for many years, and here he begins from a consideration of the general issues in sampling methodology that he sees as central to the analysis of multivariate network data. A common method in network analysis has been implicit or explicit snowball sampling, and Frank looks at the use of this method in relation to line (edge) sampling as well as point (vertex) sampling, and he shows that the limitations of this method can be partly countered through the use of probabilistic network models (i.e., basing the sampling on population model assumptions). These are examined through the method of random graphs, especially the uniform and Bernoulli models, and the more interesting models such as Holland-Leinhardt's p_1, p^*, and Markov random graphs.

Frank gives greatest attention, however, to dyad-dependence models that explicitly address the issue of how points and lines are related. These are models in which network structure is determined by the latent individual preferences for local linkages, and Frank suggests that these can be seen as generalizations of the Holland-Leinhardt p_1 model and that they are equally useful for Bayesian models. He examines log-linear and clustering approaches to choosing such models, arguing that the most effective practical solution may be to combine the two. These general conclusions are illustrated through actual studies of drug abuse, the spread of AIDS, participation in crime, and social capital.

The next group of chapters turns from issues of data design and collection to structural measurement and analysis. Centrality has been one of the most important areas of investigation in substantive studies of social networks. Not surprisingly, many measures of centrality have been proposed. The chapter by Martin Everett and Stephen Borgatti, "Extending Centrality," notes that these measures have been limited to individual actors and one-mode data. Their concern is with the development of novel measures that would enlarge the scope of centrality analysis, seeking to generalize the three primary concepts of centrality (degree, closeness, and betweenness) and Freeman's notion of centralization. They first show that it is possible to analyze the centrality of groups, whether these are defined by some external attribute such as ethnicity, sex, or political affiliation, or by structural network criteria (as cliques or blocks). A more complex procedure is to shift the measurement of centrality from one-mode to two-mode data, such as, for example, both individuals and the events in which they are involved. Although such measures are more difficult to interpret substantively, Everett and Borgatti note that they involve less loss of the original data and do not require any arbitrary dichotomizing of adjacency matrices. Finally, they look at a core-periphery approach to centrality, which identifies those sub-graphs that share common structural locations within networks.

Patrick Doreian, Vladimir Batagelj, and Anuška Ferligoj, in "Positional Analyses of Sociometric Data," examine blockmodeling procedures, reviewing both structural equivalence and regular equivalence approaches. Noting that few empirical examples of exact partitioning exist, they argue that the lack of fit between model and reality can be measured and used as a way of comparing the adequacy of different models. Most importantly, they combine this with a generalization of the blockmodeling method that permits many types of models to be constructed and compared. Sets of "permitted" ideal blocks are constructed, and the model that shows minimum inconsistency is sought. In an interesting convergence with the themes raised by Everett and Borgatti, they use their method on Little League data and discover evidence for the existence of a center-periphery structure. They go on to explore the implications of imposing pre-specified models (such as a center-periphery model) on empirical data, allowing the assessment of the extent to which actual data exhibit particular structural characteristics. They argue that this hypothesis-testing approach is to be preferred to the purely inductive approach that is usually employed to find positions in a network.

Thomas Valente's "Network Models and Methods for Studying the Diffusion of Innovations" turns to the implications of network structure for the flow of information through a network. In this case, the flow considered is information about innovations, and Valente reviews existing studies in search of evidence for diffusion processes. His particular concern is for the speed of diffusion in different networks and the implications of this for rates of innovation. A highly illuminating comparison of available mathematical models with existing empirical studies in public health using event history analysis shows that network influences are important, but that the available data prevent more definitive conclusions from being drawn. Valente argues for the collection of more adequate data, combining evidence on both information and network structure, and the construction of more adequately theorized models of the diffusion process.

Katherine Faust's "Using Correspondence Analysis for Joint Displays of Affiliation Networks" convincingly shows the need for formal and strict representational models of the joint space of actors and relational ties. Correspondence analysis (a scaling method), she argues, allows a high level of precision in this task. Having specified the nature of the method and its relevance for social network data, rather than the more typical "actors x variable" data with which it is often used, Faust presents a novel analysis of a global trading network, consisting of international organizations and their member countries. This discloses a clear regional structure in which the first dimension separates South American from Central American countries and organizations, whereas the second dimension separates North American and North Atlantic countries from all others.

The exponential family of random graphs, p^*, has received a lot of attention in recent years, and in "An Introduction to Random Graphs, Dependence Graphs, and p^*," Stanley Wasserman joins with Garry Robins to review this recent work. Wasserman and Robins made the important generalization of the model from Markov random graphs to a larger family of models. In this chapter, however, they begin with dependence graphs to further clarify the models. They see the great value of p^* models as making possible an effective and informed move from local, micro phenomena to overall, macro phenomena. Using maximum likelihood and pseudolikelihood (based on logit models) estimation techniques, they show that the often-noted tendency towards model degeneracy (the production of trivial or uninteresting results) can be offset by using more complex models in which 3- or 4-star configuration counts are used. That is, the model incorporates the first three or four moments of the degree distribution to produce more realistic models. Evidence from simulation studies confirms the power of this approach. Indeed, degenerate models may not always be trivial, but may point to regions where stochastic processes have broken down. In making this point, they make important connections with recent developments in small world networks.

Although analyses of two-mode, affiliation networks involve one significant move away from the conventional one-mode analysis of relational, adjacency data, analyses of multiple networks involves a complementary broadening of approach. Laura Koehly and Philippa Pattison ("Random Graph Models for Social Networks: Multiple Relations or Multiple Raters?") turn to this issue of multiple networks, arguing that most real networks are of this kind. Building on simpler, univariate p^* models, they make a generalization to random graph models for multiple networks using dependence graphs. They examine both actual relations and cognitive perceptions of these relations among managers in high-technology industries, showing that the multiple network methods lead to conclusions that simply would not be apparent in a conventional single network approach. Their work is the first step toward richer models of generalized relational structures.

The idea of dependence graphs was central to the chapters of Wasserman and Robins and of Koehly and Pattison. Garry Robins and Philippa Pattison join forces to explore this key idea in "Interdependencies and Social Processes: Dependence Graphs and

Generalized Dependence Structures." They make the Durkheimian point that dependence must be seen as central to the very idea of sociality and use this to reconstruct the idea of social space. As they correctly point out, the element or unit in social space is not the individual but the ties that connect them, and they hold that the exploration of dependence models allows the grasping of the variety of ties that enter into the construction of social spaces. From this point of view, dependence graphs are to be seen as representations of proximity in social space, and network analysts are engaged in social geometry.

The analysis of social networks over time has long been recognized as something of a Holy Grail for network researchers, and Tom Snijders reviews this quest in "Models for Longitudinal Network Data." In particular, he examines ideas of network evolution, in which change in network structure is seen as an endogenous product of micro-level network dynamics. Exploring what he terms the independent arcs model, the reciprocity model, the popularity model, and the more encompassing actor-oriented model, Snijders concludes that the latter offers the best potential. In this model, actors are seen as changing their outgoing ties (choices), each change aiming at increasing the value derived from a particular network configuration. Such changes are "myopic," concerned only with the immediate consequences. A series of such rational choices means that small, incremental changes accumulate to the point at which substantial macro-level transformations of structure occur. He concludes with the intriguing suggestion that such techniques can usefully be allied with multiple network methods such as those discussed by Koehly and Pattison.

The final two chapters in the book are reviews of available software sources for visualization and analysis of social networks. The visualization of networks began with Moreno and the early sociograms, but the use of social network analysis for larger social networks has made the task of visualization more difficult. For some time, Linton Freeman has been concerned with the development of techniques, and in "Graphical Techniques for Exploring Social Network Data," he presents the latest and most up-to-date overview. The two families of approaches that he considers are those based on some form of multidimensional scaling (MDS) and those that involve an algebraic procedure. In MDS, points are optimally located in a specified, hopefully small, number of dimensions, using metric or non-metric approaches to proximity. In the algebraic methods of correspondence analysis and principal component analysis, points are located in relation to dimensions identified through procedures akin to the analysis of variance. Using data on beachgoers, Freeman shows that the two techniques produce consistent results, but an algebraic method produces a more dramatic visualization of the structure. Importantly, he also notes that wherever a network is plotted as a disc or sphere, it has few interesting structural properties. Freeman goes on to examine the use of specific algorithms for displaying and manipulating network images, focusing on MAGE, which allows points to be coded for demographic variables such as gender, age, and ethnicity. The use of this method is illustrated from a number of data sets. The longitudinal issues addressed by Snijders are also relevant to the visualization issue, and Freeman considers the use of MOVIEMOL as an animation device for representing small-scale and short-term changes in network structure. He shows the descriptive power of this technique for uncovering social change, but also shows how it can be used in more analytical ways to begin to uncover some of the processes at work.

The final chapter turns to the issue of the software available for different kinds of network analysis. Mark Huisman and Marijtje van Duijn, in "Software for Social Network Analysis," present what is the most up-to-date review of a continually changing field. A total of twenty-seven packages are considered, excluding the visualization software considered by Freeman. Detailed attention is given to six major packages: UCINET, Pajek, MultiNet, NetMiner, STRUCTURE, and StOCNET. Wherever possible, the packages are compared using the same data set (Freeman's EIES network). This is a true road test, with interesting and somewhat surprising results. The authors conclude that there is no single "best buy" and that the package of choice depends very much on the particular questions that are of interest to the analyst.

References

Barabasi, A.-L. 2002. *Linked: The New Science of Networks*. Cambridge, Mass.: Perseus.

Breiger, R. L., Carley, K., and Pattison, P. 2003. *Dynamic Social Network Modeling and Analysis: Workshop Summary and Papers*. National Academy of Sciences/National Research Council, Committee on Human Factors. Washington, DC: National Academies Press.

Buchanan, M. 2002. *Nexus: Small Worlds and the Groundbreaking Science of Networks*. New York: Norton.

Burt, R. S. 1978. "Stratification and Prestige Among Elite Experts in Methodological and Mathematical Sociology *Circa* 1975." *Social Networks*, 1, 105–8.

Degenne, A., and Forsé, M. 1999. *Introducing Social Networks*. London: Sage.

Freeman, L. C., White, D. R., and Romney, A. K. 1989. *Research Methods in Social Network Analysis*. New Brunswick: Transaction Books.

Holland, P., and Leinhardt, S. (eds.) 1979. *Perspectives on Social Networks*. New York: Academic.

Hummon, N., and Carley, K. 1993. "Social Networks as Normal Science," *Social Networks*, 15, 71–106.

Mullins, N. C. 1973. *Theories and Theory Groups in American Sociology*. New York: Harper and Row.

Scott, J. 2000. *Social Network Analysis*, 2nd ed. London: Sage. (Originally published in 1992).

Scott, J. (ed.) 2002. *Social Networks: Critical Concepts in Sociology*, 4 vols. London: Routledge.

Wasserman, S., and Faust, K. 1994. *Social Network Analysis: Methods and Applications*. New York: Cambridge University Press.

Watts, D. 1999. *Small Worlds: The Dynamics of Networks Between Order and Randomness*. Princeton, N.J.: Princeton University Press.

Watts, D. 2003. *Six Degrees: The Science of a Connected Age*. New York: Norton.

Wellman, B., and Berkowitz, S. (eds.) 2003 [1988]. *Social Structures: A Network Approach*. Toronto: Canadian Scholars' Press. (Originally published in 1988 by Cambridge University Press.)

2

Recent Developments in Network Measurement

Peter V. Marsden

Harvard University

This chapter considers study design and data collection methods for social network studies, emphasizing methodological research and applications that have appeared since an earlier review (Marsden 1990). It concentrates on methods and instruments for measuring social relationships linking actors or objects. Many analytical techniques discussed in other chapters identify patterns and regularities that measure structural properties of networks (such as centralization or global density), and/or relational properties of particular objects/actors within them (such as centrality or local density). The focus here is on acquiring the elementary data elements themselves.

Beginning with common designs for studying social networks, the chapter then covers methods for setting network boundaries. A discussion of data collection techniques follows. Survey and questionnaire methods receive primary attention: they are widely used, and much methodological research has focused on them. More recent work emphasizes methods for measuring egocentric networks and variations in network perceptions; questions of informant accuracy or competence in reporting on networks remain highly salient. The chapter closes with a brief discussion of network data from informants, archives, and observations, and issues in obtaining them.

2.1 Network Study Designs

The broad majority of social network studies use either "whole-network" or "egocentric" designs. Whole-network studies examine sets of interrelated objects or actors that are regarded for analytical purposes as bounded social collectives, although in practice network boundaries are often permeable and/or ambiguous. Egocentric studies focus on a focal actor or object and the relationships in its locality.

Freeman (1989) formally defined forms of whole-network data in set-theoretic, graph-theoretic, and matrix terms. The minimal network database consists of one set of objects (also known as *actors* or *nodes*) linked by one set of relationships observed at one occasion; the cross-sectional study of women's friendships in voluntary associations given by Valente (Figure 6.1.1, Chapter 6, this volume) is one example. The matrix representation of this common form of network data is known as a "who to whom" matrix or a "sociomatrix." Wasserman and Faust (1994) termed this form a *one-mode* data set because of its single set of objects.

Elaborations of the minimal design consider more than one set of relationships, measure relationships at multiple occasions, and/or allow multiple sets of objects (which may change over occasions). Data sets with two sets of objects – termed *two-mode* by Wasserman and Faust (1994) – are common; Table 7.4.1 of Chapter 7 in this volume gives an example, a network of national memberships in trade and treaty organizations. Many studies also measure multiple relations, as in Lazega's (1999) study of collaboration, advising, and friendships among attorneys. As Snijders (Chapter 11, this volume) indicates, interest in longitudinal questions about social networks is rising; most extant data sets remain single occasion, however. In addition to relationships, almost all network data sets measure attributes (either time constant or time varying) of objects, but this chapter does not consider issues of measurement for these.

A further variation known as a *cognitive social structure* (CSS) design (Krackhardt 1987) obtains measurements of the relationship(s) under study from multiple sources or observers. Chapter 9 in this volume presents models for such data. The CSS design is widely used to study informant variations in the social perception of networks. In applications to date, observers have been actors in the networks under study, but in principle the sets of actors and observers could be disjoint.

Egocentric network designs assemble data on relationships involving a focal object (*ego*) and the objects (*alters*) to which it is linked. Focal objects are often sampled from a larger population. The egocentric network data in the 1985 General Social Survey (GSS; see Marsden 1987), for example, include information on up to five alters with whom each survey respondent "discusses important matters."

Egocentric and whole-network designs are usually distinguished sharply from one another, but they are interrelated. A whole network contains an egocentric network for each object within it (Marsden 2002). Conversely, if egos are sampled "densely," whole networks may be constructed using egocentric network data. Kirke (1996), for instance, elicited egocentric networks for almost all youth in a particular district, and later used them in a whole-network analysis identifying within-district clusters. Egocentric designs in which respondents report on the relationships among alters in their egocentric networks may be seen as restricted CSS designs – in which informants report on clusters of proximate relationships, rather than on all linkages.

Aside from egocentric designs and one-mode (single-relation or multirelational), two-mode, and CSS designs for whole networks, some studies sample portions of networks. Frank discusses network sampling in depth in Chapter 3 (this volume). One sampling design observes relationships for a random sample of nodes (Granovetter 1976). Another, known as the "random walk" design (Klovdahl et al. 1977; McGrady et al. 1995), samples chains of nodes, yielding insight into indirect connectedness in large, open populations.

2.2 Setting Network Boundaries

Deciding on the set(s) of objects that lie within a network is a difficult problem for whole-network studies. Laumann, Marsden, and Prensky (1989) outlined three generic boundary specification strategies: a positional approach based on characteristics of objects or formal membership criteria, an event-based approach resting on participation in some class of activities, and a relational approach based on social connectedness.

Employment by an organization (e.g., Krackhardt 1990) is one positional criterion. The "regulars" at a beach depicted by Freeman (Figure 12.2.3, Chapter 12, this volume; see also Freeman and Webster 1994) were identified via an event-based approach; regulars were defined as persons observed 3 or more days during the study period.

Doreian and Woodard (1992) outlined a specific version of the relational approach called *expanding selection*. Beginning with a provisional "fixed" list of objects deemed to be in a network, it then adds objects linked to those on the initial list. This approach is closely related to the snowball sampling design discussed by Frank in Chapter 3, this volume; Doreian and Woodard, however, added a new object only after finding that it had several links (not just one) to elements on the fixed list. They review logistical issues in implementing expanding selection, and compare it with the fixed-list approach in a study of social services networks. More than one-half of the agencies located via expanding selection were not on the fixed list. Added agencies were closely linked to one another, although the fixed-list agencies were relatively central within the expanded network. The fixed-list approach presumes substantial prior investigator knowledge of network boundaries, whereas expanding selection draws on participant knowledge about them.

Elsewhere, Doreian and Woodard (1994) suggested methods for identifying a "reasonably complete" network within a larger network data set. They used expanding selection to identify a large set of candidate objects, and then selected a dense segment of this for study. They adopted Seidman's (1983) "k-core" concept (a subset of objects, each linked to at least k others within the subset) as a criterion for setting network boundaries. By varying k, investigators can set more and less restrictive criteria for including objects.

Egocentric network studies typically set boundaries during data collection. The "name generator" questions discussed in this chapter accomplish this.

2.3 Survey and Questionnaire Methods

Network studies draw extensively on survey and questionnaire data. Surveys allow investigators to decide on relationships to measure and on actors/objects to be approached for data. In the absence of archival records, surveys are often the most practical alternative: they make much more modest demands on participants than do diary methods or observation, for example. Surveys do introduce artificiality, however, and findings rest heavily on the presumed validity of self-reports.

Both whole-network and egocentric network studies use survey methods, but the designs typically differ in how they obtain network data and in what they ask of respondents. A whole-network study usually compiles a roster of actors before data collection begins. Survey and questionnaire instruments incorporate the roster, allowing respondents to recognize rather than recall their relationships. Egocentric studies, however, are often conducted in large, open populations. The alters in a respondent's network are not known beforehand, so setting network boundaries must rely on respondent recall.

Whole-network studies ordinarily seek interviews with all actors in the population, and ask respondents to report only on their direct relationships. (The CSS studies discussed later are an exception; they ask for much more data.) In egocentric studies, however, practical and resource considerations usually preclude interviewing a respondent's alters. Such studies ask respondents for data on their own relationships to alters, and also often ask for information on linkages between alters; moreover, they commonly request proxy reports about alters.

Surveys and questionnaires in whole-network studies use several response formats to obtain network data: binary judgments (often termed *sociometric choices*) about whether respondents have a specified relationship with each actor on the roster, ordinal ratings of tie strength, or rankings. Binary judgments are least difficult for respondents; ranking tasks are most demanding. Eudey, Johnson, and Schade (1994) found that a large majority of respondents preferred rating over ranking tasks. Ferligoj and Hlebec (1999) reported the reliability of ratings to be somewhat higher than that of binary judgments.

Batchelder (1989) considered network data of different scale types (dichotomous, ordinal, interval, ratio, absolute) and the inferences about network-level properties (e.g., reciprocation, presence of cliques) that can be drawn meaningfully from them. Among other things, Batchelder showed that findings may be affected if respondents have differing thresholds for claiming a given type of tie when making dichotomous judgments; Feld and Carter (2002) referred to this as *expansiveness bias* (see also Kashy and Kenny 1990). Likewise, implicit respondent-specific scale and location constants for rating relationship strength can complicate inferences. Eudey et al. (1994), however, used both ratings and rankings in studying a small group, and found quite high correlations between measures based on the two response formats.

Surveys sometimes include "global" items asking respondents about the size, density, or composition of their egocentric networks. Such questions pose extensive cognitive demands. To answer a global network density question, for instance, respondents must decide who their alters are, ascertain relationships among alters, and aggregate (Burt 1987). Sudman (1985) measured network size using both a global item and a recognition instrument; the measures had similar means, but the global item had a far greater variance. Instead of global items, contemporary studies usually measure egocentric networks using multiple-item instruments that ask respondents for only one datum at a time.

(A) *Name Generator Instruments for Egocentric Networks*

Surveys have long collected data on a respondent's social contacts and relationships (Coleman 1958). Such egocentric network instruments typically include two types of questions (Burt 1984): *name generators* that identify the respondent's alters, and *name interpreters* that obtain information on the alters and their relationships. Name generators are free-recall questions that delineate network boundaries. Name interpreters elicit data about alters and both ego–alter and alter–alter relationships. Many indices of network form and composition are based on such data.

Instruments for egocentric networks use both single and multiple name generators. A single-generator instrument focusing on alters with whom respondents "discuss important matters" first appeared in the 1985 GSS, and later in several other studies (Bailey and Marsden 1999). It tends to elicit small networks of "core" ties; Marsden (1987) reported a mean network size of 3.0 for U.S. adults in 1985, whereas Ruan et al. (1997) reported a mean of 3.4 for adults in a Chinese city in 1993. Hirsch's (1980) Social Network List (SNL) for social support networks is another one-generator instrument. Respondents list up to twenty persons they regard as "significant" and have seen during the prior 4 to 6 weeks.

Any given name-generating relationship elicits only a fraction of a respondent's social contacts. Moreover, many conceptual understandings of networks extend beyond "core" ties to include more mundane forms of social support. Fischer (1982a), for example, used name generators for instrumental aid and socializing, as well as confiding. Fischer and Shavit's (1995) U.S.–Israel support network comparison used a multiple-generator instrument. Another example is the Social Support Questionnaire (SSQ; Sarason et al. 1983), a twenty-seven-generator instrument eliciting persons to whom respondents can turn and on whom they can rely in differing circumstances.

The first consideration in choosing between single and multiple name generator instruments must be a study's conceptualization of a network. Single-generator methods may be sufficient for core networks, but more broadly defined support networks almost certainly require multiple name generators. A practical issue is the availability of interview time. Multiple-generator instruments that elicit many alters can be quite long, and measuring egocentric networks must be a central focus of studies including them.

More extensive definitions of "a network" include alters and relationships that do not provide even minor social support. McCarty et al. (1997) sought to measure features of "total personal networks," including all alters "known" by a respondent, those who "would recognize the respondent by sight or by name" (p. 305). Networks thus defined are too large to enumerate fully. McCarty et al. sampled total network alters by selecting a series of first names and asking if respondents know anyone by those names; they posed name interpreter questions about the sampled alters. The authors acknowledge that age, gender, and race/ethnic differences in naming practices may limit the representativeness of their samples. Nonetheless, their sampled total networks are less dense and less kin centered than are core or support networks, as one would anticipate. Further investigation of this technique as a means of measuring extensively defined egocentric networks seems warranted.

Because name generator instruments are complex by comparison with conventional survey items (Van Tilburg 1998), they often are administered in person so interviewers can assist respondents who need help completing them. Such instruments have, however, appeared in both paper-and-pencil (Burt 1997) and computerized questionnaires (Bernard et al. 1990; Podolny and Baron 1997). Little research has examined differences in data quality by data collection mode.

Methodological research on name generator instruments rarely addresses questions of validity because criterion data from other sources are unavailable. Some test–retest studies of instrument reliability are reviewed subsequently. Most research, however, examines the in-practice performance of instruments: how name generators differ, how respondents handle sometimes challenging tasks that instruments pose, and how key terms are understood. Much of this research reflects attention to cognitive and communicative processes involved in answering survey questions (Sudman, Bradburn, and Schwarz 1996).

Comparing Name Generators

Several studies systematically compare properties of name generators. Campbell and Lee (1991), Milardo (1992), and Van der Poel (1993) highlighted conceptual differences between generators in criteria for including alters. Some refer to specific social exchanges, such as discussing important matters or borrowing household items; others use affective criteria ("closeness"); others specify particular role relations such as kinship or neighboring; and still others measure frequent interaction. Also, some generators specify temporal (e.g., contact within the prior 6 months) or spatial/organizational restrictions on eligible alters (Campbell and Lee 1991).

Varying name generator content influences egocentric network size, among other features. Campbell and Lee (1991) and Milardo (1992) showed that intimate name generators – whether affective or exchange based – elicit smaller networks than those specifying less intense thresholds for naming alters. Mean network sizes reported in seven intimate generator studies (all in North American settings) range between three and seven. Multiple-generator exchange-based instruments produce appreciably larger networks; across seven studies using such instruments, mean network size ranged between ten and twenty-two. Studies using exchange-based name generators tended to produce networks having smaller fractions of family members than did those using intimate generators.

Bernard et al. (1990) administered the GSS name generator and an eleven-generator social support instrument within a single study. The GSS instrument elicited smaller networks than did the social support instrument. These were core contacts: about 90% of GSS alters were also named for the social support instrument.

Instruments with many name generators impose appreciable respondent burden. Three studies suggest small sets of name generators for measuring support networks. Van der Poel (1993) identified subsets of name generators that best predict the size and composition of networks elicited using a ten-generator instrument. A three-generator subset consists of items on discussing a major life change, aid with household tasks, and monthly visiting; a five-generator version adds borrowing household items and going out socially. Bernard et al. (1990) isolated questions about social activities, hobbies, personal problems, advice about important decisions, and closeness as a "natural group" of name generators. Burt (1997) used a construct validity criterion – the association between network constraint and achievement – in an organizational setting. He concluded that a minimal module of name generators should measure both intimacy and activity; it might consist of the GSS "important matters" item, socializing, and discussion of a job change.

Recall, Recognition, and Forgetting

Brewer (2000) reviewed nine studies that asked respondents first to freely recall lists of persons, and then to supplement their lists after consulting an inventory listing all eligible persons. For instance, Brewer and Webster (1999) asked dormitory residents to recall their best friends, close friends, and other friends; the respondents then reviewed a dormitory roster and could add to each list of friends. Friends recognized on the roster were deemed to have been "forgotten" in the recall task.

Across studies, Brewer reported an appreciable level of forgetting, although it varied substantially across groups and relationships. In the dormitory study, one-fifth of all friends were not named in the recall task. As in several other studies Brewer reviewed, the likelihood of forgetting alters varied inversely with tie strength: students forgot only 3% of best friends and 9% of close friends, but added 26% of other friends after inspecting the dormitory listing.

Brewer's review makes it clear that name generators elicit only a fraction of those persons having a criterion relationship to a respondent, and that intimate name generators enumerate a larger fraction of eligible alters than do weaker ones. Implications of these findings depend on the purposes for which network data are used. If one seeks to describe a network precisely or to contact alters (e.g., partner notification concerning an infectious disease; Brewer, Garrett, and Kulasingam 1999), then any shortfall in the enumeration of alters is an obvious drawback. If instead a study seeks indices contrasting the structure and composition of networks, then forgetting is more serious to the extent that indices based on the recalled and recalled/forgotten sets of alters diverge. Brewer and Webster (1999), for example, reported relatively high correlations between measures of centrality, egocentric network size, and local density based on recalled alters only, and the same measures based on recalled and recognized alters. They found appreciable differences in some network-level properties, however.

Brewer (2000) suggested several steps toward reducing the level of forgetting. These include the use of recognition rather than recall when possible and, if using recall methods, nonspecific probes for additional alters. Using multiple name generators may limit forgetting because persons forgotten for one generator are often named in response to others.

Test–Retest Studies

Brewer (2000) also reviewed eight test–retest studies. These used a variety of affective, support, and exchange name generators. Most test–retest intervals were 1 month or less. In all but one study, more than 75% of first-occasion alters were also cited at the second occasion. Brewer suggested that respondents may have forgotten the uncited alters.

Two studies examine over time stability in network size for social support instruments. Rapkin and Stein (1989) measured networks over a 2-month interval using both closeness and "importance" criteria. Between-occasion correlations of network size were 0.72 and 0.56, respectively. Size declined over time for both criteria, however, suggesting that respondents were unenthusiastic about repeating the task on the second occasion. Bass and Stein (1997) found higher 4-week stability in network size for the support-based SSQ (Sarason et al. 1983) than for the affective SNL (Hirsch 1980).

Morgan, Neal, and Carder (1997) conducted a seven-wave panel study of widows, using an importance criterion to elicit networks every 2 months. Core networks were very stable – 22% of alters were named on all seven occasions. These were often family members. There was also much flux at the periphery because 24% of alters were named only once. Morgan et al. found network properties to be more stable across occasions than were alters. They suggest that between-occasion differences in alters mix unreliability (or forgetting) and genuine turnover.

Patterns in the Free Recall of Persons

Several studies of social cognition have examined the free recall of persons under different conditions. Their findings suggest strongly that social relationships organize memories for persons. Understanding these principles of memory organization can improve instruments such as name generators that seek to tap into such memories.

Bond, Jones, and Weintraub (1985) asked subjects to name acquaintances ("people you know") and recorded the order in which acquaintances were named. Successive nominations tended to be clustered by affiliations with social groups, rather than by similarity in physical or personality characteristics. Moreover, the time intervals separating names within a given group tended to be short; subjects paused for longer periods between names of persons in different groups. Social relations thus appear to be an important basis for remembering persons: Bond et al. concluded that "the person cognizer is more a sociologist than an intuitive psychologist" (p. 336). Fiske (1995) reported results for two similar studies; clusters of persons named by his subjects were grouped much more strongly by relationships than by similarity of individual features such as gender, race, or age.

Brewer (1995) conducted three studies asking subjects to name all persons within a graduate program, a religious fellowship, and a small division of a university. He too found that memory for persons reflects social relational structures: names of graduate students, for example, tended to be clustered by entering cohort, and shorter time intervals intervened between the naming of persons within a cohort than those in different cohorts. More generally, perceived social proximity appears to govern recall of persons. Brewer also found that subjects tended to name persons in order of salience. Those in groups proximate to the subject tended to be named first, as were persons of high social status and those frequently present in a setting.

These studies suggest that respondents recall alters in social clusters when answering name generators. The basis for clustering likely varies across situations, but it is plausible that foci of activity such as families, neighborhoods, workplaces, or associations (Feld 1981) offer a framework for remembering others. Aiding respondent recall with reminders of such foci might encourage more complete delineation of alters. Brewer's studies also indicate that respondents tend to order their nominations of alters by tie strength (see Burt 1986).

The Meaning and Interpretation of Name Generators

Name generators always refer to a specific type of social tie, and researchers assume that respondents share their understanding of this criterion. Fischer (1982b) questioned this assumption for "friends" (see Kirke 1996, however). He and others suggested that meanings are more apt to be shared for specific exchanges than for role labels or affective criteria. This calls for studies of the meanings attributed to exchange name generators.

Because it has been widely used, several studies have examined the GSS "important matters" name generator. Respondents decide what matters are "important" while answering, so the content of the specific exchanges it measures may vary. Ruan (1998) investigated the intersection between the sets of alters named for the GSS name generator and those for several subsequently administered exchange name generators. In her Chinese urban sample, the GSS name generator elicited social companions and persons with whom private issues are discussed, but not alters providing instrumental aid.

Bailey and Marsden (1999) used concurrent think-aloud probes to investigate how respondents interpret the GSS name generator. Their convenience sample of U.S. adults offered a variety of interpretations: some respondents referred to specific matters, but others translated the question into one about intimacy, frequent contact, or role labels. When probed about the matters regarded as "important," most respondents referred to personal relationships; health, work, and politics were other often-mentioned categories. Differences in interpretive framework or definitions of important matters were not strongly associated with the types of relationships elicited, however.

Straits (2000) conducted an experiment: one-half of his student sample answered the GSS name generator, whereas the other half answered a generator about "people especially significant in your life." The two question wordings produced virtually identical numbers of alters. Only modest compositional differences were observed: women named a somewhat greater number of male alters for the "significant people" question than for the "important matters" question. Overall, however, Straits concluded that the "important matters" criterion also elicits "significant people."

McCarty (1995) investigated respondent judgments of how well they "know" others. Indicators of tie strength – closeness, duration, friendship, kinship – were associated with knowing alters well. Frequent contact was linked to knowing others moderately well. Low levels of knowing were distinguished by awareness of factual (but not personal) information and acquaintanceship.

Interview Context Effects

When name generators contain terms requiring interpretation, respondents may look to the preceding substantive content of an interview for cues about their meaning. A context experiment was embedded in the Bailey and Marsden (1999) study. One-half of the respondents answered a series of questions about politics before the "important matters" name generator; the other half began with questions about family. When subsequently debriefed about what types of matters were "important," family-context respondents were considerably more likely to mention family matters than were political-context respondents. Because this study is based on a small sample, these findings only suggest the prospect that context influences the interpretation of a name generator.

Interviewer Effects

Three nonexperimental studies document sizable interviewer differences in the size of egocentric networks elicited by name generator methods. Van Tilburg (1998) studied a seven-generator instrument with an elderly Dutch sample, reporting a within-interviewer correlation of network size of more than 0.2. This fell only modestly after controls for respondent and interviewer characteristics. Marsden (2003) studied a single-generator instrument eliciting "good friends" administered in the 1998 GSS, finding a somewhat smaller (0.15) intraclass correlation than Van Tilburg's. Straits (2000) reported a similar figure (0.17) for the GSS "important matters" name generator administered by his student interviewers.

These interviewer differences are much larger than typical for survey items (Groves and Magilavy 1986). Large interviewer effects are, however, common for questions like name generators that ask respondents to list a number of entities. One conjecture is that interviewer differences reflect variations in the extent of probing. The findings highlight the need for careful interviewer training to ensure standardized administration of name generators. They also suggest the potential value of computer-assisted methods for obtaining network data, which operate without interviewers.

Name Interpreters

Although name generators have attracted much methodological interest, name interpreter items provide much of the data on which measures of egocentric network form and composition rest. Once alters are enumerated, most instruments follow up with questions about each alter and about pairs of alters.

The survey research literature on proxy reporting (e.g., Moore 1988) includes many studies comparing self-reports with proxy reports. In most of these, proxy respondents report on others in their households, so findings may not apply directly to reports about alters in an egocentric network. Sudman et al. (1994) observed that memories about others (especially distant others) are less elaborate, less experientially based, and less concerned with self-presentation than are memories of the self. This implies that self- and proxy reporters use different tactics to answer questions. Proxy respondents are prone, for example, to anchor answers on their own behavior, rather than retrieving answers directly from memory (Blair, Menon, and Bickart 1991). Sudman et al. (1994) hypothesized that the quality of proxy reports rises with respondent–alter interaction, and offered supportive data from a study of spouses.

Studies in the network literature establish that survey respondents can report on many characteristics of their alters with reasonable accuracy (Marsden 1990). White and Watkins (2000) found that Kenyan village women could report observable data on their alters – such as number of children or household possessions – relatively well. Ego–alter agreement was much lower for use of contraception, something often kept secret. Respondents often projected their own contraceptive behavior onto alters.

Shelley et al. (1995) studied networks of HIV[+] informants. Most sought to limit knowledge of their HIV status to certain alters; only one-half of the relatives in these networks were said to know the informant's HIV status. Nonetheless, informants reported that this was a better-known datum than several others, including political party affiliation and blood type. Such findings call for caution in formulating name interpreters because respondents may often lack certain information about their alters.

In addition to proxy reports, important name interpreters refer to ego–alter and alter–alter ties. Studies of network perception discussed subsequently are relevant to understanding answers to such questions.

Providing name interpreter data about a series of alters can be a repetitive, tedious task. White and Watkins (2000) noted that their respondents quickly became bored when answering such questions, and they therefore asked about no more than four alters. A useful step toward limiting respondent burden is to ask some or all name interpreter items only about a subset of alters (or dyads), as in Fischer (1982a) and McCarty et al. (1997). Acceptably reliable measures of network density and composition are often available from data on only three to five alters (Marsden 1993).

(B) *Additional Instruments for Egocentric Networks*

Many name generator instruments do not elicit weak ties that are crucial in extending network range. In addition, even single-generator instruments require substantial interview time and pose notable respondent burdens. This section reviews alternative instruments developed to address such limitations.

Instruments for Measuring Extensive Network Size

Estimating the size of extensive egocentric networks, including all alters someone "knows," is difficult in large, open populations. Several survey instruments have been developed for network size. The "summation" method (McCarty et al. 2001) uses global network questions to estimate the numbers of persons with whom respondents have sixteen relationships (e.g., family, friendship, neighboring), taking the sum of a respondent's answers as total network size. Two U.S. surveys using this method estimate that mean network size lies between 280 and 290.

Killworth et al. (1998b) developed "scale-up" methods that estimate extensive network size using data on the known size of subpopulations, such as people named "Michael" or people who are postal workers. These methods rest on the proposition that egocentric network composition resembles population composition, that is,

$$\frac{m}{c} = \frac{e}{t},$$

where m is the number of alters from some subpopulation in an egocentric network, c is network size, e is subpopulation size, and t is population size. Survey data on m, together with data on e and t from official statistics or other archives, lead to scale-up estimates of network size c.

The previous proposition will not, of course, hold precisely for all persons and subpopulations. Implementations of the scale-up approach estimate c using data on m and e for several subpopulations. Studies using the approach yield a range of values for mean network size. Killworth et al. (1990) obtained a mean of around 1,700 for U.S. informants, and one of about 570 for Mexico City informants; these estimates assume a broad definition of "knowing" ("ever known during one's lifetime"). Killworth et al. (1998a) reported the mean size of "active networks" (involving mutual recognition and contact within the prior 2 years) to be about 108 for Floridians; Killworth et al. (1998a) obtained a mean active network size of 286 from a U.S. survey. The authors note that scale-up methods depend heavily on a respondent's abilities to report accurately on the numbers of persons known within subpopulations.

The *reverse small world* (RSW) method (see, e.g., Killworth et al. 1990) is still another approach to measuring extensive networks. It presents respondents with many (often 500) "target" persons described by occupation and location, asking for an alter more likely than the respondent to know each target. RSW identifies alters who could be instrumentally useful; it omits those who are known, but not judged to be useful. Bernard et al. (1990) reported mean RSW network sizes of 129 for Jacksonville, Florida, informants, and 77 for Mexico City informants.

Position Generators

Rather than identifying particular alters and later ascertaining their social locations using name interpreters, the "position generator" measures linkages to specific locations directly. It asks respondents whether they have relationships with persons in each of a set of social positions. For example, Lin, Fu, and Hsung (2001) asked respondents if they have any relatives, friends, or acquaintances who hold fifteen different occupations. Follow-up questions may ascertain the strength of links to locations. Position generator data allow construction of indices of network range (e.g., number of occupations contacted) and composition (e.g., most prestigious occupation contacted).

Several empirical studies (e.g., Erickson 1996) use the position generator effectively. It identifies weak and strong contacts, if the threshold for contact with locations is of low intimacy; Erickson, for example, asked respondents to "count anyone you know well enough to talk to even if you are not close to them" (1996: p. 227). Because position generators do not ask about individual alters, they require less interview time than do many name generator instruments. However, position generators measure network range and composition only with respect to the social positions presented. Most applications focus on class or occupational positions; thus, the resulting data do not reflect racial or ethnoreligious network diversity, for example.

Smith (2002) experimentally compared measures of interracial friendship based on a one-item position generator, a name generator instrument, and a global approach in the 1998 GSS. His global items asked for a respondent's number of "good friends" and the number who are of a different race. Percentages of respondents claiming interracial good friends were highest for the position generator (whites, 42%; blacks, 62%), intermediate for the global approach (whites, 24%; blacks, 45%), and lowest for the name generator instrument (whites, 6%; blacks, 15%). Smith suggested that the name generator approach provides the most valid figures because it enumerates friends first, and later determines their race. The other approaches focus attention on the particular social location (race) of interest, encouraging respondents to inventory their memories for anyone who might meet the "good friend" criterion. Respondents seeking to present themselves favorably might alter their definition of "good friend" so they can report an interracial friend. Smith's findings may or may not apply to position generators measuring contact with occupational positions. Further instrument comparisons like this are needed.

The Resource Generator

Very recently, Van der Gaag and Snijders (2004) proposed the "resource generator" as an instrument for measuring individual-level social capital, which they defined as "resources owned by the members of an individual's personal social network, which may become available to the individual" (p. 200). Their instrument focuses on whether a survey respondent is in personal contact with anyone having specific possessions or capacities, such as the ability to repair vehicles, knowledge of literature, or high income. The resource generator does not enumerate specific social ties: in its most elementary version it measures only whether a respondent "knows" anyone having each resource. Follow-up questions may ask about the number of ties to each resource, or qualities of the strongest tie to each resource. Using data from a Dutch survey, Van der Gaag and Snijders identify four social capital subscales, which they label prestige, information, skills, and support.

(C) *CSS Data*

As defined by Krackhardt (1987), CSS data consist of judgments by each of several perceivers about each dyadic relationship in a whole network. Such data offer many potential measurements of a network. Krackhardt called attention to three: a single observer's "slice" of judgments, a "locally aggregated structure" of judgments by the two actors directly involved in each dyad, and a "consensus structure" based on all judgments about a given dyad.

CSS data have been collected via several survey/questionnaire methods. Krackhardt (1987) used a checklist of dichotomous items about the outgoing ties of each actor in the network. Casciaro (1998) presented informants with a labeled matrix, asking that they mark pairs linked by directed ties. Batchelder (2002) used a questionnaire about outgoing ties, asking for dichotomous judgments at two thresholds of tie strength. A third response task asked informants to rank the three closest contacts of each network actor; some informants did not or could not complete the rankings, however. Johnson and Orbach (2002) asked informants for the three most frequent ties of each actor, but did not request a ranking.

These designs entail a considerable respondent burden that rises with network size, as Krackhardt (1987) noted. For example, Krackhardt asked twenty-one workplace informants for 400 dichotomous judgments about each of two types of tie (friendship and advice). Batchelder's ranking task or Johnson and Orbach's "pick three" task make fewer demands: each would require 126 judgments per informant for Krackhardt's group. Freeman and Webster's (1994) pile sort – which first asks that informants identify groups of closely related actors, and later permits them to combine groups linked at lower-intensity thresholds – is another less burdensome approach. Freeman (1994) suggested a graphic interface: informants position actors with respect to one another within a two-dimensional space. This requires only as many judgments as there are actors, albeit much more complex ones than those of other CSS tasks.

Batchelder (2002) found strong similarities among consensus structures based on dichotomous ratings, trichotomous ratings, and her ranking task. She concluded that dichotomous ratings may be sufficient for CSS data, given the volume of data in the design. The high between-task similarity found in her study, however, may result in part because informants could consult their responses on the rating tasks when providing rankings.

(D) *Informant Biases in Network Perception*

Several patterns recur in studies based on CSS data. These findings hold both sub-stantive and methodological interest. They advance substantive understanding of social perception by revealing schemas or models on which informants draw when describing their social environments, and indicate tendencies to anticipate when informants report on their own social ties and those of others.

Studying informants in an organizational department, Kumbasar, Romney, and Batchelder (1994) compared individual CSS slices to a consensus structure. Informants occupied more central locations in their slices than in the consensus structure; more than one-half placed themselves first or second in degree centrality, for example. Johnson and Orbach (2002) replicated this finding of "ego bias" in their study of a political network, finding it to be strongest among peripheral informants.

Kumbasar et al. (1994) also examined differences between reporting on relationships among adjacent alters and on ties involving actors not directly linked to informants. Reports about adjacent alters had higher density, reciprocity, and transitivity. The authors concluded that informants experience cognitive pressures toward reporting balanced local environments. This echoes Freeman's (1992) claim that informants simplify observations of interaction, imposing a "group" or "balance" schema by selectively creating or neglecting relationships among alters. His experimental evidence indicates that subjects had difficulty recalling relationships in unbalanced structures. Krackhardt and Kilduff (1999) too found that perceptions of relationships draw on a balance schema. Their studies of four CSS data sets, however, found higher levels of reciprocity and transitivity for both close *and* distant alters; perceived balance was lowest for alters at intermediate geodesic distances from the informant. Krackhardt and Kilduff reason that informants lacking detailed memories about distal relationships fill in details about them using the balance schema as a heuristic.

Johnson and Orbach (2002) suggested that, when information about social ties is limited, reports draw on a "status" schema giving positions of prominence to high-status actors. Webster (1995) too suggested that status considerations influence reports about relationships, and Brewer (1995) noted that high-status persons tend to be salient within informant memories.

Notwithstanding the various perceptual biases isolated, Kumbasar et al. (1994: p. 488) concluded that their informants were "fairly reliable" judges of the affiliation pattern in the group studied. Findings that informants employ a balance schema nonetheless suggest that relatively high local densities will be obtained using name interpreter items about relationships among alters because informants overstate the degree of closeness among alters they cite.

2.4 Informant Accuracy and Competence

Landmark studies by Bernard, Killworth, and Sailer (BKS; 1981) problematized the validity of respondent reports on social ties, documenting a far-from-complete correspondence between survey reports of interaction frequencies ("cognitive" data) and contemporaneous observations ("behavioral" data). BKS drew pessimistic conclusions about the utility of self-reported network data, stimulating many responses and much further research. Freeman, Romney, and Freeman (1987), for instance, showed that discrepancies between survey reports and time-specific observations of interaction were not random, but instead biased toward longer-term regularities. They argued that informants can make largely accurate reports about enduring patterns of interaction (see also Freeman 1992).

Research on the cognitive-behavioral correspondence continued throughout the 1990s. Closely related work examines variations in cognition about networks as a phenomenon in and of itself, revealing variations in reporting "competence" that might offer aid in selecting informants.

(A) *Correspondence Between Reports and Observations*

In a reexamination of the BKS data, Kashy and Kenny (1990) showed that actors who received many cognitive citations had high observed interaction levels; moreover, behavioral data tended – although not inevitably – to corroborate pairwise reports of unusually high or low interaction. There was little correspondence, however, between an actor's number of outgoing citations and observed interaction levels. Thus, a major source of inaccuracy lies in the different response sets or thresholds that respondents use when making citations. Kashy and Kenny nonetheless concluded that cognitive network data contain useful information about interactions.

Freeman and Webster (1994) compared cognitive data from a pile sort task with observations of interaction. They too found substantial correspondence between the two measurements. Freeman and Webster noted, however, that the structure of their cognitive data was simpler than that of their observations; discernable clusters in the observations were much more marked in the sort. They contended that cognitive data are based on observed interactions, but reflect the use of a "group" schema storing information about categorical affiliations rather than dyadic ties. Freeman and Webster observed, moreover, that informants made more nuanced distinctions about proximate actors, smoothing over details about ties among distant ones.

Corman and Bradford (1993) recorded interactions among participants in a simulation game, and subsequently asked them to recall their interactions. Highly active participants tended to omit observed interactions from their self-reports, an outcome attributed to communication overload. Corman and Bradford theorized that participants who are highly identified with a group will tend to overreport, but their study did not measure identification directly.

These studies provide some confidence in self-reports as a valid source of network data, albeit with caution. They also suggest that observing social ties is itself difficult. Kashy and Kenny (1990), for instance, noted that time sampling introduces random elements into observed interaction records. A limited cognitive-behavioral correspondence, then, may reflect flaws both in observations and in self-reports.

(B) *Studies of Informant Competence*

In an early reexamination of the BKS data, Romney and Weller (1984) found that reliable informants (whose cognitive data resemble those of other informants) tend to be accurate (i.e., their cognitive data are close to aggregated observational data).

They posited that some informants may be better sources than others in reporting on interaction patterns. Romney, Weller, and Batchelder (1986) subsequently developed a general model for inferring shared cultural knowledge from informant reports, in which informants have differential "competence" to the extent that their reports correspond with those of others. This notion of competence parallels Romney and Weller's (1984) "reliability."

Several studies using CSS data investigate variations in informant competence in reporting on a whole network. These studies often refer to an informant's "accuracy." Their assessments of accuracy, however, do not compare cognitive data to an external referent, as in the BKS studies or Romney and Weller (1984). Instead, they usually examine the difference between an informant's slice of CSS data and some representation (e.g., a locally aggregated or a consensus structure) based on data from all informants. Such comparisons reflect what Romney et al. (1986) termed competence. To avoid ambiguity, the following remarks refer to "competence" rather than "accuracy."

These studies consistently find that centrally positioned informants tend to have higher competence (Krackhardt 1990; Bondonio 1998; Casciaro 1998; Johnson and Orbach 2002). Central informants have more opportunities to observe and to exchange information with others. Casciaro's (1998) finding that part-time workers are less competent reflects similar considerations.

Bondonio (1998) pointed to proximity as a source of competence: informants were more competent in reporting on the networks of close than of distal alters. Casciaro (1998) suggested that individual differences in motivation might lead informants to be differentially attentive to their social environments. High need for achievement was associated with greater competence in her CSS study.

(C) *Prospective Uses of Informants*

Network researchers implicitly take reports by actors involved in a dyad to be more valid than those by third-party informants. Apart from CSS data and name interpreters on alter–alter ties in egocentric instruments, little use has been made of informant reports about relationships of others. Torenvlied and Van Schuur (1994), however, suggested a procedure for eliciting CSS-like data from key informants. Burt and Ronchi (1994) measured egocentric networks for a subset of managers in an organization, some of whom offered data on the same relationships. Burt and Ronchi used this overlap in reports to develop imputations for unmeasured relationships in the full managerial network.

Competence studies also suggest intriguing prospects for using informants. For instance, a whole network might be measured by asking a small number of informants to complete CSS-like instruments, rather than seeking self-reports from all participants. This would be viable if CSS data reveal a strong correspondence between, for example, a consensus structure based on reports by all informants and one based on reports of some subset of highly competent informants. It would also require data – on likely centrality or need for achievement, for example – with which to screen prospective informants for competence.

2.5   Archival Network Data

Network studies use much information residing in archives that were not created expressly for social research. Such data provide unobtrusive measures of social ties. They sometimes trace relationships of actors who are reluctant to grant interviews. Archival data are often inexpensive, especially when in electronic form; if maintained over time, archives support longitudinal network studies. Archival materials are a mainstay source for studying networks in the past.

Some recent examples illustrate the range of applications for archival network data. Podolny (1993) measured the status of investment banks based on their relative positions in "tombstone" announcements of syndicated securities offerings. Using patent citations, Podolny and Stuart (1995) developed indicators of niche differentiation for innovations. Alexander and Danowski (1990) coded links between actors in Roman society recorded in Cicero's letters. Hargens (2000) depicted the structure of research areas via citations linking scientific papers. Adamic and Adar (2003) mined homepages on the World Wide Web for connections among university students. Two-mode data on membership relations (e.g., Table 7.4.1, Chapter 7, this volume) often are to be found in archives.

Relatively few explicitly methodological studies of archival data appear in the network literature. Although properties surely vary from source to source, a few generic issues and questions can be raised about such data.

The validity of archival data rests on the correspondence between measured connections and the conceptual ties of research interest. Sometimes this can be quite close; Podolny's interest in tombstone advertisements lies in the status signals (bank affiliations) they convey to third-party observers, and observers see exactly the information Podolny coded. In other cases, there may be slippage. Rice et al. (1989) observed that researchers often assume that academic citations track the flow of scientific information, but that in practice citations have many purposes, including paying homage to pioneers, correcting or disputing previous work, and identifying methods or equipment, among many others. Hargens (2000) conducted citation-context analyses revealing differences in citation practices – and the possible meanings of citations – across research areas.

Attention to the conditions under which archives are produced may be helpful in judging their likely validity with respect to any given conceptual definition of relationships. For example, Meyer (2000) reviewed the social processes underlying patent citations. Such citations acknowledge "prior art" related to a given invention, thereby distinguishing and narrowing an applicant's legal claims to originality. Interactions among applicants, patent examiners, and patent attorneys determine prior art citations. Examiners can add citations to an application before a patent is granted; applicants often claim to be unaware of the added works, although they do acknowledge other materials not included among the examiner's "front page" citations. Patent citations, then, are not simple traces of the process leading to an invention.

Likewise, the conditions under which objects come to be included in an archive merit attention. There are some reasons to anticipate that citation databases will be relatively comprehensive: authors have clear incentives to publish their works, much as inventors have for guarding their claims. Rice et al. (1989), however, reminded us that editorial policies determine what journals are tracked by abstracting and indexing services, and thus what outgoing citations are recorded. In some instances, availability of archival materials may be quite selective. Adamic and Adar's (2003) homepage study, for example, notes that students decide whether to maintain a page. Moreover, some student pages exist, but reside in domains other than the one they examined.

Problems analogous to expansiveness bias in survey data (Feld and Carter 2002) arise by virtue of varying criteria for recording relationships in archives. Many affiliation data – such as corporate board memberships – may be relatively clear-cut. Patent citations should satisfy a common standard of "relevance" (Meyer 2000), although one might envision "examiner effects" on the number of outgoing citations. Academic citation practices, however, may differ appreciably across authors and fields. Authors of homepages have full discretion over page content, and pages almost certainly vary greatly in whether and why they include links. Adamic and Adar (2003) reported outgoing links for 14% and 33% of personal homepages in two universities.

Rice et al. (1989) also noted various mechanical problems that can introduce error into archival network measures. Journal-to-journal citation counts, for example, may be inaccurate if journal names change or if databases include "aberrant" journal abbreviations. Similar difficulties can affect author-to-author counts. Problems of this sort are easily overlooked, especially for electronically available archives.

Computer-mediated systems (Rice 1990) offer potentially rich data on human communication that network analysts have only begun to exploit. Such records are, however, medium specific: e-mail archives, for instance, exclude face-to-face communication that may be highly significant. The volume and detail of the data recorded in some such sources raises important issues of how to protect the privacy of monitored communication.

2.6 Observation

Observations made as part of extended fieldwork were important sources of data in some early network studies (Mitchell 1969). Relatively fewer recent network studies have drawn on such data, by comparison with survey and archival sources. Gibson's (2003) real-time observations of conversations in managerial meetings are one recent example.

The difficulty of obtaining observational data should not be understated. Corman and Bradford (1993) experienced problems in coding dyadic interactions from video- and audiotapes; it was not always possible for coders to discern who was addressing whom. Webster (1994) commented on problems in focal behavior sampling as an observational method, remarking that the relevant behaviors must be readily visible in the context studied and of sufficiently low frequency to allow an observer to record all relevant instances. Corman and Scott (1994) added that observation of large groups may require multiple observers positioned in all locations of group activity. They suggested that wireless microphones might be used in place of human observers; using a small set of recordings, they illustrated a procedure for establishing dyadic communications by matching digitized signal patterns.

2.7 Conclusion

Notable advances in network measurement have occurred since 1990, especially for survey and questionnaire data. Instruments for measuring egocentric networks are now much better understood, and much has been learned about cognitive processes and biases involved in answering questions about social relationships.

Important questions of validity and reliability for survey/questionnaire data remain. The number and range of network studies that draw on archival materials has risen. Given the opportunities that archival sources present, it is important to scrutinize the quality of such data as closely as data from self-reports. Assessments of data quality, regardless of source, will be facilitated if researchers clearly articulate their concepts of the "true scores" they seek to capture with empirical indicators of network ties.

Acknowledgments

For helpful comments, I am grateful to Devon Brewer, Peter Carrington, Freda Lynn, and Joel Podolny. Thanks to Hilary Levey and Freda Lynn for research assistance.

References

Adamic, Lada A., and Eytan Adar (2003) "Friends and Neighbors on the Web." *Social Networks* 25: 211–230.

Alexander, Michael C., and James A. Danowski (1990) "Analysis of an Ancient Network: Personal Communication and the Study of Social Structure in a Past Society." *Social Networks* 12: 313–335.

Bailey, Stefanie, and Peter V. Marsden (1999) "Interpretation and Interview Context: Examining the General Social Survey Name Generator Using Cognitive Methods." *Social Networks* 21: 287–309.

Bass, Lee Ann, and Catherine H. Stein (1997) "Comparing the Structure and Stability of Network Ties Using the Social Support Questionnaire and the Social Network List." *Journal of Social and Personal Relationships* 14: 123–132.

Batchelder, Ece (2002) "Comparing Three Simultaneous Measurements of a Sociocognitive Network." *Social Networks* 24: 261–277.

Batchelder, William H. (1989) "Inferring Meaningful Global Network Properties from Individual Actor's Measurement Scales," pp. 89–134. In Linton C. Freeman, Douglas R. White, and A. Kimball Romney (eds.), *Research Methods in Social Network Analysis*. Fairfax, VA: George Mason University Press.

Bernard, H. Russell, Eugene C. Johnsen, Peter D. Killworth, Christopher McCarty, Gene A. Shelley, and Scott Robinson (1990) "Comparing Four Different Methods for Measuring Personal Social Networks." *Social Networks* 12: 179–215.

Bernard, H. Russell, Peter Killworth, and Lee Sailer (1981) "Summary of Research on Informant Accuracy in Network Data and on the Reverse Small World Problem." *Connections* 4(2): 11–25.

Blair, Johnny, Geeta Menon, and Barbara Bickart (1991) "Measurement Effects in Self vs. Proxy Responses to Survey Questions: An Information Processing Perspective," pp. 145–166. In Paul P.

Biemer, Robert M. Groves, Lars E. Lyberg, Nancy A. Mathiowetz, and Seymour Sudman (eds.), *Measurement Errors in Surveys*. New York: John Wiley & Sons.

Bond, Charles F., Jr., Rosalind L. Jones, and Daniel L. Weintraub (1985) "On the Unconstrained Recall of Acquaintances: A Sampling-Traversal Model." *Journal of Personality and Social Psychology* 49: 327–337.

Bondonio, Daniele (1998) "Predictors of Accuracy in Perceiving Informal Social Networks." *Social Networks* 20: 301–330.

Brewer, Devon D. (1995) "The Social Structural Basis of the Organization of Persons in Memory." *Human Nature* 6: 379–403.

Brewer, Devon D. (2000) "Forgetting in the Recall-Based Elicitation of Personal Networks." *Social Networks* 22: 29–43.

Brewer, Devon D., Sharon B. Garrett, and Shalini Kulasingam (1999) "Forgetting as a Cause of Incomplete Reporting of Sexual and Drug Injection Partners." *Sexually Transmitted Diseases* 26: 166–176.

Brewer, Devon D., and Cynthia M. Webster (1999) "Forgetting of Friends and Its Effects on Measuring Friendship Networks." *Social Networks* 21: 361–373.

Burt, Ronald S. (1984) "Network Items and the General Social Survey." *Social Networks* 6: 293–339.

Burt, Ronald S. (1986) "A Note on Sociometric Order in the General Social Survey Network Data." *Social Networks* 8: 149–174.

Burt, Ronald S. (1987) "A Note on the General Social Survey's Ersatz Network Density Item." *Social Networks* 9: 75–85.

Burt, Ronald S. (1997) "A Note on Social Capital and Network Content." *Social Networks* 19: 355–373.

Burt, Ronald S., and Don Ronchi (1994) "Measuring a Large Network Quickly." *Social Networks* 16: 91–135.

Campbell, Karen E., and Barrett A. Lee (1991) "Name Generators in Surveys of Personal Networks." *Social Networks* 13: 203–221.

Casciaro, Tiziana (1998) "Seeing Things Clearly: Social Structure, Personality, and Accuracy in Social Network Perception." *Social Networks* 20: 331–351.

Coleman, James S. (1958) "Relational Analysis: The Study of Social Organizations with Survey Methods." *Human Organization* 17: 28–36.

Corman, Steven R., and Lisa Bradford (1993) "Situational Effects on the Accuracy of Self-Reported Communication Behavior." *Communication Research* 20: 822–840.

Corman, Steven R., and Craig R. Scott (1994) "A Synchronous Digital Signal Processing Method for Detecting Face-to-Face Organizational Communication Behavior." *Social Networks* 16: 163–179.

Doreian, Patrick, and Katherine L. Woodard (1992) "Fixed List Versus Snowball Selection of Social Networks." *Social Science Research* 21: 216–233.

Doreian, Patrick, and Katherine L. Woodard (1994) "Defining and Locating Cores and Boundaries of Social Networks." *Social Networks* 16: 267–293.

Erickson, Bonnie H. (1996) "Culture, Class, and Connections." *American Journal of Sociology* 102: 217–251.

Eudey, Lynn, Jeffrey C. Johnson, and Edie Schade (1994) "Ranking Versus Ratings in Social Networks: Theory and Praxis." *Journal of Quantitative Anthropology* 4: 297–312.

Feld, Scott L. (1981) "The Focused Organization of Social Ties." *American Journal of Sociology* 86: 1015–1035.

Feld, Scott L., and William C. Carter (2002) "Detecting Measurement Bias in Respondent Reports of Personal Networks." *Social Networks* 24: 365–383.

Ferligoj, Anuška, and Valentina Hlebec (1999) "Evaluation of Social Network Measurement Instruments." *Social Networks* 21: 111–130.

Fischer, Claude S. (1982a) *To Dwell Among Friends: Personal Networks in Town and City*. Chicago: University of Chicago Press.

Fischer, Claude S. (1982b) "What Do We Mean by 'Friend': An Inductive Study." *Social Networks* 3: 287–306.

Fischer, Claude S., and Yossi Shavit (1995) "National Differences in Network Density: Israel and the United States." *Social Networks* 17: 129–145.

Fiske, Alan Page (1995) "Social Schemata for Remembering People: Relationships and Person Attributes in Free Recall of Acquaintances." *Journal of Quantitative Anthropology* 5: 305–324.

Freeman, Linton C. (1989) "Social Networks and the Structure Experiment," pp. 11–40. In Linton C. Freeman, Douglas R. White, and A. Kimball Romney (eds.), *Research Methods in Social Network Analysis*. Fairfax, VA: George Mason University Press.

Freeman, Linton C. (1992) "Filling in the Blanks: A Theory of Cognitive Categories and the Structure of Social Affiliation." *Social Psychology Quarterly* 55: 118–127.

Freeman, Linton C. (1994) "MAP: A Computer Program for Collecting Network Data." *Connections* 17 (1): 26–30.

Freeman, Linton C., A. Kimball Romney, and Sue C. Freeman (1987) "Cognitive Structure and Informant Accuracy." *American Anthropologist* 89: 310–325.

Freeman, Linton C., and Cynthia M. Webster (1994) "Interpersonal Proximity in Social and Cognitive Space." *Social Cognition* 12: 223–247.

Gibson, David R. (2003) "Participation Shifts: Order and Differentiation in Group Conversation." *Social Forces* 81: 1335–1380.

Granovetter, Mark S. (1976) "Network Sampling: Some First Steps." *American Journal of Sociology* 81: 1287–1303.

Groves, Robert M., and Lou J. Magilavy (1986) "Measuring and Explaining Interviewer Effects in Centralized Telephone Surveys." *Public Opinion Quarterly* 50: 251–266.

Hargens, Lowell L. (2000) "Using the Literature: Reference Networks, Reference Contexts, and the Social Structure of Scholarship." *American Sociological Review* 65: 846–865.

Hirsch, Barton J. (1980) "Natural Support Systems and Coping with Major Life Changes." *American Journal of Community Psychology* 8: 159–172.

Johnson, Jeffrey C., and Michael K. Orbach (2002) "Perceiving the Political Landscape: Ego Biases in Cognitive Political Networks." *Social Networks* 24: 291–310.

Kashy, Deborah A., and David A. Kenny (1990) "Do You Know Whom You Were with a Week Ago Friday? A Re-Analysis of the Bernard, Killworth, and Sailer Studies." *Social Psychology Quarterly* 53: 55–61.

Killworth, Peter D., Eugene C. Johnsen, H. Russell Bernard, Gene Ann Shelley, and Christopher McCarty (1990) "Estimating the Size of Personal Networks." *Social Networks* 12: 289–312.

Killworth, Peter D., Eugene C. Johnsen, Christopher McCarty, Gene Ann Shelley, and H. Russell Bernard (1998a) "A Social Network Approach to Estimating Seroprevalence in the United States." *Social Networks* 20: 23–50.

Killworth, Peter D., Christopher McCarty, H. Russell Bernard, Gene Ann Shelley, and Eugene C. Johnsen (1998b) "Estimation of Seroprevalence, Rape, and Homelessness in the United States Using a Social Network Approach." *Evaluation Review* 22: 289–308.

Kirke, Deirdre M. (1996) "Collecting Peer Data and Delineating Peer Networks in a Complete Network." *Social Networks* 18: 333–346.

Klovdahl, Alden S., Z. Dhofier, G. Oddy, J. O'Hara, S. Stoutjesdijk, and A. Whish (1977) "Social Networks in an Urban Area: First Canberra Study." *Australian and New Zealand Journal of Sociology* 13: 169–172.

Krackhardt, David (1987) "Cognitive Social Structures." *Social Networks* 9: 109–134.

Krackhardt, David (1990) "Assessing the Political Landscape: Structure, Cognition, and Power in Organizations." *Administrative Science Quarterly* 35: 342–369.

Krackhardt, David, and Martin Kilduff (1999) "Whether Close or Far: Social Distance Effects on Perceived Balance in Friendship Networks." *Journal of Personality and Social Psychology* 76: 770–782.

Kumbasar, Ece, A. Kimball Romney, and William H. Batchelder (1994) "Systematic Biases in Social Perception." *American Journal of Sociology* 100: 477–505.

Laumann, Edward O., Peter V. Marsden, and David Prensky (1989) "The Boundary Specification Problem in Network Analysis," pp. 61–87. In Linton C. Freeman, Douglas R. White, and

A. Kimball Romney (eds.), *Research Methods in Social Network Analysis*. Fairfax, VA: George Mason University Press.

Lazega, Emmanuel (1999) "Generalized Exchange and Economic Performance: Social Embeddedness of Labor Contracts in a Corporate Law Partnership," pp. 237–265. In Roger T. A. J. Leenders and Shaul M. Gabbay (eds.), *Corporate Social Capital and Liability*. Boston: Kluwer.

Lin, Nan, Yang-chih Fu, and Ray-May Hsung (2001) "The Position Generator: Measurement Techniques for Investigations of Social Capital," pp. 57–81. In Nan Lin, Karen Cook, and Ronald S. Burt (eds.), *Social Capital: Theory and Research*. New York: Aldine de Gruyter.

Marsden, Peter V. (1987) "Core Discussion Networks of Americans." *American Sociological Review* 52: 122–131.

Marsden, Peter V. (1990) "Network Data and Measurement." *Annual Review of Sociology* 16: 435–463.

Marsden, Peter V. (1993) "The Reliability of Network Density and Composition Measures." *Social Networks* 15: 399–421.

Marsden, Peter V. (2002) "Egocentric and Sociocentric Measures of Network Centrality." *Social Networks* 24: 407–422.

Marsden, Peter V. (2003) "Interviewer Effects in Measuring Network Size Using a Single Name Generator." *Social Networks* 25: 1–16.

McCarty, Christopher (1995) "The Meaning of Knowing as a Network Tie." *Connections* 18(2): 20–31.

McCarty, Christopher, H. Russell Bernard, Peter D. Killworth, Gene Ann Shelley, and Eugene C. Johnsen (1997) "Eliciting Representative Samples of Personal Networks." *Social Networks* 19: 303–323.

McCarty, Christopher, Peter D. Killworth, H. Russell Bernard, Eugene C. Johnsen, and Gene A. Shelley (2001) "Comparing Two Methods for Estimating Network Size." *Human Organization* 60: 28–39.

McGrady, Gene A., Clementine Marrow, Gail Myers, Michael Daniels, Mildred Vera, Charles Mueller, Edward Liebow, Alden Klovdahl, and Richard Lovely (1995) "A Note on Implementation of a Random-Walk Design to Study Adolescent Social Networks." *Social Networks* 17: 251–255.

Meyer, Martin (2000) "What Is Special About Patent Citations? Differences Between Scientific and Patent Citations." *Scientometrics* 49: 93–123.

Milardo, Robert M. (1992) "Comparative Methods for Delineating Social Networks." *Journal of Social and Personal Relationships* 9: 447–461.

Mitchell, J. Clyde (1969) *Social Networks in Urban Situations: Analyses of Personal Relationships in Central African Towns*. Manchester, UK: Manchester University Press.

Moore, J. C. (1988) "Self-Proxy Response Status and Survey Response Quality: A Review of the Literature." *Journal of Official Statistics* 4: 155–172.

Morgan, David L., Margaret B. Neal, and Paula Carder (1997) "The Stability of Core and Peripheral Networks Over Time." *Social Networks* 19: 9–25.

Podolny, Joel M. (1993) "A Status-Based Model of Market Competition." *American Journal of Sociology* 98: 829–872.

Podolny, Joel M., and James N. Baron (1997) "Resources and Relationships: Social Networks and Mobility in the Workplace." *American Sociological Review* 62: 673–693.

Podolny, Joel M., and Toby E. Stuart (1995) "A Role-Based Ecology of Technological Change." *American Journal of Sociology* 100: 1224–1260.

Rapkin, Bruce D., and Catherine H. Stein (1989) "Defining Personal Networks: The Effect of Delineation Instructions on Network Structure and Stability." *American Journal of Community Psychology* 17: 259–267.

Rice, Ronald E. (1990) "Computer-Mediated Communication System Network Data: Theoretical Concerns and Empirical Examples." *International Journal of Man–Machine Studies* 32: 627–647.

Rice, R. E., Christine L. Borgman, Diane Bednarski, and P. J. Hart (1989) "Journal-to-Journal Citation Data: Issues of Validity and Reliability." *Scientometrics* 15: 257–282.

Romney, A. Kimball, and Susan C. Weller (1984) "Predicting Informant Accuracy from Patterns of Recall Among Informants." *Social Networks* 6: 59–77.

Romney, A. Kimball, Susan C. Weller, and William H. Batchelder (1986) "Culture as Consensus: A Theory of Culture and Informant Accuracy." *American Anthropologist* 88: 313–338.

Ruan, Danching (1998) "The Content of the General Social Survey Discussion Networks: An Exploration of General Social Survey Discussion Name Generator in a Chinese Context." *Social Networks* 20: 247–264.

Ruan, Danching, Linton C. Freeman, Xinyuan Dai, Yunkang Pan, and Wenhong Zhang (1997) "On the Changing Structure of Social Networks in Urban China." *Social Networks* 19: 75–89.

Sarason, Irwin G., Henry M. Levine, Robert B. Basham, and Barbara R. Sarason (1983) "Assessing Social Support: The Social Support Questionnaire." *Journal of Personality and Social Psychology* 44: 127–139.

Seidman, Stephen B. (1983) "Network Structure and Minimum Degree." *Social Networks* 5: 269–287.

Shelley, Gene A., H. Russell Bernard, Peter Killworth, Eugene Johnsen, and Christopher McCarty (1995) "Who Knows Your HIV Status? What HIV+ Patients and Their Network Members Know About Each Other." *Social Networks* 17: 189–217.

Smith, Tom W. (2002) "Measuring Inter-Racial Friendships." *Social Science Research* 31: 576–593.

Straits, Bruce C. (2000) "Ego's Important Discussants or Significant People: An Experiment in Varying the Wording of Personal Network Name Generators." *Social Networks* 22: 123–140.

Sudman, Seymour (1985) "Experiments in the Measurement of the Size of Social Networks." *Social Networks* 7: 127–151.

Sudman, Seymour, Barbara Bickart, Johnny Blair, and Geeta Menon (1994) "The Effect of Participation Level on Reports of Behavior and Attitudes by Proxy Reporters," pp. 251–265. In Norbert Schwarz and Seymour Sudman (eds.), *Autobiographical Memory and the Validity of Retrospective Reports.* New York: Springer-Verlag.

Sudman, Seymour, Norman M. Bradburn, and Norbert Schwarz (1996) *Thinking About Answers: The Application of Cognitive Processes to Survey Methodology.* San Francisco: Jossey-Bass.

Torenvlied, René, and Wijbrandt H. Van Schuur (1994) "A Procedure for Assessing Large Scale 'Total' Networks Using Information from Key Informants: A Research Note." *Connections* 17 (2): 56–60.

Van der Poel, Mart G. M. (1993) "Delineating Personal Support Networks." *Social Networks* 15: 49–70.

Van der Gaag, Martin, and Tom Snijders (2004) "Proposals for the Measurement of Individual Social Capital," pp. 199–218. In Henk Flap and Beate Völker (eds.), *Creation and Returns of Social Capital: A New Research Program.* London: Routledge.

Van Tilburg, Theo (1998) "Interviewer Effects in the Measurement of Personal Network Size." *Sociological Methods and Research* 26: 300–328.

Wasserman, Stanley, and Katherine Faust (1994) *Social Network Analysis: Methods and Applications.* New York: Cambridge University Press.

Webster, Cynthia M. (1994) "Data Type: A Comparison of Observational and Cognitive Measures." *Journal of Quantitative Anthropology* 4: 313–328.

Webster, Cynthia M. (1995) "Detecting Context-Based Constraints in Social Perception." *Journal of Quantitative Anthropology* 5: 285–303.

White, Kevin, and Susan Cotts Watkins (2000) "Accuracy, Stability, and Reciprocity in Informal Conversational Networks in Kenya." *Social Networks* 22: 337–355.

3

Network Sampling and Model Fitting

Ove Frank

Stockholm University

3.1 Introduction

Survey methodology has a tradition in statistics of focusing on populations and samples. Samples of population units are selected according to probabilistic sampling designs. By controlling the design, selection bias and uncertainty of estimators and tests can be quantified so inference can be drawn with confidence. Early publications in the field were dedicated to explaining the benefits of probability sampling designs as opposed to convenience sampling of various sorts. *Probability sampling* is the term usually used when the selection probabilities are known for all samples and each population unit has a nonzero probability of being selected. The focus on controlled randomization can be contrasted with probabilistic uncertainty modeling. In many surveys, sampling variation is not the main source of uncertainty. There is variation due to measurement errors, response imperfections, observation difficulties, and other repetitive factors that can be specified by probabilistic assumptions. The superpopulation concept can also be seen as a way to include probabilistic modeling for such uncertainty that is not a consequence of imposed randomization or variation due to repetitive incidents. Modern statistical survey methodology distinguishes between design- and model-based approaches, and often uses an intermediate approach with model-assisted techniques in combination with design-based inference. A pure probabilistic model approach focuses on data and tries to imitate how data are generated. A good model fit is important for reliable inference, but does not necessarily mean that the sampling design is an explicit part of the model's data generating mechanism. For further information, see Särndal, Swensson, and Wretman (1992) and Smith (1999).

Both the design and the pure modeling perspectives have been used in network surveys. See, for instance, the review articles by Frank (1980, 1988a, 1997). As a background to the subsequent presentation of network sampling, Section 3.2 reviews some central concepts and fundamental problems in survey sampling. Multivariate network data comprising attributes of population units and relational structures between the units are introduced in Section 3.3. Section 3.4 gives various examples of sampling and data collection in networks. Snowball sampling and other link-tracing designs are briefly discussed. When such designs get too involved, a model approach might be necessary. There is a huge literature on basic random graph models of importance for understanding structural properties of networks. Some standard models and some general references are given in Section 3.5. Often the random graph models do not suffice for applications with multivariate network data, and more elaborate multiparametric

31

models are needed. In particular, the relational structure often implies that there is need for a random graph model with specific dependence among the network variables. Section 3.6 presents a class of network models for multivariate data with so-called dyad dependence. Section 3.7 discusses such a model with normally distributed structural attributes, and Section 3.8 specifies a version for discrete data. It is suggested that network structure is governed by latent individual preferences for local structure, and this new approach is shown to lead to interesting interpretations and generalizations of the Holland-Leinhardt model (Holland and Leinhardt 1981). The local structure assumption also makes the model very appropriate for Bayesian extensions. To fit the discrete model to data, two exploratory tools are described in Sections 3.9 and 3.10. Section 3.9 considers log-linear interaction analysis adapted to multivariate network data. Section 3.10 presents a clustering method that could either be used separately or as a preparation for interaction analyses. Finally, Section 3.11 briefly mentions some fields of application for network surveys.

3.2   Preliminaries on Survey Sampling

Populations of many kinds are unknown or incompletely known, and survey methods are needed to get information about them. Surveys that provide data about only parts of the population can help us draw conclusions about the whole population, but these conclusions are uncertain and we want to know how uncertain they are. By collecting data from units in the population that are selected by controlled probability sampling methods, it is possible to measure with what confidence population properties can be assessed from sample data. Thus, probability sampling methods play a key role in investigating populations with good surveys.

Much effort in survey sampling has been devoted to how auxiliary information can be used to improve sampling designs. Auxiliary information is a concept of special concern when populations are imbedded in networks of relationships between the population units.

Other issues of relevance and possible importance in survey sampling are non-sampling errors caused by nonresponse and response imperfections of various kinds. Särndal et al. (1992) provide a thorough discussion. In so-called total survey designs, one is concerned with the sources of variation considered to be relevant for obtaining the data to be investigated. It is customary to distinguish between design specifications and model assumptions. Design specifications refer to the random sampling mechanism only, whereas model assumptions are intended to provide a sufficiently accurate mathematical description of population data when all sources of nonsampling variation are taken into account. According to the model approach, sample data can be conceived as observations on random variables that explain the total uncertainty due to both sample selection and other sources of variation.

To be more specific about concepts and terminology in survey sampling, the basic setup is now introduced. This presentation also serves the purpose of pointing out the specific features of data obtained by survey sampling that make it possible to apply statistical methods that are not generally available for observations on random variables.

Consider a finite population U of N units. The units are labeled by integers $1, \ldots, N$, and without restriction we identify the units with their labels and define the population as $U = \{1, \ldots, N\}$. There is a variable of interest y defined for the units in the population, and the value of y for unit i is denoted y_i for $i = 1, \ldots, N$. The variable y might be univariate or multivariate. In the univariate case its values might be numeric or categorical, and in the multivariate case they might be any combination of such values. The variable y is observable, but its values are unknown prior to the survey. Auxiliary information in the form of a variable x with values x_i for unit $i = 1, \ldots, N$ is known prior to the survey. This variable x might, like y, be a multivariate combination of numeric and categorical variables.

Any probabilistic selection mechanism that does not depend on y can be used to draw a sample of units from the population U. If the units are sequentially drawn, we have random variables $S_1, S_2, \ldots$ that are the (labels of the) units selected at the first draw, second draw, and so on. The sample is defined by a sequence

$$(S_1, S_2, \ldots, S_n)$$

of randomly drawn units where the number of draws n is generally a random variable defined by the selection mechanism. Note that generally $n, S_1, \ldots, S_n$ are random variables with a multivariate probability distribution not depending on the population values of y, but possibly on those of x. If the selected units $S_1, \ldots, S_n$ are all distinct with probability 1, the draws are said to be without replacement; otherwise, the draws are said to be with replacement.

Instead of specifying the sample by the sequence $(S_1, \ldots, S_n)$, an equivalent representation is given by the matrix of indicators

$$S_{ij} = I(S_i = j)$$

which are 1 or 0 according to whether the ith draw selects unit j for $i = 1, \ldots, n$ and $j = 1, \ldots, N$.

The variable of interest y is observed for each selected unit in the sample. By writing $y_j = y(j)$, we can define $Y_i = y(S_i)$ for $i = 1, \ldots, n$. The observation Y_i is random because it is a function of the random variable S_i. If $S_i = j$, then $Y_i = y_j$. The sample provides the sequence of y-values given by

$$(Y_1, \ldots, Y_n).$$

This sequence is a multivariate random variable with a probability distribution that depends on the population values $y_1, \ldots, y_N$ via the random selection mechanism that does not depend on these values. The essential difference between standard statistical data given by observations on random variables $(Y_1, \ldots, Y_n)$ and survey sample data is the knowledge of the labels of the units selected $(S_1, \ldots, S_n)$. This information is often beneficial and can be used to improve inference on the population values $y_1, \ldots, y_N$. In the survey sampling setup, we have data both on labels and y-values for the units in the sample sequence. Moreover, we might have auxiliary information about labels and x-values for all units in the population. Formally, survey sample data and auxiliary data consist of

$$(S_i, Y_i) \quad \text{for} \quad i = 1, \ldots, n \quad \text{and} \quad (j, x_j) \quad \text{for} \quad j = 1, \ldots, N.$$

Note that knowledge of labels is required for proper matching of auxiliary data to observed sample data.

There is obviously some redundancy in reporting y-values for the same unit more than once, which occurs if selections with replications are made. However, the locations in the sample sequence of such repetitions carry some sort of information, and it might not be evident whether it is needed or not. Likewise, it is perhaps not clear whether the order of selection carries some sort of useful information. To explore this, consider the matrix of selection indicators $S_{ij} = I(S_i = j)$ defined previously. The column sum

$$S_{.j} = S_{1j} + \cdots + S_{nj}$$

reports how many times unit j is included in the sample sequence, and it is called the multiplicity of unit j for $j = 1, \ldots, N$. Define indicators $I_j = I(S_{.j} > 0)$, which are 1 or 0 according to whether unit j is included in the sample sequence $(S_1, \ldots, S_n)$. Let s be the set of distinct units sampled, that is

$$s = \{j \in U : S_i = j \quad \text{for some} \quad i = 1, \ldots, n\} = \{j \in U : I_j = 1\}.$$

The sample set s is a subset of U. The indicator sequence $(I_1, \ldots, I_N)$ has a sum m equal to the size of s. The multiplicity sequence $(S_{.1}, \ldots, S_{.N})$ has a sum equal to the number of draws n in the sample sequence $(S_1, \ldots, S_n)$. If labels and y-values are given for distinct units in the sample only, data reported consist of

$$\{(j, y_j) : j \in s\}$$

and the information about selection order and multiplicity is missing. If multiplicities are also given so

$$\{(j, y_j, S_{.j}) : j \in s\}$$

is given, then the information about selection order is still missing. It is a well-known fact in survey sampling proved by Basu and Ghosh (1967) and Basu (1969) that neither selection order nor multiplicity is needed and that

$$t = \{(j, y_j) : j \in s\}$$

is a minimal sufficient statistic for $(y_1, \ldots, y_N)$. The statistic t is sufficient and it is a function of any other sufficient statistic. Moreover, any function of t that is not a bijection cannot be sufficient. Many convenient estimators used in survey sampling are not functions of the minimal sufficient statistic t. For example, in simple random sampling with replacement from a finite population of known size N, the ordinary sample mean

$$(Y_1 + \cdots + Y_n)/n = \sum_{j \in s} y_j S_{.j}/n$$

is an unbiased estimator of the population mean. Because it depends on the multiplicities, it is not a function of t. Therefore, it is possible, in principle, to improve any such estimator by Rao-Blackwellization, that is, by replacing it by its expected value conditional on t. For the example considered, it is possible to show that the Rao-Blackwell method leads to the unbiased estimator

$$e_1(t) = \sum_{j \in s} y_j/m$$

which is the mean of the y-values of the distinct sample units and consequently a function of the minimal sufficient statistic t. For many sample selection procedures, it is complicated to apply Rao-Blackwellization and it is convenient in special situations to consider particular estimators based on the minimal sufficient statistic. For instance, the so-called Horvitz-Thompson estimator of the population total $y_1 + \cdots + y_N$ is an unbiased estimator based on t given by

$$\sum_{j \in s} (y_j/\pi_j)$$

where π_j is the probability that the sample set s contains unit j. This probability is called the inclusion probability of unit j. In the example considered, we have

$$\pi_j = 1 - (1 - 1/N)^n$$

and the population mean has an unbiased estimator given by

$$e_2(t) = \sum_{j \in s} (y_j/N\pi_j).$$

Thus, there are two distinct unbiased estimators of the population mean in this case, $e_1(t)$ and $e_2(t)$, and they are both based on the minimal sufficient statistic t. From this fact, and similar findings in other cases, implications are that the minimal sufficient statistic t is not complete. The lack of completeness of the minimal sufficient statistic t makes it difficult in general to obtain optimal estimators in survey sampling without turning to model assumptions for the y-values.

3.3 Variables in Network Surveys

Design-based survey sampling can be criticized for treating population values as if they are fixed unrelated quantities, even if it is known that they are related for units that are close in some sense. For instance, neighboring geographic units might have similar characteristics in terms of natural resources, and people who are friends might share certain values. Sometimes such similarities between population units can be handled by auxiliary variables defined for the units themselves, but in a more general setting it could be advantageous to consider relational variables defined for pairs of population units. For instance, contact frequencies between people and amount of goods transferred between different sites are examples of dyadic relationships. To take such relationships into account, it is convenient to consider the population units as vertices in a graph. Variables defined for population units and variables defined for pairs of population units are then referred to as vertex variables and edge variables. A dyadic relationship is symmetric if it never depends on the order of the population units in the pair. It is sometimes important to distinguish between symmetric and unsymmetric (not symmetric for all pairs) relationships, and this can be done by referring to edge and arc variables in the two cases, respectively. A special case of an unsymmetric relationship is one that is not symmetric for any pair – it is called *asymmetric*.

Vertex, edge, and arc variables could be variables of interest to be investigated in a survey or could be known prior to the survey and useful as auxiliary variables. The variables could be multivariate combinations of numeric and categorical variables. Numeric variables could sometimes be formally treated as discrete variables with a finite number of possible values. Regardless of the scales of the variables, it is for some purposes convenient to label their values by integers $0, 1, \ldots$. Binary variables have values in $\{0, 1\}$, trinary in $\{0, 1, 2\}$, etc. A bivariate variable consisting of two trinary variables has nine possible values, which can be represented as trinary numbers $(0, 0) = 0, (0, 1) = 1, (0, 2) = 2, (1, 0) = 3, (1, 1) = 4, (1, 2) = 5, (2, 0) = 6, (2, 1) = 7, (2, 2) = 8$. Applying this labeling or coding principle in general, a p-variate variable $x = (x_1, x_2, \ldots, x_p)$ consisting of variables x_i having a_i values $0, 1, \ldots, a_i - 1$ for $i = 1, \ldots, p$ has $a = a_1 \ldots a_p$ values $0, 1, \ldots, a - 1$ obtained according to

$$x = x_1 a_2 \ldots a_p + x_2 a_3 \ldots a_p + \cdots + x_p.$$

Conversely, the p-variate representation can be obtained from the integer representation x by first defining x_1 as the integer part of $x/a_2 \ldots a_p$, then defining x_2 as the integer part of $(x - x_1 a_2 \ldots a_p)/a_3 \ldots a_p$, and so on. When $(a_1, \ldots, a_p)$ is specified, it is convenient to use x interchangeably as a notation for the p-variate sequence and its integer representation. Here x is said to be a p-variate variable of type $(a_1, \ldots, a_p)$.

Consider a network with a p-variate vertex variable x of type $(a_1, \ldots, a_p)$, a q-variate edge variable y of type $(b_1, \ldots, b_q)$, and an r-variate arc variable z of type $(c_1, \ldots, c_r)$. Let

$$a = a_1 \ldots a_p, b = b_1 \ldots b_q, \quad \text{and} \quad c = c_1 \ldots c_r$$

denote the numbers of values on x, y, and z. We can consider the network to be a colored complete multigraph with N vertices, $N(N - 1)/2$ edges, and $N(N - 1)$ arcs having vertices of at most a different colors, edges of at most b different colors, and arcs of at most c different colors. The variable x takes value x_i at vertex i for $i = 1, \ldots, N$. The variable y takes value $y_{ij} = y_{ji}$ at edge $\{i, j\}$ with $i \neq j$ for $i = 1, \ldots, N$ and $j = 1, \ldots, N$. The variable z takes value z_{ij} at arc (i, j) with $i \neq j$ for $i = 1, \ldots, N$ and $j = 1, \ldots, N$. It is convenient to put $y_{ii} = z_{ii} = 0$ for $i = 1, \ldots, N$. The notation here is in slight conflict with the multivariate notation $x = (x_1, \ldots, x_p)$, but it should be clear by context whether x_i is a component variable in x or a value of x at vertex i. In the latter case, we use notation $x_i = (x_{1i}, \ldots, x_{pi})$ and similarly $y_{ij} = (y_{1ij}, \ldots, y_{qij})$ and $z_{ij} = (z_{1ij}, \ldots, z_{rij})$.

The dyad involving vertices i and j is characterized by the five values

$$(x_i, x_j, y_{ij}, z_{ij}, z_{ji})$$

representing the color type of the dyad. Frank (1988b) gave the number of distinct color types when isomorphic dyads are not distinguished. There are $a^2 bc^2$ possible color types when isomorphic dyads are distinguished and they reduce to

$$d = abc(ac + 1)/2$$

possible color types for nonisomorphic dyads. In particular, a network with two binary vertex variables, no edge variable, and a binary arc variable has $a = 4, b = 1$, and $c = 2$, which implies that there are $d = 36$ nonisomorphic dyads for a simple digraph on vertices of four kinds. Note that $b = 1$ means that there is no edge variable.

3.4 Sample Selection in Network Surveys

Some early references to network sampling are the papers by Bloemena (1964), Capobianco (1970), Frank (1969, 1970, 1971), Stephan (1969), Granovetter (1976), and Morgan and Rytina (1977). Some more recent references are Jansson (1997), Karlberg (1997), and Spreen (1998). Many references to various network sampling problems can be found in the author's review articles (Frank 1980, 1988a, 1997). The general framework for network surveys in this presentation is defined as a multivariate complete multigraph with N vertices of at most $a = a_1 \ldots a_p$ different kinds, $N(N-1)/2$ edges of at most $b = b_1 \ldots b_q$ different kinds, and $N(N-1)$ arcs of at most $c = c_1 \ldots c_r$ different kinds. The multivariate vertex, edge, and arc variables are denoted x, y, and z with values x_i, $y_{ij} = y_{ji}$, and z_{ij} at vertex i, edge $\{i, j\}$, and arc (i, j) for $i = 1, \ldots, N$ and $j = 1, \ldots, N$. Here for convenience $y_{ii} = z_{ii} = 0$ for $i = 1, \ldots, N$. The multivariate values are referred to as colors labeled by integers $0, 1, 2, \ldots$, as explained in the previous section. The vertices are also referred to as the population units.

Consider a probabilistic sampling mechanism for selecting vertices. Let s be the set of distinct vertices in the sample. There are several different possibilities for making observations in the network, and we consider just a few here. If the variables x, y, and z are observed within the sample s, this means that data comprise

$$\{(i, x_i): i \in s\} \quad \text{and} \quad \{(i, j, y_{ij}, z_{ij}): i \in s, j \in s\}.$$

If y and z are observed not only within s, but also at all edges and arcs out from s, this yields data

$$\{(i, j, y_{ij}, z_{ij}): i \in s, j \in U\},$$

and if they are observed within and into s, data are given by

$$\{(i, j, y_{ij}, z_{ij}): i \in U, j \in s\}.$$

For numeric variables, population totals

$$\sum x_i, \sum \sum_{i<j} y_{ij}, \quad \text{and} \quad \sum \sum z_{ij}$$

are estimated without bias by Horvitz-Thompson estimators. For instance, if arc values are observed from and to a vertex sample s with inclusion probabilities

$$\pi_i = P(i \in s) \quad \text{and} \quad \pi_{ij} = P(i \in s, j \in s),$$

the arc value population total has the Horvitz-Thompson estimator

$$\sum\sum[z_{ij}/(\pi_i + \pi_j - \pi_{ij})],$$

where summation is over all pairs of vertices (i, j) having at least one of i and j contained in s. Many different sampling designs and estimators of population totals are treated by Frank (1977a, b, c, 1978a, b, 1979) and Capobianco and Frank (1982). Properties of various estimators are investigated and comparisons are made between estimators based on different sample designs.

Of particular interest are the designs in which the sample selection depends on auxiliary edge or arc variables. Snowball sampling is such a design. We can describe it in the following way. Let $Z = (Z_{ij})$ be the adjacency matrix of a directed simple graph on U. For any subset s of U, the subsets of vertices after and before s are defined according to

$$A(s) = \{j \in U : Z_{ij} = 1 \quad \text{for some} \quad i \in s\}$$
$$\text{and } B(s) = \{j \in U : Z_{ji} = 1 \quad \text{for some} \quad i \in s\}.$$

A snowball vertex sample with one wave after an initial vertex sample s_0 is given by $s_1 = s_0 \cup A(s_0)$ provided $s_1 \neq s_0$. The vertices in s_1 that are not in s_0 constitute the first wave. A two-wave snowball sample is given by $s_2 = s_1 \cup A(s_1)$ provided $s_2 \neq s_1$. The second wave consists of the vertices in s_2 that are not in s_1. If waves are joined until no further increase of the sample size is possible, a total or full-wave snowball sample is obtained. The inclusion probability of vertex i in the snowball sample s_1 can be expressed as the probability that s_0 has at least one vertex in common with $B(i)$. The complementary event that s_0 and $B(i)$ are disjoint means that $B(i)$ is excluded from s_0. Thus,

$$P(i \in s_1) = P(B(i) \cap s_0 \neq \emptyset) = 1 - P(B(i) \text{ excluded from } s_0).$$

Exclusion probabilities can be obtained from inclusion probabilities according to the general formula

$$P(B \text{ excluded}) = \sum (-1)^{\text{size}(A)} P(A \text{ included}),$$

where A runs through all subsets of B and the inclusion probability of the empty set is 1. It follows that if the graph given by Z is available as auxiliary information or if the sets $B(i)$ can be observed for i belonging to the snowball, then it is possible to determine the inclusion probabilities for the snowball s_1 in terms of the inclusion probabilities for the initial sample s_0. Consequently, the Horvitz-Thompson estimator e_1 based on the snowball s_1 can be used to estimate any population total of a numeric vertex variable. Frank (1977c) compared this Horvitz-Thompson estimator e_1 with the Horvitz-Thompson estimator e_0 based on the initial sample s_0 and showed that generally neither of them dominates the other. Either e_0 or e_1 can have a strictly smaller variance. It was also shown that e_0 is dominated by the estimator e_2 obtained as the expected value of e_0 conditional on the snowball. However, e_2 depends in a rather complicated way on the sampling design of the initial sample and is computationally not very attractive.

So far, we have discussed vertex sampling. Edge and arc sampling can be alternatives or even the only possibilities available. If a population of people is considered, and we are interested in those who committed a crime together, it might be natural to sample incidents of crime from some police records. Another example for which it could be convenient to use edge or arc sampling is a situation when mail or phone calls are easy to sample in order to get information from senders and receivers in a communication network.

Consider a sampled set of edges from the population network. Data obtained could be the values of the vertex variables at all vertices incident to the sampled edges. Such data consist of

$$\{(i, x_i) : i \in U(s)\},$$

where $U(s)$ is the union of all edges in s considered as two-vertex subsets of U. Another possibility is that data consist of the edge values at all edges that are contained in the subgraph induced by the vertices that are incident to the sampled edges. This is generally much more than just the values of the edge variables at the sampled edges. All edges between any two vertices belonging to the sampled edges are included. Even more information could be gathered if all edges incident to any of the vertices in the sampled edges also provide their values of the edge variable. Formally this means that data are given by

$$\{(i, j, y_{ij}): i \in U(s), j \in U\}.$$

These examples of data can be considered as obtained by some kind of snowballing or link tracing in the population. When snowballing is generalized as it is here, and it seems to be difficult to determine the inclusion probabilities of the design, likelihood-based inference could still be possible if the data available make the design ignorable in the sense discussed by Sugden and Smith (1984) and Thompson and Frank (2000). Another possibility to avoid the complications due to an involved design could be to adhere to a model approach.

3.5 Probabilistic Network Models

The lack of uniform optimality for the design-based estimators considered in the previous section is mainly due to their dependence on the vertex labels. This dependence is even more pronounced in the network setting than in ordinary survey sampling. A way to avoid these problems in ordinary survey sampling is to introduce population model assumptions. A similar approach now requires probabilistic network models. We first review some of the common random networks and discuss the need for multivariate network models. In the following section, a flexible class of models is presented that can fairly easily be fit to multivariate network data. If it is possible to get a good fit in an actual application, then this allows us to use the model approach in the data analysis and avoid some of the complications caused by having an involved sampling design.

Some very simple, yet much used, random graph models are uniform models and Bernoulli models. Palmer (1985) gave an elementary exposition. Bollobas (1985) and Janson, Luczak, and Rucinski (2000) are more advanced texts. Uniform models assign equal probabilities to all graphs in a specified class of graphs, for instance, all graphs with N labeled vertices and M edges or all trees on N labeled vertices. Bernoulli graph models on N labeled vertices select edges independently and with a common probability p for all unordered vertex pairs. Bernoulli digraph models are defined similarly for ordered vertex pairs. Slight generalizations are obtained by restricting the edge selections to a subset G of the vertex pairs. In this way, a Bernoulli (G, p) graph is obtained that can be considered as the random subgraph of G remaining when its edges are independently kept or removed with probability p and $1 - p$, respectively. A further generalization to a Bernoulli (G, α, β) graph is obtained if edges in G are independently removed with probability α and nonedges in G are independently replaced by new edges with probability β. The Bernoulli (G, α, β) graph can be considered as a version of G perturbed by independent errors making present edges disappear and false edges appear with probabilities α and β, respectively. Models like these have been used for reliability problems and communication networks. Random graph theory is also much influenced by problems in computer science. The use of martingales and other stochastic processes in graph theory is a rapidly expanding area of research, which is also of importance for the development of combinatorics in general. Alon and Spencer (1992) and Janson et al. (2000) are modern monographs on probabilistic methods in combinatorics and asymptotic properties of random structures.

In many applications from the social and behavioral sciences, multivariate network data require models of another type. To handle survey data on multivariate network variables, there is a general class of probabilistic network models available that includes as special cases the Holland-Leinhardt model, the p^*-model, Markov graph models, and various block models. The models can be specified as log-linear models with the log-likelihood function given as a linear combination of some chosen network statistics. The Holland-Leinhardt model for a simple digraph has as statistics the out- and in-degrees at every vertex and the total numbers of arcs and mutual arcs. The coefficients of the statistics are the parameters of the model. The Holland-Leinhardt model on N vertices has $2N$ degrees of freedom since the $2N + 2$ parameters are subject to two restrictions due to the fact that both the out-degrees and the in-degrees sum to the total number of arcs. The parameters can be considered as individual effects of activity and attraction, and as two overall effects of relation and reciprocity in the network. Block models are generalizations of the Holland-Leinhardt model taking into account different effects for units in different categories. When the categories are unknown latent characteristics, the parameters are not so easily estimated as when categories are observable. Fienberg and Wasserman (1981); Holland, Laskey, and Leinhardt (1983); Wasserman and Anderson (1987); Wang and Wong (1987); Anderson, Wasserman, and Faust (1992); Snijders and Nowicki (1997); Tallberg (2000); and Nowicki and Snijders (2001) treat block models. Markov graph models introduced by Frank and Strauss (1986) are log-linear with statistics based on dyad and triad counts. Frank (1989), Frank and Nowicki (1993),

Robins (1998), and Corander, Dahmström, and Dahmström (1998) treat estimation for Markov graphs.

The next section presents a class of network models defined by explicit assumptions about how vertex, edge, and arc variables are related. An important feature of the class is that it consists of multiparametric models allowing tie dependence. Sections 3.7 and 3.8 present examples of continuous and discrete versions of the dyad dependence models. With many parameters, there might be too many degrees of freedom for fitting the models to data. It is well-known that overfitting might lead to irrelevant models. There should be a proper balance between the degrees of freedom and the goodness of fit. To choose an appropriate model from the class, there are two main exploratory methods available. The first method, which is based on log-linear representations of discrete models, is described in Section 3.9, and the second method, which is based on clustering of dyad distributions, is described in Section 3.10. Both log-linear interaction testing and clustering are techniques that are widely available in standard statistical computer packages for data analysis. The convenience of the methods in this context is, to a large extent, dependent on that they work directly on the network variables without any need for supplementary network programs.

3.6 A Class of Network Models with Dyad Dependence

To define the dyad dependence, we need to include latent or manifest vertex variables that influence the dyad structure. A dyad dependence model is specified by giving a probability distribution for the vertex variables x_i for $i = 1, \ldots, N$, and, conditionally on the outcomes of $x_1, \ldots, x_N$, the $N(N-1)/2$ dyad variables (y_{ij}, z_{ij}, z_{ji}) are assumed to be independent. The conditional probability distribution of the dyad variable (y_{ij}, z_{ij}, z_{ji}) may be dependent on i and j, but is independent of x_k for all k different from i and j. Formally, we write the probability or probability density function of all network variables as follows

$$f(x_1, \ldots, x_N) \, \Pi_{i<j} \, g_{ij}(y_{ij}, z_{ij}, z_{ji}|x_i, x_j).$$

In a graphical model representation (Whittaker 1990; Edwards 1995; Cox and Wermuth 1996 or Lauritzen 1996), there are $N(N+1)/2$ nodes (not to be confused with the vertices in the network) for the N vertex variables and the $N(N-1)/2$ dyad variables. There are no links (not to be confused with the edges or arcs in the network) between the dyad variables, but there are generally links between the vertex variables themselves and between the vertex variables and the dyad variables. There are at most $3N(N-1)/2$ links in graphical models representing this type of dyad dependence models on N vertices. Note that lack of links means not marginal, but conditional independence. Therefore, the dyad variables are generally dependent. Figure 3.6.1 shows a graphical model representation of a general network on $N = 5$ vertices, and Figure 3.6.2 is a schematic diagram for four vertices drawn in a way that is easily adapted to an arbitrary number N of vertices.

If the vertex variables are assumed to be independent, the graphical model is further restricted, but the dyad variables can still be dependent. By introducing latent variables

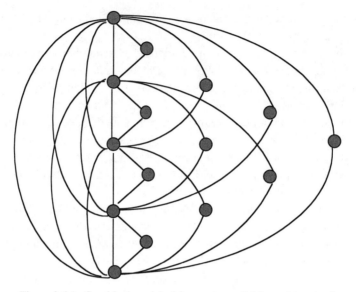

Figure 3.6.1. Graphical model of five vertex variables and ten dyad
variables.

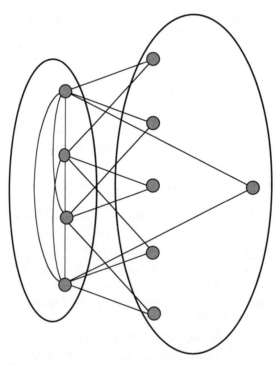

Figure 3.6.2. Graphical model illustrating a set of vertex
variables with complete links, a set of dyad variables
with no links, and two links between each dyad variable
and its vertex variables.

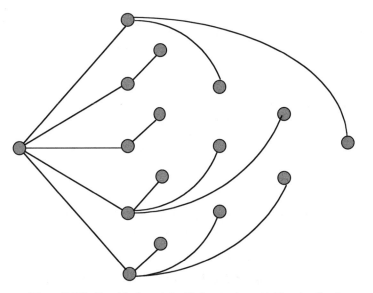

Figure 3.6.3. Graphical model with five vertex variables, ten dyad
variables, and a latent variable.

it is also possible to create dependence between any variables that are conditionally
independent. An example is given in Figure 3.6.3.

3.7 Continuous Dyad Dependence Models

We consider a dyad dependence model for continuous variables, which is of some
interest in connection with other log-linear models considered in network analysis and
deserves to be further investigated. Assume that $x_i = (x_{1i}, x_{2i})$ are independent vertex
variables with a common bivariate normal distribution

$$N(\mu_1, \mu_2, \sigma_1, \sigma_2, \rho).$$

The two components of the vertex variable represent out- and in-effects or out- and
in-capacities of the vertex. Conditionally on the vertex variables, the dyad variables
have a trivariate normal distribution that is given by

$$y_{ij} = \alpha_0 + \alpha_1(x_{1i} + x_{1j}) + \alpha_2(x_{2i} + x_{2j}) + \sigma_3\varepsilon_{3ij},$$
$$z_{ij} = \beta_0 + \beta_1 x_{1i} + \beta_2 x_{2i} + \beta_3 x_{1j} + \beta_4 x_{2j} + \sigma_4\varepsilon_{4ij},$$
$$z_{ji} = \beta_0 + \beta_1 x_{1j} + \beta_2 x_{2j} + \beta_3 x_{1i} + \beta_4 x_{2i} + \sigma_4\varepsilon_{4ji},$$

where the ε-variables are standardized normally distributed with covariances

$$C(\varepsilon_{3ij}, \varepsilon_{4ij}) = C(\varepsilon_{3ij}, \varepsilon_{4ji}) = \gamma_3, \, C(\varepsilon_{4ij}, \varepsilon_{4ji}) = \gamma_4.$$

The edge variable is linearly dependent on the out- and in-effects of its two vertices,
and by symmetry the two vertices are equally weighted. The arc variables are also
linearly dependent on the out- and in-effects of their two vertices. Here the weights are

allowed to differ, but by symmetry they are interchanged for the two arcs. The coefficients in front of the ε-variables are conditional standard deviations. By symmetry, two of them are equal. The distribution of the vertex variables is determined by five parameters, and the conditional distributions of the dyad variables involve twelve more parameters. From the assumptions, it follows that the dyad variables are marginally normally distributed. The marginal distribution is determined by the expected values, variances, and covariances, which are given by the following functions of the parameters

$$E(y_{ij}) = \alpha_0 + 2\alpha_1\mu_1 + 2\alpha_2\mu_2,$$
$$E(z_{ij}) = E(z_{ji}) = \beta_0 + (\beta_1 + \beta_3)\mu_1 + (\beta_2 + \beta_4)\mu_2,$$
$$V(y_{ij}) = 2(\alpha_1^2\sigma_1^2 + \alpha_2^2\sigma_2^2 + 2\alpha_1\alpha_2\sigma_1\sigma_2\rho) + \sigma_3^2,$$
$$V(z_{ij}) = V(z_{ji}) = \beta_1^2\sigma_1^2 + \beta_2^2\sigma_2^2 + 2\beta_1\beta_2\sigma_1\sigma_2\rho + \beta_3^2\sigma_1^2 + \beta_4^2\sigma_2^2$$
$$+ 2\beta_3\beta_4\sigma_1\sigma_2\rho + \sigma_4^2,$$
$$C(y_{ij}, z_{ij}) = C(y_{ij}, z_{ji}) = \alpha_1(\beta_1 + \beta_3)\sigma_1^2 + \alpha_2(\beta_2 + \beta_4)\sigma_2^2$$
$$+ [\alpha_1(\beta_2 + \beta_4) + \alpha_2(\beta_1 + \beta_3)]\sigma_1\sigma_2\rho + \sigma_3\sigma_4\gamma_3,$$
$$C(z_{ij}, z_{ji}) = 2[\beta_1\beta_3\sigma_1^2 + \beta_2\beta_4\sigma_2^2 + (\beta_1\beta_4 + \beta_2\beta_3)\sigma_1\sigma_2\rho] + \sigma_4^2\gamma_4.$$

The seventeen parameters can be estimated by the moment method. The required equation system with seventeen moment equations consists of six equations corresponding to the previous parametric expressions, together with eleven equations corresponding to the parametric expressions among the following moments:

$$E(x_{1i}) = \mu_1, \; E(x_{2i}) = \mu_2,$$
$$V(x_{1i}) = \sigma_1^2, \; V(x_{2i}) = \sigma_2^2,$$
$$C(x_{1i}, x_{2i}) = \sigma_1\sigma_2\rho,$$
$$C(x_{1i}, y_{ij}) = C(x_{1j}, y_{ij}) = \alpha_1\sigma_1^2 + \alpha_2\sigma_1\sigma_2\rho,$$
$$C(x_{2i}, y_{ij}) = C(x_{2j}, y_{ij}) = \alpha_2\sigma_2^2 + \alpha_1\sigma_1\sigma_2\rho,$$
$$C(x_{1i}, z_{ij}) = C(x_{1j}, z_{ji}) = \beta_1\sigma_1^2 + \beta_2\sigma_1\sigma_2\rho,$$
$$C(x_{2i}, z_{ij}) = C(x_{2j}, z_{ji}) = \beta_2\sigma_2^2 + \beta_1\sigma_1\sigma_2\rho,$$
$$C(x_{1i}, z_{ji}) = C(x_{1j}, z_{ij}) = \beta_3\sigma_1^2 + \beta_4\sigma_1\sigma_2\rho,$$
$$C(x_{2i}, z_{ji}) = C(x_{2j}, z_{ij}) = \beta_4\sigma_2^2 + \beta_3\sigma_1\sigma_2\rho.$$

The parametric expressions that apply to two different moments are equated to the average of the two moments. The others are just equated to their moments. For the resulting equations, replace the expected values, variances, and covariances by empirical quantities obtained from data and solve the equation system numerically for the parameters.

To derive the maximum likelihood estimates, one has to solve a similar equation system obtained by differentiating the log-likelihood function with respect to the parameters. It should be noted that the seventeen parameters introduced via the linearity assumptions for the conditional distributions correspond to the seventeen parameters that determine a seven-dimensional normal distribution for $(x_{1i}, x_{2i}, x_{1j},$ $x_{2j}, y_{ij}, z_{ij}, z_{ji})$ when appropriate symmetries are taken into account. In fact, there are seven means with three restrictions, seven variances with three restrictions, and twenty-one covariances with twelve restrictions, so in total thirty-five moments with eighteen restrictions making the degrees of freedom equal to seventeen. Some natural attempts to further simplify the model would be to test hypotheses like $\beta_2 = \beta_3 = 0, \alpha_1 > \alpha_2, \beta_1 > \beta_2$, and $\beta_1 = \beta_3$, corresponding to easily interpreted structural effects of the vertex variables on the edge and arc variables.

So far, we have considered networks that have simultaneously both edge and arc variables. Without this combined occurrence of symmetric and unsymmetric relationships, the degrees of freedom are reduced. If there is no edge variable but only vertex and arc variables, twelve of the seventeen parameters remain. If there is no arc variable but only vertex and edge variables, nine parameters remain. In all these cases, the model is a log-linear network model with a log-likelihood function that is a linear function of moment statistics of the types considered previously.

3.8 Discrete Dyad Dependence Models

A particular version of the dyad dependence model for categorical edge and arc variables generalizes in a nice way the Holland-Leinhardt model for a simple digraph. At the same time, it provides an interpretation of the model in terms of actor preferences for local structure. It also suggests an extension of the Holland-Leinhardt model with tie dependence, which is not so evident with the usual formulation of the model. To demonstrate these results, we now consider the following dyad dependence model.

Let $x_1, \ldots, x_N$ be independent identically distributed categorical variables of type $(a_1, \ldots, a_p)$ with $a = a_1 \ldots a_p$ categories. Thus, their log-likelihood equals

$$\log f(x_1, \ldots, x_N) = \Sigma_i \log f(x_i) = \Sigma_x N(x) \log f(x),$$

where $N(x)$ is the number of vertices with $x_i = x$ for $i = 1, \ldots, N$. Conditionally on $(x_1, \ldots, x_N)$ the $N(N-1)/2$ dyad variables (y_{ij}, z_{ij}, z_{ji}) are independent and (y_{ij}, z_{ij}, z_{ji}) has a distribution that does not depend on x_k for any k different from i and j. Assume first that the dyad distributions are also independent of the labels i and j. Thus, the log-likelihood of the dyad variables is given by

$$\Sigma\Sigma_{i<j} \log g_{ij}(y_{ij}, z_{ij}, z_{ji} \mid x_i, x_j)$$
$$= \Sigma_{xx'yzz'} R(x, x', y, z, z') \log g(y, z, z' \mid x, x'),$$

where $R(x, x', y, z, z')$ is the number of dyads of category (x, x', y, z, z'). To count the dyads in each one of the d nonisomorphic categories, it is convenient to list all the dyads $(x_i, x_j, y_{ij}, z_{ij}, z_{ji})$ for $i < j$ and denote by $M(x, x', y, z, z')$ the number of them equal to (x, x', y, z, z') for each one of the $a^2 bc^2$ different categories. Then define

$$R(x, x', y, z, z') = M(x, x', y, z, z') + M(x', x, y, z', z)$$
$$- \delta_{xx'}\delta_{zz'} M(x, x, y, z, z),$$

where $\delta_{uv} = I(u = v)$ indicates whether $u = v$. Figures 3.8.4 and 3.8.5 illustrate the transformation from M- to R-frequencies. Summing $R(x, x', y, z, z')$ over y, z, z' yields the number $N(x, x')$ of unordered pairs of vertices of categories x and x'. Thus,

$$N(x, x') = N(x)N(x') \quad \text{for} \quad x < x',$$
$$N(x, x) = N(x)[N(x) - 1]/2.$$

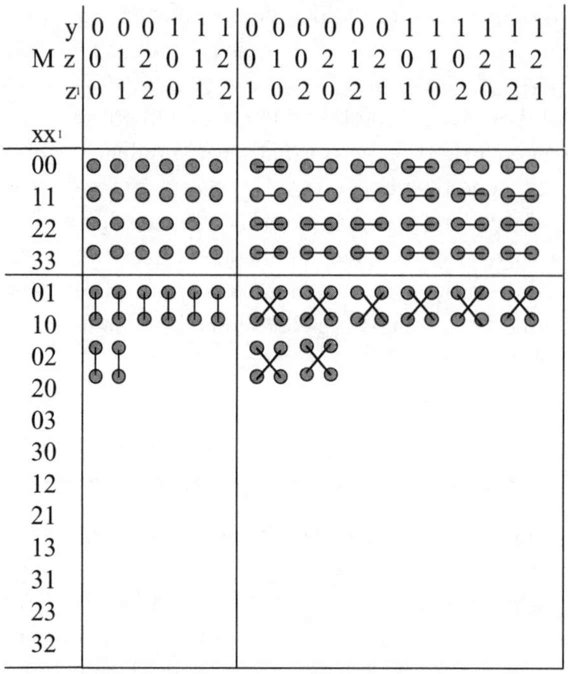

```
      y|0 0 0 1 1 1|0 0 0 0 0 0 1 1 1 1 1 1
   M z|0 1 2 0 1 2|0 1 0 2 1 2 0 1 0 2 1 2
     z'|0 1 2 0 1 2|1 0 2 0 2 1 1 0 2 0 2 1

  xx'
   00
   11
   22
   33

   01
   10
   02
   20
   03
   30
   12
   21
   13
   31
   23
   32
```

Figure 3.8.4. M-frequencies in 288 cells for $a = 4$, $b = 2$ and $c = 3$. The cells are arranged so neighboring cell frequencies should be added as indicated.

The relative frequencies $N(x)/N$ and $R(x, x', y, z, z')/N(x, x')$ are the maximum likelihood estimators of $f(x)$ and $g(y, z, z'|x, x')$ when the model has independent identically distributed vertex variables and conditional dyad distributions dependent on vertex categories, but not on vertex identities.

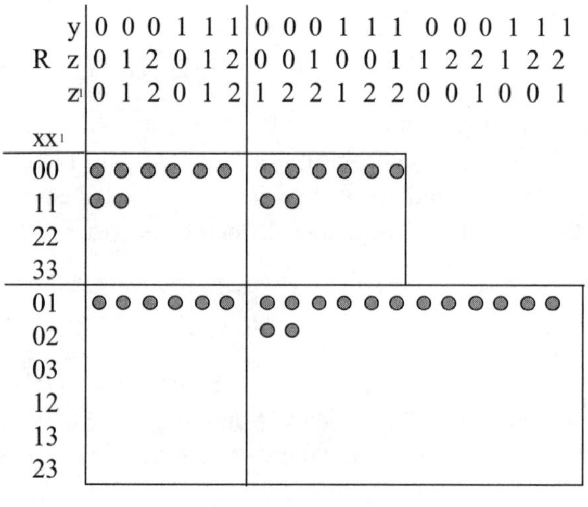

```
      y|0 0 0 1 1 1|0 0 0 1 1 1 0 0 0 1 1 1
   R z|0 1 2 0 1 2|0 0 1 0 0 1 1 2 2 1 2 2
     z'|0 1 2 0 1 2|1 2 2 1 2 2 0 0 1 0 0 1

  xx'
   00
   11
   22
   33

   01
   02
   03
   12
   13
   23
```

Figure 3.8.5. R-frequencies in 156 cells obtained from Figure 3.8.4.

Assume now that we allow the dyad distributions to depend on vertex identities and that there is a latent vertex variable θ_i specifying preference weights for local structure at vertex i for $i = 1, \ldots, N$. More specifically, $\theta_i = (\theta_i(y, z, z'|x_i, x'))$ for all x', y, z, z' consists of preference weights assigned to alternative dyad structures at vertex i. There are abc^2 weights for each vertex. Assume that the probability assigned to a dyad is proportional to the preference weights of the two vertices involved so

$$g_{ij}(y, z, z'|x_i, x_j) = \lambda_{ij}\, \theta_i(y, z, z'|x_i, x_j)\, \theta_j(y, z', z|x_j, x_i),$$

where λ_{ij} is a normalizing constant. Note that dyad structure (y, z, z') viewed from i is the same as (y, z', z) viewed from j. It follows that

$$\Sigma\Sigma_{i<j} \log g_{ij}(y_{ij}, z_{ij}, z_{ji}|x_i, x_j)$$
$$= \Sigma\Sigma_{i<j} \log \lambda_{ij} + \Sigma_i \Sigma_{x'yzz'} M_i(x', y, z, z') \log \theta_i(y, z, z'|x_i, x'),$$

where $M_i(x', y, z, z')$ is the number of $j \neq i$ with $(x_j, y_{ij}, z_{ij}, z_{ji}) = (x', y, z, z')$. Again, the model is a log-linear one with statistics $N(x)$ and $M_i(x', y, z, z')$ for $i = 1, \ldots, N$ and all values of the variables. The model has

$$d_0 = a - 1 + Na(bc^2 - 1) - 1$$

degrees of freedom. If we assume for each x' a Dirichlet distribution for the preference weights for different (y, z, z'), and these distributions may vary with x but not with i, then degrees of freedom are further reduced to

$$d_1 = a - 1 + a^2bc^2.$$

In particular, the case of a single digraph on vertices of different categories leads to $b = 1, c = 2, d_0 = a - 1 + 3aN - 1$, and $d_1 = a - 1 + 4a^2$. For $a = 1$, this is $d_0 = 3N - 1$ and $d_1 = 4$. In this case, we have

$$\Sigma\Sigma_{i<j} \log g_{ij}(z_{ij}, z_{ji}) = \Sigma\Sigma_{i<j} \log \lambda_{ij} + \Sigma_i \Sigma_{zz'} M_{izz'} \log \theta_{izz'},$$

where

$$M_{i00} = \Sigma_{j\neq i}(1 - z_{ij})(1 - z_{ji}) = N - 1 - z_{i.} - z_{.i} + z_{ii}^2,$$
$$M_{i01} = \Sigma_{j\neq i}(1 - z_{ij})z_{ji} = z_{.i} - z_{ii}^2,$$
$$M_{i10} = \Sigma_{j\neq i} z_{ij}(1 - z_{ji}) = z_{i.} - z_{ii}^2,$$
$$M_{i11} = \Sigma_{j\neq i} z_{ij}z_{ji} = z_{ii}^2.$$

The four statistics $M_{izz'}$ sum to $N - 1$ and can be replaced by the three statistics $z_{i.}, z_{.i}$, and z_{ii}^2, which are the numbers of out-arcs, in-arcs, and mutual arcs at vertex i. The log-likelihood function expressed with these statistics is equal to

$$\lambda + \Sigma_i(\alpha_i z_{i.} + \beta_i z_{.i} + \gamma_i z_{ii}^2),$$

where

$$\alpha_i = \log(\theta_{i10}/\theta_{i00}),$$
$$\beta_i = \log(\theta_{i01}/\theta_{i00}),$$
$$\gamma_i = \log(\theta_{i11}\theta_{i00}/\theta_{i10}/\theta_{i01}),$$

and λ is a normalizing constant. The new parameters are the log-odds of out-arc with no in-arc, the log-odds of in-arc with no out-arc, and the log-odds ratio of out-arc with and without in-arc (or, equivalently, of in-arc with and without out-arc). We can assume $\Sigma_i \alpha_i = 0$ and $\Sigma_i \beta_i = 0$ if a new term $\mu z_{..}$ is added to the log-likelihood. In this way, we have $3N + 1$ parameters with two restrictions matching the $3N - 1$ degrees of freedom. The Holland-Leinhardt model assumes all γ_i equal and has $2N$ degrees of freedom. Without having to assume equal reciprocity effects, the number of parameters can be reduced so the degrees of freedom do not depend on N. This is achieved by introducing a Dirichlet distribution for the latent preference weights. As a consequence, we get tie dependence governed by the Dirichlet parameters. For the case $a = 1, b = 1, c = 2$, there are four Dirichlet parameters ($\nu_{00}, \nu_{01}, \nu_{10}, \nu_{11}$) that control the choice of preference weights at each vertex i. The Dirichlet parameters are positive, and if their sum $\nu_{..}$ is large, each preference weight θ_{ikl} is close to $\nu_{kl}/\nu_{..}$. If all $\nu_{kl} = 1$, then all possible combinations of preference weights are given the same probability density. Furthermore, each preference weight is expected to be $1/4$ with a variance of $3/80$, and any two preference weights at the same vertex have a correlation coefficient of $-1/3$. This implies, for instance, that $E(\alpha_i) = 0$ and $V(\alpha_i) \approx 3/5$. It should be interesting to investigate the prior on the parameters ($\mu, \alpha_i, \beta_i, \gamma_i$) that is induced by a general Dirichlet prior on the preference weights. It does not seem very natural to start with a prior on ($\mu, \alpha_i, \beta_i, \gamma_i$) and deduce the consequences for the preference weights, but this could also be of interest. The reduction of the degrees of freedom from $3N - 1$ (or $2N$ for the Holland-Leinhardt model) to 4 might be too drastic in many practical situations. A reduction to $d_1 = a - 1 + 4a^2$ might be more feasible and could be achieved if different vertex categories are used to differentiate between preference patterns.

3.9   Log-Linear Representations of Models with Dyad Dependence

The dyad dependence model with all variables categorical, the vertex variables independent, and the dyad distributions independent of vertex labels has a log-likelihood function given by

$$\Sigma_x N(x) \log f(x) + \Sigma R(x, x', y, z, z') \log g(y, z, z'|x, x'),$$

where the second sum is over the d nonisomorphic dyads (x, x', y, z, z'). Consider now the vertex variable as multivariate and expand the log-likelihood function of the vertex variables according to

$$\log f(x) = \Sigma_A \lambda_A(x_A),$$

where A runs through all subsets of variables among the p vertex variables and x_A is the subsequence of x restricted to variables in A. The term corresponding to the empty set $A = \emptyset$ is a normalizing constant and the other terms are interaction effects between the variables in A. With

$$a = a_1 \ldots a_p = \Sigma_A \Pi_{i \in A}(a_i - 1)$$

values of x, there are $\Pi_{i \in A}(a_i - 1)$ free parameters for the a interactions corresponding to the nonempty subsets A. This allows us to impose

$$\Pi_{i \in A} a_i - \Pi_{i \in A}(a_i - 1)$$

restrictions on the interaction effects $\lambda_A(x_A)$. It is customary to put $\Sigma \lambda_A(x_A) = 0$ for summations over the values x_i of any of the variables in A. If we assume that all interactions with three or more variables are zero and keep only those with one or two variables (main effects and second-order interactions), then the degrees of freedom are reduced from $a - 1$ to

$$\Sigma_i(a_i - 1) + \Sigma\Sigma_{i<j}(a_i - 1)(a_j - 1)$$

for the distribution of the vertex variables.

For the dyad variables, a similar approach leads to

$$\log \; g(y, z, z'|x, x') = \Sigma_{BCC'} \lambda_{BCC'}(y_B, z_C, z'_{C'}|x, x'),$$

where B runs through all subsets of variables among the q edge variables, and C and C' both run through all subsets of variables among the r arc variables. Because only nonisomorphic dyads are considered, there should be certain symmetries present in the interactions. For $x = x'$, it holds that $\lambda_{BCC'} = \lambda_{BC'C}$ for all values of the arguments. This implies that for $x = x'$ there are only

$$\binom{q+r}{k} + \binom{2r}{k}\Big/2 - \binom{r}{k} + \binom{r}{k/2}\Big/2$$

k-order interactions, whereas for $x < x'$ there are $\binom{q+2r}{k}$. It may seem natural to try to restrict attention to the models with main effects and second-order interactions only. For $x = x'$, there are $q + r$ main effects corresponding to the variables $y_1, \ldots, y_q, z_1, \ldots, z_r$, and $r^2 + qr + q(q-1)/2$ second-order interactions corresponding to the pairs of variables (y_i, y_j) for $i < j$, (y_i, z_j) for all i and j, (z_i, z_j) for $i < j$, and (z_i, z'_j) for $i \leq j$. For $x < x'$, there are $q + 2r$ main effects and $(q + 2r)(q + 2r - 1)/2$ second-order interactions corresponding to all single variables and all unordered pairs of variables. If the interactions are restricted in the ordinary way to match the degrees of freedom, then for $x = x'$ the degrees of freedom are reduced from $bc(c + 1)/2 - 1$ to

$$d_1 = \Sigma(b_i - 1) + \Sigma(c_j - 1) + \Sigma\Sigma_{i<j}(b_i - 1)(b_j - 1) + \Sigma\Sigma(b_i - 1)(c_j - 1)$$
$$+ \Sigma\Sigma_{i<j}(c_i - 1)(c_j - 1) + \Sigma\Sigma_{i\leq j}(c_i - 1)(c_j - 1),$$

and for $x < x'$ the degrees of freedom are reduced from $bc^2 - 1$ to

$$d_2 = \Sigma(b_i - 1) + 2\Sigma(c_j - 1) + \Sigma\Sigma_{i<j}(b_i - 1)(b_j - 1) + 2\Sigma\Sigma(b_i - 1)(c_j - 1)$$
$$+ 2\Sigma\Sigma_{i<j}(c_i - 1)(c_j - 1) + \Sigma\Sigma(c_i - 1)(c_j - 1).$$

It follows that the saturated log-linear model with

$$d_{max} = abc(ac + 1)/2 - a(a - 1)/2 - 1$$

degrees of freedom is replaced by a model with

$$d_0 = a - 1 + ad_1 + a(a - 1)d_2/2$$

degrees of freedom if no more than second-order interactions are needed. This is a substantial reduction in degrees of freedom. For instance, consider the case of two binary vertex variables, one binary edge variable, and two binary arc variables. Here, $p = 2, q = 1, r = 2, a_1 = a_2 = b_1 = c_1 = c_2 = 2$, and it follows that $a = 4$, $b = 2, c = 4, d = 272, d_{max} = 265$, and $d_0 = 129$. In practice, there is no need to force the degrees of freedom to be d_1 for all x and d_2 for all pairs (x, x') with $x < x'$. The formula for d_0 still applies if d_1 and d_2 are interpreted as the average degrees of freedom among the dyad distributions for equal and unequal vertex categories, respectively.

Consider now univariate edge and arc variables. Then, $q = r = 1$. For $x = x'$

$$d_1 = b - 1 + c - 1 + (b - 1)(c - 1) + c(c - 1)/2,$$

and for $x < x'$

$$d_2 = b - 1 + 2(c - 1) + 2(b - 1)(c - 1) + (c - 1)^2,$$

so

$$d_{max} - d_0 = a(b - 1)(c - 1)(ac - a + 1)/2.$$

There is obviously no reduction in degrees of freedom if $b = 1$ or $c = 1$ because then there are no third-order interactions. Otherwise, the reduction $d_{max} - d_0$ equals the number of nonisomorphic dyads with a vertex categories, $b - 1$ edge categories, and $c - 1$ arc categories.

3.10   Clustered Versions of Models with Dyad Dependence

The general dyad dependence model given by independent identically distributed $x_1, \ldots, x_N$ with $P(x_i = x) = f(x)$ for $x = 0, \ldots, a - 1$ and $P(y_{ij} = y, z_{ij} = z$, $z_{ji} = z'|x_i = x, x_j = x') = g_{ij}(y, z, z'|x, x')$ for $y = 0, \ldots, b - 1, z = 0, \ldots, c - 1$, and $z' = 0, \ldots, c - 1$ consists of $a(a + 1)/2$ conditional dyad distributions, one for each value (x, x') with $x \le x'$. Those conditioned by two equal vertex categories have $bc(c + 1)/2$ distinct dyads, and the others have bc^2 distinct dyads.

Initially, we have $N(N - 1)/2$ conditional dyad distributions. By distinguishing them by their two vertex categories only and not by the vertex labels, we merge $N(x, x')$ of the distributions into a cluster of distributions with relative dyad frequencies $R(x, x', y, z, z')/N(x, x')$. If all numbers $N(x, x')$ are positive, there are $a(a + 1)/2$ clusters. We can continue to merge distributions that are similar according to some similarity measure. To apply cluster analysis with the distributions as objects to be clustered, each distribution is represented by its sequence of relative dyad frequencies. The dissimilarity between two distributions is defined as the Euclidean distance between their sequences of relative dyad frequencies. We calculate all pairwise distances between the sequences

$$u(x) = (R(x, x, y, z, z')/N(x, x) \quad \text{for all} \quad y \quad \text{and} \quad z \le z')$$

for $x = 0, \ldots, a - 1$, say $D(x, x')$ is the distance between $u(x)$ and $u(x')$ for $x < x'$. Moreover, we calculate all pairwise distances between the sequences

$$v(x, x') = (R(x, x', y, z, z')/N(x, x') \quad \text{for all} \quad y, z, z')$$

for all pairs (x, x') with $x < x'$, say $D(x, x', \xi, \xi')$ is the distance between $v(x, x')$ and $v(\xi, \xi')$ for $x \leq \xi$ and $x' < \xi'$.

Cluster analysis is applied separately to the $u(x)$ and $v(x, x')$ sequences. By applying hierarchical clustering methods such as single linkage, average linkage, or complete linkage, we might be able to scan the dendrograms and select appropriate numbers of clusters. We could also apply partitioning clustering methods such as k-means clustering into k clusters. By trying different numbers of clusters and comparing the results, we might be able to choose appropriate numbers of clusters. Assume that we find that k_1 of the $u(x)$-sequences and k_2 of the $v(x, x')$-sequences are distinct. The distinct distributions have relative dyad frequencies that are given by weighted averages of the relative dyad frequencies for the distributions belonging to each cluster. These weighted averages are generally not equal to the so-called centroids of the clusters if these are given as unweighted averages. The clustered model has

$$d_0 = a - 1 + k_1[bc(c + 1)/2 - 1] + k_2(bc^2 - 1)$$

degrees of freedom. Here, $1 \leq k_1 \leq a$ and $1 \leq k_2 \leq a(a - 1)/2$. A total clustering into one cluster for all dyad distributions between equal vertex categories and one cluster for all dyad distributions between unequal vertex categories implies a minimal number of

$$d_{min} = a + 2bc + 3bc(c - 1)/2 - 3$$

degrees of freedom. Compared with no clustering with

$$d_{max} = abc(ac + 1)/2 - a(a - 1)/2 - 1$$

degrees of freedom, there is a substantial maximal reduction possible by clustering. For instance, consider the case of two binary vertex variables, one binary edge variable, and two binary arc variables. Here, $a = 4, b = 2, c = 4, d_{max} = 265$, and $d_{min} = 53$.

In practice, it may be beneficial to combine clustering and log-linear interaction analysis. We should first reduce the dyad distributions to a reasonable number of clusters, say k_1 and k_2, and then try to eliminate high-order interactions within clusters. Note that different interactions might be needed in different clusters. Say that the degrees of freedom reduce from $bc(c + 1)/2 - 1$ to an average of d_1 among the k_1 clusters, and reduce from $bc^2 - 1$ to an average of d_2 among the k_2 clusters. As a consequence, the combined procedures imply that the degrees of freedom are reduced from d_{max} to

$$d_0 = a - 1 + k_1 d_1 + k_2 d_2.$$

Two illustrations of the clustering approach to dyad distribution modeling are found in Frank, Komanska, and Widaman (1985) and Frank, Hallinan, and Nowicki (1985).

3.11 Applications

There are numerous possibilities for applications of survey methods in a network context. This section gives some flavor of the variety by giving references to various areas. The selection of applications is heavily biased toward my own experience and work in the field. There are certainly network areas of central importance not covered here.

Drug abuse populations provide a field of research that makes much use of network methods. Populations of heroin users, multidrug users, drug injectors, or drug dealers are examples of populations that are hard to access. They consist of individuals that are not likely to be found in sufficient numbers by standard sampling procedures. Various network methods have been applied. Initial samples from treatment centers or other sites that drug users frequent are typically interviewed and asked to name friends or acquaintances that are drug users. In such cases, the network has the role of helping the investigator to find the hidden population. There could also be a direct interest in the network structure itself or in some network variables. Examples are substance abusers' recruiting routes and frequencies of needle sharing. Neaigus et al. (1995, 1996) and Kaplan et al. (1999) investigated problems in this area. For more specific statistical problems related to drug abuse, see, for instance, Spreen (1992), Frank and Snijders (1994), Spreen and Zwaagstra (1994), Jansson (1997), Spreen (1998), and Frank et al. (2001).

Network methods are common in social epidemiology (see Klovdahl 1985 and Rothenberg et al. 1995). The epidemiology of sexually transmitted diseases and the spread of HIV and other viruses is a vivid current area of research using network methods. Neaigus et al. (1995, 1996) and Klovdahl et al. (1994) reported on investigations in this area. In particular, interesting statistical issues come up in the analysis of data from a longitudinal data collection over 5 years in the latter study. Five samples of individuals followed from different starting years are interviewed every year about their current contact patterns. The longitudinal dependencies between individual contacts imply special difficulties. Proper modeling has to consider networks changing with time. Some attempts by Frank (1991) and Frank and Nowicki (1993) to study network processes used Markov graphs with parameters changing with time.

The social and behavioral sciences have long provided the theoretical framework for problems that have been a major source of inspiration for developers of network survey methodology. Well-known early examples include work by Heider (1946), Cartwright and Harary (1956), Harary, Norman, and Cartwright (1965), Davis (1967), Holland and Leinhardt (1971), Granovetter (1973, 1976), and Freeman (1979). More recent examples are Wellman (1988), Wasserman and Faust (1994), and Friedkin (1998).

Sarnecki (1986, 1999) considered network surveys in criminology. Police crime surveys usually do not report data on networks of offenders. There are special methodological challenges if one wants to use available data on crimes and offenders to infer about joint participation in crimes (co-offending) and repeated criminal activity (re-offending). Carrington (2000) and Frank (2001) discussed such issues.

Social capital is an important modern concept in sociology extensively treated by Lin (1999). At a more recent conference on social capital, van der Gaag and Snijders (2004) and Frank (2004) considered measurement problems and other quantitative aspects of social capital. The role, in this context, of centrality measurements in social networks was discussed. Freeman (1979) and Wasserman and Faust (1994) described various centrality measures, and Snijders (1981), Hagberg (2000), Tallberg (2000), and Frank (2002) studied some of their statistical properties. It should be interesting to investigate how these statistics can be used for survey sample inference when manifest centrality is modeled as stochastically generated from individual centrality characteristics. Such models are similar in spirit to the preference models introduced in Section 3.8 and should provide substantial alternatives to the null models of no centrality considered in centrality testing by Hagberg (2000) and Tallberg (2000).

References

Alon, N., and Spencer, J. (1992) *The Probabilistic Method*. New York: Wiley.

Anderson, C. J., Wasserman, S., and Faust, K. (1992) Building stochastic blockmodels. *Social Networks* 14, 137–161.

Basu, D. (1969) Role of the sufficiency and likelihood principles in sample survey theory. *Sankhya* A31, 441–454.

Basu, D., and Ghosh, J. K. (1967) *Sufficient Statistics in Sampling from a Finite Universe*. Proceedings of the 36th Session of the International Statistical Institute, 850–859.

Bloemena, A. R. (1964) *Sampling from a Graph*. Amsterdam: Mathematisch Centrum.

Bollobas, B. (1985) *Random Graphs*. London: Academic Press.

Capobianco, M. (1970) Statistical inference in finite populations having structure. *Transactions of the New York Academy of Sciences* 32, 401–413.

Capobianco, M., and Frank, O. (1982) Comparison of statistical graph-size estimators. *Journal of Statistical Planning and Inference* 6, 87–97.

Carrington, P. (2000) *Age and Group Crime*. Waterloo, Ontario, Canada: University of Waterloo, Department of Sociology.

Cartwright, D., and Harary, F. (1956) Structural balance: A generalization of Heider's theory. *Psychological Review* 63, 277–292.

Corander, J., Dahmström, K., and Dahmström, P. (1998) *Maximum Likelihood Estimation for Markov Graphs*. Stockholm: Stockholm University, Department of Statistics.

Cox, D. R., and Wermuth, N. (1996) *Multivariate Dependencies*. London: Chapman & Hall.

Davis, J. A. (1967) Clustering and structural balance in graphs. *Human Relations* 20, 181–187.

Edwards, D. (1995) *Introduction to Graphical Modelling*. New York: Springer-Verlag.

Fienberg, S. E., and Wasserman, S. (1981) Categorical data analysis of single sociometric relations. In Leinhardt, S. (ed.) *Sociological Methodology*. San Francisco: Jossey-Bass, 156–192.

Frank, O. (1969) Structure inference and stochastic graphs. *FOA-Reports* 3:2, 1–8.

Frank, O. (1970) Sampling from overlapping subpopulations. *Metrika* 16, 32–42.

Frank, O. (1971) *Statistical Inference in Graphs*. Ph.D. Thesis. Stockholm University, Stockholm, Sweden.

Frank, O. (1977a) Estimation of graph totals. *Scandinavian Journal of Statistics* 4, 81–89.

Frank, O. (1977b) A note on Bernoulli sampling in graphs and Horvitz-Thompson estimation. *Scandinavian Journal of Statistics* 4, 178–180.

Frank, O. (1977c) Survey sampling in graphs. *Journal of Statistical Planning and Inference* 1, 235–264.

Frank, O. (1978a) Sampling and estimation in large social networks. *Social Networks* 1, 91–101.

Frank, O. (1978b) Estimation of the number of connected components in a graph by using a sampled subgraph. *Scandinavian Journal of Statistics* 5, 177–188.

Frank, O. (1979) Estimation of population totals by use of snowball samples. In Holland, P., and Leinhardt, S. (eds.) *Perspectives on Social Network Research*. New York: Academic Press, 319–347.

Frank, O. (1980) Sampling and inference in a population graph. *International Statistical Review* 48, 33–41.

Frank, O. (1988a) Random sampling and social networks – A survey of various approaches. *Mathematique, Informatique et Sciences Humaines* 26:104, 19–33.

Frank, O. (1988b) Triad count statistics. *Discrete Mathematics* 72, 141–149.

Frank, O. (1989) Random graph mixtures. *Annals of the New York Academy of Sciences* 576, 192–199.

Frank, O. (1991) Statistical analysis of change in networks. *Statistica Neerlandica* 45, 283–293.

Frank, O. (1997) Composition and structure of social networks. *Mathematique, Informatique et Sciences Humaines* 35:137, 11–23.

Frank, O. (2001) statistical estimation of co-offending youth networks. *Social Networks* 23, 203–214.

Frank, O. (2002) Using centrality modeling in network surveys. *Social Networks* 24, 385–394.

Frank, O. (2004) Measuring social capital by network capacity indices. In Flap, H., and Völker, B. (eds.) *Creation and Returns of Social Capital*. London: Routledge.

Frank, O., Hallinan, M., and Nowicki, K. (1985) Clustering of dyad distributions as a tool in network modeling. *Journal of Mathematical Sociology* 11, 47–64.

Frank, O., Jansson, I., Larsson, J., Reichmann, S., Soyez, V., and Vielva, I. (2001) Addiction severity predictions using client network properties. *International Journal of Social Welfare* 10, 215–223.

Frank, O., Komanska, H., and Widaman, K. (1985) Cluster analysis of dyad distributions in networks. *Journal of Classification* 2, 219–238.

Frank, O., and Nowicki, K. (1993) Exploratory statistical analysis of networks. *Annals of Discrete Mathematics* 55, 349–366.

Frank, O., and Snijders, T. (1994) Estimating the size of hidden populations using snowball sampling. *Journal of Official Statistics* 10, 53–67.

Frank, O., and Strauss, D. (1986) Markov graphs. *Journal of the American Statistical Association* 81, 832–842.

Freeman, L. (1979) Centrality in social networks. Conceptual clarification. *Social Networks* 1, 215–239.

Friedkin, N. (1998) *A Structural Theory of Social Influence*. Cambridge: Cambridge University Press.

Granovetter, M. (1973) The strength of weak ties. *American Journal of Sociology* 81, 1287–1303.

Granovetter, M. (1976) Network sampling: Some first steps. *American Journal of Sociology* 81, 1287–1303.

Hagberg, J. (2000) *Centrality Testing and the Distribution of the Degree Variance in Bernoulli Graphs*. Licentiate Thesis. Department of Statistics, Stockholm University, Stockholm, Sweden.

Harary, F., Norman, R. Z., and Cartwright, D. (1965) *Structural Models: An Introduction to the Theory of Directed Graphs*. New York: Wiley.

Heider, F. (1946) Attitudes and cognitive organization. *Journal of Psychology* 21, 107–112.

Holland, P., and Leinhardt, S. (1971) Transitivity in structural models of small groups. *Comparative Group Studies* 2, 107–124.

Holland, P., and Leinhardt, S. (1981) An exponential family of probability distributions for directed graphs (with discussion). *Journal of the American Statistical Association* 76, 33–65.

Holland, P. W., Laskey, K. B., and Leinhardt, S. (1983) Stochastic blockmodels: Some first steps. *Social Networks* 5, 109–137.

Janson, S., Luczak, T., and Rucinski, A. (2000) *Random Graphs*. New York: Wiley.

Jansson, I. (1997) *On Statistical Modeling of Social Networks*. Ph.D. Thesis. Stockholm University, Stockholm, Sweden.

Kaplan, C., Broekaert, E., Frank, O., and Reichmann, S. (1999) Improving psychiatric treatment in residential programs for emerging dependency groups: Approach and epidemiological findings in Europe. In *Epidemiological Trends in Drug Abuse*. Vol. II Proceedings of the Community Epidemiology Work Group. Bethesda, MD: National Institutes of Health, 323–330.

Karlberg, M. (1997) *Triad Count Estimation and Transitivity Testing in Graphs and Digraphs*. Ph.D.Thesis. Stockholm University, Stockholm, Sweden.

Klovdahl, A. S. (1985) Social networks and the spread of infectious diseases: The AIDS example. *Social Science & Medicine* 21, 1203–1216.

Klovdahl, A. S., Potterat, J. J., Woodhouse, D. E., Muth, J. B., Muth, S. Q., and Darrow, W. W. (1994) Social networks and infectious disease: The Colorado Springs study. *Social Science & Medicine* 38, 79–88.

Lauritzen, S. (1996) *Graphical Models*. Oxford: Clarendon Press.

Lin, N. (1999) Building a network theory of social capital. *Connections* 22, 28–51.

Morgan, D. L., and Rytina, S. (1977) Comments on "Network sampling: some first steps" by Mark Granovetter. *American Journal of Sociology* 83, 722–727.

Neaigus, A., Friedman, S. R., Goldstein, M. F., Ildefonseo, G., Curtis, R., and Jose, B. (1995) Using dyadic data for a network analysis of HIV infection and risk behaviors among injection drug users. In Needle, R. H., Genser, S. G., and Trotter II, R. T. (eds.) *Social Networks, Drug Abuse, and HIV Transmission*. Rockville, MD: National Institute of Drug Abuse, 151, 20–37.

Neaigus, A., Friedman, S. R., Jose, B., Goldstein, M. F., Curtis, R., Ildefonso, G., and Des Jarlais, D. C. (1996) High-risk personal networks and syringe sharing as risk factors for HIV infection among new drug injectors. *Journal of Acquired Immune Deficiency Syndromes and Human Retrovirology* 11, 499–509.

Nowicki, K., and Snijders, T. (2001) Estimation and prediction for stochastic blockstructures. *Journal of the American Statistical Association* 96, 1077–1087.

Palmer, E. (1985) *Graphical Evolution*. New York: Wiley.

Robins, G. L. (1998) *Personal Attributes in Inter-Personal Contexts: Statistical Models for Individual Characteristics and Social Relationships*. Ph.D. Thesis. University of Melbourne, Melbourne, Australia.

Rothenberg, R. B., Woodhouse, D. E., Potterat, J. J., Muth, S. Q., Darrow, W. W., and Klovdahl, A. S. (1995) Social networks in disease transmission: The Colorado Springs study. In Needle, R. H., Genser, S. G., and Trotter II, R. T. (eds.) *Social Networks, Drug Abuse, and HIV Transmission*. Rockville, MD: National Institute of Drug Abuse, 151, 3–19.

Särndal, C.-E., Swensson, B., and Wretman, J. (1992) *Model Assisted Survey Sampling*. New York: Springer-Verlag.

Sarnecki, J. (1986) *Delinquent Networks*. Stockholm: The Swedish Council for Crime Prevention.

Sarnecki, J. (1999) *Co-Offending Youth Networks in Stockholm*. Stockholm: Stockholm University, Department of Criminology.

Smith, T. M. F. (1999) *Some Recent Developments in Sample Survey Theory and Their Impact on Official Statistics*. Proceedings of the 52nd Session of the International Statistical Institute, 3–15.

Snijders, T. (1981) The degree variance: An index of graph heterogeneity. *Social Networks* 3, 163–174.

Snijders, T., and Nowicki, K. (1997) Estimation and prediction for stochastic blockmodels for graphs with latent block structure. *Journal of Classification* 14, 75–100.

Spreen, M. (1992) Rare populations, hidden populations, and link-tracing designs: What and why? *Bulletin de Methodologie Sociologique* 36, 34–58.

Spreen, M. (1998) *Sampling Personal Network Structures: Statistical Inference in Ego-Graphs*. Ph.D. Thesis. University of Groningen, Groningen, The Netherlands.

Spreen, M., and Zwaagstra, R. (1994) Personal network sampling, outdegree analysis, and multilevel analysis: Introducing the network concept in studies of hidden populations. *International Sociology* 9, 475–491.

Stephan, F. F. (1969) Three extensions of sample survey technique: Hybrid, nexus, and graduated sampling. In Johnson, N. L., and Smith, H. (eds.) *New Developments in Survey Sampling*. New York: Wiley, 81–104.

Sugden, R. A., and Smith, T. M. F. (1984) Ignorable and informative designs in survey sampling inference. *Biometrika* 71, 495–506.

Tallberg, C. (2000) *Centrality and Random Graphs*. Licentiate Thesis. Department of Statistics, Stockholm University, Stockholm, Sweden.

Thompson, S., and Frank, O. (2000) Model-based estimation with link-tracing sampling designs. *Survey Methodology* 26, 87–98.

van der Gaag, M., and Snijders, T. (2004) Measurement of individual social capital. In Flap, H., and Völker, B. (eds.) *Creation and Returns of Social Capital*. London: Routledge.

Wang, Y. J., and Wong, G. Y. (1987) Stochastic blockmodels for directed graphs. *Journal of the American Statistical Association* 82, 8–19.

Wasserman, S., and Anderson, C. (1987) Stochastic a posteriori blockmodels: Construction and assessment. *Social Networks* 9, 1–36.

Wasserman, S., and Faust, K. (1994) *Social Network Analysis*. Cambridge: Cambridge University Press.

Wellman, B. (1988) Structural analysis: From method and metaphor to theory and substance. In Wellman, B., and Berkowitz, S. D. (eds.) *Social Structures: A Network Approach*. Cambridge: Cambridge University Press, 19–61.

Whittaker, J. (1990) *Graphical Models in Applied Multivariate Statistics*. Chichester: Wiley.

4

Extending Centrality

Martin G. Everett
University of Westminster

Stephen P. Borgatti
Boston College

4.1 Introduction

Centrality is one of the most important and widely used conceptual tools for analyzing social networks. Nearly all empirical studies try to identify the most important actors within the network. In this chapter, we discuss three extensions of the basic concept of centrality. The first extension generalizes the concept from that of a property of a single actor to that of a group of actors within the network. This extension makes it possible to evaluate the relative centrality of different teams or departments within an organization, or to assess whether a particular ethnic minority in a society is more integrated than another. The second extension applies the concept of centrality to two-mode data in which the data consist of a correspondence between two kinds of nodes, such as individuals and the events in which they participate. In the past, researchers have dealt with such data by converting them to standard network data (with considerable loss of information); the objective of the extension discussed here is to apply the concept of centrality directly to the two-mode data. The third extension uses the centrality concept to examine the core-periphery structure of a network.

It is well-known that a wide variety of specific measures have been proposed in the literature dating back at least to the 1950s with the work of Katz (1953). Freeman (1979) imposed order on some of this work in a seminal paper that categorized centrality measures into three basic categories – degree, closeness, and betweenness – and presented canonical measures for each category. As a result, these three measures have come to dominate empirical usage, along with the eigenvector-based measure proposed by Bonacich (1972). Although many other measures of centrality have been proposed since, these four continue to dominate, and so this chapter concentrates on just these. In addition, for the sake of clarity and simplicity, we discuss only connected undirected binary networks. However, it should be noted that much of the work can be extended without difficulty to directed graphs, valued graphs, and graphs with more than one component.

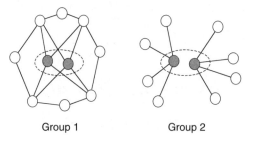

Group 1   Group 2

Figure 4.2.1. Two equal sized groups with the
same degrees but different numbers of contacts.

4.2 Group Centrality

Traditionally, centrality measures have been applied to individual actors. However, there are many situations when it would be advantageous to have some measure of the centrality of a set of actors. These sets may be defined by attributes of the actors, such as ethnicity, age, club membership, or occupation. Alternatively, the sets could be emergent groups identified by a network method such as cliques or structural equivalence. Thus, we can examine informal groups within an organization and ask which ones are most central, and use that in an attempt to account for their relative influence.

In addition, the notion of group centrality can be used to solve the inverse problem: how to construct groups that have maximal centrality. A manager may want to assemble a team with a specific set of skills; if the team were charged with some innovative project, it would be an additional benefit if they could draw on the wider expertise available within the organization. The more central the group, the better-positioned they would be to do this.

The notion of group centrality also opens up the possibility of examining the membership of a group in terms of contribution to the group's centrality. If an individual's ties are redundant with those of others, they can be removed from the group without reducing the group's centrality, creating more efficient groups in this respect.

Everett and Borgatti (1999) proposed a general framework for generalizing in this way the three centrality measures discussed in Freeman's paper. They noted that for any group centrality measure to be a true generalization of an individual measure, when applied to a group consisting of a single actor it should obtain the same result as the standard individual measure. This immediately implies that a group centrality measure is a measure of the centrality of the whole group, with respect to the individuals in the rest of the network, rather than to other groups.

One simple approach that satisfies this condition would be to sum or average the centrality scores in the group. Summing is clearly problematic. Larger groups will tend to have higher scores, and when trying to construct a group of maximum centrality, we would need to restrict the size or the method would always group the entire network together. Averaging solves this problem; however, it does not take account of redundancy or, to put it differently, the fact that actors within the group may be central with respect to or due to the same or different actors. For example, consider two groups of just two actors each, as shown in Figure 4.2.1. In each group, both actors have degree four. In one group the pair are structurally equivalent (i.e., adjacent to exactly the same four actors), whereas in the second group the pair are adjacent to four different actors. Simple aggregation methods would result in both these groups having the same centrality score. Clearly the second group, with its larger span of contacts, should have a better score. Thus, the problem is more complicated than simply choosing the k individuals with greatest individual centrality because much of their centrality could be due to ties with the same third parties or with each other.

(A) *Degree*

We define *group degree centrality* as the number of actors outside the group that are connected to members of the group. Because it is a count of the number of actors as opposed to the number of edges, then multiple ties to the same actors by different group members are only counted once. If C is a group that is a subset of the set of vertices V, then we denote by $N(C)$ the set of all vertices that are not in C, but that are adjacent to a member of C. This measure needs to be normalized so we can compare different groups on the same set of actors. Clearly, the maximum possible is when every actor outside the group is connected to an actor in the group (in graph theory, such a set is said to be dominating). We can therefore normalize by dividing the degree of the group by the number of actors outside the group. The formula in (4.1) provides expressions for group degree centrality:

$$\text{Group degree centrality} = |N(C)|$$
$$\text{Normalized group degree centrality} = \frac{|N(C)|}{|V| - |C|}. \tag{4.1}$$

As an example, we examine data collected by Freeman and Freeman (1979). These data arose from an early experiment on computer-mediated communication. Fifty academics interested in interdisciplinary research were allowed to contact each other via an Electronic Information Exchange System (EIES). The data collected consisted of all messages sent plus acquaintance relationships at two time periods (collected via a questionnaire). The data included the thirty-two actors who completed the study. In addition, attribute data on primary discipline and number of citations was recorded. The data are available in UCINET 6 (Borgatti, Everett, and Freeman 2002). We look at the acquaintance relationship at the start of the study. Two actors are adjacent if they both reported that they have met. The actors are divided into four primary disciplines, namely, sociology, anthropology, psychology, and statistics. We use these disciplines to form the groups. The results are given in Table 4.2.1.

Although sociology has the lowest (unnormalized) group degree centrality, it is a dominating set and so has a normalized group degree centrality of 1.0. Normalization is of greater significance in group centrality than in individual centrality. In individual centrality, the primary purpose of normalization is to enable comparison of centrality scores for individuals in different networks. Within the same network, normalizing centrality makes little difference because normalization is (except in the case of closeness) a linear transformation affecting all nodes equally. However, in group centrality, different

Table 4.2.1. *Group Degree Centrality for the EIES Data*

Discipline	Number of Actors	Group Degree	Normalized Group Degree (%)
Anthropology	6	21	81
Psychology	6	25	96
Sociology	17	15	100
Statistics	3	23	80

groups in the same network will have different sizes, so normalization is necessary to compare scores.

Smaller groups need more connections to obtain the same normalized score as larger groups. We can see that the extra connections the statisticians have over the anthropologists do not quite compensate for their smaller size. For small groups to be central, they need to work harder than large groups; this has to be taken into consideration when analyzing real data. The converse of this is that it is easier for large groups to have higher centrality scores. There are two reasons for this. First, large groups contain more actors so each actor requires fewer contacts outside the group in order for the group as a whole to reach more of the outsiders. Second, the more actors there are in the group the fewer there are outside, so the whole group needs to connect to fewer actors to be a dominating set. This effect is particularly strong in small networks.

In the example given, the groups were identified by attributes rather than structural properties. When using network methods to first find the groups and then analyze their centrality, care needs to be taken in interpreting the results, particularly if this is done on the same relation. Suppose we had searched the EIES data for factions, that is, searched for groups of actors that are well-connected to each other, but the groups have few connections between them. In this case, group degree centrality would have to be carefully interpreted because the search method deliberately tries to minimize this value.

It is interesting to note that an analysis of individual centrality in the EIES data set shows that one particular sociologist has direct contact with all nonsociologists. In a sense, then, the connections of the other sixteen sociologists are redundant in terms of contributing to the degree group centrality. Similarly, two of the anthropologists, two of the psychologists, and one of the statisticians do not directly contribute to the group centrality measures of their respective groups. The presence of actors who do not contribute to the group centrality score can be measured in terms of the efficiency of the group. Efficient groups do not have redundancy in terms of supporting actors who do not contribute. We now give a general formulation of this concept.

Let *gpc* be any unnormalized group centrality score, such as group degree centrality. The contribution of a subset K of a group C to $gpc(C)$ in a network G is the group centrality score of K with respect to the nodes in G-C. With a slight abuse of notation, we denote this by $gpc(K)$. A group centrality score is *monotone* if, in any graph, for every group C and subset K $gpc(K) \leq gpc(C)$. In essence, monotone group centrality means that each actor provides a nonnegative contribution. (Provided, that is, that we are using measures in which larger values indicate more centrality; if the reverse were true, the inequality would need to be reversed.) A subset K of C in which $gpc(K) = gpc(C)$ is said to be making a *full contribution*. Let k be the size of the smallest subset of C that makes a full contribution. The *efficiency e* of a group C with respect to a monotone group centrality measure can be defined as:

$$e = \frac{k}{|C|}. \tag{4.2}$$

We can see from the EIES data and the previous observations that the sociologists have an efficiency of 1/17 (0.06), whereas the efficiencies for the three other groups are 2/3 (0.67). The efficiency is a normalized measure of the maximum number of actors that can be deleted before affecting the group centrality score. A low efficiency means that quite a few actors can be deleted without changing the group centrality value (if they are chosen with care).

(B) *Closeness*

We can extend the measure of closeness to the group context in a similar way. That is, our extension considers the group as a whole and does not try to reduce the group to a single entity. Computationally, for degree centrality this would not make any difference, but for closeness it does. We define group closeness as the normalized inverse sum of distances from the group to all nodes outside the group. As is well-known in the hierarchical clustering literature (Johnson, 1967), there are many ways to measure the distance from a group to a node outside the group. Let D be the set of all distances (defined in the graph theoretic sense as the length of the shortest path) from a node x to a set of nodes C. Then we can define the distance from x to C as the maximum of D, the minimum of D, the mean of D, the median of D, or any of a number of other variants. Each gives rise to a different group centrality measure, and each is a proper generalization of individual closeness centrality because, if the group were a single actor, all of these would be identical to each other and to ordinary individual closeness. We can then normalize the group closeness by dividing the summed distance score into the number of nongroup members. This is given in (4.3). (This value represents the theoretical minimum for all measures mentioned here; if a more esoteric distance is used, then this should be replaced by the corresponding optimum value.)

$$D_x = \{d(x, c), c \in C\} \, x \in V - C.$$
$$d_f(x, C) = f(D_x)$$

where $f = $ min, max, mean, or median.

$$\text{Group closeness} = \sum_{x \in V-C} d_f(x, C)$$

$$\text{Normalized group closeness} = \frac{|V - C|}{\displaystyle\sum_{x \in V-C} d_f(x, c)}. \tag{4.3}$$

The question as to which of these should be used in a particular application arises. This, of course, is dependent on the nature of the data. It is worth noting that the minimum and maximum methods share the property that the distance to a group is defined as the distance to an individual actor within the group. If the data are such that the group can be thought of as an individual unit, then the minimum method would be the most appropriate. As an example, consider the group of police informers embedded in a criminal network. Assume that as soon as any one informer knows a bit of information, the information is passed on instantaneously to the police. In this case, it is reasonable to use the minimum distance formulation of group closeness because the effectiveness of the group is a function of the shortest distance that any informer is from the origin of any bit of information.

Now let us consider the maximum method. Using the maximum method means that everyone within the group is a distance equal to or less than the group's distance to a given actor. Consider a communication network within an organization, and suppose that everyone who manages a budget needs to know about a regulatory change. If any one department head is unaware of the change, his or her department is not in compliance and may make the organization as a whole liable for penalties. In this case, the maximum method would be more appropriate because the performance of a group is a function of the time that the last person hears the news. Alternatively, rumors may travel through a network by each actor passing on the rumor to a randomly selected neighbor. The expected time until arrival of the rumor to the group will be a function of all distances from the group to all other actors. In this case, the average method makes sense. The different methods also have some mathematical properties that in different situations may make one more attractive than the others. For example, the minimum method is not very sensitive and it is relatively easy for groups to obtain the maximum value. However, of the closeness methods discussed here, it is the only one that is monotone and can thus be used to define efficiency.

(C) Betweenness

The extension to betweenness is in the same vein as the extensions discussed previously. Group betweenness centrality measures the proportion of geodesics connecting pairs of nongroup members that pass through the group. Let C be a subset of nodes of a graph with node set V, let $g_{u,v}$ be the number of geodesics connecting u to v, and let $g_{u,v}(C)$ be the number of these geodesics that pass through C. Then the group betweenness centrality of C is given by (4.4):

$$\text{Group betweeness centrality} = \sum_{u<v} \frac{g_{u,v}(C)}{g_{u,v}} \quad u, v \notin C. \tag{4.4}$$

This value can then be normalized by dividing by $\frac{1}{2}(|V| - |C|)(|V| - |C| - 1)$, which is the maximum possible.

$$\text{Normalized group betweeness centrality} = \frac{2\sum_{u<v} \frac{g_{u,v}(C)}{g_{u,v}}}{(|V| - |C|)(|V| - |C| - 1)}, \tag{4.5}$$

where $u, v \notin C$

(D) *Social Capital*

The notion of group centrality provides a measure of the social capital of an embedded group. Most discussions of social capital distinguish between individual capital and group capital. Individual social capital is easily thought of in terms of centrality. Group social capital is typically thought of in terms of the pattern of ties within the group (e.g., cohesion). This is perhaps because theorists concerned with group social capital typically regard the group as the social universe. However, in organizational theory, the groups in which we are interested (e.g., teams, task forces, departments, divisions, whole organizations) are typically embedded in a larger social network (e.g., the organization as a whole, the industry, the economy). This means that the social capital of the group could refer as much to the ties of the group to the network it is embedded in as it does to the ties within the group. The new measures of group centrality provide an effective way to measure this external form of group social capital.

4.3   Two-Mode Centrality

We now shift our attention to the application of centrality to a different kind of data, namely, two-mode data. In two-mode data, there are two kinds of entities, which we call actors and events, and a binary relation, such as membership or participation, that connects the actors to the events. The data may be represented by a two-way, two-mode affiliation matrix, in which the rows represent actors and the columns represent events, and a 1 in row i column j indicates that actor i attended event j. Two-mode data can also be represented as a bipartite graph – a graph in which the nodes can be divided into two classes and the only ties in the network are between nodes of different classes. This type of data is of interest to network analysts when it can reasonably be supposed that two actors participating in the same event indicates the existence or potential for some form of social bond between them.

Bonacich (1991) looked at two-mode centrality, but his methods were not direct extensions of the traditional measures. Because the bipartite graph is simply a graph, we can apply the traditional centrality measures directly to this graph. This approach has been taken by a number of authors, particularly with respect to degree centrality, and Faust (1997) discussed this conceptualization and suggested some alternatives using Galois lattices. Here, we concentrate on the work of Borgatti and Everett (1997) and their approach to normalizing these measures and developing indices of graph centralization. We assume that the bipartite graph representation is of the form $G(A + E, R)$, where A and E are the sets of actors and events respectively, and R is the set of ties connecting them. Let n be the size of the node set A and m be the size of node set E.

(A) *Degree*

In the two-mode context, the degree centrality for an actor is simply the number of events they attend, and for an event, it is the number of actors attending that event. Clearly, the maximum degree for an actor is the total number of events and the maximum degree for an event is the total number of actors. These are given in equation 4.6. We can use this

Table 4.3.2. *Two-Mode Degree Centrality for the Davis Data*

Name	Degree	Normalized Degree	Two-Mode Normalized Degree
Evelyn	8	25.81	57.14
Laura	7	22.58	50.00
Theresa	8	25.81	57.14
Brenda	7	22.58	50.00
Charlotte	4	12.90	28.57
Frances	4	12.90	28.57
Eleanor	4	12.90	28.57
Pearl	3	9.68	21.43
Ruth	4	12.90	28.57
Verne	4	12.90	28.57
Myrna	4	12.90	28.57
Katherine	6	19.36	42.86
Sylvia	7	22.58	50.00
Nora	8	25.81	57.14
Helen	5	16.13	35.71
Dorothy	2	6.45	14.29
Olivia	2	6.45	14.29
Flora	2	6.45	14.29
E1	3	9.68	16.67
E2	3	9.68	16.67
E3	6	19.36	33.33
E4	4	12.90	22.22
E5	8	25.81	44.44
E6	8	25.81	44.44
E7	10	32.26	55.56
E8	14	45.16	77.78
E9	12	38.71	66.67
E10	5	16.13	27.78
E11	4	12.90	22.22
E12	6	19.36	33.33
E13	3	9.68	16.67
E14	3	9.68	16.67

information to normalize the degree centrality scores. Davis et al. (1941) collected data on a series of social events attended by society women. The data consisted of eighteen women and fourteen events so that $n = 18$ and $m = 14$:

$$\text{Actor } x \text{ normalized centrality} = \frac{C_D(x)}{m}$$

$$\text{Event } y \text{ normalized centrality} = \frac{C_D(y)}{n}. \tag{4.6}$$

In Table 4.3.2, the second column is the raw degrees of the nodes, and the third column gives the standard normalization proposed by Freeman for ordinary single-mode data. The fourth column is the two-mode normalization. This is calculated by taking the women's degree and dividing by the number of events (fourteen in this case) and the event's degree, and dividing by the number of women (eighteen in this case) and expressing the answers as a percentage. The two-mode normalization takes account of the special nature of the data and allows the centrality scores to take on the full range of values from 0 to 100. It should be noted that the two-mode normalization is nonlinear in the sense that actors and events can be scaled differently. As an example, actor Theresa and event E5 both have degree 8, but Theresa has a higher normalized score reflecting the fact that there are fewer events than women. Comparing these scores without the normalization would have given a false impression, and the score for Theresa would have been unrepresentative of the real situation.

(B) *Closeness and Betweenness*

We can take exactly the same approach for closeness and betweenness as we have taken for degree – that is, apply the original measures as before, but change the way they are normalized to reflect the fact that there are restrictions on which nodes can be adjacent. For ordinary closeness, we take the raw score and divide this value into the size of the network minus one. In the bipartite case, we have a theoretical minimum value of $m + 2n - 2$ for the actors and $n + 2m - 2$ for the events. We therefore take an event node, calculate its raw closeness centrality score, and divide this value into $n + 2m - 2$. For an actor node we do the same thing, but divide the raw score into $m + 2n - 2$. Clearly, as in the degree case, this is a normalization procedure that is nonlinear. These are given in (4.7):

$$\text{Actor } x \text{ closeness centrality} = \frac{m + 2n - 2}{C_c(x)}$$

$$\text{Event } y \text{ closeness centrality} = \frac{2m + n - 2}{C_c(y)}. \tag{4.7}$$

Betweenness is treated in the same way, but the formulas are more complicated. We normalize the events by dividing by $\frac{1}{2}[n^2(p + 1)^2 + n(p + 1)(2r - p - 1) - r(2p - r + 3)]$, where p is the integer portion of the result of dividing $(m - 1)$ by n, and r is the remainder. We normalize the actors by dividing by $\frac{1}{2}[m^2(s + 1)^2 + m(s + 1)(2t - s - 1) - t(2s - t + 3)]$, where s is the integer portion of the result of dividing $(n - 1)$ by m, and t is the remainder. This is given in (4.8):

Actor x betweenness centrality

$$= \frac{C_B(x)}{\frac{1}{2}\left[m^2(s + 1)^2 + m(s + 1)(2t - s - 1) - t(2s - t + 3)\right]}$$

$$s = \left\lceil \frac{(n - 1)}{m} \right\rceil, t = (n - 1) \bmod m$$

Event y betweenness centrality

$$= \frac{C_B(y)}{\frac{1}{2}\left[n^2(p+1)^2 + n(p+1)(2r-p-1) - r(2p-r+3)\right]}. \tag{4.8}$$

$$p = \left\lceil \frac{(m-1)}{n} \right\rceil, r = (m-1) \bmod n$$

(C) Centralization

Freeman, in his original 1979 paper, proposed a general measure of centralization to try and capture the extent to which a network consisted of a highly central actor surrounded by peripheral actors. This measure is simply the sum of the differences in centrality of the most central actor to all others, normalized by the maximum possible over all connected graphs. This can be expressed as

$$\frac{\sum[c_* - c_i]}{\max\sum[c_* - c_i]}, \tag{4.9}$$

where c_i is the centrality of node i and c_* is the centrality of the most central node.

We can apply this formula directly to our two-mode centrality measures. Note that we should only apply this to the normalized centrality measures because the formula takes the difference between the centrality of one node and that of all other nodes, so we need the scores to be comparable across modes. We also need to determine the denominator in this formula because this is now the maximum over all connected bipartite graphs and not over all connected graphs. In the one-mode case, the graph that achieved the maximum was the star graph. For two-mode data, it is a little more complicated, but in general the graphs on which the maximum centralities were achieved to obtain the normalization can be used to construct this denominator. The following formulas give expressions for the maximum and assume the centralities are on the scale of 0 to 1. If percentages are used, then the formulas need to be multiplied by 100. The node that achieves the highest centrality score could be either an actor or an event. We denote by n_o the size of the node set that contains the actor with the highest centrality score (this value could be either n or m), and n_i is the size of the other mode.

Degree

$$\frac{(n_o n_i - n_i - n_o + 1)(n_i + n_o)}{n_i n_o}. \tag{4.10}$$

Closeness

$$((p+1)n_i + r) - [(1+2p)n_i + 2r]$$

$$\times \left(\frac{p(n_i - r)}{2p(2n_i - 1) + 4r + 3n_i - 2} + \frac{r(p+1)}{2p(2n_i - 1) + 4(r-1) + 3n_i} \right)$$

$$- [n_i(p+2) + r - 1]$$

$$\times \left(\frac{n_i - r}{n_i(3p+2) + 3r - 2p - 1} + \frac{r}{n_i(3p+2) + 3(r-1) - 2p} \right)$$

$$p = (n_o - 1) \text{ div } n_i, r = (n_o - 1) \bmod n_i. \tag{4.11}$$

Betweenness

$$(n_o + n_i - 1) - \frac{p(n_i - r)(2n_o + 2n_i - p - 3) + r(p + 1)(2n_o + 2n_i - p - 4)}{n_o^2(s + 1)^2 + n_o(s + 1)(2t - s - 1) - t(2s - t + 3)}$$

$$p = (n_o - 1) \text{ div } n_i, r = (n_o - 1) \mod n_i,$$

$$s = (n_i - 1) \text{ div } n_o, t = (n_i - 1) \mod n_o. \tag{4.12}$$

In the formulas for closeness and betweenness, parameters p, r, s, and t are used to simplify the expressions. The parameter p is the integer result of dividing $n_o - 1$ by n_i, and parameter r is the remainder. The parameters s and t are defined analogously.

As an example, consider the betweenness formula for the Davis data. The highest normalized score (24.38%) is achieved by event E8. Summing the difference between 0.2438 and the centrality of every other node gives us the numerator of the centralization formula and equals 6.3686. The denominator, as given by the previous equation is 30.1236, yielding a graph centralization score of 21.14%.

It is interesting to note that it is possible for an event and an actor to have the same centrality score and for this to be the highest score. In this case there are two possible centralizations, one of an actor and one for an event, and these could be quite different for the closeness and betweenness centralizations (they would agree for the degree case). This fact suggests a fundamental problem with this approach, namely, that the centralization measures the extent to which actors and events are peripheral to the most central actor or event. It could happen that the events have similar centrality scores, but there is a high degree of centralization among the actors taken on their own. Borgatti and Everett (1997) proposed an extension called single-mode centralization. For each mode, the difference between the most central node and the centralities of all other nodes in that mode is calculated. This is exactly the same formula as for all the centralizations, except we now restrict the calculation to each mode. Again, we need to calculate the formula for the denominator, and these are given as follows. Note that, because we restrict ourselves to a single mode, it is not necessary to use the normalized centrality scores for degree and betweenness, but it is necessary for closeness because the normalization is always nonlinear. Because the formula for the unnormalized cases are much simpler, we present those here. We use the same notation as for the complete centralization case.

Degree (unnormalized)

$$(n_i - 1)(n_o - 1). \tag{4.13}$$

Closeness (normalized)

$$n_o - 1 - [(1 + 2p)n_i + 2r]$$

$$\times \left[\frac{p(n_i - r)}{2p(2n_i - 1) + 4r + 3n_i - 2} + \frac{r(p + 1)}{2p(2n_i - 1) + 4(r - 1) + 3n_i} \right].$$

Betweenness (unnormalized)

$$(n_o - 1)[n_i^2(p + 1)^2 + n_i(p + 1)(2r - p - 1) - r(2p - r + 3)]/2. \tag{4.14}$$

We now apply the formula for single-mode degree centrality. There are eighty-nine edges in the data set so the sums of the degrees of the women and the events will both be eighty-nine. The woman with the highest degree has degree 8 and, because there are eighteen women, the numerator will be $8 \times 18 - 89 = 55$. The denominator is given by the previous formula and is therefore $17 \times 13 = 221$. This gives a single-mode centralization of 25%; a similar calculation for the events results in 47%. We can see that the women in this case are far less centralized than the events.

The reason for preferring single-mode centralization over the traditional method of converting to one-mode data is that this technique does not destroy information on patterns of overlap. In addition, we are also able to apply methods that are only valid on binary data to the network. In converting to one-mode, it is necessary to dichotomize the data before applying some of the centrality calculations, and this induces further information loss. As an example, suppose we convert to a single mode for the previous example and look at the resultant women-by-women and event-by-event matrices using the traditional methods. The matrices are now valued and need to be dichotomized to look for degree centralization. If we run through the full range of possible dichotomizations, that is, from zero to the maximum value in the new matrix, then we never obtain results as we have here. In this case, the maximum centralization for the women is 10% and for the events is 32%. These values seriously underestimate the true centralization scores.

4.4 Core-Periphery Measures

The notion of core-periphery structures draws on elements from the previous sections of this chapter. From the discussion of group centrality, we draw the basic notion of extending centrality to apply to a group. From the discussion of two-mode data, we draw on the notion of graph centralization, which we extend to the group case. The synthesis of these concepts is the notion of a core-periphery structure, which is simultaneously a model of a graph and a generalized measure of centrality. A graph has a core-periphery structure to the extent that it lacks subgroups. Another way of putting it is that all nodes can be regarded as belonging (to a greater or lesser extent) to a single group, either as core members or peripheral members. The extent to which a node belongs to the core can be thought of as the coreness of the node, and is an individual measure similar to centrality. The approach taken here follows the work of Borgatti and Everett (1999).

Our starting model will be a simple partition of nodes into core and periphery classes, in which the core is a complete subgraph and the periphery is a collection of actors that do not interact with each other. This leaves a number of options for the relations between core and periphery nodes, and each of these can give rise to different models. One option is to assume that everyone in the periphery is connected to every member of the core. Table 4.4.3 gives an adjacency matrix of this structure. The matrix has been blocked to emphasize the pattern.

The pattern can be seen as a generalization of Freeman's (1979) maximally centralized graph, the simple star (Figure 4.4.2). In the star, a single node (the center) is connected to all other nodes, which are not connected to each other. To move to the

Table 4.4.3. *Idealized Core-Periphery Structure*

	1	2	3	4	5	6	7	8	9	10
1		1	1	1	1	1	1	1	1	1
2	1		1	1	1	1	1	1	1	1
3	1	1		1	1	1	1	1	1	1
4	1	1	1		1	1	1	1	1	1
5	1	1	1	1		0	0	0	0	0
6	1	1	1	1	0		0	0	0	0
7	1	1	1	1	0	0		0	0	0
8	1	1	1	1	0	0	0		0	0
9	1	1	1	1	0	0	0	0		0
10	1	1	1	1	0	0	0	0	0	

core-periphery image, we simply add duplicates of the center to the graph and connect them to each other (Figure 4.4.3). The core of a core-periphery structure can also be seen as a group with maximum group centrality; in this case, the core is in fact a dominating set.

The patterns in Table 4.4.3 and Figures 4.4.2 and 4.4.3 are idealized patterns that are unlikely to be actually observed in empirical data. We can readily appreciate that real structures will only approximate this pattern, in that they will have one-blocks with less than perfect density, and zero-blocks that contain a few ties. A simple measure of how well the real structure approximates the ideal is given by (4.15) together with (4.16).

$$\rho = \sum_{i,j} a_{ij}\delta_{ij} \tag{4.15}$$

$$\delta_{ij} = \left\{ \begin{array}{l} 1 \text{ if } c_i = \text{CORE or } c_j = \text{CORE} \\ 0 \text{ otherwise} \end{array} \right\}. \tag{4.16}$$

In the equations, a_{ij} indicates the presence or absence of a tie in the observed data, c_i refers to the class (core or periphery) to which actor i is assigned, and δ_{ij} (subsequently called the *pattern matrix*) indicates the presence or absence of a tie in the ideal image. For a fixed distribution of values, the measure achieves its maximum value when and only when A (the matrix of a_{ij}) and Δ (the matrix of δ_{ij}) are identical, which occurs when A has a perfect core-periphery structure. Thus, a structure is a core-periphery

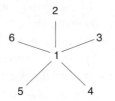

Figure 4.4.2. Freeman's star.

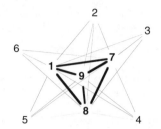

Figure 4.4.3. Core-periphery structure.

structure to the extent that ρ is large. This formulation can be used as the basis for a procedure for detecting core-periphery structures in data. The procedure, which has been implemented in UCINET (Borgatti et al. 2002) using a genetic algorithm, begins with a random partition of nodes into two classes (core and periphery), then iteratively reassigns the nodes to maximize a variant of (4.15).

We can think of the c_i as a discrete coreness measure and assign a value of 1 to the core actors and a value of 0 to the peripheral actors. In this case (4.16) can be written as $\delta_{ij} = c_i c_j$. This can be extended further by allowing the cs to take on values from a continuous range between 0 and 1. Thus, the pattern matrix $\triangle$ has large values for pairs of node that are both high in coreness, medium-size values for pairs of node in which one is high in coreness and the other is not, and low values for pairs of node that are both peripheral.

Now that we have a continuous model, the simple matching count of (4.15) would not be appropriate. (Nor, in fact, do we need to restrict the data matrix to contain only binary values.) Two possible solutions have been extensively used although many others are possible. The first is to simply correlate matrix A with matrix $\triangle$. We can then optimize the correlation of A and $\triangle$ over all values of the vector $\mathbf{c}$, where the elements of $\mathbf{c}$ are constrained between zero and one. This is a continuous optimization problem and has been implemented in UCINET (Borgatti et al. 2002) using the well-known Nelder-Mead simplex optimization procedure. An alternative is to use the sum of squared differences and optimize this. It is well-known that, if the diagonal is not ignored, this equates to finding the principal eigenvector of A and therefore is simply an eigenvector centrality measure. This gives us a new insight into eigenvector centrality and helps us understand why the smaller separate components have an eigenvector centrality of zero; they simply cannot be part of the core.

In a series of studies, Bernard, Killworth, and Sailer collected five sets of data on human interactions in bounded groups and on the actors' abilities to recall those interactions (Killworth and Bernard 1976, 1979; Bernard and Killworth 1977; Bernard, Killworth, and Sailer 1980, 1982). In each study, they obtained measures of social interaction among all actors and ranking data based on the subjects' memory of those interactions. These data concern interactions in a technical research group at a West Virginia university, again recorded by an "unobtrusive" observer. Observations were made as the observer patrolled a fixed route through the work space every 15 minutes during two 14-day periods. The coreness, using the correlation criterion, was calculated using UCINET (Borgatti et al. 2002) (which contains the data as a standard data set), and these have been placed in descending order of coreness in Table 4.4.4.

Table 4.4.4. *Coreness of Research
Workers*

ID	Coreness
23	0.62
2	0.31
16	0.30
27	0.29
3	0.27
10	0.26
22	0.20
30	0.19
31	0.16
1	0.15
8	0.15
12	0.14
28	0.11
34	0.08
13	0.08
5	0.06
32	0.05
7	0.05
14	0.02
24	0.01
9	0.00
15	0.00
33	0.00
11	0.00
25	0.00
17	0.00
26	0.00
4	0.00
6	0.00
18	0.00
21	0.00
29	0.00
20	0.00
19	0.00

We can also use the discrete form of the core-periphery model to compare these results. The results are given in Table 4.4.5. This table gives a blockmodel image of the core-periphery structure. We note that the seven actors identified in the core are precisely the top seven actors in terms of continuous coreness.[1]

As noted in our discussion of two-mode data, a way to summarize the pattern of centrality scores in a graph is the notion of centralization. Because the intuitive basis for centralization is the graph in Figure 4.4.2, it would seem natural to extend this concept to deal with the core-periphery structure given in Figure 4.4.3. We refer to this extension as *concentration*. Because centralization looks at the difference in centrality of the most central actor to all other actors, in order to extend this to the core-periphery case, we need to compare the coreness of the actors in the core with the coreness of

Table 4.4.5. *Discrete Core-Periphery Model of the Data*

	22	2	3	16	27	23	10	1	9	4	7	12	13	14	15	8	17	18	11	20	21	5	6	24	25	26	19	28	29	30	31	32	33	34
22		14	14	7	6	4	5	5	1	1	1	1	1	1		5			1					1				1		1		1		1
2	14		4	4		8	1	7	1	1	1	1	3	1	1	1						4		1			1	1		3	4	1		1
3	14	4		1	7	5	8	7	1	1	3	1	1	1	1	1						1		1				2		3	4	1	1	1
16	7	4	1		7	6	8		1		5	5			1	4						4						1	1			2	2		
27	6		7	7		7	6	1	1	3	5	6	4	1	1	4						1		1	1		1	7	1	10	6	1		
23	4	8	5	6	7		6	4		1	2		1									2						2	1	1				3
10	5	1	8	8	6	6			2	2	2	6	4	1	1	4							1			1	3	2		1	6	1	3	3
1	1	5	7		1	4			1	1	1	1	3	1	4	1			1			1	6	2		4	5	1	1		3		1	
9		1	1	1	1		2	1		1	1	2	1	1	2	6						6	14	4		4	3	5	1	1	4	3	1	
4	1	1	1	1	3	1	2	1	1		2	1	1						1				2	1				1	2	3	1		1	2
7	1	1	3	5	5	6	2			2		1	1	1	2				2			1	1		1		1	3	3		1		3	2
12	1		1	5	6	4	1									1		1				1	1	2			10		1					
13	5	1	1		1	3	4																						1	1					
8	5	1	1	4	1			1										1																
11	5			4	4	3	1		6																					2				
20	1			4	1	2		1		14	6	1	2		1							1		2		2			1				1	
21		1	1						2		2	3	1		1					1	2					1	2	1	1					
5								2		1	2	3		2	1		1							3		3		1		3			1	1
6		1	1					4		3	1	4	1											3	1	3	3							
24						10		4		1		1		3	1					2		2	2	1				2	1	1				
25						6		5		2	2	3	4	1	10		1		2		1	1	2	3	3		3	5		1	6	2	5	3
26		1	3	1		1	3	1						5			1											3	1	1		1	1	1
19	1	4	4	2	10	6	3	3		1		1		3	1		1		2			1		1		1	1	5	1	1	3	3	3	7
28											1	1		2								1		1				2	5	3		7	2		
29	1	1	1	1	1		3				1	1	2	2		1				1	1	1		1	1	1	1		1	1	1	7	2	2
30–34	1	1	1		1	3	3	3	1				2	2			1																	

those in the periphery. If there is little difference in coreness, then the graph is not highly concentrated.

Suppose that C is a coreness centrality measure on a collection of n actors, and that the actors have been arranged in descending order based on C and the network relabeled so $c_1 \leq c_2 \leq \cdots \leq c_n$. Let the first j actors comprise the membership of the core. Then we define *concentration* as in (4.17):

$$\frac{\sum_{i=1}^{j} \left(c_i - max(c_{j+1}, c_{j+2}, \ldots, c_n) \right)}{2j} + \frac{\sum_{k=j+1}^{n} \left(min(c_1, c_2, \ldots, c_j) - c_k \right)}{2(n-j)}. \quad (4.17)$$

The first term measures the difference between each core actor and the peripheral actor with the highest coreness centrality measure, whereas the second term compares each peripheral actor with the core actor with the lowest coreness centrality measure. Each term is then normalized so one does not dominate the other simply by the number of actors it contains. Clearly, the formula could be simplified because $max(c_{j+1}, c_{j+2}, \ldots, c_n)$ is just c_{j+1} given the way we have relabeled the network. Similarly, $min(c_1, c_2, \ldots, c_j)$ is equal to c_j. If we assume that the underlying coreness measure can have a maximum value of 1 for every core member and a value of zero for every peripheral member, then the concentration has a maximum value of 1.[2]

The concentration measure can be used to compare different networks, just as we typically compare networks with respect to density or centralization. Borgatti and Everett (2000) speculated that groups with high concentration may perform better in certain contexts due to the short graph theoretic distances among actors and the lack of subgroups that may develop antagonisms or alternative ways of thinking. Similarly, Schenkel, Tiegland, and Borgatti (2001) argued that communities of practice will have high concentrations.

The measure can also be used to find the best place to partition a continuous coreness measure into a discrete core and a periphery. We do this by sorting actors in descending order according to coreness, and then repeatedly calculating concentration, taking the core initially to consist of just the top actor, then the top two actors, and so on, and choosing the partition that maximizes concentration. Table 4.4.6 gives the concentration measures for the coreness scores of Table 4.4.4. The ID gives the row number of the next actor to be added into the core. Hence, row 4 of Table 4.4.6 shows that actors 23, 2, 16, and 27 as the core give a concentration score of 0.340. The maximum score is 0.461, and this indicates that the first twelve actors would give the best core. There is also a local maximum of 0.430, which includes the first six actors, and this is close to the division given by the discrete model.

4.5 Conclusion

We have discussed three extensions of the original centrality concept: one extends centrality to groups, another extends centrality to two-mode data, and the third broadens the concept to formulate a model of a core-periphery structure. Each has useful application in empirical settings. As noted earlier, group centrality provides a natural way to

Table 4.4.6. *Sorted Concentration Measure of the*
Research Workers

	ID	Conc
1	23	0.402
2	2	0.284
3	16	0.294
4	27	0.340
5	3	0.356
6	10	0.430
7	22	0.385
8	30	0.424
9	31	0.395
10	1	0.386
11	8	0.400
12	12	0.461
13	28	0.446
14	34	0.406
15	13	0.453
16	5	0.411
17	32	0.413
18	7	0.452
19	14	0.425
20	24	0.425
21	9	0.387
22	15	0.376
23	33	0.370
24	11	0.361
25	25	0.354
26	17	0.348
27	26	0.341
28	4	0.335
29	6	0.330
30	18	0.324
31	21	0.319
32	29	0.314
33	20	0.309

measure the external aspect of the social capital of groups, thus providing an independent variable in a study predicting group performance. In addition, the technique can be turned around to provide a criterion for forming groups that have maximal centrality. This could be used by organizations to staff teams or taskforces with maximum clout.

The extension to two-mode data serves a number of important functions. First, we can compare the centrality of members of different modes using a comparable metric. Second, it allows us to directly analyze two-mode data, using the tools and concepts of network analysis, without resorting to structure-destroying transformations such as multiplying the data matrix by its transpose and dichotomizing. The result is that we can measure the extent to which, for example, an event serves as a unique bridge between different groups of actors. Two-mode tools allow us to mine a wealth of data that can be obtained unobtrusively, such as participation in projects, group memberships, event attendance, and so on. This is particularly useful in large networks where data collection by survey is prohibitively expensive and yields unacceptable nonresponse rates.

The generalization to core-periphery structures represents an advance along several different fronts. First, it extends Freeman's concept of centralization to the case of multiple actors. Centralization measures the extent to which a network revolves around a single highly central actor. However, what if there are two or more actors occupying the same central position and playing that same structural role? The centralization measure, by design, gets a lower score in such a case. In contrast, our concentration measure yields the same high score regardless of how many people are in the core. Second, with the core-periphery notion, we bring a modeling perspective to the measurement of centrality. We make clear, for example, that the measure of individual coreness is only interpretable when the core-periphery model fits the observed network data (Borgatti and Everett 1999).

Our objective has been to present the concepts underlying three classes of generalization of centrality. A limitation of our study is that we have only specifically discussed the generalization of a few of the dozens of extant centrality measures. This should not be taken to imply that only the measures we discuss are generalizable. Others can and should be generalized along the lines we have presented here.

Endnotes

1. However, because it is a combinatorial algorithm, other runs can produce slightly different results. In such cases, it is wise to identify the core as the intersection of all the core members over a number of runs and move the rest into the periphery (or define a category of "semiperiphery").
2. It should be noted, however, that core-periphery measures such as the principal eigenvector are usually normalized in such a way that values as extreme as 0 and 1 are not attainable. Hence, a smaller maximum concentration should be used, or alternatively, the coreness measure should be renormalized.

References

Bernard H., and Killworth P. (1977). Informant accuracy in social network data II. *Human Communication Research*, 4:3–18.

Bernard H., Killworth P., and Sailer L. (1980). Informant accuracy in social network data IV. *Social Networks*, 2:191–218.

Bernard H., Killworth P., and Sailer L. (1982). Informant accuracy in social network data V. *Social Science Research*, 11:30–66.

Bonacich P. (1972). Factoring and weighting approaches to status scores and clique identification. *Journal of Mathematical Sociology*, 2:113–120.

Bonacich P. (1991). Simultaneous group and individual centralities. *Social Networks*, 13(2):155–168.

Borgatti S. P., and Everett M. G. (1997). Network analysis of 2-mode data. *Social Networks*, 19(3):243–269.

Borgatti S. P., and Everett M. G. (1999). Models of core/periphery structure, *Social Networks*, 21:375–395.

Borgatti S. P., and Everett M. G. (2000, June). *Graphs with Short Paths*. Presentation at Mathematical Sociology Conference, Honolulu.

Borgatti S. P., Everett M. G., and Freeman L. C. (2002). *Ucinet for Windows: Software for Social Network Analysis*. Harvard: Analytic Technologies.

Davis A., Gardner B. B., and Gardner M. R. (1941). *Deep South: A Social Anthropological Study of Caste and Class*. Chicago: University of Chicago Press.

Everett M. G., and Borgatti S. P. (1999). The centrality of groups and classes. *Journal of Mathematical Sociology*, 23(3):181–201.

Faust K. (1997). Centrality in affiliation networks. *Social Networks*, 19(2):157–191.

Freeman L. C. (1979). Centrality in networks: I. Conceptual clarification. *Social Networks*, 1:215–39.

Freeman S. C., and Freeman L. C. (1979). The networkers network: a study of the impact of a new communications medium on sociometric structure. *Social Science Research Reports*, No. 46. Irvine: University of California.

Johnson S. C. (1967). Hierarchical clustering schemes. *Psychometrika*, 32:241–253.

Katz L. (1953). A new index derived from sociometric data analysis. *Psychometrika*, 18:39–43.

Killworth B., and Bernard H. (1976). Informant accuracy in social network data. *Human Organization*, 35:269–286.

Killworth P., and Bernard H. (1979). Informant accuracy in social network data III. *Social Networks*, 2, 19–46.

Schenkel A., Tiegland R., and Borgatti S. P. (2001). *Theorizing Structural Dimensions of Communities of Practice: A Social Network Approach*. Presentation at the Academy of Management Conference, Washington, DC, August.

5

Positional Analyses of Sociometric Data

Patrick Doreian

University of Pittsburgh

Vladimir Batagelj

University of Ljubljana

Anuška Ferligoj

University of Ljubljana

One of the major goals of social network analysis is to discern fundamental structure(s) of networks in ways that (1) allow us to know the structure of a network and (2) facilitate our understanding of network phenomena. One of the most used tools for doing this is blockmodeling, a collection of methods for partitioning networks according to well-specified criteria.

Initially, we use the term "blockmodeling" or "conventional blockmodeling" to characterize the usual approach to blockmodeling, one based on the concepts of structural equivalence (Lorrain and White 1971) and regular equivalence (White and Reitz 1983)[1] using indirect methods. Our intent here is to use an optimizational approach to blockmodeling to *generalize* blockmodeling to consider indefinitely *many types* of blockmodels. Refer to Batagelj et al. (1992a,b) for an account of optimizational methods applied to blockmodeling, Doreian et al. (1994) for the extension to generalized blockmodeling, and Batagelj et al. (1998) for prespecified blockmodeling. Integral to this approach is the use of a built-in measure of the adequacy of the fit of a blockmodel and the use of direct methods. We use the term "generalized blockmodeling" for the generalized version of blockmodeling described later in this chapter. See also Doreian et al. (2005) for a more complete treatment.

5.1 Introduction

Let $\mathcal{U} = \{x_1, x_2, \ldots, x_n\}$ be a finite set of *units* representing actors. The units are related by a binary *relation*

$$R \subseteq \mathcal{U} \times \mathcal{U},$$

which determines a *network*

$$\mathbf{N} = (\mathcal{U}, R).$$

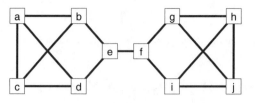

Figure 5.1.1. The Everett Network.

The network can be represented by a graph with units as vertices. In general, the statement can be extended to include several relations $\{R_t\}$ and valued networks. The *location* of an actor in a network is given by the row and/or column corresponding to that actor in the relational matrix. This extends to multiple relations. The location is the set of ties to and from all other actors in the network.

A *clustering* (partition) $\mathbf{C} = \{C_1, C_2, \dots, C_k\}$, where $\emptyset \subset C_i \subseteq \mathcal{U}$ are *clusters* (also called *positions*), partitions the relation R into *blocks*

$$R(C_i, C_j) = R \cap C_i \times C_j.$$

Each cluster, C_i, is a position occupied by all the vertices in the cluster, C_i. Each block is defined in terms of the units belonging to clusters C_i and C_j, and all the arcs leading from cluster C_i to cluster C_j. If $i = j$, a block $R(C_i, C_i)$ is called a *diagonal* block.

Each partition $\mathbf{C} = \{C_i\}, i \neq j \Rightarrow C_i \cap C_j = \emptyset$ and $\cup_i C_i = \mathcal{U}$, determines an equivalence relation $\sim$

$$u \sim v \Leftrightarrow \exists i : u, v \in C_i$$

and each equivalence relation $\sim$ determines a partition $\mathbf{C} = \{C(u) : u \in \mathcal{U}\}$

$$C(u) = \{v \in \mathcal{U} : u \sim v\}.$$

A blockmodel consists of structures obtained by identifying all units from the same cluster of the clustering $\mathbf{C}$ and can be presented by a *reduced graph* or by a relational matrix, called an *image matrix*. The vertices in the reduced graph represent the *positions*.

Blockmodeling, as a set of empirical procedures, is based on the idea that units in a network can be grouped according to the extent to which they are equivalent, in terms of some *meaningful definition* of equivalence. In general, different definitions of equivalence usually (but not always) lead to distinct partitions. Regardless of the definition of equivalence used, there are two basic approaches to the equivalence of units in a given network (Faust 1988):

- The equivalent units have the same connection pattern to the **same** neighbors.
- The equivalent units have the same or similar connection pattern to (possibly) **different** neighbors.

The first type of equivalence is formalized by the notion of structural equivalence, and the second by the notion of regular equivalence, with the latter a generalization of the former.

As a simple example, we consider the Everett Network (Borgatti and Everett 1989) shown in Figure 5.1.1 where all of the ties are reciprocated.

(A) *Structural Equivalence*

Lorrain and White (1971) provided one definition of an equivalence: units are equivalent if they are connected to the rest of the network in *identical* ways. Such units are said to be structurally equivalent. A permutation $\varphi : \mathcal{U} \to \mathcal{U}$ is an automorphism of the relation R if and only if

$$\forall x, y \in \mathcal{U} : (xRy \Rightarrow \varphi(x)R\varphi(y)).$$

The units x and y are *structurally equivalent*, we write $x \equiv y$, if and only if the permutation (transposition) $\pi = (xy)$ is an automorphism of the relation R (Borgatti and Everett 1992).

In other words, x and y are structurally equivalent if and only if:

s1.	$xRy \Leftrightarrow yRx$	s3.	$\forall z \in \mathcal{U} \setminus \{x, y\} : (xRz \Leftrightarrow yRz)$
s2.	$xRx \Leftrightarrow yRy$	s4.	$\forall z \in \mathcal{U} \setminus \{x, y\} : (zRx \Leftrightarrow zRy)$

On the left in Figure 5.1.1, a and c are structurally equivalent as are b and d. On the right, g and i are structurally equivalent and h and j form a structurally equivalent pair. Note that a and c are not structurally equivalent to h and j, and b and d are not structurally equivalent to g and i.

From the definition of structural equivalence, it follows that only four possible blocks can appear (Batagelj et al. 1992b).

Type 0.	$b_{ij} = 0$	Type 2.	$b_{ij} = 1 - \delta_{ij}$
Type 1.	$b_{ij} = \delta_{ij}$	Type 3.	$b_{ij} = 1$

where δ_{ij} is the Kronecker delta function[2] and $i, j \in C$. The blocks of types 0 and 1 are called the *null* blocks, and the blocks of types 2 and 3 the *complete* blocks.

Examples of these structural blocks are:

0	0	0	0	0		1	0	0	0		0	1	1	1		1	1	1	1	1
0	0	0	0	0		0	1	0	0		1	0	1	1		1	1	1	1	1
0	0	0	0	0		0	0	1	0		1	1	0	1		1	1	1	1	1
0	0	0	0	0		0	0	0	1		1	1	1	0		1	1	1	1	1

For the nondiagonal blocks $R(C_u, C_v)$, $u \neq v$, only blocks of type 0 and type 3 are admissible. In general, specifying a set of permitted block types defines a blockmodel *type* and, in this section, we consider only the structural equivalence type. An exact structural equivalence partition

$$C = \{\{a, c\}, \{h, j\}, \{b, d\}, \{g, i\}, \{e\}, \{f\}\},$$

of the Everett Network is shown in Table 5.1.1 with the corresponding image matrix below it. The positions are $C_1 = \{a, b\}$, $C_2 = \{h, j\}$, $C_3 = \{b, d\}$, $C_4 = \{g, i\}$, $C_5 = \{e\}$, and $C_6 = \{f\}$. Note that the blocks are either null or complete.

Table 5.1.1. *A Structural Equivalence Partition of the Everett Network with Its Image Matrix*

	a	c	h	j	b	d	g	i	e	f
a	0	1	0	0	1	1	0	0	0	0
c	1	0	0	0	1	1	0	0	0	0
h	0	0	0	1	0	0	1	1	0	0
j	0	0	1	0	0	0	1	1	0	0
b	1	1	0	0	0	0	0	0	1	0
d	1	1	0	0	0	0	0	0	1	0
g	0	0	1	1	0	0	0	0	0	1
i	0	0	1	1	0	0	0	0	0	1
e	0	0	0	0	1	1	0	0	0	1
f	0	0	0	0	0	0	1	1	1	0

	C_1	C_2	C_3	C_4	C_5	C_6
C_1	1	0	1	0	0	0
C_2	0	1	0	1	0	0
C_3	1	0	0	0	1	0
C_4	0	1	0	0	0	1
C_5	0	0	1	0	0	1
C_6	0	0	0	1	1	0

(B) *Regular Equivalence*

Attempts to generalize structural equivalence date back at least to Sailer (1978) and have taken various forms. Integral to all formulations is the idea that units are equivalent if they link in equivalent ways to other units that are also equivalent. Regular equivalence, as defined by White and Reitz (1983), is one such generalization.

The equivalence relation $\approx$ on $\mathcal{U}$ is a *regular equivalence* on network $\mathbf{N} = (\mathcal{U}, R)$ if and only if for all $x, y, z \in \mathcal{U}$, $x \approx y$ implies both

R1. $xRz \Rightarrow \exists w \in \mathcal{U} : (yRw \wedge w \approx z)$

R2. $zRx \Rightarrow \exists w \in \mathcal{U} : (wRy \wedge w \approx z)$

Another view of regular equivalence comes from using colorings. Consider a clustering $\mathbf{C} = \{C_1, C_2, \ldots, C_k\}$ of the vertices, where all vertices in a cluster, C_i, are colored the same and all vertices are colored. The clustering C determines a *coloring*, $c : x \mapsto i \Leftrightarrow x \in C_i$, and vice versa. The clustering C is regular if and only if

$$c(x) = c(y) \Rightarrow (c(R(x)) = c(R(y)) \wedge c(R^{-1}(x)) = c(R^{-1}(y))),$$

where equivalent vertices have identically colored neighbors – both use exactly the same colors (Everett and Borgatti 1996).

As was the case with structural equivalence, regular equivalence implies the existence of ideal blocks. The nature of these ideal blocks follows from the following theorem (Batagelj et al. 1992a):

Theorem 1: *Let* $\mathbf{C} = \{C_i\}$ *be a partition corresponding to a regular equivalence* $\approx$ *on the network* $\mathbf{N} = (\mathcal{U}, R)$. *Then each block* $R(C_u, C_v)$ *is either null, or it has the property*

Table 5.1.2. *A Regular Equivalence Partition of the Everett Network with Its*
Image Matrix

	a	c	h	j	b	d	g	i	e	f
a	0	1	0	0	1	1	0	0	0	0
c	1	0	0	0	1	1	0	0	0	0
h	0	0	0	1	0	0	1	1	0	0
j	0	0	1	0	0	0	1	1	0	0
b	1	1	0	0	0	0	0	0	1	0
d	1	1	0	0	0	0	0	0	1	0
g	0	0	1	1	0	0	0	0	0	1
i	0	0	1	1	0	0	0	0	0	1
e	0	0	0	0	1	1	0	0	0	1
f	0	0	0	0	0	0	1	1	1	0

	C_1	C_2	C_3
C_1	1	1	0
C_2	1	0	1
C_3	0	1	1

that there is at least one 1 in each of its rows and in each of its columns. Conversely, if for
a given clustering C each block has this property, then the corresponding equivalence
relation is a regular equivalence.

From this proposition, it follows that regular equivalence produces two types of
blocks:

- *Null blocks*, which have all entries 0
- *1-Covered blocks*, which have in each row and in each column at least one 1

We use the term "regular" for these 1-covered blocks. Specifying only null and regular
blocks for a blockmodel defines a regular equivalence type of blockmodel.

Examples of the ideal blocks for regular equivalence are:

0	0	0	0	0
0	0	0	0	0
0	0	0	0	0
0	0	0	0	0

1	0	1	0	0
0	0	1	0	1
0	1	0	0	0
1	0	1	1	0

An exact regular equivalence partition,

$$C = \{\{a, c, h, j\}, \{b, d, g, i\}, \{e, f\}\},$$

of the Everett Network is shown in Table 5.1.2 together with its image matrix under-
neath it. The three positions are $C_1 = \{a, c, h, j\}$, $C_2 = \{b, d, g, i\}$, and $C_3 = \{e, f\}$.
Note that the blocks are either null or regular and that this partition has the structural equivalence partition of Table 5.1.1 nested within it. Every structural equivalence
partition is also a regular partition.

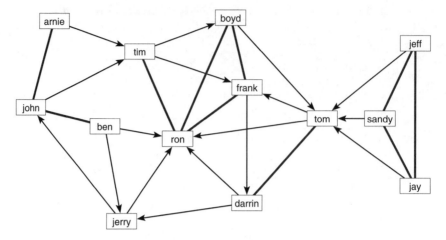

Figure 5.1.2. A Little League baseball team network.

(C) Ideal Blocks and Measures for Blockmodels

In the empirical world, few exact partitions based on structural or regular equivalence ideas exist. In general, such blockmodels fit approximately in the sense that there is a nonzero number of inconsistencies when an empirical blockmodel is compared with a nearest ideal blockmodel. As an example, consider the network of the Little League team shown in Figure 5.1.2 in terms of structural equivalence. In this figure, and for all other empirical networks considered in this chapter, thick solid lines represent reciprocated ties between pairs of actors.[3] Thin lines represent unreciprocated ties, with the arrow indicating the direction of the relational tie. The only actors that are structurally equivalent are {jay, jeff, sandy}, and any clustering together of other actors yields a blockmodel with inconsistencies when compared with an ideal blockmodel, in this case, structural equivalence.

In broad terms, blockmodeling tools are empirical partitioning (clustering) procedures. Usually, in conventional blockmodeling, there are few formal assessments of how well the blockmodels fit the data. In the approach taken here, we present ways of blockmodeling that incorporate *measures of adequacy*. We do this in the following fashion.

Assume, as before, that we have a single relation network $N = (\mathcal{U}, R)$. Let Θ denote the set of all equivalence relations of a selected type (for example, regular or structural equivalence) over N. Every equivalence relation $\sim$ on $\mathcal{U}$ determines a partition C of $\mathcal{U}$, and vice versa.

Let Φ denote the set of all partitions into k clusters corresponding to the relations from Θ. This is also called the *set of feasible clusterings*. If we are able to construct a criterion function $P(C)$ with the properties:

P1. $P(C) \geq 0$
P2. $P(C) = 0 \Leftrightarrow \sim \in \Theta,$

then we can express the problem of establishing a partition of a network, in terms of a specific type of equivalence, as a clustering problem where the task is to determine the clustering(s) $C^* \in \Phi$ for which $P(C^*) = \min_{C \in \Phi} P(C)$. If there are exact equivalences in Φ, then (by P2) the minimal value of $P(\mathbf{C})$ is 0. In the case where there is no exact equivalence, then $\forall \mathbf{C} \in \Phi$, $P(\mathbf{C}) > 0$, and the optimization approach provides those solutions that differ the *least* from some ideal blockmodel. There can be multiple equally well-fitting partitions for a well-defined blockmodel type.

One of the possible ways of constructing a criterion function that *directly reflects the considered equivalence* is to measure the fit of a clustering by comparing it to an ideal one having perfect relations within each cluster and between clusters (i.e., ideal blocks), given the specified type of equivalence.

Given a clustering $\mathbf{C} = \{C_1, C_2, \ldots, C_k\}$, let $\mathcal{B}(C_u, C_v)$ denote the set of all ideal blocks corresponding to block $R(C_u, C_v)$. Then the *global* inconsistency of the clustering $\mathbf{C}$ can be expressed as

$$P(\mathbf{C}) = \sum_{C_u, C_v \in \mathbf{C}} \min_{B \in \mathcal{B}(C_u, C_v)} \delta(R(C_u, C_v), B),$$

where the term, δ, measures the inconsistency (difference) between the block $R(C_u, C_v)$ and the corresponding ideal block B. The function δ has to be compatible (Batagelj et al. 1992b) with the selected type of equivalence – it is nonnegative and is 0 exactly when $R(C_u, C_v)$ is itself an ideal (permitted) block for the selected equivalence. The term $\delta(R(C_u, C_v), B)$ is the local inconsistency (in block B) and the sum of the local inconsistencies gives the total, or global, inconsistency.

(D) *A Criterion for Structural Equivalence*

For the structural equivalence type of blockmodel, the term $\delta(R(C_u, C_v), B)$ can be expressed as

$$\delta(R(C_u, C_v), B) = \sum_{x \in C_u, y \in C_v} |r_{xy} - b_{xy}|$$

In this expression, r_{xy} is the observed tie and b_{xy} is the corresponding value in an ideal block. For binary data, this criterion function counts the number of 1s in erstwhile null blocks and the number of 0s in otherwise null blocks.[4] It is easy to verify that a criterion function $P(\mathbf{C})$ defined in this fashion is *sensitive* (Batagelj et al. 1992b) to structural equivalence:

$$P(\mathbf{C}) = 0 \Leftrightarrow \mathbf{C} \text{ defines structural equivalence.}$$

(E) *A Clustering Algorithm*

In the direct clustering approach, an appropriate criterion function to capture the selected equivalence is constructed, and a local optimization clustering procedure (a relocation algorithm) is used to solve the given blockmodeling problem (Batagelj et al. 1992a):

> Determine the initial clustering $\mathbf{C}$;
> **repeat**:
> **if** in the neighborhood of the current clustering $\mathbf{C}$
> there exists a clustering $\mathbf{C}'$ such that $P(\mathbf{C}') < P(\mathbf{C})$,
> **then** move to clustering $\mathbf{C}'$.

Usually, the *neighborhood* is determined by two transformations: *moving* a unit from one cluster to another, and *interchanging* two units between different clusters.

Table 5.1.3. *Little League Structural Equivalence Partitions*

Transatlantic Industries

			1	3	4	5	2	6	10	11	12	13	7	8	9
C_1	Ron	1	0	1	1	1	0	0	0	0	0	0	0	0	0
	Frank	3	1	0	1	0	0	0	0	1	0	0	0	0	0
	Boyd	4	1	1	0	0	1	0	0	0	0	0	0	0	0
	Tim	5	1	1	1	0	0	0	0	0	0	0	0	0	0
C_2	Tom	2	1	1	0	0	0	0	0	1	0	0	0	0	0
C_3	John	6	0	0	0	1	0	0	0	0	1	1	0	0	0
	Jerry	10	1	0	0	0	0	1	0	0	0	0	0	0	0
	Darrin	11	1	0	0	0	1	0	1	0	0	0	0	0	0
	Ben	12	1	0	0	0	0	1	1	0	0	0	0	0	0
	Arnie	13	0	0	0	1	0	1	0	0	0	0	0	0	0
C_4	Jeff	7	0	0	0	0	1	0	0	0	0	0	0	1	1
	Jay	8	0	0	0	0	1	0	0	0	0	0	1	0	1
	Sandy	9	0	0	0	0	1	0	0	0	0	0	1	1	0

To obtain a "good" solution and some impression of its quality, we repeat this procedure with different (random) initial partitions **C**. If the procedure is repeated many times (some hundreds of times or thousands of times, depending on the size of the network), all or most of the partitions of a selected type of equivalence (e.g., structural or regular) in a given network can be found.

The Little League Network
We use the Little League network of Figure 5.1.2 to illustrate the clustering algorithm with the criterion function for structural equivalence.

The unique best-fitting partition of the Little League network (for four positions based on structural equivalence) is shown in Table 5.1.3. Note that the four positions define the sixteen blocks in the blockmodel. The pattern of block types is:

complete	null	null	null
null	null	null	null
null	null	null	null
null	complete	null	complete

One product of the direct partitioning approach is a count of the inconsistencies, by block, of the partition. Corresponding to Table 5.1.3, the distribution of inconsistencies is:

2	1	1	0
2	0	1	0
5	1	7	0
0	0	0	0

There are eight empirical blocks with zero inconsistencies. Put differently, they are also ideal blocks. There is a total of twenty inconsistencies that are distributed across

Table 5.2.4. *Block Types*

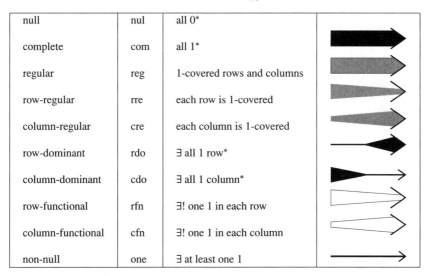

null	nul	all 0*
complete	com	all 1*
regular	reg	1-covered rows and columns
row-regular	rre	each row is 1-covered
column-regular	cre	each column is 1-covered
row-dominant	rdo	∃ all 1 row*
column-dominant	cdo	∃ all 1 column*
row-functional	rfn	∃! one 1 in each row
column-functional	cfn	∃! one 1 in each column
non-null	one	∃ at least one 1

* Except for diagonal blocks, which may differ slightly.

the other eight blocks. For C_1, there are two inconsistencies in its block. There are no ties from Frank and Boyd to Tim in what should be a block of type 2. For the link from C_1 to C_2, there is one inconsistency: Boyd sends a tie to Tom in what, otherwise, would be a null block (type 0). Similarly, the lone link from Frank in C_1 to Darrin in C_3 is an inconsistency. For the ties from Tom (in C_2) to boys in C_1, either the two 0s or the two 1s can be viewed as contributing two inconsistencies to the total count of inconsistencies. When we treat the corresponding ideal block as null, the ties from Tom to Ron and Frank are the inconsistencies. The tie from Tom to Darrin (in cluster C_3) is another inconsistency. There are five ties from boys in C_3 to boys C_1 and they are all inconsistent with a null block. In a similar fashion, the seven ties among the boys in cluster C_3 are all inconsistencies. There are no inconsistencies among the ties from boys in cluster C_4. For now, we note that twelve of the errors are concentrated in two of the cells. It seems reasonable that, for the model as a whole, the errors are distributed across the cells in roughly the same fashion (controlling for block size). Having the errors piling up in a small number of cells suggests that we take a closer look at the partition and the distribution of inconsistencies.

5.2 The Generalized Blockmodeling Approach

The logic and history of blockmodeling took the form of defining types of equivalences and then searching for partitions that were believed to be consistent with the specified equivalences. Under the so-called indirect approach (for example, in Burt 1976 and Breiger et al. 1975), a relational matrix is turned into a matrix of (dis)similarities and clustered. The direct approach to blockmodeling (Batagelj et al. 1992a,b) takes advantage of the result that structural and regular equivalence each implied a (small) set of permitted blocks in an ideal blockmodel image. In this way, it was straightforward

Table 5.2.5. *Examples of Blocks with Types of Connections*

	C_j				
C_i	1	1	1	1	1
	1	1	1	1	1
	1	1	1	1	1
	1	1	1	1	1

complete

	C_j				
C_i	0	1	0	0	0
	1	1	1	1	1
	0	0	0	0	0
	0	0	0	1	0

row-dominant

	C_j				
C_i	0	0	1	0	0
	0	0	1	1	0
	1	1	1	0	0
	0	0	1	0	1

column-dominant

	C_j				
C_i	0	1	0	0	0
	1	0	1	1	0
	0	0	1	0	1
	1	1	0	0	0

regular

	C_j				
C_i	0	1	0	0	0
	0	1	1	0	0
	1	0	1	0	0
	0	1	0	0	1

row-regular

	C_j				
C_i	0	1	0	1	0
	1	0	1	0	0
	1	1	0	1	1
	0	0	0	0	0

column-regular

	C_j				
C_i	0	0	0	0	0
	0	0	0	0	0
	0	0	0	0	0
	0	0	0	0	0

null

	C_j				
C_i	0	0	0	1	0
	0	0	1	0	0
	1	0	0	0	0
	0	0	0	1	0

row-functional

	C_j			
	1	0	0	0
C_i	0	1	0	0
	0	0	1	0
	0	0	0	0
	0	0	0	1

column-functional

to specify a criterion function that captured the difference between an empirical block-model and a (or the) nearest ideal blockmodel. Doreian et al. (1994) presented evidence that shows that blockmodeling partitions established with the direct approach are usually better – and are never worse – than those established with indirect methods.

The logic of generalized blockmodeling is to *start with sets of permitted ideal blocks*. An appropriate generalization of the equivalence idea is one where each block of a particular blockmodel is free to conform to its own block type. This led Batagelj (1997) and Doreian et al. (1994) to the definition of several types of connection inside and between the clusters as different types of blocks. Some of them are characterized in Table 5.2.4, where the right-hand column shows a pictorial way of representing blocks as connections when image diagrams are drawn. Table 5.2.5 shows these block types in more detail. The measures of inconsistency $\delta(R(C_u, C_v), B; T)$ are defined specifically for each type, T, of ideal blocks.

(A) *Revisiting the Little League Network*

With this expanded set of block types in mind, reconsider the partition shown in Table 5.1.3. We could recode the nearest ideal block types as:

reg	column-regular	null	null
row-regular	null	row-regular	null
row-regular	column-regular	row-regular	null
null	complete	null	complete

Table 5.2.6. *A Generalized Partition of the Little League Network*

			1	2	5	6	10	11	12	13	7	8	9	3	4
C_1	Ron	1	0	0	1	0	0	0	0	0	0	0	0	1	1
	Tom	2	1	0	0	0	0	1	0	0	0	0	0	1	0
	Tim	5	1	0	0	0	0	0	0	0	0	0	0	1	1
	John	6	0	0	1	0	0	0	1	1	0	0	0	0	0
	Jerry	10	1	0	0	1	0	0	0	0	0	0	0	0	0
	Darrin	11	1	1	0	0	1	0	0	0	0	0	0	0	0
C_2	Ben	12	1	0	0	1	1	0	. 0	0	0	0	0	0	0
	Arnie	13	0	0	1	1	0	0	0	0	0	0	0	0	0
C_3	Jeff	7	0	1	0	0	0	0	0	0	0	1	1	0	0
	Jay	8	0	1	0	0	0	0	0	0	1	0	1	0	0
	Sandy	9	0	1	0	0	0	0	0	0	1	1	0	0	0
C_4	Frank	3	1	0	0	0	0	1	0	0	0	0	0	0	1
	Boyd	4	1	1	0	0	0	0	0	0	0	0	0	1	0

regular	row-dominant	null	row-dominant
column-dominant	null	null	null
column-dominant	null	complete	null
column-dominant	null	null	complete

and the pattern of inconsistencies becomes:

$$
\begin{array}{cccc}
0 & 0 & 1 & 0 \\
0 & 0 & 0 & 0 \\
0 & 0 & 0 & 0 \\
0 & 0 & 0 & 0
\end{array}
$$

Of course, we do *not* advocate that blockmodels obtained under one set of permitted block types then be reinterpreted with a different set of block types. We use this example as a simple way of thinking about *alternative* block types.

As another example, consider the set of permitted block types as complete, regular, row-dominant, column-dominant, and null. This specification leads to the generalized blockmodel in Table 5.2.6, where there are no inconsistencies with the specified ideal blockmodel.

Pictorially, we have the partitioned network as shown on the left of Figure 5.2.3 and the image network as shown on the right side of Figure 5.2.3. This image provides an alternative (generalized) blockmodel with a different interpretation compared with the blockmodel image in Table 5.1.3. (Note that the ties representing block types in this figure come from Table 5.2.5.) Figure 5.2.3 reveals a very clear center-periphery structure defined in terms of row dominance and column dominance. The core of the team is found in cluster C_1, whose diagonal block is regular. The row-dominant link from C_1 to C_2 comes from john's ties to arnie and ben, and the column-dominant link from C_2 to C_1 comes from the ties from arnie and ben (in C_2) to john (in C_1). The tie from C_1 to C_3 is null because there are no ties from boys in C_1 to boys in C_3. The column-dominant tie from C_3 to C_1 comes from all the boys in C_3 choosing tom in C_1.

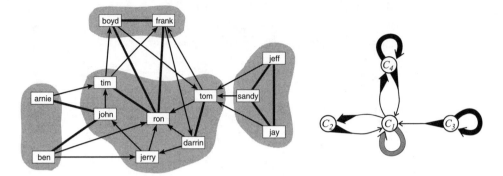

Figure 5.2.3. Generalized partition of the Little League network and its image graph.

The row-dominant link from C_1 to C_4 comes from ron choosing both frank and boyd (as does Tim). The column-dominant link to C_1 from C_4 comes from frank and boyd in C_4 both choosing ron in C_1. Finally, both C_3 and C_4 form complete (diagonal) blocks.

We note an additional feature of generalized blockmodeling. In generating Table 5.2.6, we gave preference to row and column dominance as block types. It is possible to view the ties from C_1 to both C_2 and C_4 as row-regular. Similarly, all the ties from C_2, C_3, and C_4 to C_1 can be viewed as row-regular. If preference was given to those block types and *if* the same partition was returned, we could interpret these blocks as row- and column-regular blocks. However, the "if" in the previous sentence should be noted – the generalized blockmodel as a whole is specified *prior* to an analysis given *that* specification. It is not reinterpreted after some other analysis.

5.3   Prespecified Blockmodels

In revisiting the Little League baseball team network, we began doing more than just specifying block types. In addition to such a specification, it is possible to also require that particular block types go in particular places in the blockmodel. This can vary between specifying the location of *every* block type and specifying the location of only *some* of them. When a blockmodel (conventional or generalized) has this additional specification, we call it a *prespecified blockmodel*. Refer to Doreian et al. (in press) for an extended discussion of prespecification. Our first illustration of this takes the form of a baboon grooming network.

(A) *A Baboon Network as a Center-Periphery Structure*

Table 5.3.7 (in permuted form) shows a two-cluster (four blocks) partition of a baboon grooming network. An initial examination of these ties provided a strong clue as to how to partition this network: males do not groom other males. This suggests that the grooming structure is centered on the females, and this observation is a first step in constructing a blockmodel as a "center-periphery" structure. We retain the idea of a core as a block whose ties are sufficiently dense. One operationalization of this could be that a core block is complete. However, this may be too stringent if belonging to a

Table 5.3.7. *Permuted Grooming Ties for a Two-Cluster Model*

		1	3	4	6	8	10	11	2	5	7	9	12
f_1	1	.	.	1	.	.	.	1	1	1	.	.	1
f_2	3	.	.	1	1	.	1	1	.	1	1	.	1
f_3	4	1	1	.	1	.	1	.	.	1	1	.	1
f_4	6	.	1	1	.	.	1	.	.	1	.	.	1
f_5	8	.	.	.	.	.	1	.	.	1	1	1	.
f_6	10	.	1	1	1	1	.	.	.	.	.	.	.
f_7	11	1	1	.	.	.	.	.	.	.	.	.	.
m_1	2	1	.	.	.	.	.	.	.	.	.	.	.
m_2	5	1	1	1	1	1	.	.	.	.	.	.	.
m_3	7	.	1	1	.	1	.	.	.	.	.	.	.
m_4	9	.	.	.	.	1	.	.	.	.	.	.	.
m_5	12	1	1	1	1	.	.	.	.	.	.	.	.

regular or complete	column-regular
row-regular	null

core does not require that *all* core actors are mutually linked. For social cohesion in the core, *enough* pairs need to be in mutual ties. Another possible specification is that the core block is regular – in the sense of regular equivalence – so each member of the core is linked to at least one other member of the core. Hence, the specification of a regular diagonal block for the female baboons. The males in the periphery do not groom each other so their diagonal block is null.

For the specification of the off-diagonal blocks, we note that the males are linked to the females in the core in such a way that each male baboon is groomed by at least one female baboon. Consistent with this, the upper off-diagonal block is specified as column-regular and the lower off-diagonal block is specified as row-regular. Table 5.3.7 shows the prespecified model implied by this argument below the empirically fitted blockmodel. The distribution of ties in Table 5.3.7 conforms exactly to the pattern of the prespecified blockmodel. In this sense, the prespecified blockmodel has been "tested" and supported as an empirical hypothesis.

It is possible to fit a finer-grained partition (with more positions). Both the female and male baboons show some internal variation. Some of the females do not groom males, and there is a pair of males that are each groomed only by a single female baboon. The finer-grained prespecified blockmodel is:

regular	column-regular or null	column-regular or null	column-regular or null
row-regular or null	regular or null	column-regular or null	column-regular or null
row-regular or null	row-regular or null	null	null
row-regular or null	row-regular or null	null	null

With this specification in mind, fitting the generalized blockmodel resulted in the partition shown in Table 5.3.8. The fitted blockmodel has two inconsistencies in the diagonal block for C_2. The females, f_1 and f_7, groom each other in an otherwise null block. We

Table 5.3.8. *A Four-Position Model Fitted to Baboon Network*

		3	4	10	1	6	8	11	5	7	12	2	9
f_2	3	.	1	1	.	1	.	1	1	1	1	.	.
f_3	4	1	.	1	1	1	.	.	1	1	1	.	.
f_6	10	1	1	.	.	1	1	.	.	.	.	.	.
f_1	1	.	1	.	.	.	.	1	1	.	1	1	.
f_4	6	1	1	1	.	.	.	.	1	.	1	.	.
f_5	8	.	.	1	.	.	.	.	1	1	.	.	1
f_7	11	1	.	.	1	.	.	.	.	.	.	.	.
m_2	5	1	1	.	1	1	1	.	.	.	.	.	.
m_3	7	1	1	.	.	.	1	.	.	.	.	.	.
m_5	12	1	1	.	1	1	.	.	.	.	.	.	.
m_1	2	.	.	.	1	.	.	.	.	.	.	.	.
m_4	9	.	.	.	.	.	1	.	.	.	.	.	.

	C_1	C_2	C_3	C_4
C_1	regular	column-regular	column-regular	null
C_2	row-regular	null	column-regular	column-regular
C_3	row-regular	row-regular	null	null
C_4	null	row-regular	null	null

note also that the off-diagonal blocks for C_1 and C_2 happen to be regular. As a regular block is both row-regular and column-regular, this does not violate the prespecification. However, we think that a prespecification of regular is too strong for a general specification of core-periphery models. A more extended discussion of core-periphery models is provided in Doreian et al. (2005).

(B) *Ranked-Clusters Models of Stratified Sociometric Systems*

A line of research was started by Davis and Leinhardt (1972) when they formulated a "ranked-clusters" model for stratified sociometric systems. In their formulation, there are distinct patterns in the location of mutual, asymmetric, and null ties in a ranked-clusters model. The mutual ties are only in cliques (as maximal complete subgraphs). These cliques are distributed across ranks so asymmetric ties always go in one direction (usually up) and never occur in the opposite direction. Null ties can be anywhere except within cliques. Put differently, diagonal blocks are complete, blocks above the diagonal are always null, and only blocks below the diagonal have asymmetric ties.

A classical result from Harary et al. (1965) states that any directed graph factored by its strong connectivity relation gives an acyclic structure (model). Based on this, Doreian et al. (2000) proposed a slightly more general blockmodel for ranked-clusters systems. All that differs in their version is the specification of *symmetric* diagonal blocks as a way of weakening the requirement of complete cliques in the diagonal blocks. Formally, the new symmetric block is specified as follows. A block[5] is symmetric if

$$\forall x, y \in C_i \times C_j : (xRy \Leftrightarrow yRx).$$

Table 5.3.9. *Social Relation as a Ranked-Clusters System*

	a	b	c	d	e	j	k	l	m	n	o	f	g	h	i	p	q	r	s
a	·	1	1	·	·	·	·	·	·	·	·	·	**1**	·	·	·	·	·	·
b	1	·	1	·	·	·	·	·	·	·	·	·	·	·	·	·	·	·	·
c	1	1	·	·	·	·	·	·	·	·	·	·	·	·	·	·	·	·	·
d	·	1	·	·	1	·	·	·	·	·	·	·	·	·	·	·	·	·	·
e	·	·	1	1	·	·	·	·	·	·	·	·	·	·	·	·	·	·	·
j	·	·	·	1	·	·	*1*	1	·	·	·	·	·	·	·	·	·	·	·
k	·	·	·	·	1	·	·	1	·	·	·	·	·	·	·	·	·	·	·
l	·	·	·	·	1	1	1	·	·	·	·	·	·	·	·	·	·	·	·
m	·	·	1	1	·	·	·	·	·	1	1	·	·	·	·	·	·	·	1
n	·	·	1	·	1	·	·	·	1	·	·	·	·	·	·	·	·	·	·
o	·	·	·	·	·	·	·	·	1	*1*	·	·	·	·	·	·	·	·	·
f	1	1	1	·	·	·	·	·	·	·	·	·	1	·	·	·	·	·	·
g	1	·	·	·	·	·	·	·	·	·	·	1	·	1	1	·	·	·	·
h	1	1	·	·	·	·	·	·	·	·	·	·	1	·	1	·	·	·	·
i	1	1	1	·	·	·	·	·	·	·	·	·	1	1	·	·	**1**	·	·
p	·	·	·	1	1	·	·	·	·	1	·	·	·	1	·	·	1	·	·
q	·	·	·	1	1	·	·	·	·	·	·	·	·	1	·	1	·	1	1
r	·	·	·	1	1	·	·	·	·	·	1	·	·	·	·	*1*	1	·	1
s	·	·	·	1	1	·	·	·	·	·	·	·	1	·	·	·	1	1	·

The *new blockmodel type* specifies symmetric or null blocks on the diagonal and null blocks above the diagonal. The bulk of Doreian et al.'s paper was devoted to symmetric-acyclic decompositions of networks with generalized blockmodels in a complementary (but secondary) role. The acyclic requirement is captured by having null blocks above the diagonal. We emphasize that using more block types expands the number of blockmodel types. The ranked-clusters blockmodel is defined by a distinctive *pattern* of the location of block types.

A hypothetical ranked-clusters blockmodel is given in Table 5.3.9 and blocked in a way to show the ranked-clusters structure. The italicized elements in the diagonal blocks are ties that are inconsistent with the symmetric diagonal block requirement. The bolded ties above the diagonal are inconsistencies with the acyclic requirement that there be no cycles linking nondiagonal blocks.

Another departure with regard to generalized blockmodeling is illustrated by the ranked-clusters model used here. We can view the two types of inconsistencies as differentially important and weight them accordingly. Inconsistencies with the strict ranking (acyclic) requirement seem more consequential and are weighted more heavily than inconsistencies with the symmetry requirement.[6]

A Trust Relation in an Organization

Figure 5.3.4 shows an exact ranked-clusters model taken from Doreian (2001). The data come from a study by French (1963) of salesmen in a competitive working environment where trust was of great importance. The relation depicted is trust ties for the first of three time points. [As before, the heavy lines depict the symmetric (mutually trusting) ties and the thin lines represent unreciprocated trust ties.] The actors linked only by symmetric ties go into a set of six positions whose (diagonal) blocks are symmetric.[7]

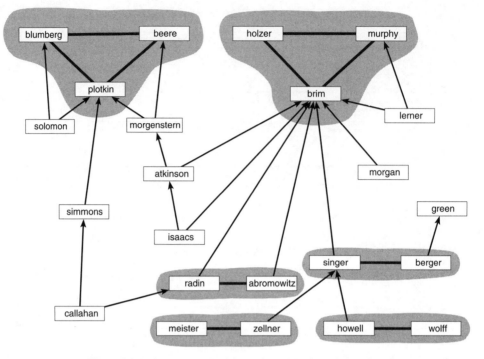

Figure 5.3.4. An exact ranked-clusters model of a trust relation.

These are shaded in Figure 5.3.4. The overall structure can be described roughly as one with parallel ranked-clusters subsystems. One has {blumberg, beere, plotkin} as its top, whereas {holzer, murphy, brim} tops the other. Multiple ranked-clusters systems are possible. For example, {meister, zellner} and {howell, wolff} can be merged into a single cluster without violating the acyclic requirement. We have reported the finest-grained ranked-clusters system in Figure 5.3.4 for the trust network that is possible.

A Children's Network

Figure 5.3.5 shows a network for a group of girls in a sixth-grade children's network where the data come from Jennings (1948). Although there are boys in the classroom, there are hardly any ties going between children of different genders. So, for this class-room, focusing on just the girls does not distort their network. As for the trust example, the thick lines depict symmetric ties, whereas the thinner lines (with arrows) represent unreciprocated ties. There are two inconsistencies with a ranked-clusters model. One is the unreciprocated link from g_{14} to g_{12} within a diagonal block, whereas the other is the link from g_{12} in a high-ranking cluster to g_{16} in a low-ranking cluster. Figure 5.3.5 shows the ranked-clusters model, where $G_1 = \{g_{12}, g_{13}, g_{14}, g_{18}\}$; $G_2 = \{g_{19}, g_{20}, g_{21}\}$; $G_3 = \{g_6, g_8\}$; $G_4 = \{g_3, g_{15}, g_{16}, g_{17}\}$; and $G_5 = \{g_1, g_2\}$. These clusters having more than one member are represented as circles in the image graph on the right of Figure 5.3.5. To keep the image simple, we have omitted the self-loops for these positions. The remaining clusters are singletons and have been represented as squares in Figure 5.3.5.

   We suggest the use of ranked-clusters models as an effective way of characterizing ranked or hierarchical sociometric systems (when they fit).

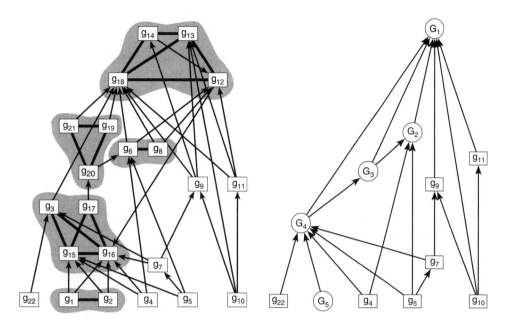

Figure 5.3.5. A network of ties for girls and its ranked-clusters model.

5.4　Formalization of Blockmodeling

We finish by providing a formal statement of generalized blockmodeling that is applicable to all types of blockmodels. The point of departure is, as before, a network with a set of units, $\mathcal{U}$, and a relation $R \subseteq \mathcal{U} \times \mathcal{U}$. Let $\mathcal{Z}$ be a set of positions or images of clusters of units. Let $\mu : \mathcal{U} \to \mathcal{Z}$ denote a mapping that maps each unit to its position. The cluster of units $C(t)$ with the same position $t \in \mathcal{Z}$ is

$$C(t) = \mu^{-1}(t) = \{x \in \mathcal{U} : \mu(x) = t\}.$$

Therefore,

$$\mathbf{C}(\mu) = \{C(t) : t \in \mathcal{Z}\}$$

is a partition (clustering) of the set of units $\mathcal{U}$. This is illustrated in Figure 5.4.6, where clusters C_i and C_j are mapped under μ to their positions in the image. The general problem is to determine the nature of the tie between the positions i and j (to which C_i and C_j are mapped in the image). To do this, we have to determine the type, T, of tie that reflects the structure of the block $R(C_i, C_j)$ and the value a of the tie that summarizes the values $\{a_{xy}\}$.

A *(generalized) blockmodel* is an ordered quintuple $\mathbf{M} = (\mathcal{Z}, K, \mathcal{T}, \pi, \alpha)$, where:

- $\mathcal{Z}$ is a set of positions.
- $K \subseteq \mathcal{Z} \times \mathcal{Z}$ is a set of *connections* between positions.
- $\mathcal{T}$ is a set of predicates used to describe the types of connections between clusters in a network; we assume that nul $\in \mathcal{T}$.
- A mapping $\pi : K \to \mathcal{T} \setminus \{\text{nul}\}$ assigns predicates to connections.
- A mapping $\alpha : K \to Q$, where Q is a set of "averaging rules."

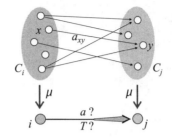

Figure 5.4.6. Generalized blockmodeling.

A (surjective) mapping $\mu : \mathcal{U} \to \mathcal{Z}$ determines a blockmodel, **M**, of a network **N** iff it satisfies the conditions:

$$\forall (t, w) \in K : \pi(t, w)(C(t), C(w))$$

and

$$\forall (t, w) \in \mathcal{Z} \times \mathcal{Z} \setminus K : \mathrm{nul}(C(t), C(w)).$$

For each connection, (t, w), the corresponding block, $R(C(t), C(w))$, is of the type $\pi(t, w)$, and if positions t and w are not linked, then the corresponding block, $R(C(t), C(w))$, is a null block.

Let $\sim$ be an equivalence relation over $\mathcal{U}$. It partitions the set of units $\mathcal{U}$ into clusters

$$[x] = \{ y \in \mathcal{U} : x \sim y \}.$$

We say that $\sim$ is *compatible* with $\mathcal{T}$ or a $\mathcal{T}$-equivalence over a network **N** iff

$$\forall x, y \in \mathcal{U}, \exists T \in \mathcal{T} : T([x], [y])$$

It is easy to verify that the notion of compatibility for $\mathcal{T} = \{\mathrm{nul}, \mathrm{reg}\}$ reduces to the usual definition of regular equivalence. Similarly, compatibility for $\mathcal{T} = \{\mathrm{nul}, \mathrm{com}\}$ reduces to structural equivalence.

For a compatible equivalence $\sim$, the mapping $\mu{:}x \mapsto [x]$ determines a blockmodel with $\mathcal{Z} = \mathcal{U}/\sim$.

(B) *Criterion Functions*

One possible way of constructing a criterion function that directly reflects the selected type of equivalence is to measure the fit of a clustering to an ideal one with perfect relations within each cluster and between clusters according to the selected type of equivalence. Notationally, this is the same as described in Section 5.1 (C). For generalized blockmodels, we add the following specification: given a set of types of connection $\mathcal{T}$ and a block $R(C_u, C_v)$, $C_u, C_v \subseteq \mathcal{U}$, we can determine the strongest (according to the ordering of the set $\mathcal{T}$) type $t \in \mathcal{T}$, which is satisfied the most by $R(C_u, C_v)$. In this case, we set

$$\pi(\mu(C_u), \mu(C_v)) = t.$$

Given the specification of a generalized blockmodel and the specification of an appropriate criterion function, as written in Section 5.1 (C), but with a richer set of connection types, the blockmodeling problem is solved by the use of a local optimization procedure [in the form of a relocation algorithm as described in Section 5.1 (E)]. For a general approach to clustering relational and multivariate data, see Batagelj and Ferligoj (2000).

5.5 Conclusion

Starting with new block types (and hence new blockmodel types) and allowing each block to have its own characterization means that the number of blockmodel types can be increased indefinitely. New block types can be defined formally (as done in Table 5.2.4) or can have substantive foundations (as is the case with the ranked-clusters model). Structural balance theory provides an example of a substantively based (generalized) blockmodel, where an ideal blockmodel takes the form of having diagonal blocks containing only positive and null ties and off-diagonal blocks having only negative and null ties (Doreian and Mrvar 1996). The way is clear for using a much richer set of blocks and blockmodel types and the construction of richer social theories.

There are two broad caveats to this sweeping claim. First, the choice of block types and blockmodel types must be specified on substantive grounds prior to an analysis. This specification can take a weak form where only the block types are specified or a strong form where *both* the block types and their locations in a generalized blockmodel are specified. In this context, we use the term "prespecified" (generalized) blockmodel to emphasize that in this strong specification, more is involved than selecting block types. The weak specification corresponds to an *inductive* use of generalized blockmodeling, whereas strong specification corresponds to a *deductive* use of generalized blockmodeling where the blockmodel is prespecified and *fitted*. In this sense, the prespecified blockmodel is viewed as a hypothesis and is tested. If there are too many inconsistencies when this blockmodel is fitted, the hypothesis is not supported in the relational data. Second, with a rich array of block types available, it is always possible to locate/fit a generalized blockmodel that fits exactly (with zero inconsistencies). When generalized blockmodels are established "blindly" (i.e., with many block types switched on), it seems that this is an analogue to "capitalizing on chance" in fitting statistical relations. We doubt that generalized blockmodels established blindly have any substantive or practical value. We acknowledge that we do not have a "theory of errors" in fitting generalized blockmodels at this time. As a result, the boundary between generalized blockmodels that fit and those that do not fit is fuzzy. However, we argue that placing substance first goes a long way in protecting us against the risk of fitting nonsense generalized blockmodels. Establishing a procedure for fitting generalized blockmodels with a well-founded theory of errors is a future task. For now, our attention is on the substantive gains that become available with an expanded set of block and blockmodel types.

In general, for a given network, a set of ideal blocks is selected, a reduced graph (image) is formulated, and partitions are established by solving a clustering problem through the minimization of a criterion function. The use of the optimization procedure is crucial and provides some additional benefits that include:

- For conventional blockmodels in inductive mode, it permits the establishment of empirical blockmodels with a measure of fit.
- Given a specific type of blockmodel, and through time data, the value of the criterion function can be tracked to measure the quality of fit of the blockmodel through time. Structural balance theory provides an obvious application of this idea (see Doreian and Mrvar 1996, and Doreian et al. 1997, for examples.)
- When prespecified models are used in deductive mode, optimizational methods permit the testing of these models as discussed previously. The prespecified blockmodeling starts with a blockmodel specified on the basis of substance and/or empirical knowledge *prior to the analysis*.

All fitted blockmodels discussed in this chapter were obtained by using Pajek, a program for network analysis and visualization that was developed by Batagelj and Mrvar (2003). A key feature of the design of Pajek is its ability to handle large networks. An accessible introduction to network analyses using Pajek is provided by de Nooy et al. (2004).

Endnotes

1. Included here are variants like automorphic equivalence (Faust 1988; Pattison 1988). See also Everett and Borgatti (1994).
2. This is defined as $\delta_{ij} = 0$ if $i \neq j$ and $\delta_{ij} = 1$ if $i = j$.
3. We leave both arrowheads out of the figures for these ties.
4. These two types of inconsistencies can be weighted differently. See Batagelj et al. (1992b).
5. Although this can be extended to include nondiagonal blocks, this extension is not relevant here.
6. We are experimenting with different weighting regimes but, in the main, have weighted the inconsistencies with the acyclic requirement at ten times the weight for the inconsistencies with symmetry. In essence, we solve a two-criteria clustering problem by reducing it to a single criterion problem.
7. In this specific blockmodel, the clusters happen to be complete. Of course, a complete diagonal block is consistent with the symmetric specification. In the French (1963) data, for a subsequent time point, there are diagonal blocks that are not complete.

References

Batagelj, V. (1997). "Notes on Blockmodeling." *Social Networks, 19*, 143–155.
Batagelj, V., Doreian, P., and Ferligoj, A. (1992a). "An Optimizational Approach to Regular Equivalence." *Social Networks, 14*, 121–135.
Batagelj, V., and Ferligoj, A. (2000). "Clustering Relational Data," pp. 3–15 in W. Gaul, O. Opitz, and M. Schader (Eds.), *Data Analysis: Scientific Modeling and Practical Application*. Berlin: Springer.
Batagelj, V., Ferligoj, A., and Doreian, P. (1992b). "Direct and Indirect Methods for Structural Equivalence." *Social Networks, 14*, 63–90.
Batagelj, V., Ferligoj, A., and Doreian, P. (1998). "Fitting Pre-specified Blockmodels," pp 199–206 in Hayashi, N., Yajima, K., Bock, H-H., and Baba, Y. (Eds.), *Data Science, Classification and Related Methods*. Tokyo: Springer-Verlag.

Batagelj, V., and Mrvar, A. (2003). "Pajek – A Program for Large Nework Analysis." *Connections, 21,* 47–57.

Borgatti, S. P., and Everett, M. G. (1989). "The Class of All Regular Equivalences: Algebraic Structure and Computation." *Social Networks, 11,* 65–88.

Borgatti, S. P., and Everett, M. G. (1992). "Notions of Positions in Social Network Analysis," pp. 1–35 in P. V. Marsden (Ed.), *Sociological Methodology.* San Francisco: Jossey-Bass.

Breiger, R. L., Boorman, S. A., and Arabie, P. (1975). "An Algorithm for Clustering Relational Data with Applications to Social Network Analysis and Comparison to Multidimensional Scaling." *Journal of Mathematical Psychology, 12,* 328–383.

Burt, R. S. (1976). "Positions in Networks." *Social Forces, 55,* 93–122.

Davis, J. A., and Leinhardt, S. (1972). "The Structure of Positive Interpersonal Relations in Small Groups," pp. 218–251 in J. Berger, M. Zelditch, Jr., and B. Anderson (Eds.), *Sociological Theories in Progress, Volume 2.* Boston: Houghton Mifflin.

de Nooy, W., Mrvar, A., and Batagelj, V. (in press). *Exploratory Social Network Analysis with Pajek.* Cambridge: Cambridge University Press.

Doreian, P. (2001). "Ranked Clusters Models of Stratified Sociometric Systems." Pittsburgh: University of Pittsburgh, Department of Sociology.

Doreian, P., Batagelj, V., and Ferligoj, A. (1994). "Partitioning Networks on Generalized Concepts of Equivalence." *Journal of Mathematical Sociology, 19,* 1–27.

Doreian, P., Batagelj, V., and Ferligoj, A. (2000). "Symmetric-Acyclic Decompositions of Networks." *Journal of Classification, 17,* 3–28.

Doreian, P., Batagelj, V., and Ferligoj, A. (in press). *Generalized Blockmodeling.* Cambridge: Cambridge University Press. (2005).

Doreian, P., Kapuscinski, R., Krackhardt, D., and Szczypula, J. (1997). "A Brief History of Balance Through Time," pp. 129–147 in Doreian, P., and Stokman, F. N. (Eds.), *Evolution of Social Networks.* New York: Gordon and Breach.

Doreian, P., and Mrvar, A. (1996). "A Partitioning Approach to Structural Balance." *Social Networks, 18,* 149–168.

Everett, M. E., and Borgatti, S. P. (1994). "Regular Equivalence: General Theory." *Journal of Mathematical Sociology, 19,* 29–52.

Everett, M. E., and Borgatti, S. P. (1996). "Exact Colorations of Graphs and Digraphs." *Social Networks, 18,* 319–331.

Faust, K. (1988). "Comparison of Methods for Positional Analysis: Structural and General Equivalences." *Social Networks, 10,* 313–341.

French, C. (1963). "Some Structural Aspects of a Retail Sales Group." *Human Organization, XXII,* 146–151.

Harary, F., Norman, R. Z., and Cartwright, D. (1965). *Structural Models: An Introduction to the Theory of Directed Graphs.* New York: John Wiley & Sons.

Jennings, H. H. (1948). *Sociometry in Group Relations: A Manual for Teachers.* Westport, CT: Glenwood Press.

Lorrain, F., and White, H. C. (1971). "Structural Equivalence of Individuals in Social Networks." *Journal of Mathematical Sociology, 1,* 49–80.

Pattison, P. (1988). "Network Models: Some Comments on Papers in This Special Issue." *Social Networks, 10,* 383–411.

Sailer, L. D. (1978). "Structural Equivalence: Meaning and Definition, Computation and Application." *Social Networks, 1,* 73–90.

White, D. R., and Reitz, K. P. (1983). "Graph and Semigroup Homomorphisms on Networks of Relations." *Social Networks, 5,* 193–234.

6

Network Models and Methods for Studying the Diffusion of Innovations

Thomas W. Valente

University of Southern California

6.1 Introduction

Diffusion of innovations theory attempts to explain how new ideas and practices spread within and between communities. The theory has its roots in anthropology, economics, geography, sociology, and marketing, among other disciplines (Hägerstrand 1967; Robertson 1971; Brown 1981; Rogers 2003), and has in some ways been adapted from epidemiology (e.g., Bailey 1975; Morris 1993). The premise, confirmed by empirical research, is that new ideas and practices spread through interpersonal contacts largely consisting of interpersonal communication (Ryan and Gross 1943; Beal and Bohlen 1955; Katz, Levine, and Hamilton 1963; Rogers 1995; Valente 1995; Valente and Rogers 1995).

In their pioneering study, Ryan and Gross (1943) laid the groundwork for the diffusion paradigm by showing that, among other things, social factors rather than economic ones were important influences on adoption (Valente and Rogers 1995). Hundreds of diffusion studies were conducted in the 1950s and early 1960s to examine the diffusion process in more detail across a variety of settings (Rogers 2003). Many studies sought to understand how information created in government or otherwise sponsored programs could be disseminated more effectively. Diffusion research peaked in the early 1960s, but has been reinvigorated more recently with the advent of more sophisticated network models and technology making it possible to study the diffusion process more explicitly.

Most diffusion studies focus on trying to understand the factors that lead some members of a population to adopt a new idea and others do not. Further, studies try to understand why some people adopt the behavior early, whereas others wait a substantial amount of time before accepting the new practice. For example, Ryan and Gross (1943) wanted to know why some farmers purchased hybrid seed corn almost immediately upon its availability, whereas others waited until almost all the farmers in the area purchased it before they were willing to do so. Similarly, Coleman, Katz, and Menzel (1966) wanted to know why some physicians began prescribing tetracycline as soon as it was available, whereas others waited until most physicians prescribed it before they were willing to do so.

This chapter describes a variety of mathematical and network models used to study the diffusion of these and other innovations. The Coleman and others (1966) study provided a conceptual leap from other diffusion studies by explicitly measuring who talked to whom within the community about the innovation. (NB: Rogers also collected such data in his dissertation on the diffusion weed spray in Iowa.) Burt (1987) unearthed the Coleman and other (1966) data and made it available to the network community so scholars could debate various models used to describe the network diffusion process. Although having data has been useful for clarifying diffusion models, the limitations of these data and this study make it a poor choice for studying adoption behavior. Rather, scholars should have focused on collecting better data or reanalyzing diffusion network data in which contagion are more likely.

This chapter chronicles the development of network diffusion models and indicates where such progress is being made. I first present macro models used to estimate the speed of diffusion and, with the Bass (1969) model, to estimate rates of innovation and imitation. Next, spatial autocorrelation is presented that is used to estimate the degree to which contiguous nodes adopt innovations. Spatial autocorrelation led to the network autocorrelation model, which is presented statically (cross-sectional data only) and then with one time lag. I then discuss event history analysis applications of network autocorrelation and its extension by including time-based network interaction terms. Throughout the chapter, I attempt to provide a review of more recent research conducted in a variety of domains, but mostly drawn from the public health field.

(A) *Macro Models*

One consistent finding of diffusion research has been that the cumulative pattern of diffusion follows a growth pattern approximated by a simple one-parameter logistic function such as:

$$y_t = b_0 + \frac{1}{1 + e^{-b_1 t}}, \tag{6.1}$$

where y is the proportion of adopters, b_0 the y intercept, t is time, and b_1 the rate parameter to be estimated. This simple model can be used to compare growth rates for various innovations, but is extremely limited in its applicability. A considerable improvement was advanced by Bass (1969) and many others (see Hamblin, Jacobsen, and Miller 1973; Mahajan and Peterson 1985; Valente 1993) by creating a two-parameter model:

$$y_t = b_0 + (b_1 - b_0)Y_{t-1} - b_1(Y_{t-1})^2, \tag{6.2}$$

where y is the proportion of adopters, b_0 a rate parameter for innovation, and b_1 a rate parameter for imitation (the degree of adoption due to prior adopters). The Bass model incorporates the percentage adopters at each time point and thus makes a better estimate of the growth attributable to personal network persuasion. The mathematical model in (6.2) can be used to (1) forecast expected levels of diffusion (Mahajan and Peterson 1985), (2) estimate the rate of diffusion attributed to different theoretical aspects of the diffusion processes, b_0, external influence or innovativeness, and b_1, internal influence or interpersonal persuasion (Bass 1969; Hamblin et al. 1973; Valente 1993). This model can be used to estimate rate of disease spread from a central source such as contaminated food or from infections spread through interpersonal contact. In

Table 6.1.1. *Diffusion Rate Parameter Estimates and Moran's* I *Estimates for Two Data Sets*

	Medical Innovation	Cameroon Tontine 1 Simulation
One-parameter model		
Coefficient (95% CI)[a]	0.23 (−.053–0.51)	0.06 (.01–0.12)
N	17	50
R^2	0.76	0.71
Two-parameter (Bass) model		
Innovation coefficient (95% CI)	−0.43(−0.83–0.03)	−0.20 (−0.30–0.09)
Imitation coefficient (95% CI)	4.09 (3.05–5.12)	2.96 (2.58–3.34)
N	16	49
R^2	0.89	0.89
Moran's I	−.13	−.08
z-Score	−6.73	−7.80

[a] CI, Confidence Interval.

the social realm, one can use the model to estimate rate of adoption from a mass media advertisement or from interpersonal influence. Rate parameter estimates from both models for two diffusion data sets are provided in Table 6.1.1. Interpretation of these estimates is highly dependent on the time scale used to measure diffusion.

These rate parameter estimates can be used as outcomes to study factors associated with diffusion at the macrolevel by comparing rates between groups and/or populations. For example, parameter estimates for different countries can be compared in order to study factors associated with the spread of behaviors in different countries. Modeling at this macrolevel, however, is imprecise at best because it assumes perfect social mixing, everyone interacting with everyone else (Granovetter 1978; Van den Bulte and Lillien 1997). These macro models do not measure whether people who are connected to one another engage in the same behaviors. Geographers have devoted considerable attention to trying to determine whether innovations spread between contiguous areas.

(B) *Spatial Autocorrelation*

Rather than just estimate rate of diffusion, spatial models measure whether artifacts, diseases, farming practices, and other behaviors spread between contiguous areas (Hägerstrand 1967; Cliff and Ord 1981; Griffith et al. 1999). Proximity data are easy to obtain and are relatively unambiguous, thus providing a network of connections based on distance. Moran's I (1956) was an early model developed to test for spatial association, geographic clustering of adoption:

$$I = \frac{N \sum_i^N \sum_j^N D_{ij}(y_i - \bar{y})(y_j - \bar{y})}{S \sum_i^N (y_i - \bar{y})^2},$$

(6.3)

where N is the sample size, D a distance matrix (as proximities), y indicates adoption, and S the sum of the distances in the distance matrix. Moran's I measures the degree to which nodes that are connected to one another deviate from the average behavior in the network similarly or differently. Moran's I is high when connected nodes (positive elements of D) are either positively or negatively different from the average score. The statistical significance of Moran's I can be calculated in two ways – via permutation methods or analytically.

To use a permutation method to calculate the significance of Moran's I, assume adoption (y_i) is randomly distributed and calculate I repeatedly to get a sample of estimates based on D and the number of adopters. If Moran's I calculated is significantly different than the random sample generated, Moran's I is considered significant (z-scores can be obtained). The logic then is to calculate the degree to which neighbors (however defined) have similar adoption behavior compared with that expected if adoption were distributed randomly. Variance estimators for Moran's I can be found in spatial statistics textbooks (Cliff and Ord 1981; Bailey and Gatrell 1995) and used to calculate exact significance tests. Moran's I is useful and has been extended considerably (Nyblom, Borgatti, Roslakka, and Salo 2003), yet this approach often assumes that geographic proximity equates with communication and influence, which may not be true.

The spatial autocorrelation methodology was seen as a useful approach to measuring network autocorrelation, the bias inherent in a regression model when y appears as both the dependent and independent variable. Erbing and Young (1979) wrote an influential paper on measuring network effects and using network autocorrelation methods. Dow (1986) demonstrated the effects of network autocorrelation on estimate errors, and Doriean, Teuter, and Wang (1984) found considerable bias in the point estimates and their standard errors. Exactly how network autocorrelation applied to diffusion of innovations was not clear because spatial autocorrelation measured diffusion at the macrolevel, but did not show whether specific individuals were more or less likely to adopt based on their network position. Further, spatial autocorrelation did not show how network structure influenced diffusion. To do so, we turn to network models.

(C) *Network Models*

Figure 6.1.1 displays two networks from a study conducted in Cameroon among women in voluntary organizations (Valente et al. 1997). Women were asked to name their friends in the organization in an attempt to determine if friendship ties were associated with contraceptive choices (they were). The diffusion network model posits that initial contraceptive choices would be made by some women based on their innovativeness and exposure to outside sources of influence such as their cosmopoliteness, media use, or greater need for the innovation. The new idea, and its practice, then spreads through the network as users persuade nonusers to adopt either by exhortation, entreaty, enticement, or example.

Network influences are captured by an exposure or contagion model (Figure 6.1.2), and each individual's likelihood of adoption increases as the proportion (or number) of users in his or her personal network increases. Personal network exposure is the proportion or number of adopters in each person's network that provide information

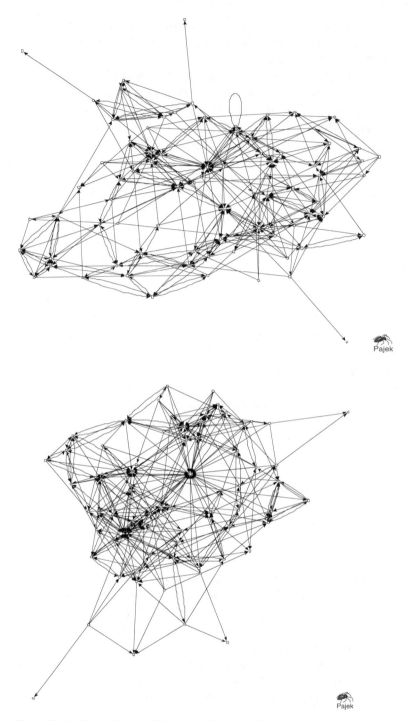

Figure 6.1.1. Networks 1 and 2 from the Cameroon Voluntary Association Study.

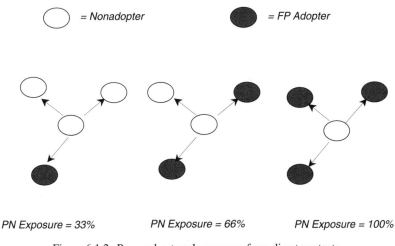

Figure 6.1.2. Personal network exposure from direct contacts.

and influence with regard to some behavior. The equation for nonrandom mixing, or personal network exposure, is:

$$E_i = \frac{\sum w_{ij} y_j}{\sum w_i}, \qquad (6.4)$$

where w is the social network weight matrix and y is vector of adoptions. For an individual who reported three contacts, network exposure (E_i) is the proportion of those contacts that have adopted (Figure 6.1.2). When network exposure is measured on direct contacts, it captures social influence conveyed through overt transmission of information, persuasion, or direct pressure. Alternatively, exposure can be calculated by transforming the social network, W, to reflect other social influence processes. For example, W can be transformed to represent the degree of structural equivalence (similarity in network position) among people in the network. Exposure calculated on this network captures social influence conveyed via comparison to equivalent others by social comparison or competition (Burt 1987). Exposure can also be weighted by network properties such as centrality to reflect social influence by opinion leaders.

These three social influence processes are modeled with three different classes of network weight matrices (relational, positional, and central) constructed from the same social network data (Table 6.1.2). All three can be justified theoretically as sources of influence on adoption behavior, and all three can be calculated various ways (there are at least ten centrality measures). It is possible that all three operate for different people or at different times during the diffusion process.

In addition to the social influence process, a second dimension to these influence mechanisms is the weight attached to each based on social distance. For example, in relational influence models, different weights can be assigned to direct ties, ties of ties, and even the ties of ties of ties; in positional equivalence models, different weights can be assigned to those that are more equivalent than others (Valente 1995). A potential line of diffusion network research then is to compare different network weighting mechanisms in order to model and compare different social influence processes.

Table 6.1.2. *Social Network Influence Weightings*

Relational	Positional	Central
1. Direct ties	1. Percent positive matches (tie overlap)	1. Degree
2. Indirect ties	2. Euclidean distance	2. Closeness
3. Joint participation in groups or events	3. Regular equivalence	3. Betweenness
		4. Flow
		5. Integration/radiality
		6. Information
		7. Power

Diffusion was simulated through the two Cameroon networks in Figure 6.1.1 to illustrate how network exposure and network structure influence diffusion. At each time period, adoption occurred for the nonadopter with the most nominations received, then network exposure was calculated, all nodes with exposure of 50% or higher were categorized as adopters, and the process repeated. We compared diffusion in this network with that simulated in a network of the same size and density, but with links allocated randomly. Both conditions were averaged across 1,000 runs. Figure 6.1.3 shows that, in network 1, initially the diffusion trajectories are similar, but at about time 10, diffusion in the actual network accelerated.

The network accelerated diffusion because it is somewhat centralized (in-degree 21.7%), and once diffusion reaches the center of the network it can propagate rapidly. Notice that at about time 20 diffusion slowed, accelerated again at about 25, and then slowed from about time 30 to 40. These "fits and starts" are a product of the network structure: diffusion reaches pockets of interconnectivity and spreads rapidly within these dense pockets, but slows between groups. Network 2 (Figure 6.1.3) had more rapid and sustained diffusion because it was even more centralized (in-degree, 47.2%). Note that, in the spatial autocorrelation model, adoptions were randomized to measure statistical significance, and in this simulation, the network structure was randomized to illustrate its influence on the rate of diffusion.

Simulation assumptions regarding influences on adoption could easily be changed to achieve different outcomes. For example, when adoptions were assigned randomly, diffusion was constant in network 1 (and saturation lower) and similar to the random network in network 2. The validity of these diffusion models rests partly on determining whether network exposure influences adoption. To that end, a number of empirical studies have been conducted to measure the degree to which social network exposure is associated with adoption.

6.2 Empirical Studies

Empirical support for an association between one's own behavior and that of one's peers can be found throughout the behavioral sciences literature. Although many scholars assume adoption is associated with network exposure, few studies have traced an innovation through a network of social contacts to empirically validate this proposition.

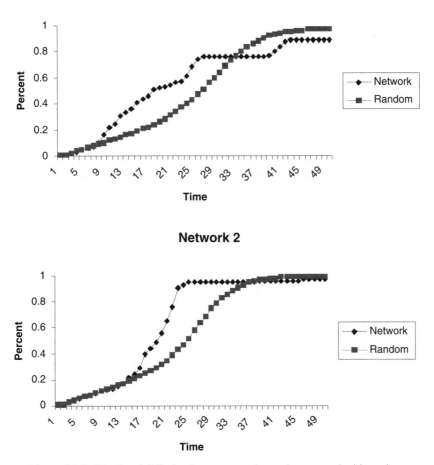

Figure 6.1.3. Simulated diffusion in two networks, each compared with random networks of the same size and density. Network 2 is more centralized.

The lack of data on diffusion within an entire network stems largely from the difficulty of trying to collect data over a time period long enough for diffusion to occur. Consequently, most studies have relied on retrospective data that introduces some but not much bias (Coughenour 1965; Nischan et al. 1993). It has also meant that several scholars have reanalyzed two studies that collected network and adoption data: (1) medical innovation study (Coleman et al. 1966), reanalyzed by Burt (1987), Marsden and Podolny (1990), Strang and Tuma (1993), Valente (1995, 1996), and Van den Bulte and Lillien (2001); and (2) Korean family planning study (Rogers and Kincaid 1981), reanalyzed by Dozier (1977), Montgomery and Chung (1999), Kohler (1997), and Valente (1995, 1996). More recent studies in the fields of reproductive health (Casterline 2001) and substance abuse (Neaigus et al. 2001) have provided new data, but these classics remain classic.

Because collecting complete network data is difficult, most empirical research has been egocentric (Marsden 1987, 1990), based on respondent reports of their behavior and that of their network peers who are not necessarily connected to one another and not interviewed. Social influence is often based on respondent reports of perceptions of peer behavior or perceptions of peer influence (Valente and Saba 1998, 2001; Valente and Vlahov 2001). Comparison of exposure scores based on respondent perceptions with alters' reports in one study found that perceptions were more strongly related to behavior than exposure based on alter reports (Valente et al. 1997; also see Urberg, Degirmencioglu, and Pilgrim 1997; Montgomery and Chung 1999).

Sociometric studies interview members of a bounded community and attempt to gather information from everyone in the community (typically conducted in schools, organizations, and small communities) and record their time of adoption (Coleman et al. 1966; Becker 1970; Rogers and Kincaid 1981; Wasserman and Faust 1994; Scott 2000). Sociometric studies are useful for understanding how an innovation flows within the community and how certain network structural variables influence the diffusion process. Sociometric data capture network influences by the alters' reports because they were also interviewed. For example, sociometric studies can determine whether structural positions such as centrality are associated with adoption and/or whether centralization is associated with more rapid diffusion (Valente 1995).

A number of more recent diffusion network studies have been cross-sectional and, in many cases, retrospective involving only one time point. For example, a study in Thailand by Entwisle and others (1996) found that contraceptive choices made by early adopters contributed significantly to the contraceptive choices made by later adopters (also see Rogers and Kincaid 1981). Valente and others (1997) collected sociometric data on contraceptive use among women in voluntary associations in Cameroon and showed that perceptions of these friends' behavior, and in particular, perceptions that these friends encouraged contraceptive use, were significantly associated with behavior. In general, these statistical analyses use the following model:

$$\log \frac{\Pr(y_t = 1)}{(1 - \Pr(y_t = 1))} = \alpha + \sum B_k X_k + B_{(k+1)}\omega y_t, \tag{6.5}$$

where y is a binary vector of adoption behavior, α is the intercept, β_k are parameter estimates for vectors of K sociodemographic characteristics (Xs), and ω represents the social network matrix. The ωy_t term represents the calculation of contemporaneous network exposure, and this vector is usually divided by a count of the number of nominations sent (alternatively, the number of nominations can be entered into the regression separately).

Significant estimates for β_{k+1} indicate contagion effects by showing that network exposure is associated with adoption. The variances for these estimates, however, are usually biased because the observations are not independent; hence, the errors in prediction are not independent. One partial solution is to obtain robust estimates by controlling for clustering. Clustering is the degree that elements from the same cluster are similar compared with those of different clusters. For example, two individuals chosen at random from the same organization are more likely to be similar than two chosen at random from different organizations. Table 6.2.3 reports regression results of the Cameroon data with and without correction for clustering. Without correction, network exposure is strongly and significantly associated with adoption, but with the correction it is only marginally statistically significant ($p = .04$). Controlling for clustering is

Table 6.2.3. *Logistic Regression on the Likelihood of Contraceptive Behavior on Controls and Network Exposure with and without Correction for Clustering* (N = 555; Groups = 9)

	Contraceptive Method Use			
	Without Correction		With Correction	
	Adjusted Odds Ratios	*P*-Value	Adjusted Odds Ratios	*P*-Value
Age	0.97	0.001	0.97	0.010
Education	0.91	0.247	0.91	0.184
Possessions	1.39	0.000	1.39	0.000
Network exposure	1.14	0.005	1.14	0.047

particularly important in network exposure models because network choices are often restricted to the cluster.

Even with clustering controlled, social influence as measured through social networks seems to be strongly associated with behavior. For example, a school-based sociometric study was conducted by Alexander and colleagues (2001) using adolescent health data (Bearman, Jones, and Udry 2000) to show that students with a majority of network ties who were smokers were almost two times as likely to smoke themselves, with an additional two times greater likelihood of smoking for those with best friends who smoke. Intra-school clustering was controlled and the multilevel model accurately captured microlevel effects within the context of macrolevel influences. The study measured the influence of peers on smoking, while conditioning on the smoking rate within the school (Alexander et al. 2001).

Estimating the network exposure (autocorrelation) term with a multilevel model can provide contagion estimates across settings and estimate the degree it varies between settings (i.e., communities, schools, organizations, etc.). The models are incomplete, however, because there may be factors that influence both adoption and choice of social network contacts. For example, the decision to smoke and to nominate friends who smoke may both be a function of delinquency or rebellion. Hence, an association between behavior and peer behavior can be spurious. Testing social influence with network methods then requires longitudinal data involving at least two time points. Boulay and Valente (in press) collected data among women in three villages of Nepal and found that having discussion partners who used contraception influenced information-seeking behavior and contraceptive choice. Having data from two time points allows testing of a simple dynamic model on adoption:

$$\log \frac{\Pr(y_t = 1)}{(1 - \Pr(y_t = 1))} = \alpha + \sum B_k X_k + B_{(k+1)}\omega_t y_t + B_{(k+2)}\omega_{(t-1)}y_{(t-1)}, \quad (6.6)$$

where y is a binary indicator of behavior, α is the intercept, β_k are parameter estimates for vectors of K sociodemographic characteristics (Xs), and ω represents the social network matrix. A positive and significant β_{k+2} indicates that respondents with high network exposure at baseline were more likely to adopt at time two. A positive and significant β_{k+1} indicates that change in network exposure is associated with change in behavior. This may indicate contagion, but still may be a product of some omitted factor. Panel data collected at two time periods are adequate for most research needs and can provide evidence of network influences on behavior. However, because there is often a considerable time between the two measures, many factors may account for simultaneous change in behavior and network exposure. To cope with this threat, data can be collected on time of adoption, expanding the microlevel dynamic analysis by using event history analysis (Tuma and Hannan 1984).

(A) *Event History Analysis*

Event history analysis techniques have been developed to analyze data with a substantive number of time points, estimating coefficients with maximum likelihood estimators (Bartholomew 1982; Allison 1984; Tuma and Hannan 1984; Strang and Tuma 1993; Teachman and Hayward 1993). There are two types of event history analysis, discrete time, in which the outcome is binary, and continuous time, in which the outcome is time to an event. Because diffusion occurs over time, there is an explicit time dimension in diffusion studies captured by both discrete and continuous time models. The time of adoption variable is the dependent variable and may be influenced by both time-varying and time-constant factors. Some individuals may not have adopted by the time of data collection giving rise to time-censored observations (right censoring occurs when the data are collected before the innovation has finished diffusing or does not diffuse to all members of the community or study).[1]

There are a variety of event history techniques, including hazard models developed in epidemiology, used to understand the hazard or risk to disease or injury over time. Hazard and/or event history analysis generally requires that the data are reshaped from simple observations to a case–time format, such that there is a case in the data for each individual at each time period of study up to and including that person's time of adoption (Table 6.2.4). The time-varying and time-constant independent variables are included in each case, as well as a binary indicator for whether the individual adopted the behavior (or got sick).

Maximum-likelihood estimation can determine whether the independent variables are associated with the dependent variable (adopt/not adopt) (Eliason 1993). A study of 100 people with an average adoption time of seven translates into 700 person–time cases. Each person–time case has a variable for the network exposure at that time period plus an indicator for whether the person adopted (plus additional time-constant and time-varying covariates as desired). The event history model is:

$$\log \frac{\Pr(y_t = 1)}{(1 - \Pr(y_t = 1))} = \alpha + \sum B_j X_j + \sum B_{kt} X_{kt} + \sum B_{(k+1)} \omega y_t, \qquad (6.7)$$

where y is a binary indicator of behavior, α is the intercept, β_j are parameter estimates for vectors of J sociodemographic characteristics (X_j), β_{kt} are parameter estimates for the matrix of time-varying sociodemographic characteristics (X_{kt}), ω represents the social network weight matrix, and t a time indicator. Note here we have assumed a

Table 6.2.4. *Event History Analysis of Factors Associated with Adoption for the Three Diffusion Network Datasets (Coefficients Are Adjusted Odds Ratios for Likelihood of Adoption).*

	Medical Innovation ($N = 947$)	Brazilian Farmers ($N = 10,092$)	Korean Family Planning ($N = 7,103$)
Time (recoded as proportion)	0.21	0.72	0.31
Time logistically transformed	0.68	1.94	0.67
Infection	11.8*	10.9**	9.26**
Susceptibility	2.31	2.24*	2.44*
Number sent	0.91	0.90†	0.96
Number received	1.06†	1.02†	1.06**
Exposure via direct contacts	0.64	1.07	1.19
Exposure via structural equivalence	0.93	2.47**	1.12
Attitude toward science	0.65**		
Journals	1.84*		
Income		1.17**	
Visits		1.00	
No. of children			1.25**
Campaign exposure			1.03†

† $p < .10$; * $p < .01$; ** $p < .001$.

static (constant) network. Standard statistical packages allow testing of event history or survival data in a relatively straightforward manner, once the data are reformatted. Event history analysis requires the construction of exposure matrices for each time period, which can be a formidable task, particularly if one uses more than one network weight matrix (Valente 1995).

Marsden and Podolny (1990) used event history analysis and tested network exposure's association with adoption in the medical innovation data. Results showed that exposure was not associated with adoption in that study. Strang and Tuma (1993) revisited the issue with the same data by postulating time variance in network influence (i.e., how much lag time, if any, is there in the influence). Strang and Tuma (1993) found evidence of contagion. Van den Bulte and Lillien (2001) supplemented the medical innovation data with archival data on media promotion by pharmaceutical firms at the time of the original study and showed that network contagion effects disappear once these data are added. Their analysis demonstrates the importance of omitted variables when studying diffusion through networks. The rapid diffusion measured in the medical innovation study indicates that contagion was probably not the primary factor driving diffusion.

To illustrate, I conducted event history analysis of three classic diffusion network data sets. The analysis controlled for within village and within person covariation, as well as terms for time and a logistic transformation of time, were included to control for macrolevel effects. Terms for infection and susceptibility (Strang and Tuma 1993; Myers 2000) were included to measure whether adoption by central individuals (high in-degree) influenced subsequent adoption – infection – and whether centrality (out-degree) influenced a person's likelihood to adopt as diffusion occurred – susceptibility.

In- and out-degree were also included in the model. Two network exposure terms were computed – direct ties and structural equivalence.[2] For this analysis, network exposure was calculated using contemporaneous measures because two of the data sets recorded adoption in 1-year intervals. Two control variables representing individual characteristics were included. Analysis was conducted only on those who adopted. The following model was estimated:

$$\log(\Pr(y_t = 1)) = \alpha + \sum \beta_{lm} X_{lm} + \sum \beta_{lmt} V_{lmt} + \sum \beta_{lmt} \omega_s y_t$$
$$+ \lambda_{lm1} C_D(y_+) + \lambda_{lm2} C_D(y_+), \tag{6.8}$$

where y is a binary indicator of behavior; α is the intercept; Xs are vectors or time-constant sociodemographic and network characteristics; V represents vectors of time-varying terms, in this case, time and its transformation; ω_s represents the social network matrices; and λ estimates the effects of centrality degree variables multiplied by the time-varying proportion of adopters in the network (infection and susceptibility). Results are mixed, but seem to indicate that both infection and susceptibility effects are present. In all three data sets, infection is positively associated with adoption indicating that, as those with high in-degree adopt, it increases the likelihood others in the network will adopt. In two studies, Brazilian farmers and Korean women, susceptibility is associated with adoption, indicating that those with a high number of nominations sent are more likely to adopt as the innovation diffuses. Ties sent and received are marginally associated with adoption, and only for the Brazilian data is exposure, through structural equivalence, associated with adoption. These results, however, change dramatically when nonadopters are included or when a term for the average exposure at each time period is included such that infection and susceptibility effects disappear.

The event history analysis approached has also been used by Montgomery and others (2001) using egocentric data to study network exposure's influence on contraceptive use in Ghana. Current analysis of four rounds of data over 2 years has shown that contraceptive use is strongly associated with use by social network peers. The Ghana field study provides some of the most conclusive evidence of the magnitude of social influence on behavior change by showing that, as the number of social network contacts who use contraceptives increases, the likelihood of contraceptives use by ego also increases. Of all variables, the network exposure variables were the most significant influences on contraceptive adoption. Another longitudinal field study in Kenya found similar results, again based on egocentric network data (Behrman, Kohler, and Watkins 2003).

Montgomery and others (2001) also reported preliminary analysis of network influences weighted by tie characteristics, such as the frequency of communication. They found that adding these weights did not change the strength of peer influence. Similar results have been reported in Valente (1995) and Valente and Saba (1998: p. 109). Consequently, it seems that the influence of social networks on behavior (contraceptive use in these cases) seems broad in nature and is not conditioned on specific factors such as the frequency of communication between dyads or their sociodemographic similarity. These factors may play a strong and even pervasive role in determining who is connected to whom (White and Watkins 2000), but they do not seem to determine the degree of influence social contacts provide.

Network exposure and adoption may not always be strongly correlated for a number of reasons. First, exposure may not be associated with adoption for everyone, but may be most influential during the middle stages of diffusion, when awareness and uncertainty about its relative advantages are both high (Carley 2001). Exposure may have less of an effect early in the process when there are few adopters and obvious advantages to waiting, and late in the process when most people have a majority of adopters in their personal network anyway. Second, individuals may have varying thresholds to adoption, such that some are innovative and others are not (Granovetter 1978). Valente (1995, 1996) posited a social network threshold model in which contagion (majority rule) is a special case. Most simulation models assume majority influence on adoption decisions as was done in the beginning of this chapter. It is reasonable, however, to expect that individuals vary in the amount of network exposure needed to adopt an innovation. Disproving thresholds may not be possible, but construct validity for the concept has been demonstrated (Valente 1996). Valente and Saba (1998) replicated the threshold model using egocentric data and showed that people with a minority of network members using contraception had higher campaign recall, indicating that the media campaign could substitute for interpersonal sources of influences. If thresholds vary, network exposure is needed for people to reach those thresholds; if they do not and the special case of contagion exists, network exposure will determine when individuals adopt.

In spite of the impressive list of studies showing some support for an association between one's own behavior and network exposure, and the theoretical simulations of network structure and thresholds, significant work remains to be done. Most scholars and lay people would agree that social networks influence behavior. The barriers to demonstrating this effect, however, have been challenges of data collection and agreement on appropriate statistical methodology. The most commonly analyzed data set, Medical Innovation, is 50 years old, consists of only 125 respondents, and arguably is not a diffusion study at all. Further, and perhaps most damaging, is that we have probably approached the problem wrong all along.

Although the distinction between dimensions of social influence (Table 6.1.2) represents a rich sociological map of influences on behavior, empirical investigations to date have found little variation in their role in the adoption process. Most network studies of diffusion are small bounded communities and hence do not differentiate much between cohesive and structurally equivalent alters. Therefore, measuring the influence of direct ties on adoption is probably sufficient for most studies, although future research comparing social network influence mechanisms could still be quite interesting, particularly in business settings where positional equivalence is likely to be a stronger influence, the majority of attention will still be paid to understand how direct contact influences adoption decisions.

6.3 Network-Based Interventions

Debate concerning network tie selection and the difficulty of specifying the time order of adoption will be hard to resolve. In addition, many behavioral scientists will argue over the meaning of any associations between network exposure and adoption. Specifying the direction of causal influences is likely to be difficult, no matter how complete the data. It may be that the best use of network data and the best way to demonstrate network influences on adoption is to design behavior change interventions. If these network-based interventions are successful, the value in understanding network models of diffusion will be apparent.

Several studies (Lomas et al. 1991; Latkin 1998; Soumerai et al. 1998; Kincaid 2000; Sikkemma et al. 2000) have identified opinion leaders using network data and had these leaders implement successful behavior change programs. Valente and Davis (1999) further suggested that leaders could be matched to others in the network based on minimum distances, and a randomized trial using this technique for preventing smoking among middle school students found it to be successful (Valente et al. 2003). Broadhead et al. (1998) and Latkin (1998) demonstrated the utility of networks for recruitment into behavioral change programs. Given the challenges inherent in collecting full diffusion network data, using networks as intervention points may present the best opportunity for understanding how networks influence behavior change.

A second network-based intervention is to target promotional programs to subgroups defined by social network affiliations. The subgroup becomes a source of social support and behavioral reinforcement not available if behavior change is spread out among people in the larger group. Critical mass is more likely to be achieved in the subgroup than in the community as a whole. A third approach would be to locate network bridges – linking agents – between organizations and subgroups, and to provide the support they need to transport new ideas and procedures between groups. A fourth approach is to locate isolates who may be at risk of not receiving information through the network or who may feel "left out" of activities. Finally, promotional programs might try to match structurally equivalent individuals and groups so messages and programs are appropriately tailored. In sum, most marketing programs have segmented audiences on demographic characteristics, and some on psychographic ones, but a new era of sociometric segmentation is now possible.

6.4   Conclusion

Much progress has been made since 1943 when Ryan and Gross first laid the foundation for diffusion of innovations theory. Rogers (2003) chronicled the many studies conducted since then and helped create a general diffusion model with wide applicability now being renewed and reinvigorated with fresh theory and analytic models. Overall, results indicate that social network influences on behavior are important and have consequences for the health and well-being of populations and individuals. These new insights have shed light on important aspects of how new ideas and practices spread within and between communities.

Along with new insights have come new questions and new perspectives to be addressed. It is clear that a lack of data on both time of adoption and network influences has hampered developments. Few diffusion or behavioral studies collect information on networks, and conversely few network studies record time of adoption. There are advantages to marrying these two ideas, however, and future research will hopefully try to collect both types of data.

It is also clear that our understanding of how diffusion occurs is still somewhat limited. The Medical Innovation data have often been used to demonstrate the importance of networks in adoption, yet analyses by Valente (1995) and Van den Bulte and Lillien (2001) have shown that contagion via social influence in this setting was unlikely. Given the number of confounding factors and some of the data requirements, it may be prohibitively difficult to substantiate the role of social networks in innovation adoption via survey methods alone. Purposively intervening on social networks, however, may prove to be a fruitful avenue of research. If network-based interventions can be used to accelerate innovation diffusion, then a stronger case can be made for the importance of social contagion in the diffusion process.

Nonetheless, it is clear that networks are important influences on behavior because most people acknowledge that they receive information and influence via their social networks and that they model the behavior of others. What is less clear is how to capture that influence in quantitative terms that mimic the theoretical progress made in the network field. Further, verbal accounts on how people make decisions and adopt behaviors usually reveal nonlinearities, chance circumstances, and whims that are not independent of networks, but not easily captured in social influence models.

The link between micro- and macrolevels of analysis represents an opportunity for study of diffusion processes. The opportunity lies in the fact that multilevel modeling techniques enable the separation of microlevel network exposure influences from macrolevel contextual factors. Yet both are social network influences and both represent elements of the diffusion paradigm. It is hoped that by controlling for contextual effects we do not "throw the baby out with the bathwater" by eliminating the microlevel influences that provide expressions for those contextual effects.

In spite of controls for macrolevel contextual effects, microlevel associations between peer network behavior and those of respondents are still sometimes strong. Debate remains about the meaning of these associations; is it peer influence, peer selection, or further contextual effects? More rigorous studies may eventually tease this out; in the interim, better study designs and interventions will need to be created. This review has attempted to point out some of the challenges diffusion scholars face and some of the promising new directions it may take. It is hoped that such organization will clear the way for promising new studies to be conducted. Social networks are fundamental influences on human behavior and conduits for the diffusion of ideas and practices, yet their roles are varied and complex and defy easy categorization.

Acknowledgments

My thanks to Christophe Van den Bulte, John Casterline, Chih-ping Chou, and Peter Marsden for helpful comments on earlier drafts. Support for this research was provided by NIDA grant no. DA10172 and DA16094.

Endnotes

1. Left censoring occurs when the data are incomplete at the beginning of the process. For example, adoption data for the period 1993 to 2000 may have some people who adopted in 1989 to 1992 classified as 1992 adopters.
2. Structural equivalence was computed as in Burt's (1987) measure, and Euclidian distance was raised to the sixteenth power.

References

Alexander, C., Piazza, M., Mekos, D., and Valente, T. W. (2001). Peer networks and adolescent cigarette smoking: An analysis of the national longitudinal study of adolescent health. *Journal of Adolescent Health, 29,* 22–30.

Allison, P. D. (1984). *Event History Analysis.* Newberry Park, CA: Sage.

Bailey, N. T. J. (1975). *The Mathematical Theory of Infectious Diseases and Its Applications.* London: Charles Griffen.

Bailey, T. C., and Gatrell, A. C. (1995). *Interactive Spatial Data Analysis.* Essex, UK: Longman.

Bartholomew, D. J. (1982). *Stochastic Models for Social Processes.* New York: John Wiley and Sons.

Bass, F. M. (1969). A new product growth model for consumer durables. *Management Science, 15*(5), 215–227.

Beal, G. M., and Bohlen, J. M. (1955). *How Farm People Accept New Ideas.* Cooperative Extension Service Report 15: Ames, IA: Iowa State University.

Bearman, P. S., Jones, J., and Udry, J. R. (2000). *The National Longitudinal Study of Adolescent Health: Research Design.* Available from: http://www.cpcp.unc.edu/projects/addhealth/design.html.

Becker, M. H. (1970). Sociometric location and innovativeness: Reformulation and extension of the diffusion model. *American Sociological Review, 35,* 267–282.

Behrman, J. R., Kohler, H.-P. and Watkins, S., "Social Networks, HIV/AIDS and Risk Perceptions" (February 18, 2003). PIER Working Paper No. 03-007. http://ssrn.com/abstract=382844.

Boulay, M., and Valente, T. W. (in press). Dynamic sources of information and dissonance in the discussion networks of women in rural Nepal. *Journal of Health Communication.*

Broadhead, R. S., Hechathorn, D. D., Weakliem, D. L, Anthony, D. L., Madray, H., Mills, R. J., and Hughes, J. (1998). Harnessing peer networks as an instrument fo raids prevention: Results from a peer-driven intervention. *Public Health Reports, 113*(S1), 42–57.

Brown, L. (1981). *Innovation Diffusion: A New Perspective.* New York: Methuen.

Burt, R. (1987). Social contagion and innovation: Cohesion versus structural equivalence. *American Journal of Sociology, 92,* 1287–1335.

Carley, K. M. (2001). Learning and using new ideas: A socio-cognitive approach. In J. Casterline (Ed.), *Diffusion Processes and Fertility Transition: Selected Perspectives.* Washington, DC: National Academy Press.

Casterline, J. (2001). (Ed.) *Diffusion Processes and Fertility Transition: Selected Perspectives.* Washington, DC: National Academy Press.

Cliff, A., and Ord, J. K. (1981). *Spatial Processes: Models and Applications.* London: Pion.

Coleman, J. S., Katz, E., and Menzel, H. (1966). *Medical Innovation: A Diffusion Study.* New York: Bobbs Merrill.

Coughenour, C. M. (1965). The problem of reliability of adoption data in survey research. *Rural Sociology, 30,* 184–203.

Doreian, P., Teuter, K., and Wang, C. (1984). Network autocorrelation models: Some Monte Carlo results. *Sociological Methods and Research, 13,* 155–200.

Dow, M. (1986). Model selection procedures for network autocorrelated disturbance models. *Sociological Methods and Research, 14,* 403–422.

Dozier, D. M. 1977. *Communication Networks and the Role of Thresholds in the Adoption of Innovations*. Ph.D. Thesis, Stanford University, Stanford, CA.

Eliason, S. R. (1993). *Maximum Likelihood Estimation: Logic and Practice*. Newbury Park, CA: Sage.

Entwisle, B., Rindfuss, R. D., Guilkey, D. K., Chamratrithirong, A., Curran, S. R., and Sawangdee, Y. (1996). Community and contraceptive choice in rural Thailand: A case study of Nang Rong. *Demography, 33*, 1–11.

Erbing, L., and Young, A. (1979). Individuals and social structure: Contextual effects as endogenous feedback. *Sociological Methods and Research, 7*, 396–430.

Granovetter, M. (1978). Threshold models of collective behavior. *American Journal of Sociology, 83*, 1420–1443.

Griffith, D. A., Layne, L. J., Ord, J. K., and Sone, A. (1999). *A Casebook for Spatial Statistical Data Analysis: A Compilation of Analyses of Different Thematic Data Sets*. New York: Oxford University Press.

Hägerstrand, T. (1967). *Innovation Diffusion as a Spatial Process*. (A. Pred, Trans.) Chicago: University of Chicago Press.

Hamblin, R. L., Jacobsen, R. B., and Miller, J. L. L. (1973). *A Mathematical Theory of Social Change*. New York: John Wiley and Sons.

Katz, E., Levine, M. L., and Hamilton, H. (1963). Traditions of research on the diffusion of innovation. *American Sociological Review, 28*, 237–253.

Kincaid, D. L. (2000). Social networks, ideation, and contraceptive behavior in Bangladesh: A longitudinal analysis. *Social Science and Medicine, 50*, 215–231.

Kohler, H. P. (1997). Learning in social networks and contraceptive choice. *Demography, 34*, 369–383.

Latkin, C. (1998). Outreach in natural setting: The use of peer leaders for HIV prevention among injecting drug users' networks. *Public Health Reports, 113*(S1), 151–159.

Lomas, J., Enkin, M., Anderson, G. M., Hanna, W. J., Vayda, E., and Singer, J. (1991). Opinion leaders vs. audit feedback to implement practice guidelines: Delivery after previous cesarean section. *Journal of American Medical Association, 265*, 2202–2207.

Mahajan, V., and Peterson, R. A. (1985). *Models of Innovation Diffusion*. Newbury Park, CA: Sage.

Marsden, P. V. (1987). Core discussion networks of Americans. *American Sociological Review, 52*, 122–131.

Marsden, P. V. (1990). Network data and measurement. *Annual Review of Sociology, 16*, 435–463.

Marsden, P. V., and Podolny, J. (1990). Dynamic analysis of network diffusion processes. In J. Weesie and H. Flap (Eds.), *Social Networks Through Time*. Utrecht, The Netherlands: ISOR.

Montgomery, M. R., Agyeman, D., Aglotise, P., Hewett, P., and Kiros, G. (2001). *Social Networks and Contraceptive Dynamics in Southern Ghana*. Paper presented at the annual meeting of the Population Association of America, Washington, DC.

Montgomery, M. R., and Chung, W. (1999). Social networks and the diffusion of fertility control in the Republic of Korea. In R. Leete (Ed.), *Dynamics of Values in Fertility Change*. Oxford, UK: Oxford University Press.

Morris, M. (1993). Epidemiology and social networks: Modeling structured diffusion. *Sociological Methods and Research, 22*, 99–126.

Myers, D. J. (2000). The diffusion of collective violence: Infectiousness, susceptibility, and mass media networks. *American Journal of Sociology, 106*, 173–208.

Neiagus, A., Friedman, S. R., Kottiri, B. J., and Des Jarlais, D. C. (2001). HIV risk networks and HIV transmission among injecting drug users. *Evaluation and Program Planning, 24*, 221–226.

Nischan, P., Ebeling, K., Thomas, D. B., and Hirsch, U. (1993). Comparison of recalled and validated oral contraceptive histories. *American Journal of Epidemiology, 138*(9), 697–703.

Nyblom, J., Borgatti, S., Roslakka, J. and Salo, M. A. (2003). Statistical analysis of network data – an application to diffusion of innovation. *Social Networks, 25*, 175–195.

Robertson, T. S. (1971). *Innovative Behavior and Communication*. New York: Holt, Rinehart and Winston.

Rogers, E. M. (2003). *Diffusion of Innovations* (5th ed.). New York: Free Press.

Rogers, E. M., and Kincaid, D. L. (1981). *Communication Networks: A New Paradigm for Research.* New York: Free Press.

Ryan, R., and Gross, N. (1943). The diffusion of hybrid seed corn in two Iowa communities. *Rural Sociology, 8*(1), 15–24.

Scott, J. (2000). *Network Analysis: A Handbook.* Newbury Park, CA: Sage.

Sikkema, K. J., Kelly, J. A., Winett, R. A., Solomon, L. J., Cargill, V. A., Roffman, R. A., et al. (2000). Outcomes of a randomized community-level HIV prevention intervention for women living in 19 low-income housing developments. *American Journal of Public Health, 90*, 57–63.

Soumerai, S. B., McLaughlin, T. J., Gurwitz, J. H., et al. (1998). Effect of local medical opinion leaders on quality of care for acute myocardial infarction: A randomized controlled trial. *Journal of the American Medical Association, 279*, 1358–1363.

Strang, D., and Tuma, N. B. (1993). Spatial and temporal heterogeneity in diffusion. *American Journal of Sociology, 99*, 614–639.

Teachman, J. D., and Hayward, M. D. (1993). Interpreting hazard rate models. *Sociological Methods and Research, 21*(3), 340–371.

Tuma, N. B., and Hannan, M. T. (1984). *Social Dynamics: Models and Methods.* New York: Academic Press.

Urberg, K. A., Degirmencioglu, S. M., and Pilgrim, C. (1997). Close friend and group influence on adolescent cigarette smoking and alcohol use. *Developmental Psychology, 33*, 834–844.

Valente, T. W. (1993). Diffusion of innovations and policy decision-making. *Journal of Communication, 43*(1), 30–41.

Valente, T. W. (1995). *Network Models of the Diffusion of Innovations.* Cresskill, NJ: Hampton Press.

Valente, T. W. (1996). Social network thresholds in the diffusion of innovations. *Social Networks, 18*, 69–89.

Valente, T. W., and Davis, R. L. (1999). Accelerating the diffusion of innovations using opinion leaders. *The Annals of the American Academy of the Political and Social Sciences, 566*, 55–67.

Valente, T. W., Hoffman, B. R., Ritt-Olson, A., Lichtman, K., and Johnson, C. A. (2003). The effects of a social network method for group assignment strategies on peer led tobacco prevention programs in schools. *American Journal of Public Health, 93*, 1837–1843.

Valente, T. W., and Rogers, E. M. (1995). The origins and development of the diffusion of innovations paradigm as an example of scientific growth. *Science Communication: An Interdisciplinary Social Science Journal, 16*(3), 238–269.

Valente, T. W., and Saba, W. (1998). Mass media and interpersonal influence in a reproductive health communication campaign in Bolivia. *Communication Research, 25*, 96–124.

Valente, T. W., and Saba, W. (2001). Campaign recognition and interpersonal communication as factors in contraceptive use in Bolivia. *Journal of Health Communication, 6*, 303–322.

Valente, T. W., and Vlahov, D. (2001). Selective risk taking among needle exchange participants in Baltimore: Implications for supplemental interventions. *American Journal of Public Health, 91*, 406–411.

Valente, T. W., Watkins, S., Jato, M. N., Van der Straten, A., and Tsitsol, L. M. (1997). Social network associations with contraceptive use among Cameroonian women in voluntary associations. *Social Science and Medicine, 45*, 677–687.

Van den Bulte, C., and Lillien, G. L. (1997). Bias and systematic change in the parameter estimates of macro-level diffusion models. *Marketing Science, 16*, 338–353.

Van den Bulte, C., and Lillien, G. L. (2001). Medical innovation revisited: Social contagion versus marketing effort. *American Journal of Sociology, 106*, 1409–1435.

Wasserman, S., and Faust, K. (1994). *Social Networks Analysis: Methods and Applications.* Cambridge, UK: Cambridge University Press.

White, K., and Watkins, S. C. (2000). Accuracy, stability and reciprocity in informal conversational networks in rural Kenya. *Social Networks, 22*, 337–356.

7

Using Correspondence Analysis for Joint Displays of Affiliation Networks

Katherine Faust

University of California, Irvine

This chapter describes and illustrates methods for studying affiliation networks, with special attention to methods for spatial representations that jointly display the actors and events in the network. Although affiliation networks have been the focus of methodological research for decades (Levine 1972; Breiger 1974; Seidman 1981; McPherson 1982; Wilson 1982), more recent analyses of affiliation networks have raised a number of issues concerning appropriate methods for their study. At the same time, research has pointed to the empirical and theoretical generality of this perspective (Freeman and White 1993; Wasserman and Faust 1994; Borgatti and Everett 1997; Faust 1997; Skvoretz and Faust 1999; Breiger 2000; Mische and Pattison 2000; Roberts 2000; Brazill and Groffman 2002; Faust et al. 2002; Pattison and Breiger 2002).

7.1 Background

Representing the two modes in the affiliation network in a "joint space" in which both actors and events are depicted simultaneously is of particular interest in both earlier and more recent work on affiliation networks. Such graphic displays commonly use scaling (e.g., correspondence analysis) or algebraic approaches (e.g., lattices). An important, but often neglected, aspect of some applications is clear specification of the formal relationships embodied in the configuration and explicit description of how the result corresponds to the original data. These omissions produce rather casual depictions and consequent ambiguity in interpretation. They also contribute to misunderstanding and fuel debate about the usefulness of the approach. The following passages are typical of such descriptions for affiliation networks or similar two-mode data arrays.

In describing correspondence analysis for the joint display of actors and events in an affiliation network of Chinese political actors' involvement, Schweizer (1991) interpreted the result in terms of a "preference" model: "In this application of the model to an actor-by-event matrix, actors are placed as points into their region of maximal involvement ('preference') for certain events" (p. 33). However, he neglected to reveal what scores were used for the display.

Similarly, in their reanalysis of the classic Davis, Gardner, and Gardner (1941) observations of southern women's attendance at social events, Borgatti and Everett

(1997) described the joint display as follows:

Applied to the Davis, Gardner and Gardner data, a correspondence analysis results in a map in which (a) points representing the women are placed close together if the women attended mostly the same events, (b) points representing the social events are placed near each other if they were attended by mostly the same women, and (c) women-points are placed near event-points if those women attended those events. (p. 246)

However, as with the previous example, the authors failed to reveal which scores were used for the display, so we are left with no precise understanding of what "near" means in the plots.

Admittedly, these passages are intended as simplified descriptions to aid substantive interpretation of the results, but their informality and the absence of information about exactly which sets of scores are used in the figures prevent precise interpretation of the results. In addition, absence of formal specification contributes to debate about potential problems with correspondence analysis for studying affiliation networks. Criticisms have included application of the approach to dichotomous data, possible inadequacy of representations in two dimensions, and proper interpretations of distances in the displays (see the exchange between Borgatti and Everett 1997, and Roberts 2000).

This chapter takes the modest step of laying out some aspects of the formal basis for joint representations of actors and events in an affiliation network using correspondence analysis. The goal is to provide the precise formal specification of the model and of the relationship between the model and the input data in such a way that users can select among some possible alternatives and interpret the results appropriately. This chapter describes and illustrates some of the methodological issues using both a small hypothetical affiliation network and an affiliation network of Western Hemisphere countries and their memberships in regional trade and treaty organizations.

7.2   Affiliation Networks

Many social situations bring together actors in sets of two, three, or more in collectivities of arbitrary size. Corporate boards of directors, scientists attending sessions at a professional meeting, members of voluntary organizations in a community, activists gathered in protest demonstrations, fans watching sporting events, countries forging alliances through membership in trade and treaty organizations, and members of committees in a university are all examples of this sort of social situation. These situations are varied in nature. Some are quite informal social gatherings, whereas others are well-defined assemblages. In some situations people can be expected to interact quite intensely with one another, whereas in other situations direct interaction among all members is unlikely. Some situations are fleeting one-time events, whereas others are recurrent. Nevertheless, all the examples mentioned previously share a number of common features. In each, joint social participation brings together sets of actors rather than simply linking pairs or dyads. Thus, joint participation constitutes a social relation among *collections* of actors. Moreover, when actors participate in multiple interaction occasions, the social occasions themselves are linked to one another through their common participants. Finally, all the situations involve two different kinds of social entities: the individuals (referred to as *actors*) and the social occasions (referred to as *events*).

Affiliation networks have been used to study a wide range of social situations, and a partial list highlights their generality. A classic example is Davis et al.'s (1941) study of southern women's participation in informal social gatherings (see also Homans 1950; Breiger 1974; Doreian 1979; Freeman and White 1993; Freeman 2002). Many studies of corporate interlocks have used affiliation networks (Levine 1972; Mariolis 1975; Mariolis and Jones 1982; Mizruchi 1982), as have studies of corporate CEOs and their memberships in civic, cultural, and corporate boards (Galaskiewicz 1985). Participation in community ritual celebrations has been studied by Foster and Seidman (1984) and Schweizer, Klemm, and Schweizer (1993). Affiliation networks have also been used to study social movements (Rosenthal et al. 1985; Mische and Pattison 2000; Osa 2003) and other political situations, including roll call votes (Stokman 1977), opinions by U.S. Supreme Court justices (Breiger 2000; Brazill and Groffman 2002), winners and losers in Chinese political struggles (Schweizer 1991), and the participation of Soviet political elites in official and social occasions (Faust et al. 2002). Academic associations have been the focus of a number of affiliation network studies, including sociologists' memberships in disciplinary specialty sections (Cappell and Guterbock 1992; Ennis 1992).

The situations mentioned previously can be viewed as instances of affiliation networks (also called *membership networks*, *dual networks*, or *hypernetworks*). Affiliation networks are a general class of networks with several important properties. In particular, three characteristics distinguish affiliation networks from the more standard social network in which relations are measured on pairs of actors from a single set. Linkages in an affiliation network occur between two different kinds of social entities, referred to as "actors" and "events." As with all social networks, the actors may be any meaningful social unit, including individual or collective entities. The events in an affiliation network are collections of actors. The events may either be well-defined collectivities with official membership lists, or they may be less formal gatherings. Each of these kinds of entities constitutes a "mode" of the network. Thus, affiliation networks are *two-mode* networks. A second important characteristic is that the affiliation relation links collections of entities – actors belong to multiple events, and events may include multiple actors. Thus, affiliation networks are *nondyadic*. These two characteristics permit a third important property – the *duality* of perspectives in the relation between actors and events (Breiger 1974). Viewed from the perspective of actors, participation in events links actors to one another. Viewed from the dual perspective of events, the actors multiple memberships link events together. Putting these together gives a *joint* perspective of the simultaneous linking of actors through events and events through actors.

The distinction between social ties based on *membership relations* (seen in affiliation networks) and *social relations* (the typical one-mode network linking pairs of actors) is nicely discussed in Breiger's foundational work on membership networks (Breiger 1974). Both of these kinds of social ties give rise to networks, but networks with rather different properties. Social relations are dyadic – they link pairs of actors in a single mode directly to one another. However, membership relations link individuals to collectivities, and then indirectly to each other through these shared memberships.

These considerations provide the foundation for affiliation network methodology and highlight why methodology for affiliation networks deserves special attention, beyond that for standard one-mode networks.

Of particular importance in analyzing affiliation networks is producing an interpretable simultaneous or joint model of actors, events, and the relationships between them. This chapter describes how to do this appropriately using correspondence analysis.

7.3   Example

This chapter uses as an example the memberships of twenty-two Western Hemisphere countries in fifteen regional international organizations. The actors in this example are sovereign nations in North, Central, and South America. The events are regional international trade and treaty organizations. These organizations primarily promote economic interests or political, social, or cultural cooperation among member nations. The list of organizations and their members was compiled from *Keesing's Record of World Events*, and consists of the regional organizations listed for the Americas, excluding the Caribbean (East 1996). Membership in these organizations includes all countries that are full members, but excludes observers, nations outside the hemisphere, and territories. Organizational memberships were verified using information from the *CIA Yearbook* (CIA 2000) and publications of the individual organizations, when available. Brief descriptions of the organizations are presented in the Appendix. This substantive example illustrates the political and economic alliances among countries in one part of the world, and reveals the more local basis for some of these alliances.

7.4   Notation

An affiliation network is presented in a two-mode sociomatrix. The rows of the matrix index actors and the columns index events. The set of actors is denoted by N, with g being the number of actors, and the set of events is denoted by M, with h being the number of events. We use the notation $\mathbf{A}$ for the matrix, with entries a_{ij}, where $a_{ij} = 1$ if actor i is in event j and 0 otherwise. The sociomatrix for the twenty-two countries and fifteeen organizations is presented in Table 7.4.1. In this table, both countries and organizations are listed in alphabetical order.

In this form, it is difficult to see any patterns that might be present in the network. Representational and graphic methods can help reveal and communicate patterns in the data.

7.5   Bipartite Graph

Visualization is an integral part of social network analysis (McGrath, Blythe, and Krackhardt 1997; Freeman 2000). Well-drawn graphs or diagrams bring attention to

Table 7.4.1. *Sociomatrix of Western Hemisphere Countries and Memberships in Regional Trade and Treaty Organizations*

	ACS	ALADI	Amazon Pact	Andean Pact	CARICOM	GENPLACEA	Group of Rio	G-3	IDB	MERCOSUR	NAFTA	OAS	Parlacén	San José Group	SELA
Argentina	0	1	0	0	0	1	1	0	1	1	0	1	0	0	1
Belize	1	0	0	0	1	0	0	0	1	0	0	1	0	0	1
Bolivia	0	1	1	1	0	1	1	0	1	0	0	1	0	0	1
Brazil	0	1	1	0	0	1	1	0	1	1	0	1	0	0	1
Canada	0	0	0	0	0	0	0	0	1	0	1	1	0	0	0
Chile	0	1	0	0	0	0	1	0	1	0	0	1	0	0	1
Colombia	1	1	1	1	0	1	1	1	1	0	0	1	0	0	1
Costa Rica	1	0	0	0	0	1	0	0	1	0	0	1	0	1	1
Ecuador	0	1	1	1	0	1	1	0	1	0	0	1	0	0	1
El Salvador	1	0	0	0	0	1	0	0	1	0	0	1	1	1	1
Guatemala	1	0	0	0	0	1	0	0	1	0	0	1	1	1	1
Guyana	1	0	1	0	1	1	0	0	1	0	0	1	0	0	1
Honduras	1	0	0	0	0	1	0	0	1	0	0	1	1	1	1
Mexico	1	1	0	0	0	1	1	1	1	0	1	1	0	0	1
Nicaragua	1	0	0	0	0	1	0	0	1	0	0	1	0	1	1
Panama	1	0	0	0	0	1	0	0	1	0	0	1	0	1	1
Paraguay	0	1	0	0	0	0	1	0	1	1	0	1	0	0	1
Peru	0	1	1	1	0	1	1	0	1	0	0	1	0	0	1
Suriname	1	0	1	0	0	0	0	0	1	0	0	1	0	0	1
United States	0	0	0	0	0	0	0	0	1	0	1	1	0	0	0
Uruguay	0	1	0	0	0	1	1	0	1	1	0	1	0	0	1
Venezuela	1	1	1	1	0	1	1	1	1	0	0	1	0	0	1

important features of the network, such as the presence of subgroups, the relative importance or centrality of actors (McGrath et al. 1997), and often convey descriptive information in a form that is more easily appreciated than are numeric summaries or matrices.

Because the affiliation relation always links actors to events and vice versa, all ties in an affiliation network are between entities from different sets – the two modes of the network. This means that an affiliation network can be represented as a bipartite graph. In a bipartite graph, the nodes can be partitioned into two mutually exclusive sets and all edges link nodes from different sets.

Figure 7.5.1 presents a graph of the network of countries and their memberships in regional organizations. In this figure, the points are located to highlight the fact that the graph is bipartite. Countries are roughly arrayed from south to north in terms of their geographic position, calling attention to the regional basis for many of the organizations. Consistent with the fact that a number of organizations have regional economic or political interests as their express intent, it can be seen in the graph that

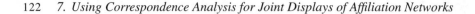

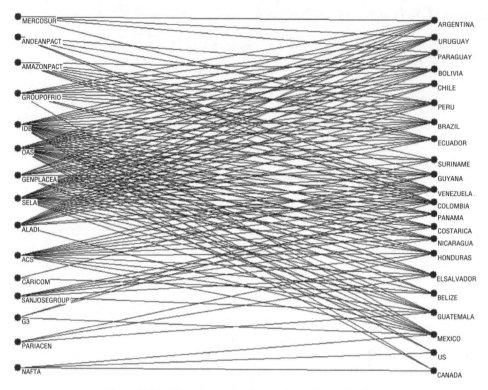

Figure 7.5.1. Bipartite graph of countries and organizations.

some organizations only have as members countries from within one region. Notably, MERCOSUR, Andean Pact, and Amazon Pact are all composed entirely of South American countries; San José Group and Parlacén include only Central American countries; and NAFTA consists entirely of North American countries. In contrast, other organizations clearly span the entire hemisphere (for example, IDB, OAS, and SELA); in fact, all countries in the set belong to IDB and OAS. (See Appendix for descriptions of these organizations.) We can also see differences among the countries in their level of participation. Some countries (for example, the United States and Canada) belong to relatively few of these organizations, whereas others belong to more than one-half of them (Ecuador, Peru, Bolivia, Colombia, Venezuela, and Mexico, for example).

In Figure 7.5.1, locations of the points are arbitrary in the sense that the formal information represented in the figure consists only of the nodes and the edges between nodes. Locations of points and the proximity of pairs or sets of points are not related in any specifiable way to the input data, nor do distances in the figure relate in an explicit way to associations between the countries and the organizations.

Alternatively, one can construct a graphic display in which location of points and distances between them convey precise information about properties of the network. The next section discusses how to accomplish this using correspondence analysis for joint graphic displays.

7.6   Joint Representation of Actors and Events

The goal is to represent the affiliation network graphically so both actors and events are presented in the same display. The problem is to find locations for points representing both actors and events so the resulting configuration provides a low-dimensional approximation to the input data and the locations of the points in the configuration correspond in an explicit way to specified aspects of the data. In the configuration, the proximity of points can show relationships among actors, among events, or between actors and events. More generally, a representation for two-mode data that include entities from both modes is called a *joint space* because it jointly displays entities from two different sets (Jacoby 1991; Coombs 1964). An important feature of the models described here is that they explicitly specify the relationship between the input data and the locations of points in the resulting configuration.

Affiliation networks are often analyzed using correspondence analysis and the resulting coordinates used in graphic displays. There is great appeal in this approach because it does provide a joint representation of the two modes in the network. Nevertheless, this approach has been the topic of considerable recent discussion and debate (Borgatti and Everett 1997; Breiger 2000; Roberts 2000; Faust et al.).

This section presents the formal basis for correspondence analysis, with special attention to how this model can be used for a joint representation of an affiliation network when interpretable distances between points from different modes are desired. Three alternatives are illustrated, first using a small hypothetical example and then using data on Western Hemisphere countries' memberships in trade and treaty organizations.

Correspondence analysis (Weller and Romney 1990; Greenacre and Blasius 1994; Blasius and Greenacre 1998) is a scaling approach usually used for studying relationships between variables in two-way arrays. It is one of a number of closely related approaches, including dual scaling (Nishisato 1994), homogeneity analysis (Gifi 1990), and optimal scaling. There are numerous articles and monographs describing the general approach. A few useful references include Weller and Romney (1990), Greenacre (1984), Greenacre and Blasius (1994), Blasius and Greenacre (1998), Nishisato (1994), Claussen (1998), and Gifi (1990).

Correspondence analysis is often used to study relationships between categorical variables in contingency tables or incidence matrices, but it has also been used to model social networks, particularly affiliation networks (Noma and Smith 1985; Wasserman and Faust 1989, 1994; Wasserman, Faust, and Galaskiewicz 1990; Schweizer 1991, 1993; Faust and Wasserman 1993; Nakao and Romney 1993; Kumbasar, Romney, and Batchelder 1994; Breiger 2000; Roberts 2000; Faust et al. 2002).

To appreciate and interpret correspondence analysis as a way of providing a joint display of an affiliation network, it is useful to clearly describe several aspects of the approach. In particular, the following points are important:

1. Decomposition of a matrix into its basic structure using singular value decomposition
2. Geometric features of correspondence analysis, especially as they pertain to the relationship between the resulting configuration and the input data

3. Alternative "scalings" that may be used for a joint representation and implica-
    tions of the alternatives
4. Dimensionality of the result

Each of these issues is described and illustrated in turn.

7.7 Matrix Decomposition

Correspondence analysis is accomplished through the decomposition of a matrix into
its basic structure (Digby and Kempton 1987; Weller and Romney 1990; Clausen 1998).
In general, singular value decomposition is defined as the decomposition of a matrix,
$\mathbf{A}$, of size g by h, as:

$$\mathbf{A} = \mathbf{X}\mathbf{\Lambda}\mathbf{Y}', \tag{7.1}$$

where $\mathbf{\Lambda}$ is a diagonal matrix of singular values, $\{\lambda_k\}$, $\mathbf{X}$ is the matrix of left singular
vectors, and $\mathbf{Y}$ is the matrix of right singular vectors. If $\mathbf{A}$ has g rows and h columns
(with h less than or equal to g), then $\mathbf{X}$ is of size $g \times h$ and $\mathbf{Y}$ is size $h \times h$. Both $\mathbf{X}$ and $\mathbf{Y}$
are orthonormal. In other words, rows of $\mathbf{X}$ and similarly columns of $\mathbf{Y}$ are orthogonal
and of unit length. Formally,

$$\mathbf{X}\mathbf{X}' = \mathbf{I} \tag{7.2}$$

$$\mathbf{Y}'\mathbf{Y} = \mathbf{I}, \tag{7.3}$$

where $\mathbf{I}$ is an identity matrix.

The same relationships can be expressed in terms of the elements of $\mathbf{X}$ and $\mathbf{Y}$:

$$\sum_{k}^{W} x_{ik}^2 = \sum_{k}^{W} y_{jk}^2 = 1 \tag{7.4}$$

$$\sum_{k}^{W} x_{ik} x_{i'k} = \sum_{k}^{W} y_{jk} y_{j'k} = 0. \tag{7.5}$$

The number of singular values and singular vectors, and hence the dimensionality of
the matrix, is equal to rank of the matrix $\mathbf{A}$. Generally, this is the number of nonnegative
singular values, which is no greater than the minimum of the number of rows (g) or
columns (h). We denote the rank of $\mathbf{A}$ as W. When the full set of W dimensions are
used, then $\mathbf{\Lambda}$, $\mathbf{X}$, and $\mathbf{Y}$ perfectly reproduce the entries in $\mathbf{A}$. When fewer than the full
set of W dimensions are used, the result approximates the entries in $\mathbf{A}$.

Correspondence analysis is a singular value decomposition not of $\mathbf{A}$, but of a "normalized" version of $\mathbf{A}$. Entries in the original matrix are divided by the square root of the
product of the row and column marginal totals prior to singular value decomposition.
Let $\mathbf{A}$ be a rectangular matrix of positive entries with g rows and h columns (where
$g \geq h$). Two diagonal matrices $\mathbf{R}^{-\frac{1}{2}}$ and $\mathbf{C}^{-\frac{1}{2}}$ have entries equal to reciprocals of the

Table 7.7.2. *Hypothetical Affiliation Network*

	Event 1	Event 2	Event 3
Affiliation matrix, **A**			
Actor 1	1	0	1
Actor 2	0	0	1
Actor 3	0	1	1
Actor 4	1	1	0
"Normalized" matrix, $\mathbf{R}^{-1/2}\,\mathbf{AC}^{-1/2}$			
Actor 1	0.500	0.000	0.408
Actor 2	0.000	0.000	0.577
Actor 3	0.000	0.500	0.408
Actor 4	0.500	0.500	0.000

row and column totals of **A**, respectively:

$$\mathbf{C}^{-\frac{1}{2}} = \text{diag}\left(\frac{1}{\sqrt{a_{+j}}}\right) \tag{7.6}$$

$$\mathbf{R}^{-\frac{1}{2}} = \text{diag}\left(\frac{1}{\sqrt{a_{i+}}}\right). \tag{7.7}$$

Correspondence analysis consists of a singular value decomposition of the matrix $\mathbf{R}^{-\frac{1}{2}}\mathbf{AC}^{-\frac{1}{2}}$ defined as:

$$\mathbf{R}^{-\frac{1}{2}}\mathbf{AC}^{-\frac{1}{2}} = \mathbf{X}\Lambda\mathbf{Y}', \tag{7.8}$$

where Λ is a diagonal matrix of singular values, $\{\lambda_k\}$, and **X** and **Y** are the left and right singular vectors (Digby and Kempton 1987; Weller and Romney 1990; Clausen 1998).

To illustrate, consider a hypothetical example of an affiliation network of four actors and three events. The matrix, **A**, is presented in Table 7.7.2, panel A. The "normalized" version of this matrix, $\mathbf{R}^{-\frac{1}{2}}\mathbf{AC}^{-\frac{1}{2}}$, is in panel B of Table 7.7.2.

The singular values, Λ, and the left and right singular vectors, **X** and **Y**, are presented in Table 7.7.3.

7.8   Relationship Between Scores and Input Data

One important feature of the decomposition is that the resulting scores (the right and left singular vectors) are explicitly related to the input data. As seen in (7.8), the decomposition $\mathbf{X}\Lambda\mathbf{Y}'$ reproduces the matrix, $\mathbf{R}^{-\frac{1}{2}}\mathbf{AC}^{-\frac{1}{2}}$. Rearranging terms shows that it also reproduces the original matrix, **A**:

$$\mathbf{A} = \mathbf{R}^{\frac{1}{2}}\mathbf{X}\Lambda\mathbf{Y}'\mathbf{C}^{\frac{1}{2}}. \tag{7.9}$$

Table 7.7.3. *Singular Value Decomposition of "Normalized" Affiliation Matrix*

	Dimension		
	1	2	3
Left singular vectors, **X**			
Actor 1	−0.535	0.120	0.707
Actor 2	−0.378	0.676	0.000
Actor 3	−0.535	0.120	−0.707
Actor 4	−0.535	−0.717	0.000
Right singular vectors, **Y**			
Event 1	−0.535	−0.463	0.707
Event 2	−0.535	−0.463	−0.707
Event 3	−0.655	0.756	0.000
Singular values, **Λ**	1.000	0.645	0.500

Or, in terms of the elements of **A**:

$$a_{ij} = \sqrt{a_{i+}a_{+j}} \sum_{k=1}^{W} x_{ik}\lambda_k y_{jk}. \tag{7.10}$$

When the number of dimensions and, hence, sets of row scores, column scores, and singular values are equal to the rank of the matrix, W, then the data are perfectly reproduced. When fewer than W dimensions are used, the data are approximated in the lower dimensional solution. Using only the first singular value and first singular vectors reproduces the expected frequencies under the model of statistical independence in the matrix **A**. Formally,

$$\frac{a_{i+}a_{+j}}{a_{++}} = \sqrt{a_{i+}a_{+j}} x_{i1}\lambda_1 y_{j1}. \tag{7.11}$$

Consequently the first "trivial" dimension is usually ignored because it is simply a function of the marginal totals and does not represent the pattern of relationship between rows and columns.

7.9 Scores for Correspondence Analysis

Correspondence analysis uses one of a number of possible rescalings of the right and left singular vectors, **X** and **Y**. The first alternative, referred to as *optimal scores*, *standard scores*, or *standard coordinates*, multiplies values in each left singular vector **X** by the square root of the reciprocal of its row proportion and multiplies each right singular vector **Y** by the square root of the reciprocal of its column proportion. These new scores, which we denote $\tilde{u}_{ik}$ and $\tilde{v}_{jk}$, are:

$$\tilde{u}_{ik} = x_{ik}\sqrt{\frac{a_{++}}{a_{i+}}} \tag{7.12}$$

for row scores, and

$$\tilde{v}_{jk} = y_{jk}\sqrt{\frac{a_{++}}{a_{+j}}} \tag{7.13}$$

for column scores. On each dimension, these scores have weighted means equal to 0.0 and weighted variances equal to 1.0:

$$\sum_{i=1}^{g} \tilde{u}_{ik}\frac{a_{i+}}{a_{++}} = \sum_{i=1}^{h} \tilde{v}_{jk}\frac{a_{+j}}{a_{++}} = 0 \tag{7.14}$$

$$\sum_{i=1}^{g} \tilde{u}_{ik}^2\frac{a_{i+}}{a_{++}} = \sum_{i=1}^{h} \tilde{v}_{jk}^2\frac{a_{+j}}{a_{++}} = 1. \tag{7.15}$$

Because the variance is equal to 1.0 on each dimension, standard scores do not express the relative importance of each dimension in accounting for the data (Weller and Romney 1990). An alternative, referred to as *principal scores* or *principal coordinates*, and which we denote u_{ik} and v_{jk}, are given by:

$$u_{ik} = \lambda_k x_{ik}\sqrt{\frac{a_{++}}{a_{i+}}} \tag{7.16}$$

for row scores, and

$$v_{jk} = \lambda_k y_{jk}\sqrt{\frac{a_{++}}{a_{+j}}} \tag{7.17}$$

for column scores. On each dimension, these scores have weighted means equal to 0.0 and weighted variances equal to the singular value squared:

$$\sum_{i=1}^{g} u_{ik}\frac{a_{i+}}{a_{++}} = \sum_{i=1}^{h} v_{jk}\frac{a_{+j}}{a_{++}} = 0 \tag{7.18}$$

$$\sum_{i=1}^{g} u_{ik}^2\frac{a_{i+}}{a_{++}} = \sum_{i=1}^{h} v_{jk}^2\frac{a_{+j}}{a_{++}} = \lambda_k^2. \tag{7.19}$$

On each dimension, the principal coordinates, u_{ik} and v_{jk}, express the importance of the dimension in terms of the singular value squared, λ_k^2. As follows, we show how the singular values are related to the inertia or total variation in the data.

In summary, correspondence analysis results in three sets of information: a set of g scores for rows of the matrix, $\mathbf{U} = \{u_{ik}\}$, for $i = 1, 2, \ldots g$ and $k = 1, 2, \ldots W$; a set of h scores for columns of the matrix, $\mathbf{V} = \{v_{jk}\}$, for $j = 1, 2, \ldots h$ and $k = 1, 2, \ldots W$; and the singular values $\Lambda = \{\lambda_k\}$ for $k = 1, 2, \ldots W$, expressing the importance of each dimension.

7.10   Asymmetric Duality

An important feature of correspondence analysis is the inherent duality in the relationship between scores for rows $\{u_{ik}\}$ and scores for columns $\{v_{jk}\}$. This relationship is critical for the "asymmetric" interpretation of some correspondence analysis displays that use $\{u_{ik}\}$ and $\{v_{jk}\}$, or some rescaling of them, as coordinates for joint display of row and column entities. The duality can be seen in that, on each dimension, the score for an object in one set is the weighted average of the scores for all objects in the other set, where the weightings are the marginal row or column proportions. This duality is expressed in the following set of equations:

$$\lambda_k u_{ik} = \sum_{j=1}^{h} \frac{a_{ij}}{a_{i+}} v_{jk} \tag{7.20}$$

and

$$\lambda_k v_{jk} = \sum_{i=1}^{g} \frac{a_{ij}}{a_{+j}} u_{ik}. \tag{7.21}$$

For an affiliation network, the score for an actor is the weighted average of the scores for the events with which it is affiliated and the score for an event is the weighted average of the scores of its constituent actors.

7.11   Chi-Square Distance Interpretations

Scores for row and column objects may be used as coordinates in graphic displays, but appropriate interpretation of the display depends on the formal relationship between distances between points representing row and/or column entities and chi-square distances calculated on the input data. This relationship is at the heart of the interpretative debate about which of a number of alternative correspondence analysis scores should be used for graphic displays. The chi-square distances also express the overall variability (inertia) in the data and are used to measure how well the configuration fits the input data.

Distances in correspondence analysis displays represent the chi-square distances between row or column profiles. The profile for a row is defined as the entry in each cell divided by its corresponding row total, $\{\frac{a_{ij}}{a_{i+}}\}$, for $j = 1, 2, \ldots h$. A column profile similarly is defined as the entry in each cell divided by the column total, $\{\frac{a_{ij}}{a_{+j}}\}$, for $i = 1, 2, \ldots g$. The row and column profiles for the hypothetical example are presented in Table 7.11.4. Profiles of different rows (or different columns) can be compared with each other to measure the distances between rows (or between columns). The chi-square distance between profiles for rows i and i', denoted, $d(i, i')$ is given by:

$$d(i, i') = \sqrt{\sum_{j=1}^{h} \frac{\left(\frac{a_{ij}}{a_{i+}} - \frac{a_{i'j}}{a_{i'+}} \right)^2}{\frac{a_{+j}}{a_{++}}}}. \tag{7.22}$$

Table 7.11.4. *Row and Column Profiles for Hypothetical Affiliation Network*

Row profiles

	Event 1	Event 2	Event 3	Sum
Actor 1	0.500	0.000	0.500	1.000
Actor 2	0.000	0.000	1.000	1.000
Actor 3	0.000	0.500	0.500	1.000
Actor 4	0.500	0.500	0.000	1.000
Average row profile	0.286	0.286	0.429	

Column profiles

	Event 1	Event 2	Event 3	Average Column Profile
Actor 1	0.500	0.000	0.333	0.286
Actor 2	0.000	0.000	0.333	0.143
Actor 3	0.000	0.500	0.333	0.286
Actor 4	0.500	0.500	0.000	0.286
Sum	1.000	1.000	1.000	

A parallel definition for the chi-square distance between two column profiles, j and j', is:

$$d(j, j') = \sqrt{\sum_{i=1}^{g} \frac{\left(\frac{a_{ij}}{a_{+j}} - \frac{a_{ij'}}{a_{+j'}} \right)^2}{\frac{a_{i+}}{a_{++}}}}. \qquad (7.23)$$

These are the interpoint distances depicted in graphic displays of correspondence analysis. The formal relationship between the chi-square distances and the row and column scores is presented in detail as follows (7.29 and 7.30).

Chi-square distances are also used to compare row or column profiles to the "average," or marginal, row or column profile to assess the total variation in the data. The average row profile is defined as the set of marginal column proportions, $i^+ = \{\frac{a_{+j}}{a_{++}}\}$ for $j = 1, 2, \ldots h$, and similarly the average column profile is defined as the set of marginal row proportions, $j^+ = \{\frac{a_{i+}}{a_{++}}\}i = 1, 2, \ldots g$,. The chi-square distance between an individual row (or column) and the average row (or column) profile is defined as:

$$d(i, i^+) = \sqrt{\sum_{j=1}^{h} \frac{\left(\frac{a_{ij}}{a_{i+}} - \frac{a_{+j}}{a_{++}} \right)^2}{\frac{a_{+j}}{a_{++}}}} \qquad (7.24)$$

and

$$d(j, j^+) = \sqrt{\sum_{i=1}^{g} \frac{\left(\frac{a_{ij}}{a_{+j}} - \frac{a_{i+}}{a_{++}} \right)^2}{\frac{a_{i+}}{a_{++}}}}. \qquad (7.25)$$

Table 7.11.5. *Chi-Square Distances Between Row Profiles and Between Column Profiles, and Distances Between Profiles and Mean Profile on Diagonal*

Chi-square distances between row profiles

	Actor 1	Actor 2	Actor 3	Actor 4
Actor 1	0.677			
Actor 2	1.208	1.155		
Actor 3	1.323	1.208	0.677	
Actor 4	1.208	2.021	1.208	0.866

Chi-square distances between column profiles

	Event 1	Event 2	Event 3
Event 1	0.866		
Event 2	1.323	0.866	
Event 3	1.462	1.462	0.745

Table 7.11.5 presents the chi-square distances between row profiles and between column profiles for the hypothetical example. These are the distances that are represented in correspondence analysis displays. On the diagonals of the arrays, Table 7.11.5 presents the distances between rows (and columns) and the average row (and column) profile.

7.12   Inertia

In correspondence analysis, *inertia* quantifies the total amount of variation in the data (Greenacre 1984; Greenacre and Blasius 1994; Clausen 1998). Inertia is calculated as the weighted sum of the squared chi-square distances between the row profiles and the average row profile, where the weights are marginal row proportions, or similarly, the weighted sum of the squared chi-square distances between the column profiles and the average column profile, where the weights are the marginal column proportions (Greenacre 1984; Greenacre and Hastie 1987). The total inertia is given by the following equations:

$$\sum_{i=1}^{g} \frac{a_{i+}}{a_{++}} d(i, i^{+})^2 \tag{7.26}$$

or

$$\sum_{j=1}^{h} \frac{a_{+j}}{a_{++}} d(j, j^{+})^2. \tag{7.27}$$

These expressions show that total inertia can be decomposed into the contributions from each of the entities (rows or columns) in the data. The total inertia is also equal to the sum of the squared singular values:

$$\sum_{k=1}^{W} \lambda_k^2. \tag{7.28}$$

This allows another decomposition of the total inertia into the amount of variation that is accounted for by each dimension in the model by considering each λ_k^2, for $k = 1, 2, \ldots W$.

7.13   Within-Set Distance Comparisons

Distances between points in graphic display using correspondence analysis scores are interpretable with respect to specific patterns in the input data, but proper interpretation requires both correct selection of scores and recognition that the distances are chi-square distances. First, consider the distance between two rows, i and i'. This distance is the chi-square distance between the profiles for rows i and i' (7.22). The reproduced or fitted distance, $\hat{d}(i, i')$, is calculated from the correspondence analysis row scores, $\{u_{ik}\}$ and $\{u_{i'k}\}$ as:

$$\hat{d}(i, i') = \sqrt{\sum_{k=1}^{W} (u_{ik} - u_{i'k})^2}. \tag{7.29}$$

Similarly, the distance between two columns, j and j' (7.23), is calculated from the column scores $\{v_{jk}\}$ and $\{v_{j'k}\}$ as:

$$\hat{d}(j, j') = \sqrt{\sum_{k=1}^{W} (v_{jk} - v_{j'k})^2}. \tag{7.30}$$

When the full set of W dimensions is used, the chi-square distances between row profiles and between column profiles are perfectly reproduced, so $\hat{d}(i, i') = d(i, i')$ and $\hat{d}(j, j') = d(j, j')$ for all pairs of rows and all pairs of columns. When fewer than W dimensions are used, the fitted distance approximates the chi-square distance between row or column profiles in the original data. These distance interpretations hinge on correct selection of scores. The relationship between chi-square distances between row (or column) profiles and fitted distances (7.29 and 7.30) holds when scores are scaled as principal coordinates (7.16 and 7.17).

7.14   Between-Set Comparisons

Equations (7.29) and (7.30) express distances between entities within the same set. The problem of interpreting distances arises when comparing locations of points from different sets. The general problem has been widely discussed in the correspondence analysis literature (Carroll, Green, and Schaffer 1986, 1987, 1989; Greenacre 1989). In fact, some authors argue that interset distance comparisons are not even justified

(Nishisato 1994: p. 113). Unfortunately, these are the distances between actors and events in an affiliation network, and are exactly the comparisons of most interest if we take seriously the duality argument and the goal of constructing an interpretable joint space. Under what conditions are these interset relationships interpretable?

Returning to (7.16) and (7.17), suppose we want to express the score for an actor, u_{ik}, as function of the scores for the events to which it belongs, v_{jk}, for $j = 1, 2, \ldots h$. This is accomplished by using actor scores expressed in principal coordinates paired with events expressed as standard coordinates. The relationship between row scores, u_{ik}, and column scores, $\tilde{v}_{jk}$, is:

$$u_{ik} = \sum_{j=1}^{h} \frac{a_{ij}}{a_{i+}} \tilde{v}_{jk}. \tag{7.31}$$

With the row scores in principal coordinates, u_{ik}, and the column scores in standard coordinates, $\tilde{v}_{jk}$, the score for a row point is the weighted average of the scores for the column points. However, the reverse is not true. If one wants to express the score for a column point, v_{jk}, as the average of the scores for the rows, u_{jk}, for $i = 1, 2, \ldots k$, then columns in principal coordinates, v_{jk}, are paired with standard coordinates for rows. The relationship between column scores, v_{jk}, and row scores, $\tilde{u}_{ik}$, is:

$$v_{jk} = \sum_{i=1}^{g} \frac{a_{ij}}{a_{+j}} \tilde{u}_{ik}. \tag{7.32}$$

With column scores in principal coordinates, v_{jk}, and row scores in standard coordinates, $\tilde{u}_{jk}$, the score for a column point is interpreted as the weighted average of the scores for the row points.

In summary, for an asymmetric joint display there are two possible sets of scores that might be used: row scores, u_{ik}, paired with column scores, $\tilde{v}_{jk}$, or column scores, v_{jk}, paired with row scores, $\tilde{u}_{jk}$. Either of these gives an "asymmetric" depiction of the relationship between entities from the two modes. The choice of which to use depends on which relationships in the data one wants to highlight. Unlike distances within sets, interset comparison is only legitimate when the location of a single point from one set is compared with the locations of *all* points in the other set, but not when two individual points from different sets are compared.

7.15   Symmetric Representation

An alternative approach, which permits a "symmetric" view of the distances between row and column points, and in which interset distance comparisons are interpretable, has been proposed by Carroll et al. (1986). Carroll et al. viewed the problem as one of *multiple correspondence analysis*. Using this approach, observations in a two-way contingency table are reexpressed as a cases-by-variables data array called a *pseudo-contingency table*. In the pseudocontingency table, a two-way contingency table with r rows, c columns, and N observations is transformed into an array in which each row in the new array is an observation in the original table, and the row and column entities in

Table 7.15.6. *Pseudocontingency Table for Hypothetical Affiliation Network*

Actor 1	Actor 2	Actor 3	Actor 4	Event 1	Event 2	Event 3
1	0	0	0	1	0	0
1	0	0	0	0	0	1
0	1	0	0	0	0	1
0	0	1	0	0	1	0
0	0	1	0	0	0	1
0	0	0	1	1	0	0
0	0	0	1	0	1	0

the new array are coded as indicator variables for the variables in the original table. The pseudocontingency table has N rows (one for each observation) and $r + c$ columns (the total number of categories of the row variable plus the total number of categories of the column variable). This arrangement is standard in multiple correspondence analysis where more than two variables can be studied by including additional sets of indicator variables. For an affiliation network, the pseudocontingency table, which we denote by **F**, has $g + h$ columns, one for each actor and one for each event, and as many rows as there are entries of 1 in the affiliation network, a_{++}.

Table 7.15.6 shows the pseudocontingency table for the hypothetical example of four actors and three events. This table has seven columns (four actors plus three events) and seven rows (the number of 1s in the affiliation matrix). Notice that the first row of the table codes actor 1 attending event 1, the second row codes actor 1 attending event 3, and so on. Each row in the table has exactly two entries equal to 1 and the remaining entries equal to 0. The column totals are the marginal row and column totals from the original affiliation network – for actors the totals are a_{i+}, and for events the totals are a_{+j}.

Correspondence analysis of this array results in two sets of scores: one for each column of the table and one for each row of the table. Usually, the scores for the rows will not be of interest. As in correspondence analysis of a two-way table, scores for categories of the column variables represent the chi-square distances between the column profiles. Because all row totals in the pseudocontingency table are equal to the number of variables (two in our case) and there are as many rows as there are observations (a_{++}), the total number of 1s in the table is equal to $2 \times a_{++}$ and all marginal row proportions are equal:

$$\frac{f_{i+}}{f_{++}} = \frac{1}{a_{++}}. \tag{7.33}$$

As a consequence, the chi-square distance between two column profiles simplifies and is equal to:

$$d(j, j') = \sqrt{a_{++} \sum_{i=1}^{N} \left(\frac{f_{ij}}{f_{+j}} - \frac{f_{ij'}}{f_{+j'}} \right)} \tag{7.34}$$

(also see Carroll et al. 1986: p. 275).

The approach proposed by Carroll, Green, and Schaffer uses correspondence analysis of the matrix, $\mathbf{F}$, through a singular value decomposition of the matrix $\mathbf{R}^{-\frac{1}{2}}\mathbf{FC}^{-\frac{1}{2}} = \mathbf{X}\Delta\mathbf{Y}'$. The scores for rows and columns using Carroll, Green, and Schaffer's approach, which we denote $\ddot{u}_{ik}$ and $\ddot{v}_{jk}$, are then scaled as principal coordinates. Because the columns of $\mathbf{F}$ index both actors and events, using these scores, distances between points from different sets are interpretable as chi-square distances between columns of the pseudocontingency table.

These scores are related to the principal coordinates and standard coordinates for a correspondence analysis of $\mathbf{A}$ by the following equations:

$$\ddot{u}_{ik} = \tilde{u}_{ik}(1+\lambda_k)^{\frac{1}{2}} = \frac{u_{ik}}{\lambda_k}(1+\lambda_k)^{\frac{1}{2}} \tag{7.35}$$

$$\ddot{v}_{jk} = \tilde{v}_{jk}(1+\lambda_k)^{\frac{1}{2}} = \frac{v_{jk}}{\lambda_k}(1+\lambda_k)^{\frac{1}{2}}. \tag{7.36}$$

The singular values, $\ddot{\lambda}_k$, from the Carroll et al. (1986) approach are related to the singular values for the original two-way contingency table as:

$$\ddot{\lambda}_k = \frac{\lambda_k + 1}{2}. \tag{7.37}$$

The Carroll, Green, and Schaffer coordinates have weighted means of zero on each dimension:

$$\sum_{i=1}^{g} \ddot{u}_{ik}\frac{a_{i+}}{a_{++}} = \sum_{i=1}^{h} \ddot{v}_{jk}\frac{a_{+j}}{a_{++}} = 0. \tag{7.38}$$

On each dimension, the weighted variances are equal to the squares of the singular values of the normalized pseudocontingency table. Carroll et al. (1986) demonstrated that for an array with two variables this is equal to $\frac{\lambda_k+1}{2}$, where the λ_k are the singular values of the original contingency table. Thus, for the Carroll, Green, and Schaffer coordinates, the weighed variances on each dimension are:

$$\sum_{i=1}^{g} \ddot{u}_{ik}^2\frac{a_{i+}}{a_{++}} = \sum_{i=1}^{h} \ddot{v}_{jk}^2\frac{a_{+j}}{a_{++}} = \frac{\lambda_k + 1}{2}. \tag{7.39}$$

There is now a *symmetric* interpretation of distances between objects from different sets. However, this symmetry comes at a cost. The chi-square distances between objects in the *same* set are completely determined by the row and column marginal totals in the original matrix, $\mathbf{A}$ (Carroll et al. 1986; Greenacre 1989). For example, the chi-square distance between rows i and i' of the original matrix is equal to:

$$d(i, i') = \sqrt{\frac{1}{\frac{a_{i+}}{a_{++}}} + \frac{1}{\frac{a_{i'+}}{a_{++}}}} \tag{7.40}$$

(Carroll et al. 1986: p. 275; Greenacre 1989: p. 359). A similar result holds for the distance between two columns of the original matrix. As Greenacre (1989) observed, because these within-set distances are fundamental to correspondence analysis of a two-way array, the fact that they are completely determined by the marginal totals in the pseudocontingency table limits the usefulness of this approach. Nevertheles,

Table 7.16.7. *Correspondence Analysis Scores for Hypothetical Network*

	Principal Coordinates		Standard Coordinates		Carroll, Green, Schaffer	
	1	2	1	2	1	2
Actor 1	−0.144	0.661	−0.224	1.323	−0.203	1.146
Actor 2	−1.155	0.000	−1.789	0.000	−1.623	0.000
Actor 3	−0.144	−0.661	−0.224	−1.323	−0.203	−1.146
Actor 4	0.866	0.000	1.342	0.000	1.217	0.000
Event 1	0.559	0.661	0.866	1.323	0.786	1.146
Event 2	0.559	−0.661	0.866	−1.323	0.786	−1.146
Event 3	−0.745	0.000	−1.155	0.000	−1.047	0.000

because of the interpretability of interset distances, it remains an option when a joint representation is desired.

7.16 Comparing Solutions

Let us now compare the results of these three possible scalings of correspondence analysis scores, beginning with the small hypothetical example. Table 7.16.7 provides sets of scores for the hypothetical example using each of the three approaches. Figures 7.16.2,

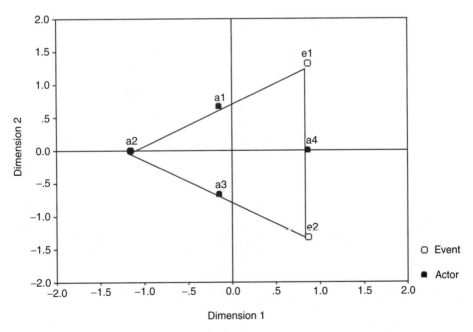

Figure 7.16.2. Correspondence analysis of hypothetical network: actors in principal coordinates and events in standard coordinates.

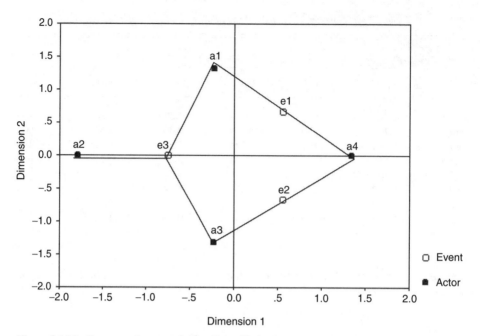

Figure 7.16.3. Correspondence analysis of hypothetical network: actors in standard coordinates and events in principal coordinates.

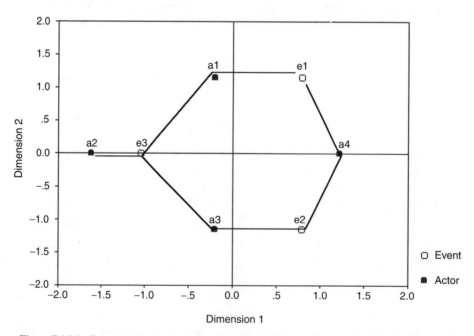

Figure 7.16.4. Correspondence analysis of hypothetical network: actors and events in Carroll, Green, and Schaffer coordinates.

7.16.3, and 7.16.4 present the first two nontrivial dimensions for each approach. Because there are four rows and three columns in the hypothetical network, the two-dimensional solution perfectly accounts for the data. The edges in the affiliation network are drawn on each figure to highlight the relationship between point locations and ties in the original network. Figure 7.16.2 shows the actors in principal coordinates and the events in standard coordinates. In this figure, the score for an actor (row) is the weighted average of the scores for the events (columns) to which it belongs. Because the two-dimensional solution perfectly fits the data, this interpretation is perfectly reflected in the two-dimensional graph, as can be seen from the fact that actors are literally "between" the events to which they belong. Notice that in this figure actor 2 and event 3 are in the same location because actor 2 only belongs to event 3. If a higher-dimensional solution were required to reproduce the data, the interpretation would only be approximated in a lower dimensions. Notice that in this figure the points for events (in standard coordinates) are around the perimeter of the figure, and points for actors (in principal coordinates) do not fall outside this polygon defined by the event points. This is generally the case because points in standard coordinates define the space onto which the other set of points are plotted (Greenacre and Hastie 1987). In contrast, Figure 7.16.3 reverses the roles of actors and events, presenting the events in principal coordinates and actors in standard coordinates. In this display, events are at the centroids of their constituent actors. The actors (in standard coordinates) are on the perimeter of the display, and events do not fall outside the polygon defined by the actor points. In both Figures 7.16.2 and 7.16.3, interpretation of the distances between actors and events is asymmetric and depends on which scaling is used. Distances relating points from different sets require situating a point from one set (in principal coordinates) in relation to *all* points from the other set (in standard coordinates). Figure 7.16.4 uses the Carroll, Green, and Schaffer scaling to produce display with a symmetric interpretation. In this figure, distance between a pair of points from different sets is interpreted as the chi-square distance between their respective column profiles in the pseudocontingency table.

7.17 Distances Versus Dimensions

Figures 7.16.2, 7.16.3, and 7.16.4 appear to provide rather different depictions of the affiliation network. Certainly, their mathematical properties and the distance interpretations allowed by the three are different. Nevertheless, it is useful to explore more fully the formal relationships among the three approaches and also to display these relationships graphically. First, notice that the principal coordinates, u_{ik} and v_{jk}; standard coordinates, $\tilde{u}_{ik}$ and $\tilde{v}_{jk}$; and the Carroll, Green, and Schaffer coordinates, $\ddot{u}_{ik}$ and $\ddot{v}_{jk}$, are, on each dimension, linear functions of one another. These relationships are:

$$\tilde{u}_{ik} = \frac{u_{ik}}{\lambda_k} \tag{7.41}$$

$$\ddot{u}_{ik} = \frac{u_{ik}}{\lambda_k}(1 + \lambda_k)^{\frac{1}{2}} \tag{7.42}$$

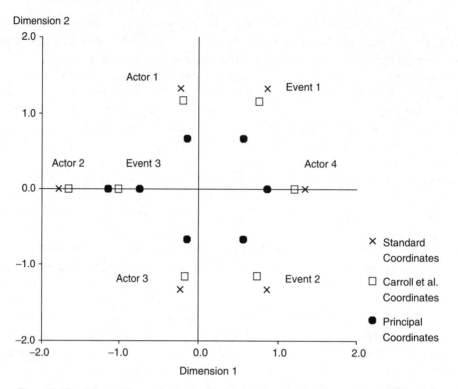

Figure 7.17.5. Three different scalings of correspondence analysis scores for hypothetical affiliation network.

$$\tilde{v}_{jk} = \frac{v_{jk}}{\lambda_k} \tag{7.43}$$

$$\ddot{v}_{jk} = \frac{v_{jk}}{\lambda_k}(1 + \lambda_k)^{\frac{1}{2}}. \tag{7.44}$$

All three sets of scores have weighted means equal to 0, but they differ in their variances. Scores in principal coordinates have weighted variance equal to the square of the singular value on each dimension (7.19). Standard coordinates have weighted variance equal to 1 on each dimension (7.15). Finally, the Carroll, Green, and Schaffer coordinates have weighted variances equal to the squares of the singular values of the normalized pseudocontingency table (7.39). The implication of these relationships is that when the scores are used to define coordinate axes for graphic displays, the effect is a "stretching" or "shrinking" of each axis, as a function of the singular values on the various dimensions (Weller and Romney 1990). The overall impact of this stretching depends on how far the singular values depart from 1.0. For the hypothetical example, $\lambda_1 = 0.645$ and $\lambda_2 = 0.5$. The variances of principal coordinates, standard coordinates, and Carroll, Green, and Schaffer coordinates on the first dimension are 0.416, 1.0, and 0.822, and on the second dimension they are 0.25, 1.0, and 0.75, respectively.

The graphic impact of these alternatives is shown in Figure 7.17.5. In this figure, points for both actors and events in the hypothetical example are presented using all three alternatives in the same plot. By focusing on the positions of a single point across the different scalings, the stretching and shrinking effect is clear. Points in standard coordinates (variance of 1.0 on each dimension) are on the outside, points using the Carroll, Green, and Schaffer scores are next (variances of 0.822 and 0.75 on first and second dimensions), and the points in principal coordinates are on the inside (variances of 0.416 and 0.25).

7.18   Correspondence Analysis of Western Hemisphere Countries

Let us now return to the example of Western Hemisphere countries and their memberships in trade and treaty organizations. The affiliation network matrix for this example was presented in Table 7.4.1. Scores from the three different approaches are presented in Tables 7.18.8 and 7.18.9. Figures 7.18.6, 7.18.7, and 7.18.8 display the first two dimensions of each solution. Figure 7.18.6 uses principal coordinates for organizations and standard coordinates for countries. In this figure, each organization is the centroid of its member countries. In Figure 7.18.7, countries are presented in principal coordinates and organizations in standard coordinates. In this figure, each country is at the centroid of the organizations to which it belongs. Figure 7.18.8 uses the Carroll, Green, and Schaffer scores for coordinates. In this figure, the distance between a country and an organization is the chi-square distance between their respective columns in the pseudocontingency matrix (which is not presented).

Table 7.18.10 provides the squared singular values and percents of inertia for the first eleven dimensions. Using correspondence analysis of the affiliation matrix, **A**, the first five dimensions together account for 88.47% of the total inertia. In the Carroll, Green, and Schaffer approach the first five dimensions account for 94.66% of the variance. Table 7.18.10 also presents the contributions to the total inertia by each country and by each organization. Countries whose organizational memberships differ from the marginal profile (notably United States and Canada, but also Belize and Guyana) make larger contributions to the total inertia than do countries whose memberships are more similar to the marginal profile (notably, Chile, Bolivia, Ecuador, and Peru). Recall that this is measured as the chi-square distance between each profile and the marginal profile (7.22 and 7.23). Similarly, organizations whose memberships differ from the marginal distribution of members (e.g., CARICOM and NAFTA) contribute more to the total inertia than do organizations whose memberships are more similar to the marginal profile (e.g., SELA, OAS, and IDB).

Comparing Figures 7.18.6, 7.18.7 and 7.18.8, it can be seen that the major patterns are strikingly similar. Each has three clear branches reflecting the regional organization of this network. The first dimension contrasts South American countries and organizations on the one hand and Central American countries and organizations on the other hand. On the right are Parlacén and the San José Group, both organizations of Central American countries, along with El Salvador, Guatemala, and other Central American countries. On the lower left of each figure are Andean Pact, MERCOSUR, ALADI, Group of Rio, and Amazon Pact, organizations whose members are primarily in South America, along with Paraguay, Uruguay, Peru, Ecuador, and other South American countries. In all three figures, the second dimension clearly distinguishes Canada and the United States (both North American countries) along with NAFTA from other countries

Table 7.18.8. *Correspondence Analysis Scores for Organizations*

Organization	Principal Coordinates			Standard Coordinates			Carroll, Green, and Schaffer Coordinates			Contribution to Inertia	
	1	2	3	1	2	3	1	2	3	Total	Percent
ACS	0.73	-0.13	0.32	1.21	-0.24	0.71	1.08	-0.21	0.61	0.067	5.414
ALADI	-0.80	-0.15	-0.22	-1.34	-0.28	-0.49	-1.20	-0.25	-0.42	0.059	4.713
Amazon Pact	-0.52	-0.33	0.57	-0.87	-0.61	1.26	-0.77	-0.53	1.07	0.076	6.124
Andean Pact	-0.80	-0.37	0.33	-1.33	-0.69	0.73	-1.19	-0.60	0.62	0.081	6.518
CARICOM	0.74	-0.13	2.83	1.24	-0.25	6.26	1.11	-0.22	5.34	0.158	12.673
GENPLACEA	0.14	-0.22	-0.13	0.23	-0.42	-0.29	0.20	-0.36	-0.25	0.027	2.200
Group of Rio	-0.80	-0.15	-0.22	-1.34	-0.28	-0.49	-1.20	-0.25	-0.42	0.059	4.713
G-3	-0.55	0.22	0.33	-0.93	0.41	0.73	-0.83	0.36	0.62	0.083	6.696
IDB	0.08	0.23	0.01	0.14	0.43	0.01	0.12	0.38	0.01	0.015	1.209
MERCOSUR	-0.93	-0.26	-0.92	-1.56	-0.49	-2.03	-1.39	-0.43	-1.73	0.117	9.415
NAFTA	-0.02	3.41	-0.11	-0.04	6.37	-0.25	-0.04	5.58	-0.22	0.239	19.180
OAS	0.08	0.23	0.01	0.14	0.43	0.01	0.12	0.38	0.01	0.015	1.209
Parlacén	1.69	-0.38	-0.91	2.83	-0.72	-2.01	2.53	-0.63	-1.72	0.123	9.838
San José Group	1.44	-0.30	-0.61	2.40	-0.57	-1.36	2.15	-0.50	-1.16	0.114	9.167
SELA	0.08	-0.19	0.02	0.13	-0.36	0.05	0.12	-0.32	0.04	0.012	0.932
Total										1.246	100.00

Table 7.18.9. *Correspondence Analysis Scores for Countries*

Country	Principal Coordinates			Standard Coordinates			Carroll, Green, and Schaffer Coordinates			Contribution to Inertia	
	1	2	3	1	2	3	1	2	3	Total	Percent
Argentina	-0.52	-0.14	-0.46	-0.86	-0.26	-1.02	-0.77	-0.23	-0.87	0.043	3.487
Belize	0.57	0.00	1.41	0.96	0.00	3.12	0.86	0.00	2.66	0.111	8.914
Bolivia	-0.53	-0.22	0.10	-0.89	-0.41	0.22	-0.79	-0.36	0.19	0.035	2.787
Brazil	-0.56	-0.20	-0.25	-0.93	-0.37	-0.55	-0.84	-0.32	-0.46	0.041	3.288
Canada	0.08	2.41	-0.08	0.13	4.49	-0.17	0.12	3.94	-0.15	0.121	9.722
Chile	-0.45	-0.01	-0.18	-0.76	-0.02	-0.40	-0.68	-0.02	-0.34	0.031	2.469
Colombia	-0.40	-0.16	0.22	-0.66	-0.30	0.49	-0.59	-0.26	0.42	0.045	3.621
Costa Rica	0.71	-0.12	-0.14	1.18	-0.23	-0.32	1.06	-0.20	-0.27	0.035	2.811
Ecuador	-0.53	-0.22	0.10	-0.89	-0.41	0.22	-0.79	-0.36	0.19	0.035	2.787
El Salvador	1.01	-0.21	-0.41	1.69	-0.38	-0.91	1.51	-0.34	-0.77	0.065	5.224
Guatemala	1.01	-0.21	-0.41	1.69	-0.38	-0.91	1.51	-0.34	-0.77	0.065	5.224
Guyana	0.32	-0.14	1.15	0.53	-0.27	2.54	0.48	-0.24	2.16	0.083	6.657
Honduras	1.01	-0.21	-0.41	1.69	-0.38	-0.91	1.51	-0.34	-0.77	0.065	5.224
Mexico	-0.20	0.67	0.00	-0.33	1.25	0.00	-0.30	1.10	0.00	0.065	5.242
Nicaragua	0.71	-0.12	-0.14	1.18	-0.23	-0.32	1.06	-0.20	-0.27	0.035	2.811
Panama	0.71	-0.12	-0.14	1.18	-0.23	-0.32	1.06	-0.20	-0.27	0.035	2.811
Paraguay	-0.64	-0.09	-0.49	-1.07	-0.17	-1.08	-0.96	-0.15	-0.92	0.055	4.407
Peru	-0.53	-0.22	0.1	-0.89	-0.41	0.22	-0.79	-0.36	0.19	0.035	2.787
Suriname	0.15	-0.07	0.41	0.25	-0.13	0.90	0.23	-0.11	0.77	0.036	2.894
United States	0.08	2.41	-0.08	0.13	4.49	-0.17	0.12	3.94	-0.15	0.121	9.722
Uruguay	-0.52	-0.14	-0.46	-0.86	-0.26	-1.02	-0.77	-0.23	-0.87	0.043	3.487
Venezuela	-0.40	-0.16	0.22	-0.66	-0.30	0.49	-0.59	-0.26	0.42	0.045	3.621
Total										1.246	100.000

141

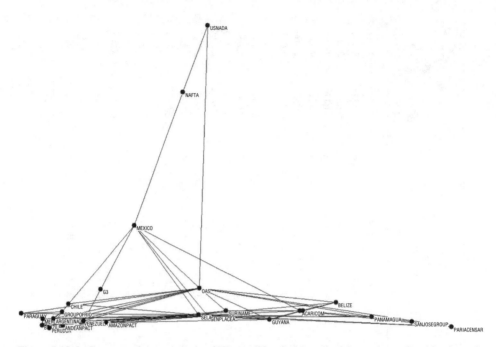

Figure 7.18.6. Correspondence analysis of Western Hemisphere countries and memberships in trade and treaty organizations. Countries in standard coordinates and organizations in principal coordinates.

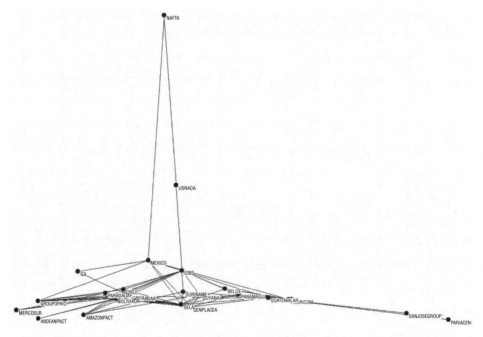

Figure 7.18.7. Correspondence analysis of Western hemisphere countries and memberships in trade and treaty organizations. Countries in principal coordinates and organizations in standard coordinates.

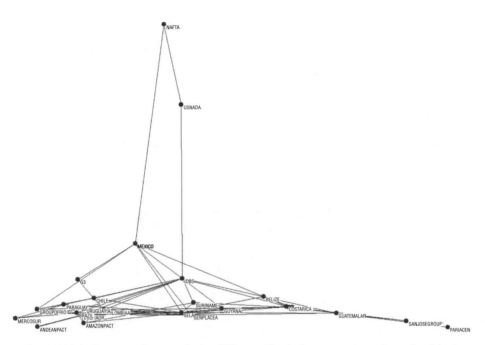

Figure 7.18.8. Correspondence analysis of Western Hemisphere countries and memberships in trade and treaty organizations, both countries and organizations in Carroll, Green, and Schaffer coordinates.

and organizations. Recall that Canada, the United States, and NAFTA all contributed substantially to the total inertia in the data. In all three figures, organizations whose members span the hemisphere (SELA, OAS, and IDB) are in the center at the bottom of the figure. As noted previously, SELA, OAS, and IDB all have membership profiles that are similar to the marginal profile, and their contributions to the total inertia are relatively small. The three figures do differ in minor details, which can be understood by recalling that the different approaches essentially stretch or shrink axes relative to one another.

7.19   Conclusion

In conclusion, let us return to the issue raised at the beginning of this chapter, in particular, the formal basis for an interpretable joint display of actors and events in an affiliation network. As the illustrations in this chapter demonstrate, joint graphic displays using correspondence analysis are possible, but require careful specification of which of a number of possible solutions is used for the display. The problem resides in appropriate interpretation of within-set and between-set distances between points. These interpretations require clear specification of which scores are used in order to avoid improper conclusions. That said, when viewed in concert, the various approaches are strikingly similar, at least for within-set comparisons.

When studying an affiliation network, the choice of which sets of scores should be used depends on theoretical and interpretative considerations. In an affiliation network,

Table 7.18.10. *Singular Values and Percent of Inertia Accounted for in Correspondence Analysis of Countries and Organizations*

Dimension	Principal Coordinates or Standard Coordinates				Carroll, Green, and Schaffer Scaling			
	Singular Values	Squared Singular Values	Percent of Inertia	Cumulative Percent of Inertia	Singular Values	Squared Singular Values	Percent of Inertia	Cumulative Percent of Inertia
1	0.598	0.358	28.69	28.69	0.894	0.799	29.71	29.71
2	0.536	0.287	23.05	51.73	0.876	0.767	28.53	58.24
3	0.452	0.204	16.39	68.12	0.852	0.726	26.99	85.23
4	0.416	0.173	13.88	82.00	0.416	0.173	6.43	91.66
5	0.284	0.081	6.47	88.47	0.284	0.081	3.00	94.66
6	0.247	0.061	4.89	93.37	0.247	0.061	2.27	96.93
7	0.196	0.038	3.08	96.45	0.196	0.038	1.43	98.35
8	0.169	0.029	2.29	98.74	0.169	0.029	1.06	99.42
9	0.110	0.012	0.97	99.71	0.110	0.012	0.45	99.87
10	0.049	0.002	0.19	99.90	0.049	0.002	0.09	99.95
11	0.035	0.001	0.10	100.00	0.035	0.001	0.05	1.000
Total		1.247				2.690		

one might view the social position of an actor as being defined by the social events in which it participates. With respect to the current example of Western Hemisphere countries, one could view a nation as described by the international organizations to which it belongs. Such a theoretical interpretation suggests that in a graphic display the location of an actor should be a function of the events with which it is affiliated. Alternatively, one could view the social location of an event as a function of its members. Again, for the current example, one would view an organization as defined by its constituent countries. A third possibility is that neither set of entities has precedence and that the relationships should be interpreted symmetrically. Correspondence analysis approaches exist for all three of these interpretations.

References

Blasius, Jorg, and Michael Greenacre. 1998. *Visualization of Categorical Data*. New York: Academic Press.

Borgatti, Stephen P., and Martin Everett. 1997. "Network analysis of 2-mode data." *Social Networks*, 19:243–269.

Brazill, Timothy J., and Bernard Groffman. 2002. "Factor analysis versus multidimensional scaling: Binary choice roll-call voting and the U.S. Supreme Court." *Social Networks*, 24:201–229.

Breiger, Ronald L. 1974. "The duality of persons and groups." *Social Forces*, 53:181–190.

Breiger, Ronald L. 2000. "A tool kit for practice theory." *Poetics*, 27:91–115.

Cappell, Charles L., and Thomas M. Guterbock. 1992. "Visible colleges: The social and conceptual structure of sociology specialties." *American Sociological Review*, 57:266–273.

Carroll, J. Douglas, Paul E. Green, and Catherine M. Schaffer. 1986. "Interpoint distance comparisons in correspondence analysis solutions." *Journal of Marketing Research*, 23:271–280.

Carroll, J. Douglas, Paul E. Green, and Catherine M. Schaffer. 1987. "Comparing interpoint distances in correspondence analysis solutions: A clarification." *Journal of Marketing Research*, 26:445–450.

Carroll, J. Douglas, Paul E. Green, and Catherine M. Schaffer. 1989. "Reply to Greenacre's commentary on the Carroll-Green-Schaffer scaling of two-way correspondence analysis solutions." *Journal of Marketing Research*, 26:366–368.

CIA. 2000. *CIA World Fact Book*. Available at: http://www.odci.gov/cia/publications/factbook/.

Claussen, Sten-Erik. 1998. *Applied Correspondence Analysis*. Thousand Oaks, CA: Sage.

Coombs, Clyde. 1964. *A Theory of Data*. New York: Wiley.

Davis, A., B. Gardner, and M. R. Gardner. 1941. *Deep South*. Chicago: University of Chicago Press.

Digby, P. G. N., and R. A. Kempton. 1987. *Multivariate Analysis of Ecological Communities*. London: Chapman and Hall.

Doreian, Patrick. 1979. "On the evolution of group and network structure." *Social Networks*, 2:235–252.

East, Roger (ed.). 1996. *Keesing's Record of World Events*. London: Longman.

Ennis, James G. 1992. "The social organization of sociological knowledge: Modeling the intersection of specialties." *American Sociological Review*, 57:259–265.

Faust, Katherine. 1997. "Centrality in affiliation networks." *Social Networks*, 19:157–191.

Faust, Katherine, and Stanley Wasserman. 1993. "Correlation and association models for studying measurements on ordinal relations." In Marsden, Peter V. (ed.), *Sociological Methodology* Vol. 23. Cambridge, MA: Blackwell, pp. 177–215.

Faust, Katherine, Karin E. Willert, David D. Rowlee, and John Skvoretz. 2002. "Scaling and statistical models for affiliation networks: Patterns of participation among Soviet politicians during the Brezhnev era." *Social Networks*, 24:231–259.

Foster, Brian L., and Stephen B. Seidman. 1984. "Overlap structure of ceremonial events in two Thai villages." *Thai Journal of Development Administration*, 24:143–157.

Freeman, Linton. 2000. "Visualizing social networks." *Journal of Social Structures*, 1(1). Available at: http://www.heinz.cmu.edu/project/INSNA/joss/index1.html.

Freeman, Linton C. 2002. *Meta Analysis of Davis, Gardner, and Gardner Data*. Unpublished manuscript, University of California, Irvine.

Freeman, Linton C., and Douglas R. White 1993. "Using Galois lattices to represent network data." In Marsden, Peter V. (ed.), *Sociological Methodology*, pp. 127–146.

Galaskiewicz, Joseph. 1985. *Social Organization of an Urban Grants Economy*. New York: Academic Press.

Gifi, Albert. 1990. *Nonlinear Multivariate Analysis*. New York: John Wiley.

Greenacre, Michael. 1984. *Theory and Applications of Correspondence Analysis*. New York: Academic Press.

Greenacre, Michael. 1989. "The Carroll-Green-Schaffer scaling in correspondence: A theoretical and empirical appraisal." *Journal of Marketing Research*, 26:358–365.

Greenacre, Michael, and Jörg Blasius. (eds.). 1994. *Correspondence Analysis in the Social Sciences: Recent Developments and Applications*. New York: Academic Press.

Greenacre, Michael, and Trevor Hastie. 1987. "The geometric interpretation of correspondence analysis." *Journal of the American Statistical Association*, 82:437–447.

Homans, George C. 1950. *The Human Group*. London: Routledge and Kegan Paul.

Jacoby, William G. 1991. *Data Theory and Dimensional Analysis*. Newbury Park, CA: Sage.

Kumbasar, Ece, A. Kimball Romney, and William H. Batchelder. 1994. "Systematic biases in social perception." *American Journal of Sociology*, 100:477–505.

Levine, Joel. 1972. "The sphere of influence." *American Sociological Review*, 37:14–27.

Mariolis, Peter. 1975. "Interlocking directorates and control of corporations: The theory of bank control." *Sociological Quarterly* 56:325–439.

Mariolis, Peter, and Maria H. Jones. 1982. "Centrality in corporate interlock networks: Reliability and stability." *Administrative Science Quarterly* 27:571–584.

McGrath, C., J. Blythe, and D. Krackhardt. 1997. "The effect of spatial arrangement on judgments and errors in interpreting graphs." *Social Networks*, 19:223–242.

McPherson, J. Miller. 1982. "Hypernetwork sampling: Duality and differentiation among voluntary organizations." *Social Networks*, 3:225–249.

Mische, Ann, and Philippa Pattison. 2000. "Composing in a civic arena: Publics, projects, and social settings." *Poetics*, 27:163–194.

Mizruchi, Mark S. 1982. *The American Corporate Network 1904–1974*. Beverly Hills, CA: Sage.

Nakao, Keiko, and A. Kimball Romney. 1993. "Longitudinal approach to subgroup formation: Re-analysis of Newcomb's fraternity data." *Social Networks*, 15:109–131.

Nishisato, Shizuhiko. 1994. *Elements of Dual Scaling: An Introduction to Practical Data Analysis*. Hillsdale, NJ: Lawrence Erlbaum.

Noma, E., and D. R. Smith. 1985. "Scaling sociomatrices by optimizing an explicit function: Correspondence analysis of binary single response sociomatrices." *Mulitvariate Behavioral Research*, 20:179–197.

Osa, Maryjane. 2003. *Solidarity and Contention: The Networks of Polish Opposition*. Minneapolis: University of Minnesota Press.

Pattison, Philippa, and Ronald Breiger. 2002. "Lattices and dimensional representations: Matrix decompositions and ordering structures." *Social Networks*, 24(4):423–444.

Roberts, John M., Jr. 2000. "Correspondence analysis of two-mode network data." *Social Networks*, 22:65–72.

Rosenthal, Naomi, Meryl Fingrutd, Michele Ethier, Roberta Karant, and David McDonald. 1985. "Social movements and network analysis: A case study of nineteenth-century women's reform in New York state." *American Journal of Sociology*, 90:1022–1054.

Schweizer, Thomas. 1991. "The power struggle in a Chinese community, 1950–1980: A social network analysis of the duality of actors and events." *Journal of Quantitative Anthropology*, 3:19–44.

Schweizer, Thomas. 1993. "The dual ordering of actors and posessions." *Current Anthropology*, 34:469–483.

Schweizer, Thomas, Elmar Klemm, and Margarete Schweizer. 1993. "Ritual as action in a Javanese community: a network perspective on ritual and social structure." *Social Networks*, 15:19–48.

Seidman, Stephen B. 1981. "Structures induced by collections of subsets: A hypergraph approach." *Mathematical Social Sciences*, 1:381–396.

Skvoretz, John, and Katherine Faust. 1999. "Logit models for affiliation networks." In Sobel, Michael E., and Mark P. Becker (eds.), *Sociological Methodology* Oxford: Basil Blackwell, pp. 253–280.

Stokman, Frans N. 1977. *Roll Calls and Sponsorship : A Methodological Analysis of Third World Group Formation in the United Nations*. Leyden, The Netherlands: A. W. Sijthoff.

Wasserman, Stanley, and Katherine Faust. 1989. "Canonical analysis of the composition and structure of social networks." In Clogg, Clifford C. (ed.), *Sociological Methodology* Vol. 19. Cambridge, MA: Basil Blackwell, pp. 1–42.

Wasserman, Stanley, and Katherine Faust. 1994. *Social Network Analysis: Methods and Applications*. Cambridge, UK: Cambridge University Press.

Wasserman, Stanley, Katherine Faust, and Joseph Galaskiewicz. 1990. "Correspondence and canonical analysis of relational data." *Journal of Mathematical Sociology*, 15:11–64.

Weller, Susan C., and A. Kimball Romney. 1990. *Metric Scaling: Correspondence Analysis*. Newbury Park, CA: Sage.

Wilson, Thomas P. 1982. "Relational networks: An extension of sociometric concepts." *Social Networks*, 4:105–116.

Appendix: List of Western Hemisphere Organizations

1. Association of Caribbean States (ACS): Trade group sponsored by the Caribbean Community and Common Market (CARICOM).
2. Latin American Integration Association (ALADI): Free trade organization.
3. Amazon Pact: Promotes development of Amazonian territories.
4. Andean Pact: Promotes development of members through economic and social integration.
5. Caribbean Community and Common Market (CARICOM): Caribbean trade organization; promotes economic development of members.
6. Group of Latin American and Caribbean Sugar Exporting Countries (GEPLACEA): Sugar-producing and exporting countries.
7. Group of Rio: Organization for joint political action.
8. Group of Three (G-3): Trade organization.
9. Inter-American Development Bank (IDB): Promotes development of member nations.
10. South American Common Market (MERCOSUR): Increases economic cooperation in the region.
11. North American Free Trade Agreement (NAFTA): Free trade organization.
12. Organization of American States (OAS): Promotes peace, security, economic, and social development in the Western Hemisphere.
13. Central American Parliament (PARLACÉN). Works for the political integration of Central America.
14. San José Group. Promotes regional economic integration.
15. Latin American Economic System (SELA): Promotes economic and social development of member nations.

8

An Introduction to Random Graphs, Dependence Graphs, and p*

Stanley Wasserman

University of Illinois

Garry Robins

University of Melbourne

We begin with a graph (or a directed graph), a single set of nodes $\mathcal{N}$, and a set of lines or arcs $\mathcal{L}$. It is common to use this mathematical concept to represent a *social network*. We use the notation of Wasserman and Faust (1994), especially Chapters 13 and 15. There are extensions of these ideas to a wide range of social networks, including multiple relations, affiliation relations, valued relations, and social influence and selection situations (in which information on attributes of the nodes is available). Later chapters in this volume discuss such generalizations.

The model p^* was first discussed by Frank and Strauss (1986), who termed it a distribution for a *Markov random graph*. Further developments, especially commentary on estimation of distribution parameters, were given by Strauss and Ikeda (1990). Wasserman and Pattison (1996) further elaborated this family of models, showing how a Markov parametric assumption provides just one of many possible sets of parameters. This family, with its variety and extensions, was named p^*, a label by which it has come to be known. The parameters reflect structural concerns, which are assumed to govern the probabilistic nature of the underlying social and/or behavioral process.

The development of p^* presented here is different from that found in Wasserman and Pattison (1996) and Anderson, Wasserman, and Crouch (1999), but similar to the presentation in Pattison and Wasserman (1999). Rather than looking at p^* as an approximate autologistic regression model, we begin with *dependence graphs* and show how this family of models follows naturally from such graphs. Dependence graphs are quite useful when distinguishing among a variety of different random graph types, with unique dependence assumptions – which is one of the goals of this chapter. This chapter provides an introduction to dependence graphs, with more detail discussed in later chapters.

8.1 Some Notation

A *social network* is a set of n actors and a collection of r social relations that specify how these actors are related to one another. As defined by Wasserman and Faust (1994,

Chapter 3), a social network can also contain a collection of attribute characteristics, measured on the actors. Such actor attribute variables can be important "explanatory" variables for relational "response variables"; due to the introductory nature of this chapter, such variables, as well as the *social influence* (Robins, Pattison, and Elliot 2001) and *social selection* (Robins, Elliot, and Pattison 2001) models, are discussed in later chapters.

Here, we let $r = 1$, focusing just on networks with single relations and assuming that relational ties take on just two values (see also Frank and Strauss 1986; Strauss and Ikeda 1990; Strauss 1992; Rennolls 1995). Extensions to multiple and valued relations (more recently presented by Pattison and Wasserman 1999, and Robins, Pattison, and Wasserman 1999) are also possible (see also Frank 1991, 1997, and Frank and Nowicki 1993).

We let $\mathcal{N} = \{1, 2, \ldots, g\}$ denote the set of actors, and $\mathcal{X}$ denote a particular relation defined on the actors. Specifically, $\mathcal{X}$ is a set of ordered pairs recording the presence or absence of relational ties between pairs of actors. This social relation can be represented by a $g \times g$ matrix $\mathbf{X}$, with elements

$$X_{ij} = \begin{cases} 1 \text{ if } (i, j) \in \mathcal{X}, \\ 0 \text{ otherwise.} \end{cases}$$

We use a variety of graph characteristics and statistics throughout this chapter; such quantities are defined in the early chapters of Wasserman and Faust (1994). We assume throughout that $\mathbf{X}$ and its elements are random variables. Typically, these variables are assumed to be interdependent, given the interactive nature of the social processes that generate and sustain a social network. In fact, one of the new ideas for social network analysis used by the p^* family of models is a *dependence graph*, a device that allows one to consider which elements of $\mathbf{X}$ are independent. We define this graph in the next section.

One of the "tricks" that allows the basic p^* model to be extended to multivariate and valued relations is the creation of new relations that are the converses, compositions, or intersections of the measured relations. Here, we define three new arrays for each relational tie, $\mathbf{X}_{ij}^+$, $\mathbf{X}_{ij}^-$, and $\mathbf{X}_{ij}^c$, which will be useful for the estimation of model parameters.

Let $\mathbf{X}_{ij}^+$ be the array formed from $\mathbf{X}$ where the tie from i to j is forced to be present:

$$(X_{ij}^+)_{mn} = X_{ij}, \text{if } (m, n) \neq (i, j)$$
$$= 1, \text{if} (m, n) = (i, j).$$

Thus, $\mathbf{X}_{ij}^+$ differs at most from $\mathbf{X}$ by the (i, j)th entry, which is forced to be 1. Define $\mathbf{X}_{ij}^-$ as the array formed from $\mathbf{X}$ where the tie from i to j is forced to be absent:

$$(X_{ij}^-)_{mn} = X_{ij}, \text{if } (m, n) \neq (i, j)$$
$$= 0, \text{if } (m, n) = (i, j).$$

Last, define $\mathbf{X}_{ij}^c$ as the matrix for the *complement* relation for $\mathbf{X}$ of the tie from i to j:

$$(X_{ij}^c)_{mn} = X_{ij}, \text{if } (m, n) \neq (i, j)$$
$$= \text{undefined, if } (m, n) = (i, j).$$

The complement relation has no relational tie coded from i to j – one can view this single variable as missing. These arrays are used when estimating the parameters of $p*$ via an approximate, maximum pseudolikelihood estimation.

8.2   Dependence Graphs

Recall that we have defined a set of random variables based on the relational ties in the network. The first step for any probabilistic model of a network is to consider the statistical dependencies among the elements of this set. To do this, we construct a dependence graph. Such a device allows us to distinguish among the many possible graph probability distributions, which can often be characterized by considering which relational ties are assumed to be statistically independent.

We define a dependence graph (as it applies to network relational variables) and then show how it can distinguish among basic graph distributions (such as those described in Wasserman and Faust 1994, Chapter 13). This dependence graph is also the starting point for the Hammersley-Clifford theorem (Besag 1974), which posits a very general probability distribution for these network random variables using the postulated dependence graph. The exact form of the dependence graph depends on the nature of the substantive hypotheses about the social network under study; we briefly discuss several such hypotheses.

(A) *Theory*

Any observed single relational network may be regarded as a realization $\mathbf{x} = [x_{ij}]$ of a random two-way binary array $\mathbf{X} = [X_{ij}]$. In general, the entries of the array $\mathbf{X}$ cannot be assumed to be independent; consequently, it is helpful to specify a dependence structure for the random variables $\{X_{ij}\}$, as originally suggested by Frank and Strauss (1986).

The dependence structure for these random variables is determined by the *dependence graph* $\mathcal{D}$ of the random array $\mathbf{X}$. $\mathcal{D}$ is itself a graph whose nodes are elements of the index set $\{(i, j); i, j \in \mathcal{N}, i \neq j\}$ for the random variables in $\mathbf{X}$, and whose edges signify pairs of the random variables that are assumed to be conditionally dependent (given the values of all other random variables).

More formally, a dependence graph for a univariate social network has node set

$$\mathcal{N}_D = \{(i, j); i, j \in \mathcal{N}, i \neq j\}.$$

The edges of $\mathcal{D}$ are given by $\mathcal{E}_D = \{((i, j), (k, l)),$ where X_{ij} and X_{kl} are not conditionally independent$\}$. This specific dependence graph is a version of an *independence graph*, as it is termed in the graphical modeling literature (for example, Lauritzen 1996; Robins 1997); see Robins (1998) for an extended discussion of the application of graphical modeling techniques to social network models.

(B) *Applications*

As Frank and Strauss (1986) observed for univariate graphs and associated two-way binary arrays, several well-known classes of distributions for random graphs may be specified in terms of the structure of the dependence graph. Pattison and Wasserman (2001) and Wasserman and Pattison (2000) noted that there are three major classes – Bernoulli graphs and conditional uniform graph distributions, dyadic dependence distributions, and p^*. Other probabilistic graph models are described by Bollobas (1985), although a primary issue in the mathematics literature is on asymptotic behavior of various graph statistics as the size of the node set increases (whereas typically in social network analysis we want to analyze social networks on a fixed-node set). We briefly focus on the first two classes mentioned previously, describing the third at length later in this chapter.

The assumption of conditional independence for all pairs of random variables representing distinct relational ties (that is, X_{ij} and X_{kl} are independent whenever $i \neq k$ and $j \neq l$) leads to the class of Bernoulli graphs (see Frank and Nowicki 1993). The dependence graph for such a distribution has no edges; it is empty. A Bernoulli graph assumes complete independence of relational ties; the probability that the tie $i \rightarrow j$ is present is P_{ij}. If the $P_{ij} = 0.5$ for all ties, the distribution is often referred to as the uniform random (di)graph distribution, U. All (di)graphs are equally likely to occur; hence, the uniform probability aspect of the distribution. A more general Bernoulli graph distribution fixes the P_{ij} at P; each edge can be viewed as the outcome of a biased coin toss, with probability P of a "success."

The uniform distribution U conditions on no graph properties, whereas the uniform distribution $U|L$ statistically conditions on the number L of edges in the graph. All (di)graphs with $L = l$ lines (arcs) are equally likely; (di)graphs with $L \neq l$ lines (arcs) have probability 0. There are many other conditional uniform distributions, including the classic $U|MAN$ distribution, which fixes the counts of the dyad states and assumes that all digraphs with the specified dyad census are equally likely, and $U|\{X_{i+}\}, \{X_{+j}\}$, which fixes the out-degrees and in-degrees. Many such conditional uniform distributions are described in Chapter 13 of Wasserman and Faust (1994). Some of these distributions have simple dependence graphs; for example, the $U|\{X_{i+}\}$ distribution, which fixes only the out-degrees, has a dependence graph with edge set $\mathcal{E}_D = \{((i, j), (i, k)),$ for all $j \neq k$ for every $i\}$.

The assumption of conditional dependence of X_{ij} and X_{kl}, if and only if $\{k, l\} = \{j, i\}$, leads to the class of dyad dependence models (see Wasserman 1987; Holland & Leinhardt 1981), the second family of graph distributions mentioned previously. These "multinomial dyad" distributions assume all dyads are statistically independent and postulate substantively interesting parameterizations for the probabilities of the various dyad states. The dependence graph for such distributions has an edge set with edges connecting only the two random variables within each dyad: $\mathcal{E}_D = \{((i, j), (j, i)),$ for all $i \neq j\}$. This class of models was termed p_1 by Holland and Leinhardt (1977, 1981) and has a long history (see Chapters 15 and 16 of Wasserman and Faust 1994). Although for some parameterizations it is easy to fit, its assumption of independence across dyads is not terribly realistic.

Consider now a general dependence graph, with an arbitrary edge set. Such a dependence graph yields a very general probability distribution for a (di)graph, which we term p^* and focus on as follows. One dependence graph, for which this distribution was first developed, assumes conditional independence of X_{ij} and X_{kl}, if and only if $\{i, j\} \cap \{k, l\} = \emptyset$. This dependence graph links any two relational ties involving the same actor(s); thus, any two relational ties are associated if they involve the same actor(s). This type of dependency resembles a Markov spatial process, so these dependencies were defined as a Markov graph by Frank and Strauss (1986). This p^* family of distributions has been extended in many ways, and estimates of its parameters scrutinized.

Of course, if the dependence graph is fully connected, then a general class of random graphs is obtained. We note, however, that any model deriving from a fully connected dependence graph is not identifiable. Later chapters introduce more complex dependence structures that permit models more general than Markov random graphs, but avoid fully connected dependence graphs.

8.3 p^*

For an observed network, which we consider to be a realization $\mathbf{x}$ of a random array $\mathbf{X}$, we assume the existence of a dependence graph $\mathcal{D}$ for the random array $\mathbf{X}$. The edges of $\mathcal{D}$ are crucial here; consider the set of edges, and determine if there are any *complete subgraphs*, or cliques, found in the dependence graph. [For a general dependence graph, a subset A of the set of relational ties $\mathcal{N}_D$ is *complete* if every pair of nodes in A (that is, every pair of relational ties) is linked by an edge of $\mathcal{D}$. A subset comprising a single node is also regarded as complete.] These cliques specify which subsets of relational ties are all pairwise, conditionally dependent on each other.

The Hammersley-Clifford theorem (Besag 1974) establishes that a probability model for $\mathbf{X}$ depends only on the cliques of the dependence graph $\mathcal{D}$. In particular, application of the Hammersley-Clifford theorem yields a characterization of $Pr(\mathbf{X} = \mathbf{x})$ in the form of an exponential family of distributions:

$$Pr(\mathbf{X} = \mathbf{x}) = \left(\frac{1}{\kappa}\right) \exp\left(\sum_{A \subseteq \mathcal{N}_D} \lambda_A \prod_{(i,j) \in A} x_{ij}\right), \qquad (8.1)$$

where:

- $\kappa = \sum_{\mathbf{x}} \exp\{\sum_{A \subseteq \mathcal{D}} \lambda_A \prod_{(i,j) \in A} x_{ij}\}$ is a normalizing quantity.
- $\mathcal{D}$ is the dependence graph for $\mathbf{X}$; the summation is over all subsets A of nodes of $\mathcal{D}$.
- $\prod_{(i,j) \in A} x_{ij}$ is the sufficient statistic corresponding to the parameter λ_A.
- $\lambda_A = 0$ whenever the subgraph induced by the nodes in A is not a clique of $\mathcal{D}$.

The set of nonzero parameters in this probability distribution for $Pr(\mathbf{X} = \mathbf{x})$ depends on the *maximal* cliques of the dependence graph (a maximal clique is a complete subgraph that is not contained in any other complete subgraph). Any subgraph of a complete subgraph is also complete (but not maximal), so if A is a maximal clique of $\mathcal{D}$, then the probability distribution for the (di)graph will contain nonzero parameters for A and all its subgraphs.

Clearly, the number of parameters can be overwhelming. Thus, it is wise to limit these numbers by either postulating a simple dependence graph or making assumptions about the parameters. Our usual assumption is *homogeneity*, in which parameters for isomorphic *configurations* of nodes are equated. As defined by Pattison and Wasserman (1999), this assumption equates parameters for the various isomorphic subgraphs that arise. For example, there can be two parameters for the isomorphic dyads (null, asymmetric, and mutual), up to fifteen parameters for the isomorphic triad states, and so forth (there is a loss of one parameter for each class of subgraph due to redundancies). See Figure 10.3.2 in Robins and Pattison (Chapter 10, this volume). Detailed definitions and consequences of homogeneity can be found in Pattison and Wasserman (1999). It is also possible to equate parameters by relying on the common practice of assuming *a priori* stochastic blockmodels (Anderson, Wasserman, and Faust 1992).

Even with homogeneity imposed, models may not be identifiable. Typically, parameters for higher-order configurations (for example, higher-order stars or triads) are set to zero (equivalent to setting higher-order interactions to zero in general linear models). An interpretation of the resulting model in terms of constrained social settings is given in later chapters.

Tables of parameters, and associated minimal sufficient statistics, can be found in the trilogy of *p** papers: Wasserman and Pattison (1996), Pattison and Wasserman (1999), and Robins et al. (1999).

The interpretation of parameters can be complicated given that higher-order configurations contain within them lower-order configurations (see Robins et al. 1999). At its simplest, a substantial positive parameter estimate for a triangle (for instance) suggests that, given the number of other configurations in the observed graph, there are more triangles present than would be expected by chance.

(A) *Estimation*

The probability distribution arising from the Hammersley-Clifford theorem, (8.1), can be written in the general form:

$$Pr(\mathbf{X} = \mathbf{x}) = \frac{\exp\{\boldsymbol{\theta}'\mathbf{z}(\mathbf{x})\}}{\kappa(\boldsymbol{\theta})} \tag{8.2}$$

where $\boldsymbol{\theta}$ is a vector of model parameters and $\mathbf{z}(\mathbf{x})$ is a vector of network statistics. $\kappa(\boldsymbol{\theta})$ is a normalizing constant, which guarantees that the distribution is proper. Which network statistics appear in the model depends on the structure of the hypothesized dependence graph, and on whether any homogeneity constraints have been proposed. One could view this model as an autologistic regression, as described by Wasserman and Pattison (1996). Regardless of the motivation, the elements of $\boldsymbol{\theta}$ are unknown and must be estimated.

The likelihood function for the distribution is quite simple:

$$L(\boldsymbol{\theta}) = \frac{\exp\{\boldsymbol{\theta}'\mathbf{z}(\mathbf{x})\}}{\kappa(\boldsymbol{\theta})}.$$

Even though it has a simple expression, the function is not easy to work with, due to the dependence of $\kappa(\boldsymbol{\theta})$ on the unknown parameters. Direct, exact differentiation of the log likelihood is difficult, if not impossible. Some exact results can be found in Walker (1995), but are specific to very small (di)graphs.

Two approaches have been used to date: (1) a maximum pseudolikelihood estimation technique, pioneered by Besag (1975, 1977a, 1977b) and refined and applied by Strauss (1986) and Strauss and Ikeda (1990); and (2) Markov chain Monte Carlo maximum likelihood estimation, being applied to $p*$ by Crouch and Wasserman (1998), Snijders (2002), and Handcock (2003).

(B) *Pseudolikelihood Estimation*

For probabilities to be computed, one must be able to calculate κ, which is just too difficult for most networks. Hence, alternative model formulations and approximate estimation techniques are important. One such alternative, which we now describe, uses log odds ratios of the conditional probabilities of each element of $\mathbf{X}$.

The Logit Model

We can turn model (8.2) into a autologistic regression model, not for the probability of the (di)graph, but for the conditional probabilities of the relational ties. This produces an approximate likelihood function that is much easier to deal with than the likelihood function described previously.

We first condition on the complement of X_{ij}, defined earlier in this chapter, and consider just the probability that the dichotomous random variable X_{ij} is unity. Specifically, consider

$$
\begin{aligned}
Pr(X_{ij} = 1|\mathbf{X}_{ij}^c) &= \frac{Pr(\mathbf{X} = \mathbf{x}_{ij}^+)}{Pr(\mathbf{X} = \mathbf{x}_{ij}^+) + Pr(\mathbf{X} = \mathbf{x}_{ij}^-)} \\
&= \frac{\exp\{\boldsymbol{\theta}'\mathbf{z}(\mathbf{x}_{ij}^+)\}}{\exp\{\boldsymbol{\theta}'\mathbf{z}(\mathbf{x}_{ij}^+)\} + \exp\{\boldsymbol{\theta}'\mathbf{z}(\mathbf{x}_{ij}^-)\}}.
\end{aligned} \tag{8.3}
$$

The odds ratio, which simplifies model (8.3), is

$$
\begin{aligned}
\frac{Pr(X_{ij} = 1|\mathbf{X}_{ij}^c)}{Pr(X_{ij} = 0|\mathbf{X}_{ij}^c)} &= \frac{\exp\{\boldsymbol{\theta}'\mathbf{z}(\mathbf{x}_{ij}^+)\}}{\exp\{\boldsymbol{\theta}'\mathbf{z}(\mathbf{x}_{ij}^-)\}} \\
&= \exp\{\boldsymbol{\theta}'[\mathbf{z}(\mathbf{x}_{ij}^+) - \mathbf{z}(\mathbf{x}_{ij}^-)]\}
\end{aligned} \tag{8.4}
$$

yielding the simple "linear" model

$$
\varpi_{ijm} = \log\left\{\frac{Pr(X_{ij} = 1|\mathbf{X}_{ij}^c)}{Pr(X_{ij} = 0|\mathbf{X}_{ij}^c)}\right\} = \boldsymbol{\theta}'[\mathbf{z}(\mathbf{x}_{ij}^+) - \mathbf{z}(\mathbf{x}_{ij}^-)]. \tag{8.5}
$$

If we define $\boldsymbol{\delta}(x_{ij}) = [\mathbf{z}(\mathbf{x}_{ij}^+) - \mathbf{z}(\mathbf{x}_{ij}^-)]$, then the logit model (8.5) simplifies succinctly to $\varpi_{ij} = \boldsymbol{\theta}'\boldsymbol{\delta}(x_{ij})$.

The important quantities here are the elements of $\boldsymbol{\delta}(x_{ij})$, that is, the vector of network statistics whose elements measure the changes in the statistics when the relational tie x_{ij} changes from 1 to 0. These odds ratios form the basis of an approximate likelihood function, which is constructed by assuming they are conditionally independent.

Estimation

An approximate estimation approach, proposed by Besag (1975, 1977b), and adopted by Strauss (1986), Strauss and Ikeda (1990), and the trilogy of p^* papers, uses a *pseudolikelihood function*

$$PL(\theta) = \prod_{i \neq j} Pr(X_{ij} = 1|\mathbf{X}_{ij}^c)^{x_{ij}} Pr(X_{ij} = 0|\mathbf{X}_{ij}^c)^{1-x_{ij}}. \tag{8.6}$$

A *maximum pseudolikelihood estimator* (MPLE) is the value of θ that maximizes (8.6). This approach assumes conditional independence of the random variables representing the relational ties. Details on the literature on approximate likelihood estimation can be found in Pattison and Wasserman (1999). Estimation of θ for single, dichotomous relations can be accomplished via logistic regression. Maximizing the pseudolikelihood given in 8.6 is equivalent to maximizing the likelihood function for the fit of logistic regression to the model (8.5) (for independent observations $\{x_{ij}\}$).

In practice, pseudolikelihood estimation is not overly complex because standard logistic regression techniques can be used. To set up the data file for pseudolikelihood estimation, each possible binary tie (X_{ij}) becomes a "case," with the "independent variables" constituted by the parameters in the model (the isomorphic configurations – for instance, stars and triads of various types). For each case, the statistic associated with a variable is the difference in the number of the relevant configurations between the graph with $x_{ij} = 1$ and the graph with $x_{ij} = 0$. Standard logistic regression can then be applied to this data file, with the observations on the ties as the dependent variable. Nevertheless, this is not a standard logistic regression because of the dependencies within the data, and the usual tests of model fit do not strictly apply. For instance, the pseudolikelihood deviance (which a standard logistic regression package will normally compute) is not necessarily an asymptotic chi-square random variable. Accordingly, measures of fit are usually taken as heuristic guides. The pseudolikelihood deviance is often presented, along with simple goodness-of-fit statistics, such as mean absolute residual.

(C) *Maximum Likelihood Estimation: Simulating p* Models and Model Degeneracy*

Maximum pseudolikelihood estimation was suggested by Besag (1975) for dealing with data in spatial statistics. It has the virtue of being relatively easy to fit, even for complicated models. Moreover, the maximum pseudolikelihood estimator satisfies un-biased estimating equations, is consistent, and is asymptotically normal under suitable conditions (Baddeley and Turner 2000; see also Geys, Molenberghs, and Ryan 1997, 1999; Le Cessie and van Houwielingen 1994). Nevertheless, because the properties of the pseudolikelihood estimator are not well-understood, a more recent body of work has developed Monte Carlo techniques for maximum likelihood estimates for p^* models.

Various approaches to Monte Carlo estimation are available. For the particular case of p^* models, the central idea is to simulate a distribution of random graphs from a starting set of parameter values, and then to refine these estimated parameter values by comparing the distribution of graphs with the observed graph. The process is repeated until the parameter estimates stabilize. Simulation procedures establish a Markov chain of graphs that, under suitable conditions, will converge to a stationary graph distribution. Two of the most popular algorithms that can produce such a Markov chain are the Gibbs sampler (Geman and Geman 1984) and the Metropolis-Hastings algorithm (which includes the Gibbs sampler as a special case; see Chib and Greenberg 1995). Geyer and Thompson (1992) presented a general Markov chain Monte Carlo maximum likelihood method (see also Besag 2000). Crouch and Wasserman (1998) described how this technique could be applied specifically to p* models (see also Snijders 2002, and Corander, Dahmström, and Dahmström 2002).

Studies on Monte Carlo techniques have thrown new light on an important issue, that of model degeneracy. For certain parameter values, a p* model may produce a distribution of graphs in which only a handful of graphs (sometimes only one) have nonzero probability; moreover, these graphs are often uninteresting, such as the full or empty graph. Such a model is termed *degenerate*. For degenerate models, estimation techniques will not perform well, irrespective of method.

Strauss (1986) was the first to use the Metropolis-Hastings algorithm to simulate Markov random graph distributions. Strauss observed a variation on the problem of degeneracy, by noting that asymptotically there may be no finite normalizing constant for a distribution with certain parameter values. For these regions of the parameter space, simulations are thus not adequate in producing a stationary distribution.

Based on the results in Besag (2000) and Handcock (2000), Hoff, Raftery, and Handcock (2002) suggested that commonly used p* models may have model degeneracy and instability problems that are not resolved by alternative forms of estimation, but rather may represent defects in the models themselves. This is a strong judgment that is not necessarily borne out in subsequent work. However, a similar point is also implied by Snijders (2002), who presented a Monte Carlo estimation technique for p* models using the Gibbs sampler and the Munro-Robbins algorithm to estimate the moments of the sufficient statistics. Snijders presented several examples of simple Markov graph models that involved degeneracy and instability. For certain parameter values, sufficient statistics had bimodal distributions. Snijders' suggestions to overcome these problems worked satisfactorily for some data sets, especially for small graphs, but the bimodality remained a limitation. Snijders and van Duijn (2002) suggested that to address bimodality, model estimation might be conditional on the number of observed edges in the graph.

The most extensive study on degeneracy for these models has been conducted by Handcock (2003). Handcock defined "near degeneracy" of a graph model as occurring when the model places disproportionate probability mass on only a few of the possible graphs (often empty or full graphs). He examined in detail the simplest Markov model for very small nondirected graphs – the two-star model with only edge and two-star parameters. He delineated the region of parameter space in which nondegeneracy occurs, where Monte Carlo estimation techniques will operate satisfactorily and the models are statistically well-behaved. This work also makes clear that the bimodality observed by Snijders (2002) is to be expected for certain parameter values that are on the edge of the nondegenerate area.

Simulation studies by Robins, Pattison, and Woolcock (in press) suggested that nondegenerate graphs may be more readily achieved with more complex models, in particular with a parameterization that includes three and four stars, that is, at least the first three moments of the degree distribution. Triangle, transitivity parameters are also desirable in a "realistic" model. Robins et al. showed that by varying values for such a parameter set, it is possible to simulate Markov graph distributions with properties akin to "small worlds" (Watts 1999), or with other global features such as long paths or a high proportion of four cycles.

Following Grenander (1993), Robins et al. (in press) demonstrated that increasing all parameter values by the same factor results in movement toward degenerate regions. Contrary to Handcock (2003), who argued that degenerate regions imply uninteresting models, Robins et al. noted that some degenerate models result in graphs of theoretical import, such as graphs of disconnected complete components (the so-called caveman graphs of Watts 1999) or complete bipartite graphs. Robins et al. interpreted degenerate regions as areas where "stochasticism" breaks down and deterministic structures emerge (see also Pattison 2002). Their simulation technique permits examination of how "close" an observed graph is to this phase transition. Most human social structures are indeed stochastic, but because of tendencies toward transitivity and structural balance, it is possible that stochastic social systems may be not too "far" from determinism (Robins 2003). Such a conclusion would accord with the small world simulation results of Watts (1999), who showed that the addition of only a small random component to a highly structured graph resulted in small world properties.

In summary, Monte Carlo estimation techniques for these models are now well-established and their development has shed new light on model behavior, particularly on model degeneracy. It is important for any estimation procedure that the model be non-degenerate; otherwise, there will not be satisfactory convergence of parameter estimates. Programs for Monte Carlo estimation are now available or becoming available; one example being the estimation procedures in the StOCNET suite of network programs (Snijders 2002). This program estimates Markov random graph models for directed and nondirected graphs with a choice of parameterizations, including reciprocity, triadic, and higher-order star parameters. Output from the program includes an assessment of convergence and reliable standard errors of parameter estimates.

(D) *Comparing Pseudolikelihood and Monte Carlo Maximum Likelihood Estimation*

Maximum likelihood estimation is undoubtedly optimal in the sense of having a principled statistical basis and producing reliable standard errors from which statistical inferences can be made. These are not qualities of pseudolikelihood estimation. However, Monte Carlo approaches to maximum likelihood estimation can be computer intensive, so estimation for networks with a large number of nodes, or for a complex model, may not be possible or may take an unacceptably long time. One very important question is "in what, if any, circumstances might pseudolikelihood be an acceptably approximate technique to obtain parameter estimates?"

There have been some interesting studies comparing the methods of estimation. Corander, Dahmström, and Dahmström (1998) used a Metropolis-Hastings algorithm, together with formulae for the first three cumulants (moments) of the sufficient statistics, to obtain maximum likelihood estimates for simple Markov random graph models (see also Corander et al. 2002). Comparing these estimates with pseudolikelihood estimates, they concluded that for graphs of up to approximately 40 nodes, the maximum likelihood estimator performed better in the nondegenerate regions of the parameter space. The pseudolikelihood estimator was more biased. In larger graphs, of 40 to 100 nodes, they concluded that the two estimators were nearly equivalent, although they showed that pseudolikelihood estimates could vary for different graphs with the same values of the sufficient statistics. Their simulation approach, however, fixed the number of edges in the graph, so it is not clear how to interpret their comparison of the two estimators because the pseudolikelihood estimation presumably included an edge parameter.

In other comparative studies, using models from Wasserman and Pattison (1996), Besag (2000) showed that a Monte Carlo goodness-of-fit test can lead to different conclusions from those that would apply if fits based on maximum pseudolikelihood estimates were treated as distributed as chi-square random variables. These results emphasize that standard hypothesis tests are simply not appropriate for pseudolikelihood estimates. Snijders (2002) presented examples where pseudolikelihood estimates were close to maximum likelihood estimates, as well as other examples where they were not.

One of the problems with assessing the performance of the maximum pseudolikelihood estimator is that of model specification. The simulation results of Robins, Pattison, and Woolcock (in press), noted previously, suggest that more complex models may have better properties in terms of avoiding degeneracy and instability. It might be expected that the maximum pseudolikelihood estimator performs less well for models that are close to degeneracy so the complexity of the models may affect the performance of the estimator. These results stress the potential importance of specification.

In summary, pseudolikelihood estimates have convenience, but are at best approximate. Whenever possible, Monte Carlo maximum likelihood approaches should be preferred. If pseudolikelihoods are to be used, estimates should be treated as exploratory, giving some possible evidence for effects that may be substantial in the network, with a clear recognition that point estimates are probably not precise. (For many research purposes, this may be sufficient.) Formal statistical inferences should not be made with pseudolikelihood estimation. Standard errors and other statistical results from the logistic regression procedure used for pseudolikelihood estimation should be treated with caution. Standard errors are likely to be too small, and at best should be viewed as very rough indicators of "scale" for the parameters. Wald statistics should not be regarded as reliable. The pseudolikelihood deviance remains a valid measure of model fit, in that models that better predict the data will have lower deviance, but it will not be distributed, even asymptotically, as chi-square; thus, statistical inference is not available. In terms of model specification, our current suggestion is that Markov random graph models should carry rather complicated parameterization, including at least a three-star parameter (three-in-star and three-out-star for directed graphs). If the highest-order star parameter has a positive estimate, beware of the possibility of degeneracy. In that case, even higher-order star parameters may be necessary.

In conclusion, an important focus for future work should be the specification of regions of degeneracy relative to model specification. Such a research approach may permit a better understanding of when pseudolikelihood procedures can be considered adequate. The outcome may be a clearer idea of the type of parameters required for sensible $p*$ model formulation. The notion that a simple Markov parameterization sufficiently models social networks is also being taken up through more substantive discussion of social settings and of construals of social space in general (see Robins and Pattison, Chapter 10, this volume; also Hoff et al. 2002, and Pattison and Robins 2002). This may be an instance where substantive considerations on the one hand and technical estimation requirements on the other hand could jointly lead to better model formulation.

Acknowledgments

This research was supported by grants from the National Science Foundation and the U.S. Office of Naval Research, and the Australian Research Council.

References

Anderson, C. J., Wasserman, S., and Crouch, B. (1999). A $p*$ primer: Logit models for social networks. *Social Networks, 21*, 37–66.

Anderson, C. J., Wasserman, S., and Faust, K. (1992). Building stochastic blockmodels. *Social Networks, 14*, 137–161.

Baddeley, A., and Turner, R. (2000). Practical maximum pseudolikelihood for spatial point processes (with discussion). *Australian and New Zealand Journal of Statistics, 42*, 283–322.

Besag, J. E. (1974). Spatial interaction and the statistical analysis of lattice systems (with discussion). *Journal of the Royal Statistical Society, Series B, 36*, 192–236.

Besag, J. E. (1975). Statistical analysis of non-lattice data. *The Statistician, 24*, 179–195.

Besag, J. E. (1977a). Some methods of statistical analysis for spatial data. *Bulletin of the International Statistical Association, 47*, 77–92.

Besag, J. E. (1977b). Efficiency of pseudo-likelihood estimation for simple Gaussian random fields. *Biometrika, 64*, 616–618.

Besag, J. E. (2000). *Markov Chain Monte Carlo for Statistical Inference*. Working Paper, University of Washington, Center for Statistics and the Social Sciences, Seattle.

Bollobas, B. (1985). *Random Graphs*. London: Academic Press.

Chib, S., and Greenberg, E. (1995). Understanding the Metropolis-Hastings algorithm. *American Statistician, 49*, 327–335.

Corander, J., Dahmström, K., and Dahmström, P. (1998). *Maximum Likelihood Estimation for Markov Graphs*. Research Report 1998:8, University of Stockholm, Department of Statistics, Stockholm, Sweden.

Corander, J., Dahmström, K., and Dahmström, P. (2002). Maximum likelihood estimation for exponential random graph models. In J. Hagberg (ed.), *Contributions to Social Network Analysis, Information Theory and Other Topics in Statistics: A Festschrift in Honour of Ove Frank on the Occasion of His 65th Birthday* (pp. 1–17). Stockholm, Sweden: Universitet Stockholms.

Crouch, B., and Wasserman, S. (1998). *Fitting p*: Monte Carlo Maximum Likelihood Estimation*. Paper presented at International Conference on Social Networks, Sitges, Spain, May 28–31.

Frank, O. (1991). Statistical analysis of change in networks. *Statistica Neerlandica, 45*, 283–293.

Frank, O. (1997). Composition and structure of social networks. *Mathematiques, Informatique, et Science Humaines, 137*, 11–23.

Frank, O., and Nowicki, K. (1993). Exploratory statistical analysis of networks. In J. Gimbel, J. W. Kennedy, and L. V. Quintas (eds.), *Quo Vadis Graph Theory? Annals of Discrete Mathematics, 55,* 349–366.

Frank, O., and Strauss, D. (1986). Markov graphs. *Journal of the American Statistical Association, 81,* 832–842.

Geman, S., and Geman, D. (1984). Stochastic relaxation, Gibbs distributions, and the Bayesian restoration of images. *IEEE Transactions on Pattern Analysis and Machine Intelligence, 6,* 721–741.

Geyer, C. J., and Thompson, E. A. (1992). Constrained Monte Carlo maximum likelihood for dependent data (with discussion). *Journal of the Royal Statistical Society Series B, 54,* 657–699.

Geys, H., Molenberghs, G., and Ryan, L. M. (1997). Pseudolikelihood inference for clustered binary data. *Communications in Statistics, Part A – Theory and Methods, 26,* 2743–2767.

Geys, H., Molenberghs, G., and Ryan, L. M. (1999). Pseudolikelihood modeling of multivariate outcomes in developmental toxicology. *Journal of the American Statistical Association, 94,* 734–745.

Grenander, U. (1993). *General Pattern Theory,* Oxford: Oxford University Press.

Handcock, M. S. (2000). *Progress in Statistical Modeling of Drug User and Sexual Networks.* Manuscript, University of Washington, Center for Statistics and the Social Sciences, Seattle.

Handcock, M. S. (2003). Statistical models for social networks: Inference and degeneracy. In R. Breiger, K. Carley, and P. Pattison (eds.), *Dynamic Social Network Modeling and Analysis* (pp. 229–240). Washington, DC: National Academies Press.

Hoff, P., Raftery, A. E., and Handcock, M. S. (2002). Latent space approaches to social network analysis. *Journal of the American Statistical Association, 97,* 1090–1098.

Holland, P. W., and Leinhardt, S. (1977). *Notes on the Statistical Analysis of Social Network Data.* Unpublished manuscript.

Holland, P. W., and Leinhardt, S. (1981). An exponential family of probability distributions for directed graphs. *Journal of the American Statistical Association, 76,* 33–65 (with discussion).

Lauritzen, S. (1996). *Graphical Models.* Oxford: Oxford University Press.

Le Cessie, S., and van Houwielingen, J. C. (1994). Logistic regression for correlated binary data. *Applied Statistics, 43,* 95–108.

Pattison, P. E. (2002). *Social networks, social space, social structure.* Keynote address, Sunbelt XXII International Social Network Conference, New Orleans, February.

Pattison, P. E., and Robins, G. L. (2002). Neighbourhood-based models for social networks. *Sociological Methodology, 32,* 301–337.

Pattison, P., and Wasserman, S. (1999). Logit models and logistic regressions for social networks: II. Multivariate relations. *British Journal of Mathematical and Statistical Psychology, 52,* 169–193.

Pattison, P., and Wasserman, S. (2001). Social network models, statistical. In Smelser, N. J., and Baltes, P. B. (eds.), *International Encyclopedia of the Social and Behavioral Sciences.* London: Elsevier Science.

Rennolls, K. (1995). $p_{\frac{1}{2}}$. In Everett, M. G., and Rennolls, K. (eds.), *Proceedings of the 1995 International Conference on Social Networks. 1* (pp. 151–160). London: Greenwich University Press.

Robins, G. L. (1997). Graphical modelling. *Chance, 10,* 37–40.

Robins, G. L. (1998). *Personal Attributes in Inter-personal Contexts: Statistical Models for Individual Characteristics and Social Relationships.* Unpublished doctoral dissertation, University of Melbourne, Department of Psychology, Melbourne, Australia.

Robins, G. L. (2003). *The Small Worlds of Small Social Networks.* Paper presented at the American Association for the Advancement of Science annual meeting, Denver, Colorado, February 13–18.

Robins, G. L., Elliot, P., and Pattison, P. (2001). Network models for social selection processes. *Social Networks, 23,* 1–30.

Robins, G. L., Pattison, P., and Elliott, P. (2001). Network models for social influence processes. *Psychometrika, 66,* 161–190.

Robins, G. L., Pattison, P., and Wasserman, S. (1999). Logit models and logistic regressions for social networks, III. Valued relations. *Psychometrika, 64,* 371–394.

Robins, G. L., Pattison, P., and Woolcock, J. (in press). Small and other worlds: Global network structures from local processes. *American Journal of Sociology*.

Snijders, T. A. B. (2002). Markov chain Monte Carlo estimation of exponential random graph models. *Journal of Social Structure*, *3*, 2.

Snijders, T. A. B., and van Duijn, M. A. J. (2002). Conditional maximum likelihood estimation under various specifications of exponential random graph models. In J. Hagberg (ed.), *Contributions to Social Network Analysis, Information Theory and Other Topics in Statistics: A Festschrift in Honour of Ove Frank on the Occasion of His 65th Birthday* (pp. 117–134). Stockholm, Sweden: Universitet Stockholms.

Strauss, D. (1986). On a general class of models for interaction. *SIAM Review*, *28*, 513–527.

Strauss, D. (1992). The many faces of logistic regression. *American Statistician*, *46*, 321–327.

Strauss, D., and Ikeda, M. (1990). Pseudolikelihood estimation for social networks. *Journal of the American Statistical Association*, *85*, 204–212.

Walker, M. E. (1995). *Statistical Models for Social Support Networks: Application of Exponential Models to Undirected Graphs with Dyadic Dependencies*. Unpublished doctoral dissertation, University of Illinois, Department of Psychology, Chicago.

Wasserman, S. (1987). Conformity of two sociometric relations. *Psychometrika*, *52*, 3–18.

Wasserman, S., and Faust, K. (1994). *Social Network Analysis: Methods and Applications*. New York: Cambridge University Press.

Wasserman, S., and Pattison, P. (1996). Logit models and logistic regressions for social networks: I. An introduction to Markov random graphs and *p**. *Psychometrika*, *60*, 401–426.

Wasserman, S., and Pattison, P. (2000). Statistical models for social networks. In Kiers, H., Rasson, J., Groenen, P., and Schader, M. (eds.), *Studies in Classification, Data Analysis, and Knowledge Organization*. Heidelberg: Springer-Verlag.

Watts, D. J. (1999). *Small Worlds: The Dynamics of Networks Between Order and Randomness*. Princeton, NJ: Princeton University Press.

9

Random Graph Models for Social Networks: Multiple Relations or Multiple Raters[1]

Laura M. Koehly

Texas A&M University

Philippa Pattison

University of Melbourne

9.1 Introduction

Several chapters in this book outline some of the significant advances that have been made in modeling networks and network-based processes (see, for example, Chapters 6, 7, 10, and 11). These models generally presuppose a single network of interest, such as a network of acquaintance ties or a network of advice-seeking ties, and they represent the interdependence of such ties with actor characteristics and other ties in some local network *neighborhood* (see, for example, Chapter 10). Yet, there are compelling theoretical and methodological reasons to extend these models to the case of multiple networks, and in this chapter we discuss the rationale and nature of these extensions, as well as a number of issues to which they give rise.

From a theoretical perspective, it is more than likely that network processes involve different kinds of relational ties; indeed, some well-known hypotheses about the nature of local network processes involve multiple types of tie. Cartwright and Harary's (1956) adaptation of Heider's (1946) balance model, for example, proposes a strong form of interdependence among positive and negative ties within triadic network structures, and Granovetter's (1973) "strength of weak ties" thesis involves an interdependence between strong, weak, and null ties. In addition, there is an impressive body of empirical work that points to the importance of multiplex ties, that is, those ties in which several types of relationships come together – such as friend and coworker, or advisor and supervisor – and also to the consequences of such ties for interpersonal processes. Indeed, theoretical arguments about such forms of interdependence are supported by a number of empirical studies. For example, Lazega and Pattison (1999) identified a number of separable forms of interdependence among three different types of ties – coworker, advisor, and friend – linking members of a law firm. Their results suggested the simultaneous presence not only of strong multiplexity and generalized reciprocity effects, but also of more complex triadic forms of interdependence involving several types of ties.

From a methodological perspective, there are also compelling reasons to develop models for multiple relational observations among network members. In insightful analyses of the problems of measuring network ties and of the impact of such measurement problems on network analyses, Marsden (1990; Chapter 2, this volume) and Batchelder (1989) identified some significant questions for network analysis that are still unresolved. For example, how can we establish the validity of network tie measurements? How can we establish the validity of more complex network substructures (such as paths and cliques) that involve multiple observations of network ties? As Batchelder observed, there are particularly strong measurement assumptions implicit in the construction of network substructures, and the plausibility of these assumptions is rarely examined. Although we can adapt more widely used psychometric approaches to address questions about the reliability and validity of network measurement (e.g., see Calloway, Morrissey, and Paulson 1993), there are particular difficulties created both by the interdependent nature of network observations, as well as by interest in more complex structural forms. The capacity to develop models for multiple observations on a single relation affords considerable leverage in evaluating such questions of validity and, to some extent, in bypassing them. Thus, we can not only investigate the degree of, say, consensus and bias in various sources of relational information, but we can also incorporate information from multiple sources into a single probabilistic model for an entire set of multiple observations.

In this chapter, therefore, we describe random graph models for multiple networks. We begin by introducing some notation and terminology, as well as an example used for illustrative analyses. We then present the general extension of the random graph models reviewed in Wasserman and Robins (Chapter 8) and Robins and Pattison (Chapter 10) to the case of multivariate random graphs. We discuss the application of this general framework to the analysis of multiple networks, as well as to multiple rater networks and cognitive social structures.

9.2 Notation and Basic Terminology

We are interested in a collection of r social relations that specify relationships of various types among members of a specified set of g social *actors*. We denote the set of actors by $N = \{1, 2, 3, \ldots, g\}$ and the *social relation* of type m by X_m. The set of relation types are denoted by $R = \{1, 2, 3, \ldots r\}$. The r relations, $X_1, X_2, X_3, \ldots X_r$ are assumed to be measured on the same set of actors. We let x_{ijm} be the value of the tie from actor i to actor j on relation m; the collection of ties of type m form a $g \times g$ adjacency matrix, denoted by X_m. We can view each of these matrices as a layer of a $g \times g \times r$ array that represents all relational measurements among all ordered pairs of actors. We denote this three-way array by X. Although it is possible to develop models for measurements with discrete values (see Robins, Pattison, and Wasserman 1999), we assume here that all observations are dichotomous, with $x_{ijm} = 1$ if there is a tie of type m from actor i to actor j, and $x_{ijm} = 0$ otherwise.

As indicated in Chapter 8, it is possible to distinguish between directional and nondirectional relations. The orientation of relational ties is relevant for *directional* relations. A tie is directed from one actor, the "sender" of the tie, to another actor, the "receiver" of the tie; in this case, X_{ijm} is distinct from X_{jim}. *Nondirectional* ties do not have a direction; we cannot distinguish between a "sender" and a "receiver." For nondirectional ties, $X_{ijm} = X_{jim}$, and the corresponding adjacency matrix X_m is symmetric.

Multiple social networks can also be represented in graphic form. For a nondirectional relation, each actor is represented by a *node* and *lines* connect any pair of nodes that are connected by a tie. A directional relation can be represented by a directed graph, or *digraph*, in which the node corresponding to the sender of a tie is connected by an *arc*, or directed arrow, to the receiver of the tie. A (directed) *multigraph* allows for more than one set of arcs: an arc with the label m is directed from node i to node j if $x_{ijm} = 1$. For ease of expression, we use the general term *multigraph* to refer to both directed and nondirected multigraphs.

(A) *Example: Krackhardt's High-Tech Managers*

Krackhardt (1987) assessed two types of network ties among managers of a small high-tech manufacturing firm. The network is comprised of the twenty-one individuals employed by the firm at the managerial level ($g = 21$). The median organizational tenure for the managers was 9.33 years. The organization consisted of four departments, and each manager was at one of three hierarchical levels in the firm (CEO, vice president, manager). Each manager was asked two questions, "Who would [you] go to for advice at work?" and "Who are [your] friends?" Each manager was given a roster of names of all the managers in the organization and asked to check the names of those individuals to whom they go for advice and regard as friends. Both relations are directional. This is a multirelational data set where $N = \{1, 2, 3, \ldots, 21\}$, $R = \{1, 2\}$, and the two relations are advice ($\mathbf{X}_1$) and friendship ($\mathbf{X}_2$). These data are available to the reader in Krackhardt's (1987) original article, UCINET 5.0 for Windows (Borgatti, Everett, and Freeman 1999), and also Appendix B of Wasserman and Faust (1994). Thus, the applications presented below can be readily replicated.

9.3   Random Graph Models for Multiple Relations

As we observed in the introduction, theoretical questions about network structures and network processes often pertain to multiple types of relations. For example, among coworkers in an organization, we might expect to see different patterns and pathways for different forms of network ties (e.g., friendship, advice seeking, and cooperation). Indeed, hypotheses concerning a set of multiple network ties often center around questions of multiplexity, exchange, and interlock. Table 9.3.1 provides graphic representations for these configurations of interest. *Multiplexity* refers to the tendency for two or more ties of different types to occur together (that is, to link the same pair of actors). For example, in support networks, one may want to investigate whether there is a tendency for multiple support relations (e.g., emotional, informational, material) to come from the same individual; among coworkers, one might be interested in whether friends also offer work-related advice. Exchange structures are those in which a network tie that flows in one direction (say from actor i) is accompanied by a tie of a different type in

Table 9.3.1. *Configurations of Interest for Multivariate Networks*

Theoretical Construct	Graphic Configuration	Network Statistic[a]
Multiplexity	$i \bullet \dashrightarrow \bullet j$	$\sum x_{ijm} x_{ijh}$
Restricted exchange	$i \bullet \rightleftarrows \bullet j$	$\sum x_{ijm} x_{jih}$
Role interlocking (two-path)	$i \bullet \dashrightarrow \bullet k$ to j	$\sum x_{ikm} x_{kjh}$
Generalized exchange (three-cycle)	(triangle i, k, j)	$\sum x_{ikm} x_{kjh} x_{jip}$
Transitivity	(triangle i, k, j)	$\sum x_{ikm} x_{kjh} x_{ijp}$

[a] Network statistics assume homogeneity of λ_A based on isomorphic configurations.

the other direction (toward actor i). It is common to distinguish direct, or restricted, exchange from indirect, or generalized, exchange. *Restricted exchange* involves the direct interchange of resources among members of a dyad (e.g., actors i and j offer support to one another). *Generalized exchange* systems, however, involve substructures larger than the dyad; there is no need for immediate reciprocity. Rather, the exchange of relations may pass through several others before returning, or cycling back, to the source (e.g., Bearman 1997). More generally, if the patterns of transfer of multiple resources or relations involve contingencies within one or more network pathways, then the resource transfers or relations are said to be *interlocked*. Thus, interlocking is seen as a more general form of relational interdependence, with restricted and generalized exchange as special cases.

(A) *Assumptions*

As in Chapter 8, the set of network actors is assumed to be fixed, and the network ties X_{ijm} linking those actors are regarded as potentially interdependent random variables. The interdependencies are likely to vary in distinctive ways according to the type of relations involved and according to various attributes of the individuals, including personal and sociodemographic characteristics and social position. Following the approach originally adopted by Frank and Strauss (1986) and described in detailed in Chapter 8, a dependence graph is proposed that specifies hypothesized conditional dependencies among the X_{ijm}. By applying the Hammersley-Clifford theorem (Besag 1974) to these postulated dependencies, a general probability model is derived for the set of random variables X_{ijm}.

In applying this general modeling framework to the modeling of multiple network relations, it is also assumed that there are systematicities in the patterns of interdependence across the network; these systematicities are assumed to arise from regularities in the local social processes by which network ties evolve. However, because these local processes are not entirely regular, a stochastic modeling framework is appropriate.

(B) *Dependence Graphs*

The dependence graph is a formal representation of hypothesized conditional dependencies among the tie variables X_{ijm}. The problem of choosing an appropriate dependence graph in any application is a substantive and potentially difficult one. To provide assistance in the choice, we discuss several dependence graphs that relate to specific structural themes commonly encountered in the literature (Pattison and Wasserman 1999). The simplest of these dependence graphs is presented first; subsequent dependence graphs incorporate additional complexity by positing additional conditional dependencies.

The dependence graph, D, is a graph whose nodes are the set of all possible ties (the random variables, X_{ijm}) and whose edges specify the pairs of random variables that are assumed to be conditionally dependent, given the values of the other random variables. Formally, the node set for the dependence graph is $N_D = \{X_{ijm} : i \neq j; i, j \in N, m \in R\}$ and the edge set is $E_D = \{(X_{ijm}, X_{klh}): X_{ijm}$ and X_{klh} are conditionally dependent given the rest of $\mathbf{X}\}$.

Bernoulli Multigraphs

The simplest dependence graphs are for the class of Bernoulli multigraphs (see Frank and Nowicki 1993; Pattison and Wasserman 2002). Bernoulli multigraphs assume conditional independence for all pairs of random variables representing distinct pairs of individuals; that is, X_{ijm} and X_{klh} are assumed to be independent whenever $i \neq k$ or $j \neq l$. In other words, X_{ijm} and X_{ijh} are assumed to be interdependent and the dependence graph contains edges connecting nodes X_{ijm} and X_{ijh}. This dependence graph allows us to pose theoretical questions concerning role sets or multiplexity. The literature on role sets suggests that there is a likely dependence between different relational ties linking any given pair of actors: the presence of one type of relation between two individuals is likely to affect the presence of other types of relations. Thus, the ties connecting a pair, i and j, of individuals are likely to occur in characteristic bundles, termed *role sets*, and the pattern of interpendencies among tie variables leads to a characterization of the tendencies for these bundles to arise.

Dyad-Independent Random Multigraphs

Multivariate dyadic independence models (see Wasserman 1987; Pattison and Wasserman 2002) assume that relations from i to j are conditionally dependent on relations from j to i (X_{ijm} and X_{jih} are interdependent). Thus, in the multivariate dyadic independence model, one can investigate hypotheses concerning restricted exchange and reciprocity in addition to multiplexity hypotheses.

Path-Dependent Random Multigraphs

Path-dependent multigraph models are a more restricted case of the Markov models described in this chapter. These models allow one to investigate hypotheses concerning certain forms of role interlocking and generalized exchange processes that involve contingencies among adjacent ties in labeled paths in a network (see Pattison 1993). The dependence graph for a path-dependent multigraph (constrained to paths of two edges) places an edge between X_{ijm} and X_{jkh} for any $i, j, k \in N; m, h \in R$. Labeled paths trace the sequence of relational ties that connect a pair of individuals through other network actors. Paths are important network configurations in that they provide the conduit for the flow of social processes or diffusion of information. The dependence graph for path-dependent multigraphs has complete subgraphs that correspond to multiplexity effects, restricted exchange effects, and generalized exchange effects involving three actors.

Markov Random Multigraphs

In a Markov random multigraph, X_{ijm} and X_{klh} are assumed to be conditionally independent if and only if $\{i, j\} \cap \{k, l\} = \emptyset$. Many forms of interdependence among network actors can be investigated on the basis of a multivariate Markov dependence assumption. In addition to the investigation of hypotheses concerning role sets, role interlocking, and generalized exchange for three actors, multivariate Markov random graphs allow one to investigate hypotheses concerning various triadic effects that may be of interest, such as generalized transitivity or intransitivity. Markov random multigraphs are more general than path-dependent multigraphs by assuming that two ties forming a *semipath* are conditionally dependent. (A pair x_{ijm} and x_{klh} of ties form a *semipath* if $\{i, j\} \cap \{k, l\} \neq \emptyset$.)

Realization-Dependent Random Multigraphs

A Markov dependence assumption constrains our investigation of role interlocking to paths of two edges and cycles of three edges. To investigate the possibility of role interlocking beyond paths and semipaths of two edges and generalized exchange beyond cycles of three edges, we note that it is necessary to move beyond Markov dependence to partial conditional dependence assumptions. For example, we might assume that X_{ijm} and X_{klh} are conditionally dependent for distinct i, j, k, l, but only if a tie of some type is actually observed from actor j to actor k, or from actor l to actor i, that is, only if $x_{jkg} = 1$ or $x_{lig} = 1$ for some type g of tie (see Pattison and Robins 2002; also Chapter 10, this volume).

(C) *The Random Multigraph Model*

The Hammersley-Clifford theorem (Besag 1974) provides the important link between the dependence graph and the structure of the model that encapsulates its dependence assumptions. The theorem establishes that the probability model for the random multigraph, **X**, depends on the complete subgraphs of the dependence graph, *D*. A *complete subgraph*, or *clique*, is a subset of nodes in the dependence graph, every pair of which is linked by an edge. A subset consisting of a single node is also regarded as complete.

Each complete subgraph corresponds to a configuration of possible ties in the network. There is a model parameter corresponding to each complete subgraph in the dependence structure (and so to each corresponding configuration of possible ties). The parameter for a particular configuration reflects the effect of observing that configuration on the likelihood of the network.

The random multigraph model is of the following exponential form:

$$P(\mathbf{X} = \mathbf{x}) = \kappa^{-1} \exp\left(\sum_{A \subseteq N_D} \lambda_A z_A(\mathbf{x}) \right), \qquad (9.1)$$

where $\mathbf{x}$ is a realization of the random multigraph, $\mathbf{X}$, $\kappa = \sum_{\mathbf{x}} \exp\left\{ \sum_{A \subseteq D} \lambda_A z_A(\mathbf{x}) \right\}$ is a normalizing quantity; the summation is over all subsets A of nodes of D; $z_A(\mathbf{x})$ is the network statistic in $\mathbf{x}$ corresponding to the subgraph A of D and is given by $z_A(\mathbf{x}) = \prod_{X_{ijm} \in A} x_{ijm}$; λ_A is the parameter corresponding to the subgraph A of D; and $\lambda_A = 0$ whenever the subgraph induced by the nodes in A is not a complete subgraph of D.

For many of the dependence graphs that have been postulated, the model may not be identified due to the large number of parameters. It is often useful to define certain equality constraints among parameters or to set certain parameters equal to zero. Generally, the hypotheses in which we are interested impose some sort of regularity condition on the model. In other words, we are not necessarily interested in the effect of a specific configuration, but in the general effect of configurations of a particular type. Therefore, it is often useful to impose homogeneity constraints on the model parameters. Accordingly, we assume that certain effects are the same for all or at least large parts of the network.

One approach is to equate parameters corresponding to *isomorphic* configurations or subgraphs. Two subgraphs, A and A' are isomorphic if there is a one-to-one mapping, ϕ from the nodes of A to the nodes of A' that preserves the adjacency of nodes. Formally, A and A' are isomorphic if there exists a mapping ϕ on the node set N such that $(i, j, m) \in A$ if and only if $(\phi(i), \phi(j), m) \in A'$ for $i, j \in N, m \in R$. To apply homogeneity constraints based on isomorphic configurations, we set $\lambda_A = \lambda_{A'}$, then

$$P(\mathbf{X} = \mathbf{x}) = \kappa^{-1} \exp\left(\sum_{[A]} \lambda_{[A]} z_{[A]}(\mathbf{x}) \right), \qquad (9.2)$$

where $[A]$ is the isomorphism class of the complete subgraphs in the dependence graph D that contains A and $z_{[A]}(\mathbf{x}) = \sum_{A \in [A]} z_A(\mathbf{x})$ is a count of the number of observed configurations in $\mathbf{x}$ corresponding to the isomorphism class $[A]$. This approach assumes that the effect of configurations on the probability of the realization $\mathbf{x}$ does not depend on the identity of the actors involved. For example, the effect of a multiplex relation between advice and friendship on the likelihood of the multigraph might be assumed to be constant for all i, j pairs.

It may be the case, however, that we want to hypothesize differential effects of multiplexity due to demographic attributes or social positions of the individuals. For example, we might suppose that it is more probable for women than for men to seek advice from their friends. In this case, equality constraints would need to take node attributes such as gender into account. Similarly, if we had classified each node into social positions based on an *a priori* blockmodeling we might want to examine position effects through more restricted homogeneity constraints. These more restricted equality constraints can be achieved by ensuring the mapping ϕ on the node set N just introduced also preserves the relevant node attributes. That is, assume that A and A' are isomorphic configurations as defined previously, and set $\lambda_A = \lambda_{A'}$ only when nodes i and $\phi(i)$ are in the same block or attribute category and nodes j and $\phi(j)$ are in the same block or attribute category, for all $i, j \in N$. Pattison and Robins (2002; see also Chapter 10) discuss further constraints that can be implemented based on *local social neighborhoods*. These neighborhood constraints may take the form of setting structures such as sociocultural space, geographic space, temporal constraints, or formal organizational constraints.

(D) *Estimation*

Estimation of the parameters of equation 9.1 is generally not straightforward. For simple models based on Bernoulli or dyad-independent multigraphs, maximum likelihood methods are available (e.g., see Wasserman 1987; Frank and Nowicki 1993). To estimate models with more complex dependence assumptions, however, direct estimation using maximum likelihood techniques may not be viable. The likelihood function for the model parameters depends on the complicated normalizing quantity, κ, which impedes direct estimation except for simple models (e.g., Bernoulli, dyad-independent models) and for small multigraphs. Thus, indirect methods need to be used to estimate model parameters. Currently, Markov chain Monte Carlo (MCMC) methods are being investigated for estimating parameters for the univariate models discussed in Chapters 8 and 10 (Snijders 2002). Although MCMC approaches hold great promise for estimation of random graph models and, in principle, can be extended readily to the multirelational case, there are likely to be a number of practical problems to be resolved before these procedures can be used to fit the model defined in (9.1). Pseudolikelihood techniques, however, have proven to be useful in estimating the model parameters and can be easily implemented in the case of multigraphs (Pattison and Wasserman 1999). The pseudolikelihood approach is only approximate and, unfortunately, the statistical properties of the pseudolikelihood estimators are only partially understood.

To estimate model parameters using the pseudolikelihood approach as described by Besag (1975, 1977), Strauss and Ikeda (1990), and Pattison and Wasserman (1999), we can use the dichotomous nature of the random variables (X_{ijm}) to respecify model (9.2) into a generalized autologistic model. To specify the conditional logit form of the model, we define

$$\mathbf{X}_{ijm}^C = \{X_{klh} : X_{klh} \in N_D \text{ and } (k, l, h) \neq (i, j, m)\}$$

$$\mathbf{x}_{ijm}^+ = \{x_{klh}^+ : x_{klh}^+ = x_{klh} \text{ for all } (k, l, h) \neq (i, j, m) \text{ and } x_{ijm}^+ = 1\}$$

$$\mathbf{x}_{ijm}^- = \{x_{klh}^- : x_{klh}^- = x_{klh} \text{ for all } (k, l, h) \neq (i, j, m) \text{ and } x_{ijm}^- = 0\}.$$

Then, the conditional probability that the random variable $X_{ijm} = 1$ is

$$P\left(X_{ijm} = 1 | \mathbf{X}_{ijm}^C\right) = \frac{P\left(\mathbf{X} = \mathbf{x}_{ijm}^+\right)}{P\left(\mathbf{X} = \mathbf{x}_{ijm}^+\right) + P\left(\mathbf{X} = \mathbf{x}_{ijm}^-\right)}$$

$$= \frac{\exp\left(\sum_{[A]} \lambda_{[A]} z_{[A]}(\mathbf{x}_{ijm}^+)\right)}{\exp\left(\sum_{[A]} \lambda_{[A]} z_{[A]}(\mathbf{x}_{ijm}^+)\right) + \exp\left(\sum_{[A]} \lambda_{[A]} z_{[A]}(\mathbf{x}_{ijm}^-)\right)},$$

which does not depend on the normalizing constant, κ. The conditional probabilities can be used to construct the log-odds of a relational tie of type m from actor i to actor j. The logit model can be expressed as

$$\varpi_{ijm} = \log\left\{\frac{P\left(X_{ijm} = 1 | \mathbf{X}_{ijm}^C\right)}{P\left(X_{ijm} = 0 | \mathbf{X}_{ijm}^C\right)}\right\}$$

$$= \sum_{[A]} \lambda_{[A]}\left[z_{[A]}(\mathbf{x}_{ijm}^+) - z_{[A]}(\mathbf{x}_{ijm}^-)\right] = \sum_{[A]} \lambda_{[A]}(d_{[A]})_{ij}^m. \qquad (9.3)$$

The $(d_{[A]})_{ij}^m$ specifies the difference in the number of subgraphs of class $[A]$ that would be observed in the network $\mathbf{x}$ if the tie of type m from actor i to actor j is present rather than absent.

The pseudolikelihood function for the multivariate random graph model is

$$PL(\lambda) = \prod_{i \neq j} \prod_{m=1}^{r} P(X_{ijm} = 1 | \mathbf{X}_{ijm}^C)^{x_{ijm}} P(X_{ijm} = 0 | \mathbf{X}_{ijm}^C)^{1 - x_{ijm}}.$$

The *maximum pseudolikelihood estimator* (MPLE) is the value of λ that maximizes $PL(\lambda)$, where λ is the vector of the parameters $\lambda_{[A]}$. Strauss and Ikeda (1990) showed that the MPLEs can be obtained by fitting the logit model in (9.3) using any standard logistic regression program; see Pattison and Wasserman (1999) for details. The response variable for the logistic regression is the vector of the observed network ties and the explanatory variables are the change statistics, $(d_{[A]})_{ij}^m$, computed for each class of complete subgraphs in the hypothesized dependence graph. For the models fitted to the first example, SPSS (2000) commands for computing values of the change statistics are set out in the Appendix.

Because estimation techniques are only approximate, assessments of the importance of structural characteristics and of model fit are based on heuristics that compare the observed values, x_{ijm}, with the fitted values, $\hat{x}_{ijm}$. The fitted values are defined as $\hat{x}_{ijm} = \hat{P}(X_{ijm} = 1 | \mathbf{X}_{ijm}^C)$. Commonly, the model "deviance" (G_{PL}^2), or pseudolikelihood ratio statistic, and comparison of deviance values for nested models are used to evaluate the importance of hypothesized network configurations. The mean of the absolute value of the difference between the observed values, x_{ijm}, and the fitted values, $\hat{x}_{ijm}$, (or mean absolute residual [MAR]) is another index that provides information with regard to model fit. Both of these indices are used in the examples discussed in this chapter. To evaluate whether a particular parameter or set of parameters is statistically important, the difference in deviance values for two nested models are often compared. For a single parameter, Robins, Pattison, and Woolcock (2002a) suggested that a parameter contributes little if removing the parameter leads to an increase in model "deviance" of no more than $-2q \log(1 - \delta)$, where $q = n(n - 1)r$ is the number of tie variables and δ is a small, tunable parameter, say 0.005 or 0.001, that allows the researcher to exert control over the size of effects regarded as large. It should be emphasized that we use heuristic approaches such as these in evaluating the importance of model parameters because the distributional properties of the pseudolikelihood ratio statistic are not currently well-understood.

9.4 General Framework for Model Construction

To summarize, the general framework for constructing a random graph model for multivariate social network data is:

1. Regard each possible tie of each possible type as a random variable. All possible X_{ijm} are random variables.
2. Formulate hypotheses about the interdependencies of the ties of different types. Which pairs of random variables are conditionally dependent given the other random variables? Are we interested in hypotheses about role sets? Role reciprocity? Role interlocking?
3. Construct a dependence graph where the nodes are the random variables (X_{ijm}) and the edges link pairs of random variables hypothesized to be conditionally dependent in step 2.
4. Invoke the Hammersley-Clifford theorem to obtain a joint probability model for the set of random variables. Each model parameter corresponds to a complete subgraph in the dependence graph.
5. Consider homogeneity constraints. Should some parameters be expected to be equal (e.g., based on isomorphism classes, actor attributes, social positions, or geography)?
6. Estimate model parameters (e.g., using MPLE).

9.5 Example: Krackhardt's High-Tech Managers

To illustrate the models just described, we obtain pseudolikelihood estimates for a number of these models for the multigraph comprising advice (X_1) and friendship (X_2) relations for Krackhardt's high-tech managers. For univariate models, there are specialized programs, such as MultiNet (Richards and Seary 2000) and SIENA (Snijders 2002) that can be used to fit random graph models using pseudolikelihood and maximum likelihood estimation, respectively (see Chapter 13, this volume).[2] Unfortunately, there are no specialized programs available for multivariate random graph models. However, as mentioned earlier, MPLEs can be obtained using any standard logistic regression procedure. To fit the models discussed here, we used SPSS 10.1 for Windows (SPSS, Inc. 2000). A program in the SPSS matrix language was written to set up the explanatory variables $((d_{[A]})_{ij}^m)$ for the logistic regression. The matrix program is provided to the reader in the Appendix and can be followed immediately by a logistic regression in SPSS with response variable "yklm" and potential explanatory variables from the list t15a, t15f,..., t9faa. The labeling of terms is explained in the following paragraphs.

Multiplexity

Suppose we were interested in multiplexity effects for the high-tech managers. For instance, we might be interested in the question: do managers tend to go to their friends for advice? If we assume that multiplexity is the only possible effect of interest, we could propose a Bernoulli multigraph dependence structure. In this case, the complete subgraphs in the dependence graph take the form of single nodes corresponding to each possible advice or friendship tie ($\{X_{ij1}\}$ and $\{X_{ij2}\}$), or of pairs of connected nodes corresponding to each possible multiplex tie ($\{X_{ij1}, X_{ij2}\}$). We impose homogeneity constraints so isomorphic configurations have equal parameters. Attributes, social positions, and other possible setting structures among the managers are therefore not incorporated into the analysis. Parameters associated with the individual advice and friendship ties control for the overall density in the two networks. We fitted the following three models:

(1) $P(\mathbf{X} = \mathbf{x}) = \kappa^{-1} \exp \left\{ \lambda_1 \sum x_{ij1} + \lambda_2 \sum x_{ij2} \right\}$

(2) $P(\mathbf{X} = \mathbf{x}) = \kappa^{-1} \exp \left\{ \lambda_{1=2} \left(\sum x_{ij1} + \sum x_{ij2} \right) \right\}$

(3) $P(\mathbf{X} = \mathbf{x}) = \kappa^{-1} \exp \left\{ \lambda_1 \sum x_{ij1} + \lambda_2 \sum x_{ij2} + \lambda_3 \sum x_{ij1} x_{ij2} \right\}.$

Model (1) fits separate parameters for the degree of choice in the advice relation and the friendship relation. Model (2) equates these choice parameters. Thus, if we compare model (1) with model (2) we can evaluate whether the advice and friendship relations differ with respect to network density. Model (3) adds the multiplexity parameter to model (1). If we compare model (1) with model (3), we can evaluate, after controlling for density, whether there is a tendency for managers to go to their friends for advice in this organization (a positive multiplexity parameter), or whether they avoid going to their friends for advice (a negative multiplexity parameter). Table 9.5.2 provides the heuristic fit statistics for these three models. We note that the number of tie variables is $q = 840$, and if δ is set at 0.005, then $-2q \log(1 - \delta) = 8.42$.

Comparing model (1) with model (2), we observe a change in G^2_{PL} of 41.1 for a difference of just one parameter; in addition, the average absolute residual increases substantially when we equate the two choice parameters. Thus, the two indices suggest that the choice parameters differ. The density for the advice relation is 0.45 and the density for the friendship relation is 0.24: there are almost twice as many advice-seeking relationships as friendship ties among the managers in the organization. The parameter estimates are -0.19 for advice and -1.14 for friendship. The negative values indicate that the density for both networks is less than 0.50.

Table 9.5.2. *Fit Statistics for Multivariate Models*

Model	G^2_{PL}	df	MAR
(1) Advice choice, friend choice	1044.083	2	.4316
(2) Advice choice = friend choice	1085.213	1	.4536
(3) Model (1) + multiplexity	1024.051	3	.4213
(4) Model (1) + advice reciprocity, friend reciprocity	1014.226	4	.4173
(5) Model (4) + multiplexity	995.594	5	.4078
(6) Model (5) + restricted exchange	995.525	6	.4078
(7) Model (5) + advice two-paths, friend 2-paths	955.507	7	.3861
(8) Model (7) + role interlocking(AF), role interlocking(FA)	947.324	9	.3822
(9) Model (8) + advice three-cycles, friend three cycles	943.540	11	.3801
(10) Model (9) + generalized exchange (AFA), generalized exchange (AFF)	933.240	13	.3752
(11) Model (7) + two-in(A), two-out(A), two-in(F), two-out(F)	700.434	11	.2686
(12) Model (11) + two-in(AF), two-out(FA)	687.185	13	.2622
(13) Transitivity model	651.911	23	.2476

If we compare the fit statistics for model (1) and model (3), we find a change in G^2_{PL} of 20.0 for a single parameter, suggesting that the multiplexity parameter makes a useful contribution to the model. The mean absolute residual reduces to 0.421 from 0.432. Although this is not a large reduction, there does appear to be a tendency for multiplex ties in the network. The estimate of the multiplexity parameter is 0.73; managers exhibit an enhanced tendency to express one type of tie if they also express the other. Managers are more likely, in other words, to list their friends as advisors and their advisors as friends.

Restricted Exchange (Role Reciprocity)

The second set of models examines restricted exchange within the organization. If restricted exchange alone was in operation, then there would be a tendency for individuals to exchange resources, but only within dyads. For example, if manager i says that manager j is a friend, we would expect an increased tendency for manager j to seek advice from manager i. This second set of models assumes dyad independence. The complete subgraphs of the dependence graph correspond to possible ties for advice and friendship ($\{X_{ij1}\}, \{X_{ij2}\}$), possible multiplex ties ($\{X_{ij1}, X_{ij2}\}$), reciprocity within the advice and friendship relation ($\{X_{ij1}, X_{ji1}\}, \{X_{ij2}, X_{ji2}\}$), and restricted exchange between advice and friendship ($\{X_{ij1}, X_{ji2}\}$). We fitted the following models:

$$(4) \; P(\mathbf{X} = \mathbf{x}) = \kappa^{-1} \exp \left\{ \lambda_1 \sum x_{ij1} + \lambda_2 \sum x_{ij2} + \lambda_4 \sum x_{ij1} x_{ji1} \right. $$
$$\left. + \lambda_5 \sum x_{ij2} x_{ji2} \right\}$$

$$(5) \; P(\mathbf{X} = \mathbf{x}) = \kappa^{-1} \exp \left\{ \lambda_1 \sum x_{ij1} + \lambda_2 \sum x_{ij2} + \lambda_3 \sum x_{ij1} x_{ij2} \right. $$
$$\left. + \lambda_4 \sum x_{ij1} x_{ji1} + \lambda_5 \sum x_{ij2} x_{ji2} \right\}$$

$$(6) \; P(\mathbf{X} = \mathbf{x}) = \kappa^{-1} \exp \left\{ \lambda_1 \sum x_{ij1} + \lambda_2 \sum x_{ij2} + \lambda_3 \sum x_{ij1} x_{ij2} \right. $$
$$\left. + \lambda_4 \sum x_{ij1} x_{ji1} + \lambda_5 \sum x_{ij2} x_{ji2} + \lambda_6 \sum x_{ij1} x_{ji2} \right\}.$$

Fit statistics for these models are presented in Table 9.5.2.

If we compare model (4) to model (1) from the previous set of analyses, the change in the pseudolikelihood ratio statistics is 29.9, for two additional parameters. Further, there appears to be a moderately large reduction in the *MAR* (from 0.432 to 0.417). The parameter estimates for reciprocity are 0.16 for advice and 1.35 for friendship. Both estimates are positive, suggesting a reciprocity tendency for both types of tie, but the effect appears to be considerably stronger for friendship than for advice. In fact, removing the reciprocity parameter for advice ties is associated with a very small change in G_{PL}^2 (of 0.7) and a small change in the *MAR* (from 0.417 to 0.418). The resulting model indicates that the reciprocity effect for friendship makes an important contribution and should not be omitted from the model.

From the first set of analyses, there appeared to be a moderately strong multiplexity effect for advice and friendship. By comparing model (5) with model (4), we can evaluate whether the multiplexity parameter is still important after controlling for reciprocity within each relation. The pseudolikelihood is reduced by 18.6 with inclusion of the multiplexity parameter, and the *MAR* for model (5) is 0.408, suggesting a moderate improvement in fit. Thus, the multiplexity effect is still evident after controlling for reciprocity within relations. Model (6) introduces the restricted exchange parameter (λ_6). The change in G_{PL}^2 and *MAR* from model (5) to model (6) is negligible. Thus, there is no evidence for restricted exchange between advice and friendship in this organization. The parameter estimates for model (5) are presented in Table 9.5.3 and suggest a tendency for multiplex ties, as well as a tendency for friendship ties to be reciprocated within dyads.

Role Interlocking and Generalized Exchange

Hypotheses concerning role interlocking and generalized exchange can be investigated by assuming at least path dependence among ties. The complete subgraphs in the dependence graph for the path-dependent model include those configurations investigated under dyadic independence, plus two-paths for advice and friendship

Table 9.5.3. *Parameter Estimates and Approximate Standard Errors for Selected Multivariate Models*

Parameter/construct	Model (5) Estimate	Model (7) Estimate	Model (12a) Estimate	Final Transitivity Model Estimate
Choice – advice (λ_1)	−0.424	1.380	−4.719	−4.635
Choice – friend (λ_2)	−1.896	−1.345	−3.655	−2.414
Multiplexity (λ_3)	0.714	0.589	1.532	1.606
Reciprocity – advice (λ_4)	0.127	1.041	1.531	0.981
Reciprocity – friend (λ_5)	1.336	1.621	2.223	1.552
Two-path – advice (λ_7)		−0.129	−0.078	
Two-path – friend (λ_8)		−0.062	−0.098	
Out-star – advice			0.310	0.186
Out-star – friendship			0.324	0.283
In-star – advice			0.282	0.273
In-star – friendship			0.189	
Two-path – AF				−0.155
Out-star – AF			−0.080	−0.082
In-star – AF				−0.119
Transitivity – AFA				0.289

($\{X_{ij1}, X_{jk1}\}, \{X_{ij2}, X_{jk2}\}$), three-cycles for advice and friendship ($\{X_{ij1}, X_{jk1}, X_{ki1}\}$, $\{X_{ij2}, X_{jk2}, X_{ki2}\}$), two-paths involving both advice and friendship ties ($\{X_{ij1}, X_{jk2}\}$, $\{X_{ij2}, X_{jk1}\}$), and three-cycles involving both advice and friendship ties ($\{X_{ij1}, X_{jk2}, X_{ki1}\}$, $\{X_{ij1}, X_{jk2}, X_{ki2}\}$).

To investigate role interlocking, we fitted two models that built on model (5). Model (7) adds the two-path subgraphs for advice and friendship and model (8) adds the two role-interlocking structures in addition to the advice and friendship two-paths. Table 9.5.2 provides the fit indices for these models. A comparison of the fit statistics for models (5) and (7) suggest that the advice and friendship two-paths are important structures in the network. The change in G^2_{PL} is 40.1 for two additional parameters, and we observe a moderate reduction in the *MAR* (from 0.408 to 0.386). Model (8) adds the two role-interlocking structures. These two parameters appear not to make a substantial contribution to the model ($\Delta G^2_{PL} = 8.18$).

To examine generalized exchange hypotheses, we fit a further sequence of models that included three-cycles. Even though the role-interlocking parameters provided a minimal improvement to the model, we included these structures in the following analyses because they are marginal to the generalized exchange subgraphs. Model (9) includes the three-cycles for advice and friendship and model (10) adds the two other structures with three-cycles. Table 9.5.2 provides the fit indices for these models. The inclusion of the three-cycles and generalized exchange structures does not appear to contribute significantly to the model. Thus, there appears to be a limited amount of role interlocking and generalized exchange among the advice-seeking and friendship relationships of managers in this organization. Table 9.5.3 provides the pseudolikelihood estimates for model (7). Based on the parameter estimates, there appears to be a tendency against two-paths for advice, when choice, reciprocity, and multiplexity are controlled for. The size of the two-path parameter estimate for friendship appears to be small, suggesting that this structure provides a negligible contribution to the model.

Markov Dependence

Under the Markov dependence model, the complete subgraphs of the dependence graph include those configurations examined in previous analyses along with a number of triadic and star effects. A subset of these structures will be examined in the next set of models. The two-path structures examined in the previous set of analyses are marginal to the transitive triad configurations that will be examined under the Markov model dependence assumption. Therefore, these configurations will be included in the analysis. The first set of models examines the contribution of in-stars and out-stars of size two to model (7). First, we fitted a model with the unirelational in-stars, $\{X_{ij1}, X_{kj1}\}$, $\{X_{ij2}, X_{kj2}\}$, and out-stars $\{X_{ij1}, X_{ik1}\}$, $\{X_{ij2}, X_{ik2}\}$ (model (11)); then, in model (12), we add the multirelational versions $\{X_{ij1}, X_{jk2}\}$, $\{X_{ij1}, X_{ik2}\}$. The inclusion of the unirelational in-stars and out-stars for the advice and friendship relations resulted in a very large reduction in the pseudolikelihood ratio statistic ($\Delta G^2_{PL} = 255.1$ for four additional parameters) and average absolute residual (from 0.386 to 0.269). The parameter estimates for all four of these effects are positive and large, suggesting that managers are differentiated in their propensities to nominate and receive both advice and friendship ties. Such differentiation is consistent with "preferential attachment" hypotheses of the type proposed for network structures more generally (e.g., see Albert and Barábasi 2002): ties are likely to emanate from (and be directed toward) those nodes who are already active in nominating and receiving ties. When the multirelational in- and out-stars are entered into the model, the change in G^2_{PL} is a moderate 13.2. Removing the multirelational in-star parameter had a negligible effect on G^2_{PL}; parameter estimates for the resulting model are shown in Table 9.5.3.

The final set of models examine the eight possible transitivity effects corresponding to:

$$\{X_{ij1}, X_{jk1}, X_{ik2}\}, \{X_{ij1}, X_{jk2}, X_{ik1}\}, \{X_{ij1}, X_{jk2}, X_{ik2}\}, \{X_{ij2}, X_{jk1}, X_{ik2}\},$$
$$\{X_{ij2}, X_{jk2}, X_{ik1}\}, \{X_{ij2}, X_{jk1}, X_{ik1}\}, \{X_{ij1}, X_{jk1}, X_{ik1}\},$$

and $\{X_{ij2}, X_{jk2}, X_{ik2}\}$. Multivariate two-paths (role interlocking) are marginal to the multivariate transitive triads, thus these structures were entered into the analysis as well, even though they did not appear to be statistically important in earlier analyses. The transitivity model included the unirelational versions of choice, reciprocity, in-stars, out-stars, two-paths, and transitive triads, the multiplexity effect, multirelational in-stars, out-stars, and two paths and the six multirelational transitive triads. We evaluated the importance of each transitivity effect in turn and eliminated those effects whose omission increased G^2_{PL} by less than 8.42. This approach led to the retention of only a single transitivity effect (that associated with triads of the form $\{X_{ij1}, X_{jk2}, X_{ik1}\}$). Further successive consideration of effects associated with maximal complete graphs in the dependence graph using the same criterion resulted in a model with twenty-three parameters; the pseudolikelihood estimates for parameters in the final model are presented in Table 9.5.3. The heuristic fit indices for this final transitivity model are $G^2_{PL} = 688.6$ and $MAR = 0.263$.

As in most of the previous models, there is evidence in this final model for strong multiplexity and reciprocity effects, as well as for differentiation among nodes in their propensities to express advice and friendship ties, and to receive advice ties. (Note that the reciprocity parameter for advice ties is also large, now that differentiation among nodes in expressing and receiving advice ties is taken into account.) In addition, the positive transitivity parameter estimate suggests an enhanced probability for networks that have a large number of triads in which a manager's advisors are linked by a friendship tie. It is impossible to infer from cross-sectional data such as these what mechanisms might give rise to such structures, but one plausible hypothesis is that friendship ties build bridges for the creation of advice ties. For example, advisors might recommend their friends as further sources of advice, or a manager might be more comfortable approaching for advice the trusted friend of an advisor. These interpretations are supported by the large negative value of the parameter for two-paths comprising an advice and friendship tie: such paths are relatively unlikely in the network. We note that effects such as these illustrate the potential importance of a multirelational perspective: it may be difficult to understand the emergence of advice ties without taking into account their dependence on friendship ties.

9.6 Multiple Rater Networks/Cognitive Social Structures

As we discussed in Section 9.1, models of multiple rater networks have important implications in network measurement. Theoretical questions concerning the same relation from multiple rater perspectives might include questions about consensus and bias in perceptions, or about individual differences in perceptions of social structure. *Consensus* refers to the agreement between two or more perceivers. Thus, consensus hypotheses allow one to evaluate whether two or more raters agree in their assessment of the social relationships within an organization or whether individuals with similar attributes or who share relational ties agree on their perceptions of the social structure. *Accuracy* and bias questions relate perceptions of social structure to some criterion network. The criterion network may have been obtained via direct observation or through some function of the perceptions of relationships (see Krackhardt 1987, and Chapter 2, this volume). One might be interested in assessing whether perceptual accuracy is related to actor attributes or network location. These models allow one to account for individual differences in perceptions of structure. Thus, we can evaluate who perceives a balanced structure, who perceives a hierarchical structure, and whether there is a tendency for structural agreement if perceivers share certain attributes, positions, or relations.

The multiple rater random graph models provide one of the few statistical approaches available for examining the structure within a set of cognitive or perceptual networks. These models allow one to incorporate interdependencies between raters within the model. Furthermore, the models provide a mechanism for model-based inference about an interrelated set of cognitive networks, allowing us to investigate questions involving perceptual congruence, accuracy, and bias, and more complex questions concerning perceptions of structure within a network. The structural analysis of perceptual networks has important implications in biobehavioral research, particularly in the areas of epidemiology, social support, quality of life, intervention, and prevention; organizational communication and research concerning job satisfaction, workplace efficiency, and diffusion of new technologies; social cognition and research concerning relational recall; and, perhaps one of the most important applications, in the arena of network measurement.

(A) *Notation and Terminology*

The models that we discuss in this section involve data where several individuals provide their perceptions of the relational ties of a single type among members of a bounded group. Thus, each perceiver provides their perceptual map of the relational ties on the node set, N, which can be represented in a $g \times g$ sociomatrix, denoted by $\mathbf{X}_p$. The perceiver set is denoted by $P = \{1, 2, 3, \dots r\}$. We assume that the sociomatrix represents the respondent's perceptions of directed binary relations where

$$X_{ijp} = \begin{cases} 1 & \text{if respondent } p \text{ perceives a relational tie from } i \text{ to } j \\ 0 & \text{if respondent } p \text{ does not perceive a relational tie from } i \text{ to } j. \end{cases}$$

We can combine this set of perceptual networks into a three-way $g \times g \times p$ array X^P. Note that the multiple rater networks are similar to the multirelational network presented in the previous section. However, in the current setting the third way refers to a particular respondent, or perceiver, rather than to a particular type of relation. The respondents may be a set of outside raters or judges providing their perceptions or observations of the interactions of a group of actors or the respondents may be the set of actors in N. If the set respondents are the actors in the network under study, then the data represent a cognitive social structure (CSS) (Newcomb 1961; Krackhardt 1987).

A CSS is a set of networks reflecting each network member's perceptions of the relationships between all actors in the network. The data can be represented in a $g \times g \times g$ array. The perceptual network for perceiver p represents actor p's perception of the entire network. It should be noted that the unirelational network data commonly collected is embedded in the CSS. The pth row of perceiver p's perceptual matrix, X_p, is the pth row of the unirelational network; Krackhardt (1987) referred to this as the row locally aggregated structure (RLAS). A column locally aggregated structure (CLAS) is the matrix that is obtained by aggregating each respondent's perception of the relational ties they have received. In other words,

$$\mathbf{X}_{RLAS} = \left\{ X_{iji} \right\} \text{ and } \mathbf{X}_{CLAS} = \left\{ X_{ijj} \right\}.$$

The intersection and union of the row and column LAS are sometimes of interest. A tie exists between i and j in the intersection if both respondent i and respondent j perceive a tie from i to j. For the union, there is a tie between i and j if either respondent i or respondent j perceives a tie from i to j.

(B) *Example: Krackhardt's High-Tech Managers*

Again, we use relational data obtained from Krackhardt's high-tech managers. The network consists of relationships and perceived relationships among twenty-one managers in a high-tech, machine manufacturing firm on the West Coast. In addition to the multirelational data that we examined earlier, CSS data were obtained for the advice-seeking relation and the friendship relations. Each manager was asked to evaluate the perceived or observed ties between all managers in the firm, not just their own relationships. Every manager in the organization answered the following questions for themselves and each of their colleagues: "Who does [actor] go to for advice and help with work?" and "Who are [actor]'s friends?" The RLAS for the advice and friendship relations was used in the multivariate random graph examples presented previously. These data are available to the reader in Krackhardt's (1987) original article and UCINET V for Windows (Borgatti et al. 1999).

9.7 Multiple Rater Random Graph Models

The specification of the multiple rater model follows Koehly's (1996) work on random graph models for CSSs. Assumptions underlying the model are similar to those assumptions specified for the multivariate random graph models; however, we now have to consider the interdependencies between the perceivers or raters.

(A) *Dependence Graphs*

The dependence graph for the multiple rater model is a graph, D_p, where the node set is defined by all possible ties (the X_{ijm}) in the array $\mathbf{X}^P$ and the edge set specifies the pairs of random variables that are assumed to be conditionally dependent, given the values of the other random variables. Formally, the nodes set for the dependence graph is $N_{D_p} = \{X_{ijm} : i \neq j; i, j \in N, m \in P\}$ and the edge set is $E_{D_P} = \{(X_{ijm}, X_{klh}) : X_{ijm} \text{ and } X_{klh} \text{ are conditionally dependent given the rest of } X^P\}$. There are two components to the dependence graph for multiple rater networks: the dependence structure within each "slice" – the perceived structure for each individual rater – and the dependence structure between "slices" or perceivers. Again, there are a large number of parameters that can be fit with these models, thus the questions investigated using these models should be defined *a priori* and driven by theory. Dependence graphs for several theoretical questions are illustrated here.

Consensus

The dependence graph for questions concerning consensus or congruence among perceivers does not specify a complex dependence structure between perceivers. Consensus dependence graphs focus on the agreement or concordance of ties between perceivers. The simplest dependence graph is similar to the dependence graphs used to investigate multiplexity for multivariate relations – the Bernoulli multigraph. Thus, the Bernoulli consensus graph assumes conditional independence for all pairs of random variables representing distinct pairs of individuals; that is, X_{ijk} and X_{lmp} are assumed to be independent whenever $i \neq l$ or $j \neq m$. In other words, X_{ijk} and X_{ijp} are assumed to be interdependent. The Bernoulli consensus graph does not investigate whether there is agreement at a structural level among perceivers.

Accuracy

Accuracy, and individual differences in accuracy, refer to the agreement between an individual's perception of the social structure and some criterion network. The criterion network may be based on some objective measurement (e.g., phone records, e-mail archives) or observation of the social relationships among actors. We denote the objective representation of the network by Y, which is assumed to be exogenous. The simplest accuracy model, given an objective criterion, assumes that the respondents are independent and that the ties are independent. However, X_{ijk} is assumed to depend on Y_{ij} (see Chapter 10 for a general discussion on the inclusion of exogenous variables in random graph models).

Another approach to the accuracy question is to define the criterion network by aggregating the information in the CSS (e.g., RLAS, CLAS, intersection or union of the RLAS and CLAS). This approach leads to a more complicated model because the criterion network is a function of the CSS, which we are modeling. If we assume that the criterion is based on the intersection or union of the RLAS and CLAS, then we assume that X_{ijk}, X_{iji}, and X_{ijj} are interdependent. However, given the unresolved questions in network measurement, we prefer to consider the agreement between an individual's perception of the social structure and the RLAS, CLAS, or some function of these two aggregated structures under the consensus models. We discuss this further in the *points of view* analysis.

Structure

There are several structural themes that might be of interest. Many of the structures discussed in the previous chapter can be extended to describe the perceived structure of multiple raters. For example, balance theory (Heider 1958) is a cognitive theory that proposes that an individual will perceive the others to whom the individual is positively linked to be positively linked to each other. Such a pattern of perceived ties is termed *balanced*, and the theory predicts that if relationships between triples of individuals are not balanced, then the respondent will alter his or her perceptions of these relationships in order to achieve cognitive balance. This suggests that balance is exhibited through the existence of transitive triads within each respondent's perceptual network. The dependence graph assumes conditional dependencies within each perceptual network – balance theory would suggest a Markov dependence within each X_p. Further, we might want to assume some interdependencies among the respondents using the RLAS, CLAS, or intersection or union of the two to define the dependence structure. Clearly, there is the potential for a lot of parameters to be entered into a structural model.

Structural questions can also be asked within a consensus framework. We may want to extend the consensus and accuracy questions to include specific structural characteristics of the network. Do the respondents appear to agree with each other with respect to reciprocal or triadic relationships? How accurate are respondents with respect to clique memberships? Are respondents more accurate about the social structure "close to home"? These questions move beyond the individual ties to organized structures, and thus extend the dependence graph to include these structural characteristics. For example, to examine consensus in reciprocity, the dependence graph would include edges between X_{ijk}, X_{ijp}, X_{jik}, and X_{jip}.

(B) *Multiple Rater Random Graph Model*

Again, we apply the Hammersley-Clifford theorem. The multiple rater model takes on the following exponential form:

$$P(\mathbf{X}^P = \mathbf{x}^P) = \kappa^{-1} \exp \left(\sum_{A \subseteq N_{D_P}} \lambda_A z_A(\mathbf{x}^P) \right), \tag{9.4}$$

where $\mathbf{x}^P$ is the realization of the multiple rater random graph, $\mathbf{X}^P$, κ is a normalizing constant defined similarly to that for the multigraph model, the summation is over all subsets A of nodes of D_P, $z_A(\mathbf{x}^P)$ is the network statistic in $\mathbf{x}^p$ corresponding to the complete subgraph A of D_P, $z_A(\mathbf{x}) = \prod_{X_{ijm} \in A} x_{ijm}$ is the sufficient statistic corresponding to the parameter λ_A, and $\lambda_A = 0$ whenever the subgraph induced by the nodes in A is not a complete subgraph of D_P.

Homogeneity constraints are necessary for the models to be identified, particularly if there are a large number of respondents and a complex structural model. One approach would be to equate model parameters for isomorphic configurations within each perceiver's cognitive network. If we equate parameters across perceivers' networks, however, we lose some of the strength in these models – the ability to investigate individual differences in perception. However, we might have particular attributes of the perceivers that we want to investigate as individual differences variables. If this is the case, we can constrain parameters across perceivers to be equal if the perceivers share particular attributes of interest.

Homogeneity constraints might also be defined according to the point of view of the perceiver. Let A be a subset of tie variables, and let N_A denote the set of nodes induced by A; that is, $N_A = \{k: X_{kij} \in A \text{ or } X_{ikj} \in A \text{ or } X_{ijk} \in A, \text{ for some } i, j \in N, k \in P\}$. (For instance, the set $A = \{X_{123}, X_{124}, X_{234}\}$ has an induced node set $\{1, 2, 3, 4\}$.) The subset A can be regarded as a *labeled configuration* in a random graph: labels are from the set N_A and the configuration has a tie labeled m from the node labeled i to the node labeled j if and only if $X_{ijm} \in A$. Let A and A' be two subsets of tie variables and let φ be a one-to-one mapping from N_A to $N_{A'}$. We say that an isomorphic mapping φ between A and A' preserves the *relative identity* of actors if $X_{ijm} \in A$ if and only if $X_{\varphi(i)\varphi(i)\varphi(m)} \in A'$. If such a mapping exists, then the labeled configuration for A' can be obtained from the labeled configuration for A by replacing the label k in A by $\varphi(k)$ in A'. Such mappings preserve *relative* identities in the configuration, but not *specific* identities (hence the term). For example, there is an isomorphism that preserves relative identities between the sets $\{X_{123}\}$ and $\{X_{214}\}$ (induced by mapping 1, 2, and 3 to 2, 1, and 4, respectively), but not between the sets $\{X_{123}\}$ and $\{X_{121}\}$ (because the induced node sets are not even of the same size). We refer to this homogeneity constraint as the *points of view* assumption.

Estimation and the evaluation of model fit are performed just as discussed in the previous section for random multigraphs. MPLE is currently the only reasonable estimation approach for these models, particularly if there is a large number of respondents and a complex model. Pseudolikelihood estimation (see previous discussion for specifics) is implemented using any standard logistic regression program. The response variable is the vector of $gp(g-1)$ perceived ties. The explanatory variables are the change statistics computed for each complete subgraph in the hypothesized dependence graph, D_P.

As was the case with the random multigraph models, pseudolikelihood estimation is an approximate estimation technique. Thus, model fit and the relative importance of particular structural characteristics are based on heuristics that compare the observed values, x_{ijm}, with the fitted values, $\hat{x}_{ijm}$. We suggest using the pseudolikelihood ratio statistic and conditional pseudolikelihood ratio statistic and the change in the MAR to evaluate model fit and the importance of particular structural characteristics. It should be emphasized that these are being used as heuristics, the distributional properties of these statistics is not understood at this time.

(C) *Example: Krackhardt's High-Tech Managers*

We obtained pseudolikelihood estimates for a number of models for the cognitive social structures comprising perceived advice and friendship relations for Krackhardt's high-tech managers. To fit the models discussed here, FORTRAN programs were used to set up the data for the logistic regressions. SPSS 10.1 for Windows (SPSS, Inc., 2000) was used to obtain the pseudolikelihood estimates, model deviances, and MARs.

Consensus

We hypothesize that individuals who share common attributes or who are relationally tied to each other will share similar cognitive representations of the advice and friendship network within the organization. The attributes that were investigated include tenure – based on a median split (median = 9.33 years) – and organizational level (upper management, comprising the CEO and vice-presidents, compared with middle management). The complete subgraphs of the dependence graph include each perceiver's individual tie $\{X_{ijp}\}$, and the interdependencies, or consensus, between each pair of perceivers $\{X_{ijk}, X_{ijp}\}$. Homogeneity constraints were made based on isomorphic configurations, although individual differences in the perceived density of the network were also permitted. Further, to examine individual differences due to tenure or organizational level, homogeneity constraints were made for the consensus statistics based on subgroup membership. To investigate whether there is consensus among respondents who are relationally tied, we equate the parameters across respondents who reciprocate friendship and advice ties. The following models were fitted:

(1) $P(\mathbf{X}^P = \mathbf{x}^P) = \kappa^{-1} \exp \left\{ \sum_{p=1}^{P} \lambda_p \sum_{i,j} x_{ijp} \right\}$

(2) $P(\mathbf{X}^P = \mathbf{x}^P) = \kappa^{-1} \exp \left\{ \sum_{p=1}^{P} \lambda_p \sum_{i,j} x_{ijp} + \lambda_o \sum x_{ijk} x_{ijp} \right\}$

(3) $P(\mathbf{X}^P = \mathbf{x}^P) = \kappa^{-1} \exp \left\{ \sum_{p=1}^{P} \lambda_p \sum_{i,j} x_{ijp} + \lambda_o \sum x_{ijk} x_{ijp} \right.$

$$\left. + \lambda_{11} \sum_{i,j;k\in1,p\in1} x_{ijk} x_{ijp} + \lambda_{22} \sum_{i,j;k\in2,p\in2} x_{ijk} x_{ijp} \right\}$$

(4) $P(\mathbf{X}^P = \mathbf{x}^P) = \kappa^{-1} \exp \left\{ \sum_{p=1}^{P} \lambda_p \sum_{i,j} x_{ijp} + \lambda_o \sum x_{ijk} x_{ijp} \right.$

$$\left. + \lambda_r \sum x_{ijk} x_{ijp} y_{kp} \right\} .$$

The importance of specific structural features was guided by the change in model deviance between two nested models and the change in MAR. Consensus was investigated for the friendship CSS. We use the criterion suggested by Robins et al. (2002a) to evaluate the importance of a single structural parameter. The criterion is $-2q\log(1 - \delta) = 17.65$, based on $q = 8820$ and $\delta = 0.001$. To evaluate whether there is overall consensus among the respondents, model (2) was compared with model (1). The change in the model deviance when the overall consensus statistic is added is 1299.4, $MAR = 0.118$, suggesting that consensus in an important structural feature. Individual differences in consensus due to tenure and organizational level were investigated via model (3). For tenure, $G_{PL}^2 = 3674.21$, which is a reduction of 12.2, for two additional parameters. For organizational level, $G_{PL}^2 = 3670.90$, $MAR = 0.1172$, which is a reduction of 15.6 for two additional parameters. Neither tenure nor organizational level appear to be important predictors of consensus. Relational consensus was investigated for mutual friendship, mutual advice, and the supervisor–subordinate relation. For each of these relations, model (4) was fitted and compared with model (2). The friendship has the largest reduction in deviance ($\Delta G_{PL}^2 = 68.90$) and the $MAR = 0.115$. Based on our criterion of 17.65, mutual friendship is an important predictor of consensus. The parameter estimate for friendship ($\hat{\lambda} = 0.25$) is positive, suggesting that there is a propensity for perceivers to agree with each other if they name each other as friends. A similar conclusion can be drawn for mutual advice ($\Delta G_{PL}^2 = 26.40$, $MAR = 0.117$, $\hat{\lambda} = 0.17$) and the supervisor subordinate relation ($\Delta G_{PL}^2 = 22.21$, $MAR = 0.117$, $\hat{\lambda} = 0.39$).

Points of View Analysis

The following models impose homogeneity on model parameters using the *points of view* homogeneity assumption. In all the following models, the parameters λ_A and $\lambda_{A'}$

are assumed to be equal if and only if there is an isomorphism between A and A' that preserves the relative identity of managers. The analysis is presented for the advice CSS.

Points of View – Bernoulli Models: The following Bernoulli models were fitted:

$$(1) \quad P(\mathbf{X}^P = \mathbf{x}^P) = \kappa^{-1} \exp \left\{ \lambda_1 \sum_{m \neq i,j} x_{ijm} + \lambda_2 \sum_{i \neq j} x_{iji} + \lambda_3 \sum_{j \neq i} x_{ijj} \right\}$$

$$(2) \quad P(\mathbf{X}^P = \mathbf{x}^P) = \kappa^{-1} \exp \left\{ \lambda_1 \sum_{m \neq i,j} x_{ijm} + \lambda_2 \sum_{i \neq j} x_{iji} + \lambda_3 \sum_{j \neq i} x_{ijj} \right.$$
$$+ \lambda_4 \sum_{m,k \neq i,j} x_{ijm} x_{ijk} + \lambda_5 \sum_{\substack{m \neq ij \\ i \neq j}} x_{iji} x_{ijm}$$
$$\left. + \lambda_6 \sum_{\substack{m \neq i,j \\ j \neq i}} x_{ijm} x_{ijj} + \lambda_7 \sum_{i \neq j} x_{iji} x_{ijj} \right\}.$$

The first model examines the propensity for ties to be perceived by third parties (λ_1), by tie senders (λ_2), and by tie receivers (λ_3). In this case, the tie senders or *sources* are advice seekers and the tie receivers or *targets* are advisors. The second model adds three consensus parameters to the model: consensus between two third parties (λ_4), consensus between the sender (advice seeker) and a third party (λ_5), consensus between a third party and the receiver (advisor) (λ_6), and consensus between the sender (advice seeker) and receiver (advisor) (λ_7). Note that parameters involving x_{iji} are examining consensus or "accuracy" based on how we usually measure network ties (RLAS). Thus, λ_5 indicates the propensity for outside observers to agree with the sender (i) whether there is a relationship between i and j, and λ_7 examines the propensity for the sender (i) and receiver (j) of a relational tie to agree whether there is a relationship between i and j (RLAS $\cap$ CLAS). The model deviance and MAR for model (1) is 10798.9 and 0.422, respectively. The parameter estimates for model (1) suggest that the respondents perceive themselves to be advisors (receivers) more than they actually ask for advice $\left(\hat{\lambda}_2 = -0.199, \ \hat{\lambda}_3 = 0.048 \right)$, and they are relatively less likely to perceive ties involving distinct others $\left(\hat{\lambda}_1 = -0.886 \right)$. If we add in the consensus parameters, the change in model deviance is 2452.5 for an additional four parameters. The *MAR* for model (2) is 0.307. All the pseudolikelihood estimates are positive, indicating that there is consensus. The largest parameter estimate is for the sender–receiver consensus $\left(\hat{\lambda}_7 = 0.486 \right)$, suggesting that consensus is strongest among advisees and advisors. Interestingly, the consensus parameters involving third parties are all positive $\left(\hat{\lambda}_4 = 0.244, \ \hat{\lambda}_5 = 0.185, \ \hat{\lambda}_6 = 0.272 \right)$, suggesting that third parties also have a tendency to agree with one another and with sender and receivers; thus, there is a bias effect. These results have interesting implications for measurement models for networks.

Points of View – Dyadic Independence: The dyadic independence model adds reciprocal structures onto the Bernoulli consensus model (2). Seven reciprocal structures were added to the model, based on the points of view of the perceivers:

$(\sum_{m \neq i,j} x_{ijm} x_{jim})$ – perceived reciprocity by a single third party;

$(\sum_{\substack{m \neq k \\ m, k \neq i, j}} x_{ijm} x_{ijk})$ – a reciprocal tie whose constituent ties are perceived by *distinct* third parties;

$(\sum_{i \neq j} x_{iji} x_{jii})$ – a reciprocal tie perceived by one of the tie partners;

$(\sum_{i \neq j} x_{iji} x_{jij})$ – reciprocity as usually defined;

$(\sum_{i \neq j} x_{jii} x_{ijj})$ – one respondent perceives a tie from a second, who in turn perceives a tie from the first;

$(\sum_{\substack{i \neq j, m \\ m \neq j}} x_{jii} x_{ijm})$ – one respondent perceives a tie from an actor with a third party perceiving an outgoing tie to the same actor; and

$(\sum_{\substack{i \neq j, m \\ j \neq m}} x_{iji} x_{jim})$ – one respondent perceives an outgoing tie to an actor with a third party perceiving an incoming tie to the same actor.

The model deviance for this dyadic independence model was 7843.3 with an $MAR = 0.286$. The change in deviance values was 503.1, for an additional seven parameters. All the pseudolikelihood estimates are relatively small and negative except for reciprocity perceived by a single third party ($\hat{\lambda} = 1.494$) and reciprocity as perceived by one of the tie partners ($\hat{\lambda} = 1.110$). The latter two parameter estimates were both large and positive. This suggests that the third parties tend to perceive reciprocal ties, that managers involved in an advice tie tend to perceive them to be reciprocated, and that these effects are to some extent separable from each other.

Points of View – Markov: Finally, we constructed a Markov model that contained six transitivity effects of interest. The six effects were of three types. The first was a transitivity effect involving a triple of managers as it is perceived by a fourth party ($\sum_{m \neq i,j,h} x_{ijm} x_{jhm} x_{ihm}$). The second was a transitivity effect perceived by one of the actors involved in a transitive triple (namely, $\sum x_{iji} x_{jhi} x_{ihi}$, $\sum x_{ijj} x_{jhj} x_{ihj}$, and $\sum x_{ijh} x_{jhh} x_{ihh}$). The third type was for transitive structures in which the constituent ties are perceived by either the senders or the receivers of the ties (that is, the effects $\sum x_{iji} x_{jhj} x_{ihi}$ and $\sum x_{ijj} x_{jhh} x_{ihh}$). Effects were also incorporated for the twelve star configurations that are subgraphs of these six transitive configurations. Because the model incorporating these effects, as well as the consensus and dyad-independent effects, had thirty two parameters in all, we successively removed higher-order effects that failed to contribute 17.65 to the model deviance, using a backward elimination strategy. (In other words, at each step, the higher-order term whose elimination increased the deviance by the smallest amount was removed, provided that the deviance did not increase by more than 17.65.) The resulting model had sixteen parameters, a deviance of 5712.2 and an *MAR* of 0.203.

The only transitivity effect to remain in the model was the first one ($\sum_{m\neq i,j,h} x_{ijm}x_{jhm}x_{ihm}$), and the corresponding positive parameter estimate of 0.099 suggested a substantial tendency for perceivers to view other parts of the advice network as transitive. Interestingly, such a perceptual tendency was not evident for the participants within a transitive triple: rather, such patterns appear to be explained by simpler lower-level effects.

Of the star configurations included in the final model, three were constituent subgraphs of the transitive triple included: an out-star effect ($\sum_{m\neq i,j,h} x_{ijm}x_{ihm}$); an in-star effect ($\sum_{m\neq i,j,h} x_{jhm}x_{ihm}$); and a mixed-star effect ($\sum_{m\neq i,j,h} x_{ijm}x_{jhm}$). The estimates for these three terms were 0.256, 0.173, and -0.122, respectively, and suggest, first, that perceivers tended to view network members as being differentiated in their tendencies to seek and to be sought out for advice and, second, that perceivers tend not to see indirect advice paths that are unaccompanied by direct ties. In addition to these, two other types of star effects were retained in the model. From the first type, we see that the managers exhibited an enhanced tendency to see themselves as both the sources and targets of multiple advice ties [with estimates of 0.326 and 0.253, respectively, for the effects ($\sum x_{iji}x_{ihi}$ and $\sum x_{ijj}x_{hjj}$)]. From the second type, we can infer a tendency for managers to see their nominated advisees as seeking advice from multiple sources (0.252 for $\sum x_{ijj}x_{ihj}$), as well as their advisors as advisors to multiple others (0.143 for $\sum x_{iji}x_{hji}$).

Only two of the exchange effects described in the dyad-independent model were retained in the current model: a substantial third-party reciprocity effect (with an estimate of 1.14 for $\sum_{m\neq i} x_{ijm}x_{jim}$); and a weaker tendency for exchange to be perceived by distinct third parties (with an estimate of .043 for $\sum_{\substack{m\neq i,j,h \\ h\neq i,j}} x_{ijm}x_{jih}$). The final model also excluded one of the consensus effects described earlier, namely, the effect $\sum x_{iji}x_{ijj}$ in which both parties to a tie confirm its presence. This may seem a curious exclusion on first sight, but in fact, it is not surprising (indeed, somewhat reassuring) that confirmed ties are perceived more broadly than by the tiepartners alone.

Taken together, the effects in this model suggest some interesting albeit tentative conclusions about cognitive network structures. First, they demonstrate substantial consensus effects. The conditional odds of a tie being reported are increased by 30% to 40% for each other report of the same tie. Moreover, these consensus effects are not simply a matter of agreement with either the sender or the receiver of a tie; rather both of these effects, as well consensus among separate third parties, are in evidence. Second, it is striking that so many "third-party" effects were retained in the model. These effects suggest that managers perceive a variety of structural effects – reciprocity, transitivity, and differentiation among managers in their tendencies to seek and be sought for advice – that are not necessarily confirmed by the sources of the ties involved in the effects. One possible interpretation of this pattern is a structural bias on the part of observers: we tend to see other parts of a network as more structured than the tie partners themselves. Interestingly, Kumbasar, Romney, and Batchelder (1994) came to the same conclusion using scaling methods to analyse CSS data. A third general effect is the tendency for actors to be seen as differentiated in their tendencies to seek and be sought for advice, but the presence of a number of such effects suggests that it is not necessarily the same differentiation perceived by all. Putting all these effects together, we obtain a view of the cognitive social structure as grounded in common perceptions, but subject to subtle cognitive biases.

9.8 Conclusion

The two applications that we have presented illustrate the importance of developing effective methods for modeling complex relational data structures. In both cases, we found evidence for interesting multirelational and/or multisource effects that would be overlooked by methods for the analysis of a single network. Indeed, there is mounting evidence that it would be valuable to contextualize models for networks by taking account of the social, geographic, and cultural settings of network ties (e.g., Pattison and Robins 2002). The development of models for three-way relational arrays of the type analyzed here can be seen as a first step in this more general program of modeling *generalized relational structures*. Such a program presents significant theoretical and methodological challenges. Theoretically, we need rich conceptualizations that can guide model development; methodologically, we need to extend the advances that have been made in fitting (e.g., Snijders 2002) and evaluating (e.g., Robins, Pattison, and Woolcock 2002b) models for complex and interdependent observations.

Endnotes

1. This chapter is based on a series of workshops presented at the annual meetings of the International Network of Social Network Analysis in Charleston in February 1999, and Vancouver in April 2000, and at the "Perspectives on Spatial Analysis in the Social Sciences" Workshop held at the University of Washington, Seattle, in June 2000. We are indebted to our various copresenters (Noshir Contractor, Martina Morris, Garry Robins, and Stanley Wasserman) for comments on these earlier presentations.
2. *Multinet* is available for download from (www.sfu.ca/~richards/Multinet/Pages/multinet.htm). Multinet can be used to fit random graph models for single relations assuming edge independence, dyadic independence models, or Markov dependence (constrained to subgraphs with three or less nodes). Homogeneity constraints based on actor attributes and social position can also be implemented relatively easily in the program.

References

Albert, R., and Barabási, A.-L. (2002). Statistical mechanics of complex networks. *Review of Modern Physics*, *74*, 47–97.

Batchelder, W. H. (1989). Inferring meaningful global network properties from individual actor's measurement scales. In L. C. Freeman, D. R. White, and A. K. Romney (Eds.), *Research Methods in Social Network Analysis* (pp. 89–134). Fairfax, VA: George Mason University Press.

Bearman, P. (1997). Generalized exchange. *American Journal of Sociology*, *102*, 1383–1415.

Besag, J. E. (1974). Spatial interaction and the statistical analysis of lattice systems. *Journal of the Royal Statistical Society, Series B*, *36*, 96–127.

Besag, J. E. (1975). Statistical analysis of non-lattice data. *The Statistician*, *24*, 179–195.

Besag, J. E. (1977). Some methods of statistical analysis for spatial data. *Bulletin of the International Statistical Association*, *47*, 77–92.

Borgatti, S. P., Everett, M. G., and Freeman, L. C. (1999). *UCINET V*. Harvard, MA: Analytic Technologies.

Calloway, M., Morrissey, J. P., and Paulson, R. I. (1993). Accuracy and reliability of self-reported data in interorganziational networks. *Social Networks*, *15*, 377–398.

Cartwright, D., and Harary, F. (1956). Structural balance: A generalization of Heider's theory. *Psychological Review*, *63*, 277–292.

Frank, O., and Nowicki, K. (1993). Exploratory statistical analysis of networks. In J. Gimbel, J. W. Kennedy, and L. V. Quintas (Eds.), *Quo Vadis Graph Theory? A Source Book for Challenges and Directions*. Amsterdam: North-Holland. (also *Annals of Discrete Mathematics*, *55*, 349–366.)

Frank, O., and Strauss, D. (1986). Markov graphs. *Journal of the American Statistical Association*, *81*, 832–852.

Granovetter, M. (1973). The strength of weak ties. *American Journal of Sociology*, *78*, 161–178.

Heider, F. (1946). Attitudes and cognitive organization. *Journal of Psychology*, *21*, 107–112.

Heider, F. (1958). *The Psychology of Interpersonal Relations*. New York: John Wiley & Sons.

Koehly, L. M. (1996). *Statistical Modeling of Congruence Between Perceptual and Complete Networks*. Unpublished doctoral dissertation, Department of Psychology, University of Illinois, Urbana-Champaign.

Krackhardt, D. (1987). Cognitive social structures. *Social Networks*, *9*, 109–134.

Kumbasar, E., Romney, A. K., and Batchelder, W. H. (1994). Systematic biases in social perception. *American Journal of Sociology*, *100*, 407–505.

Lazega, E., and Pattison, P. E. (1999). Multiplexity, generalized exchange and cooperation in organizations: A case study. *Social Networks*, *21*, 67–90.

Marsden, P. V. (1990). Network data and measurement. *Annual Review of Sociology*, *16*, 435–463.

Newcomb, T. M. (1961). *The Acquaintance Process*. New York: Holt, Rinehart, and Winston.

Pattison, P. (1993). *Algebraic Models for Social Networks*. New York: Cambridge University Press.

Pattison, P., and Wasserman, S. (1999). Logit models and logistic regressions for social networks: II. Multivariate relations. *British Journal of Mathematical and Statistical Psychology*, *52*, 169–193.

Pattison, P., and Wasserman, S. (2002). Multivariate random graph distributions: Applications to social network analysis. In J. Hagberg (Ed.), Contributions to Social Network Analysis, Information Theory and Other Topics in Statistics. *Festschrift in honour of Ove Frank on the Occasion of His 65th Birthday* (pp. 74–100). Stockholm: University of Stockholm.

Pattison, P. E., and Robins, G. L. (2002). Neighbourhood-based models for social networks. *Sociological Methodology*, *32*, 301–337.

Richards, W. D., and Seary, A. J. (2000). *MultiNet 3.0 for Windows*. Vancouver, CA: Simon Fraser University.

Robins, G. L., and Pattison, P. E. (2004). Interdependence and social processes: Dependence graphs and generalized dependence structures. In Carrington, P. J., Scott, J., and Wasserman, S. (eds.), *Models and Methods in Social Network Analysis*. New York: Cambridge University Press.

Robins, G. L., Pattison, P. E., and Wasserman, S. (1999). Logit models and logistic regressions for social networks, III. Valued relations. *Psychometrika*, *64*, 371–394.

Robins, G. L., Pattison, P. E., and Woolcock, J. (2002a). *Missing Data in Networks: Exponential Random Graph (p*) Models for Networks with Non-Respondents*. Unpublished manuscript, Department of Psychology, University of Melbourne, Melbourne, Australia.

Robins, G. L., Pattison, P. E., and Woolcock, J. (2002b). *Small and Other Worlds: Global Network Structures from Local Processes*. Unpublished manuscript, Department of Psychology, University of Melbourne, Melbourne, Australia.

Snijders, T. A. B. (2002). Markov chain Monte Carlo estimation of exponential random graph models. *Journal of Social Structure*, *3*(2).

SPSS, Inc. (2000). *SPSS 10.1 for Windows*. Chicago: SPSS.

Strauss, D., and Ikeda, M. (1990). Pseudolikelihood estimation for social networks. *Journal of the American Statistical Association*, *85*, 204–212.

Wasserman, S. (1987). Conformity of two sociometric relations. *Psychometrika*, *52*, 3–18.

Wasserman, S., and Faust, K. (1994). *Social Network Analysis: Methods and Applications*. New York: Cambridge University Press.

Wasserman, S., and Robins, G. L. (in press). An introduction to random graphs, dependence graphs, and *p**. In Carrington, P. J., Scott, J., and Wasserman, S. (Eds.), *Models and Methods in Social Network Analysis*. New York: Cambridge University Press.

Appendix: Krackhardt Multivariate Random Graph – Advice, Friendship

```
set mxloop = 10000.
show workspace.

data list file = 'C:\socnet\setup\krack.af' free/c1 to c21.

* Set up network statistics

matrix.

get x/variables=all.
compute g=ncol(x).
compute h=nrow(x).
compute a=x(1:21,1:21).
compute f=x(22:42,1:21).
compute gg=g*g.
compute rgg=h*g.
compute za=make(g,g,0).
compute zf=make(g,g,0).
compute onea=make(g,g,1)-ident(g).
compute onef=make(g,g,1)-ident(g).
compute ya=transpos(a).
compute yf=transpos(f).

*choice

compute ua={onea;za}.
compute uf={zf;onef}.
compute t15a=reshape(ua,rgg,1).
compute t15f=reshape(uf,rgg,1).

*multiplexity

compute mp={f;a}.
compute t15af=reshape(mp,rgg,1).

*reciprocity and direct exchange

compute reca={ya;za}.
```

compute recf={zf;yf}.
compute recaf={yf;ya}.
compute t11aa=reshape(reca,rgg,1).
compute t11ff=reshape(recf,rgg,1).
compute t11af=reshape(recaf,rgg,1).

*two stars – in and out

compute ina={onea*a;za}.
compute t14a=reshape(ina,rgg,1).
compute inf={zf;onef*f}.
compute t14f=reshape(inf,rgg,1).
compute inaf={onea*f;onef*a}.
compute t14af=reshape(inaf,rgg,1).

compute outa={a*onea;za}.
compute t12a=reshape(outa,rgg,1).
compute outf={zf;f*onef}.
compute t12f=reshape(outf,rgg,1).
compute outaf={f*onea;a*onef}.
compute t12af=reshape(outaf,rgg,1).

* 2-paths (role-interlocking)

compute mixa={onea*ya+ya*onea;za}.
compute t13a=reshape(mixa,rgg,1).
compute mixf={zf;onef*yf+yf*onef}.
compute t13f=reshape(mixf,rgg,1).
compute mixaf={onea*yf;ya*onef}.
compute t13af=reshape(mixaf,rgg,1).
compute mixfa={yf*onea;onef*ya}.
compute t13fa=reshape(mixfa,rgg,1).

*three cycles (generalized exchange)

compute cyca={ya*ya;za}.
compute t10a=reshape(cyca,rgg,1).
compute cycf={zf;yf*yf}.
compute t10f=reshape(cycf,rgg,1).
compute cycaaf={ya*yf+yf*ya;ya*ya}.
comopute t10aaf=reshape(cycaaf,rgg,1).
compute cycaff={yf*yf;ya*yf+yf*ya}.
compute t10aff=reshape(cycaff,rgg,1).

*transitive triads

compute tta={a*ya+ya*a+a*a;za}.
compute t9a=reshape(tta,rgg,1).
compute ttf={zf;f*yf+yf*f+f*f}.

```
compute t9f=reshape(ttf,rgg,1).
compute ttffa={f*f;a*yf+yf*a}.
compute t9ffa=reshape(ttffa,rgg,1).
compute ttaaf={f*ya+ya*f,a*a}.
compute t9aaf=reshape(ttaaf,rgg,1).
compute ttaff={f*yf;a*f+ya*f}.
compute t9aff=reshape(ttaff,rgg,1).
compute ttafa={a*yf+a*f;ya*a}.
compute t9afa=reshape(ttafa,rgg,1).
compute ttfaf={yf*f;f*ya+f*a}.
compute t9faf=reshape(ttfaf,rgg,1).
compute ttfaa={yf*a+f*a;a*ya}.
compute t9faa=reshape(ttfaa,rgg,1).
```

*row and column labels.

```
compute r=make(g,g,0).
compute c=make(g,g,0).
 loop k=1 to g.
. loop l=1 to g.
.    compute r(k,l)=k.
.    compute c(k,l)=l.
. end loop.
 end loop.

compute x=reshape(x,rgg,1).
compute rr={r;r}.
compute cc={c;c}.
compute r=reshape(rr,rgg,1).
compute c=reshape(cc,rgg,1).

compute
newmat={x,r,c,t15a,t15f,t15af,t11aa,t11ff,t11af,t11aaf,t11faf,t14a,t14f,
t14af,t12a,t12f,t12af,t13a,t13f,t13af,t13fa,t10a,t10f,t10aaf,t10aff,t9a,t9f,
t9ffa,t9aaf,t9aff,t9afa,t9faf,t9faa}.
```

*write file in a form suitable for logistic regression.

```
save
newmat/outfile='temp.lr'/variables=yklm,k,l,t15a,t15f,t15af,t11aa,t11ff,t11af,
t11aaf,t11faf,t14a,t14f,t14af,t12a,t12f,t12af,t13a,t13f,t13af,t13fa,t10a,t10f,t10aaf,
t10aff,t9a,t9f,t9ffa,t9aaf,t9aff,t9afa,t9faf,t9faa.
end matrix.
```

10

Interdependencies and Social Processes: Dependence Graphs and Generalized Dependence Structures

Garry Robins and Philippa Pattison

University of Melbourne

In this chapter, we discuss the importance of the concept of dependence in social network data. Dependence is usually treated as a technical statistical issue, but in the case of social networks, the type of dependencies that might be expected in the data reflect underlying social processes that generate network structures. Consequently, we argue that possible dependencies need to be thought about explicitly when modeling social networks. We present a hierarchy of increasingly more complex dependence assumptions and show how to represent these in terms of *dependence graphs*. We show how dependence graphs are used in exponential random graph (p^*) models for social networks. The most commonly used dependence assumption for p^* models is that of Markov random graphs, but we summarize new developments that introduce higher-order dependence structures, Markov assumptions constrained within *social settings*, and dependencies involving individual-level attributes. We conclude by conceptualizing our general approach in terms of *social space*, with different types of dependence structures construed as forms of abstract *proximity* between elements of that social space.

10.1 Social Phenomena, Networks, and Dependence

An event or process is a *social* phenomenon precisely because behaviors by the individuals involved are interrelated. The form of interrelation may be particularly complex. As Solomon Asch argued half a century ago, social phenomena have the reflexive quality of being psychologically represented in each of the participating individuals. Individuals see themselves and others as sharing the same social environment, and perceive others as also perceiving themselves as within that shared environment. Yet the very same environment is principally constituted by the actions of those individuals in response to those perceptions (Asch 1952; see also Weick and Roberts 1993).

Such a series of recursive perceptions and behaviors is necessarily implicated in any human social process. Such a recursive series implies a fundamental interdependence among the actions of the individuals concerned. So when we make observations about human social phenomena, some form of dependence is inevitable among those observations because of the mere fact that the phenomena are social.

Dependence can be taken as a statistical concept, and we often do so here. However, dependencies among observations imply substantive processes underpinning social happenings. The precise nature of the dependence will vary according to the kinds of observations that we make, and will reflect the interactive nature of the social processes that generate the observations.

The interdependent nature of social observations is a potential problem when we come to construct statistical models. In many familiar modeling contexts, we can plausibly assume that observations made on one sampled unit are independent of observations made on another. Indeed, where such independence cannot be assumed, we often treat the resulting dependence as a nuisance and seek to remove it (Baron and Kenny 1986; Snijders and Bosker 1999). Yet, in the case of social observations, the interdependence of observations is intrinsic to what we seek to model, so it is essential to build models that allow us to investigate hypotheses about forms of interdependence. In what follows, we demonstrate how to build and use such hypotheses in the development of models for interdependent social observations.

In the context of social networks, we can distinguish at least two ways in which networks might be involved in the modeling of interdependent social observations. The first underlies some well-known models for social influence (e.g., Erbring and Young 1979; Doreian 1982; Friedkin and Johnsen 1990, 1997; Friedkin 1993, 1998) and regards network ties as indicators of which pairs of actors are associated with interdependent observations. For example, the status of each actor on some attribute (e.g., an attitude) might be seen as dependent on the attribute status of all other actors to whom he or she is tied. This approach permits us to construct models for the distribution of attributes across a set of actors and is discussed further in Section 10.5. Another approach, and the one that we discuss first, is to build models for network ties themselves, recognizing that each network tie is itself an observation arising from interdependent social processes. So, in what follows, we introduce methods for modeling interdependent social observations by first considering models for the collection of network ties observed on some fixed set of actors.

The method we describe has its origins in a quite general approach to the modeling of interdependent systems of variables (Besag 1974) and was adapted for the case of social networks by Frank and Strauss (1986). Needless to say, in building models for interdependent systems of variables, we require some hypothesis about the general form of interdependencies. In what follows, we describe how to represent hypotheses about interdependence in the form of a *dependence structure* (or *dependence graph*), and we discuss various proposals for the nature of these structures.

The Hammersley-Clifford theorem (Besag 1974; see Chapter 8, this volume) provides the means for expressing the most general probability model for a system of interdependent variables that is consistent with its hypothesized dependence structure. As described in Chapter 8, the parameters of this model correspond to local subgraphs of potential network ties. In other words, hypothesizing a dependence structure leads to a model for the probability of a network in terms of certain configurations of ties. More complex dependence structures (i.e., those involving more extensive interdependencies) lead to network models that are expressed in terms of larger and more complex configurations. In Section 10.3, we consider a simple hierarchy of dependence structure hypotheses and the resulting hierarchy of network models to which they give rise. In Section 10.4, we elaborate this hierarchy of dependence assumptions by introducing setting structures and partial dependence structures. In Section 10.5, we describe models that permit directed dependence assumptions, which are particularly useful where we want to model systems of network ties together with systems of node attributes, leading to models for social influence and social selection. Finally, in Section 10.6, we argue that the hierarchy of dependence structures that we have introduced can be seen as a hierarchy of hypotheses about the nature of *social space*.[1]

(A) *Social Networks and Dependence Graphs*

When we represent aspects of human social structure in network form, we have partially made the step of thinking in terms of dependencies. By adopting a network perspective in investigating a particular social process, we are taking the theoretical ground that an understanding of that process requires an understanding of the pattern of social connections or *network ties* among individuals. This is an implicit recognition that the dependencies arising through the process are in some way captured by a network representation, rather than through other possible dependence structures, for example, by nested data within multiple levels (Bryk and Raudenbush 1992; Snijders and Bosker 1999 – of course, both network and multiple levels approaches are not mutually exclusive, see van Duijn, van Busschbach, and Snijders 1999). A decision about the type of analytical strategy to use is an implicit decision about a form of dependence structure, with consequent theoretical and conceptual implications. We need a method to represent this dependence structure, thereby makeing explicit our dependence assumptions.

To begin, let us consider a directed network. A directed tie is an observation on an ordered pair of individuals. Sometimes ties are not possible for certain ordered pairs. Within a network, we term a *couple* as an ordered pair for whom a tie is possible.[2] We see a substructure or a *network configuration*, then, as a subgraph of ties observed on sets of couples.

The patterning of certain configurations may be observable across several parts of the network, suggesting that the ties themselves may be interdependent in ways that give rise to such patterns. More formally, there are dependencies among couples that may lead to the observation or nonobservation of a tie or ties that are part of a configuration. Our argument is this: if a network represents the dependencies implicit in social happenings, then to understand the network requires an understanding of the dependencies within the network, expressed as dependencies among couples. The network is represented as a graph; the dependencies among couples can also be represented as a graph, a *dependence graph*.

Dependence structures of a sufficient complexity to represent plausible social processes have a number of difficult features. No particular couple in a network is privileged, so there is no exogenous point from which to hypothesize a type of causal chain. In that sense, dependencies among couples have a form of circularity, and in the most general representations any couple may be dependent on any other couple, a situation too undifferentiated to be useful. Accordingly, to construct dependence graphs, we use the notion of *conditional dependence* between couples. Two couples may or may not be dependent, conditional on the observations on all other couples in the network. The *dependence graph* **D** for a network can be defined as follows: the vertices of the graph comprise the set of all couples (equivalently, the set of all network variables), and there is an edge between a pair of vertices if the two couples are conditionally dependent (we elaborate this definition below in various ways). By postulating different forms of conditional dependence among couples, the researcher is in effect hypothesizing different social processes that give rise to particular network substructures. For instance, dyadic independence models imply a dependence graph where the only edges are between couples that share both actors, that is, between couples of the form (i, j) and (j, i). The Markov random graph dependence structure of Frank and Strauss (1986), however, postulates conditional dependencies (edges in the dependence graph) when couples share *at least* one actor.

The Hammersley-Clifford theorem (Besag 1974; see also Chapter 8, this volume) provides the link between the dependence structure as represented by the dependence graph and a distribution of random graphs from which an observed network is an instance. In effect, the theorem translates the dependence structure into a set of parameters that represent various substructures in the network. This parameterization describes the distribution of graphs. Parameter estimation then allows us to understand the importance of the various substructures in the overall network.

Much of what we describe here derives from the statistical *graphical modeling* literature. Good introductions to the area are provided by Cox and Wermuth (1996), Edwards (1995), Lauritzen (1996), and Whittaker (1990). Graphical modeling underpins the statistical basis for our approach, but the peculiar importance of dependence in social phenomena presents both a number of substantive issues in interpretation and model development, and a number of technical issues in implementation.

In the next section, we begin by describing some aspects of graphical modeling that will be helpful in ensuing sections. (Readers not interested in the technical details may skip this section.) We then turn to a more detailed description of dependence structures for networks. We follow this with a presentation of more recent work on higher-order dependence structures that may provide a more appropriate basis for modeling human social behavior. For this purpose, we need to generalize some of the technical aspects of graphical modeling. We follow with a description of dependence graphs that incorporate both network couples and individual attributes, permitting the development of social influence, social selection, and discrete time models. We conclude with an interpretation of dependence structures in relation to abstract social space.

10.2   Some Aspects of Graphical Modeling

This section summarizes some technical results from the field of graphical modeling that are not specific to networks, but are useful in what follows.

In a graphical model, the dependencies among the variables of a data set are represented in graphic form. Whittaker (1990) defined an *independence graph*, or more properly a *conditional independence graph*, of a set of random variables as an undirected graph with the variables represented as vertices. (Graphical modeling uses the term *independence graph*; the network literature uses the term *dependence graph*. From this point, we follow the latter practice.) An edge exists between two vertices in the dependence graph, unless – conditional on the remaining variables – the two variables corresponding to the vertices are independent.

Formally, Whittaker's (1990) definition is as follows: Let $\mathbf{X} = (X_1, X_2, \ldots X_k)$ denote a vector of random variables and $K = \{1, 2, \ldots, k\}$ the corresponding set of vertices. The conditional dependence graph of $\mathbf{X}$ is the undirected graph $G = (K, E)$ with vertices from K and edge set E, where $(i, j) \notin E$ if and only if $X_i \perp X_j \mid \mathbf{X}_{K \setminus \{i,j\}}$. Here, following Dawid (1979), the notation $X \perp Y \mid \mathbf{Z}$ signifies that variables X and Y are independent conditional on $\mathbf{Z}$, a set of variables. (Also, $\mathbf{A} \perp \mathbf{B} \mid \mathbf{Z}$ signifies that for all $A \in \mathbf{A}$ and all $B \in \mathbf{B}$, $A \perp B \mid \mathbf{Z}$.) In the definition, $\mathbf{X}_{K \setminus \{i,j\}}$ represents the set of all variables excluding X_i and X_j.

(A) *Markov Properties*

The dependence graph, as defined by Whittaker (1990), reflects one of three possible *Markov properties on undirected graphs*.[3] Lauritzen (1996) defined the three Markov properties in the following terms. For an undirected graph $G = (K, E)$ with a collection of random variables $\mathbf{X} = (X_1, X_2, \ldots X_k)$, a probability measure is said to obey:

1. The *pairwise Markov property*, relative to G, if for all nonadjacent vertices i and j, $X_i \perp X_j \mid \mathbf{X}_{K \setminus \{i,j\}}$
2. The *local Markov property*, relative to G, if for every vertex i, $X_i \perp \mathbf{X}_{K \setminus \text{cl}(i)} \mid \mathbf{X}_{\text{bd}(i)}$, where $\text{bd}(i)$, the *boundary* of i, is the set of all vertices adjacent to i, or the set of *neighbors* of i (Besag 1974), and $\text{cl}(i)$, the *closure* of i, is the set $\text{bd}(i) \cup \{i\}$ so $K \setminus \text{cl}(i)$ is the set of all vertices that are neither i nor neighbors of i
3. The *global Markov property*, relative to G, if for all disjoint subsets, A, B, and S of K, such that S separates A from B in G (that is, any path in G from a vertex in A to a vertex in B passes through a vertex in S), then $\mathbf{X}_A \perp \mathbf{X}_B \mid \mathbf{X}_S$, where $\mathbf{X}_A$ specifies the subset of variables $\{X_i : i \in A\}$

Equivalence between the three conditions basically implies that the dependence graph is a coherent representation of conditional dependency structures. Lauritzen (1996) showed that the global property implies the local property, which in turn implies the pairwise property. The reverse implications only hold under more limited conditions set out by Pearl and Paz (1987). Importantly, for the three Markov conditions to be equivalent, all probabilities have to be nonzero; that is, all observations have to be possible. A positive density precludes logical relations among variables (for instance, it precludes logical relations of the form $X_1 = Y$, $X_2 = Z$, and $X_3 = Y + Z$ for then the density is zero whenever $X_1 + X_2 \neq X_3$).

(B) *Factorization and the Hammersley-Clifford Theorem*

Equivalence of the Markov properties and factorization of the probability density are closely related. Lauritzen (1996) defined factorization along the following lines: the probability P is said to *factorize* according to a graph G if for all cliques of vertices $A \subseteq K$ there exist nonnegative functions ψ_A that depend on $\mathbf{X}$ only through $\mathbf{X}_A$, and there exists a factorization of the probability density $f(\mathbf{X}) = \prod_A \psi_A(\mathbf{X})$.[4] As factorization implies the global Markov property, it also implies the local and pairwise Markov properties. So, a well-behaved graph that represents a coherent dependence structure will have a factorization of a probability density that can be expressed in terms of functions relating solely to the cliques of the dependence graph. There is one and only one function for each clique. Moreover, the variables will not be logically related.

Factorization for the discrete case amounts to the Hammersley-Clifford theorem, first presented by Besag (1974). For networks, the factorization takes the form:

$$Pr(\mathbf{X} = \mathbf{x}) = \frac{1}{\kappa} \exp \left(\sum_{T \subseteq C} \theta_T \prod_{st \in T} x_{st} \right) \tag{10.1}$$

where $\mathbf{X}$ is the random graph with $\mathbf{x}$ as a realization [so X_{st} is a binary variable on couple (s, t) expressing the presence or absence of a tie, with x_{st} as a realization]; C is the set of couples; κ is a normalizing quantity; and the parameters θ_T are nonzero only if T is a clique of the dependence graph. The cliques represent local configurations of possible network ties. There is one and only one parameter for each clique, and the sufficient statistic pertaining to each clique ($\prod_{st \in T} x_{st}$) indicates whether the corresponding configuration of possible ties is actually observed in the network. The factorization in (10.1) is the basis of the p^* class of models for social networks (Wasserman and Pattison 1996).

Of course, for even quite simple dependence structures, the dependence graph has many cliques and so the resulting network model has many parameters. For both practical and theoretical reasons, therefore, we often consider further hypotheses that lead to a reduction in the number of model parameters. For example, if we have no information about the network actors apart from their ties, we often assume that model parameters are independent of the particular identities of the actors. Each parameter then corresponds to an *isomorphism class*, that is, to a collection of all local configurations that become identical once the node labels are removed. The sufficient statistic corresponding to the class is a count of the number of observed configurations in the class. This *homogeneity assumption* leads to a considerable reduction in the number of model parameters and amounts to an assumption that the interactive processes underlying the interdependencies among ties are universal ones. As we discuss in Section 10.5, where we have doubts about the universality of such processes, we can observe characteristics of individuals that might relate to variations in interactive effects. We can then use these individual measures to restrict homogeneity assumptions according to the measured characteristics of the actors.

Our approach to exponential random graph (or p^*) modeling of networks is to postulate a dependence structure in the form of a dependence graph. From the dependence graph, cliques can be derived. The Hammersley-Clifford theorem then provides a factorization with parameters based on the cliques. Imposing homogeneity and restricting the order of terms in the factorization (i.e., concentrating on lower-order effects) results in identifiable models. These models then have parameters and statistics relating to the presence of local network configurations.

There are two important aspects to note here. First, if a set of vertices constitute a clique of the dependence graph, then any subset of vertices will also be a clique. Accordingly, if there is a parameter in the model for a higher-order configuration (such as a triad), then the model would normally include parameters for configurations lower order to that parameter (such as various stars) so models are hierarchical. Here, the *order* of the configuration is taken as the number of couples it contains. Second, the fact that there is one and only one parameter per clique leads to a need for care in model development. Often, effects that may suggest separate parameterization in fact need to have the same parameters because they pertain to the same clique of the dependence graph.

We now examine some network dependence graphs and the models to which they give rise.

10.3   Dependence Graphs for Networks

(A) *Bernoulli Dependence Structures*

The simplest dependence hypothesis is that possible network ties are independent of one another; more properly, that there are no (conditional) dependencies among couples. The dependence graph takes a particularly simple form: the set of vertices is, as before, the set of couples, but there are no edges between vertices. The only cliques in the dependence graph relate to single vertices so the corresponding network configuration is a single tie for each vertex (couple). If homogeneity is imposed across isomorphic configurations, we have a single parameter model, with the sufficient statistic equal to the number of observed ties (i.e., reflecting the density of the graph). The resulting model is the Bernoulli graph model, with the probability of any tie being the same across the graph (see Erdös and Renyi 1959; Frank and Nowicki 1993),

$$Pr(\mathbf{X} = \mathbf{x}) = \frac{1}{\kappa} \exp \left(\sum_{ij \in C} \theta_{ij} x_{ij} \right) = \frac{1}{\kappa} \exp \left(\theta \sum_{ij \in C} x_{ij} \right) = \frac{1}{\kappa} \exp(\theta L),$$

where θ is the density parameter and L is the number of observed ties in the graph. Note how this model is achieved by imposing homogeneity such that $\theta_{ij} = \theta$ for all couples.

(B) *Dyadic Dependence Structures*

A somewhat more complex, but still very simple, dependence hypothesis is that couples are only (conditionally) dependent when they share both actors, that is, the couple (i, j) is dependent only on couple (j, i). The dependence graph is of the form in Figure 10.3.1a. With homogeneity imposed across isomorphic configurations, there are only two types of cliques here: those of the form $\{(i, j)\}$ – that is, single vertices as

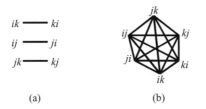

Figure 10.3.1. Dependence graphs for couples
$(i, j), (j, i), (i, k), (k, i), (j, k), (k, j)$: (a) dyadic
independence models; (b) Markov random
graphs.

in the Bernoulli graph case – and those of the form $\{(i, j), (j, i)\}$ – that is, reciprocated ties. So we have a two-parameter model, with one parameter (θ) relating to density as in the Bernoulli case and the other a mutuality parameter (ρ) relating to the presence of reciprocated ties:

$$Pr(\mathbf{X} = \mathbf{x}) = \frac{1}{\kappa} \exp\left(\theta \sum_{i,j} x_{ij} + \rho \sum_{i,j} x_{ij} x_{ji}\right) = \frac{1}{\kappa} \exp(\theta L + \rho M),$$

where M is the number of reciprocated ties in the graph.

The best known dyadic independence model in the network literature is the p_1 model of Holland and Leinhardt (1981), with expansiveness and popularity effects at the actor level. The p_1 model can be derived through our approach by loosening homogeneity constraints so the single density parameter in the previous model is replaced by a series of parameters. Rather than imposing homogeneity in the form $\theta_{ij} = \theta$, one might choose constraints of the form $\theta_{ij} = \theta + \alpha_i + \beta_j$, with the node level effects α_i and β_j relating to expansiveness and popularity, respectively. This illustrates how the imposition of different homogeneity constraints on the same dependence structure results in different models. Some form of homogeneity of course is required for identifiable models, but decisions on actual constraints are ultimately a theoretical choice.

Usually, Bernoulli and two-parameter dyadic independence models are used as baseline models against which more complex models may be compared. Most social processes are sufficiently complex to make dyadic independence a somewhat inadequate assumption (see Robins, Elliott, and Pattison 2001a, for a discussion.) Both models, however, have the virtue that, because of their relative simplicity, they can readily be estimated using maximum likelihood procedures. Although we continue to use the terminology *conditional dependence* in describing dependence graphs, the dependence structure is not conditional in these cases (at the node level for the Bernoulli case and at the dyad level for the dyadic independence case).

(C) *Markov Random Graphs*

The dependence structure for Markov random graphs was proposed by Frank and Strauss (1986). For dyadic independence models, dependencies are assumed to be only between couples with the same actors. For Markov random graphs, conditional

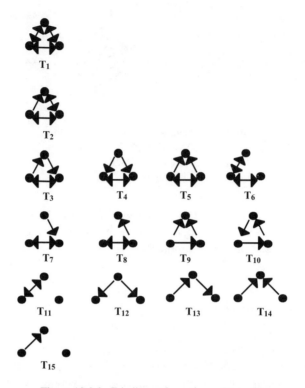

Figure 10.3.2. Triadic configurations. (Note: The
configurations are depicted in rows of decreasing order.
Parameters relating from T_9 to T_{15} configurations pertain to
transitive triad, cyclic, mutuality, out-star, mixed-star,
in-star, and density effects, respectively.)

dependencies are assumed between couples who share at least one actor. In other words, in the dependence graph, there will be an edge between vertices (i, j) and (s, t) if and only if $\{i, j\} \cap \{s, t\} \neq \emptyset$. The dependence graph is represented in Figure 10.3.1b. Frank and Strauss (1986) showed that for Markov graphs, cliques of the dependence graph related to edges, mutual dyads, triadic configurations, and various starlike configurations. Some of these configurations are depicted in Figure 10.3.2. If we consider that part of the dependence graph that involves the couple (i, j), then the dependence structure immediately implies two maximal "star" cliques: one "star" clique that includes all couples that have i as an actor, and one that includes all couples that have j as an actor. These two maximal cliques intersect at $\{(i, j), (j, i)\}$, but are otherwise distinct. However, we may also infer additional maximal cliques: one "triadic" clique for each actor $k \neq i, j$ of the form $\{(i, j), (j, i), (i, k), (j, k), (k, i), (k, j)\}$. For each k, the triadic clique is maximal because any other edge – such as (i, s), where $s \neq i, j, k$ – may be conditionally dependent on some of the edges in the clique, but is not dependent on all of them – for example, (i, s) is not conditionally dependent on (j, k) because the two couples do not have an actor in common.

The "star" cliques give rise to various types of stars. In a two-mixed-star (or two-path) clique of the form $\{(k, i), (i, j)\}$, it is tempting to try to parameterize to describe an effect for the first path of a two-path – that is, for an observed tie on (k, i) when attempting to predict a tie on (i, j) – in contrast to an effect for the second path of a two-path – that is, for an observed tie on (i, j) when attempting to predict a tie on (k, i). This temptation seems particularly strong when using pseudolikelihood methods of estimation (see Chapter 8, this volume) because the data file is set up in such a way as to suggest the possibility. It is, however, an error to do so. As noted previously, the condition that there be one and only one parameter for each clique often requires the equating of parameters relating to such apparently different effects. The clique $\{(i, j), (k, i)\}$ obviously contains both a first and second path in a possible two-path; there is one parameter for this clique; there are no grounds for privileging either (i, j) or (k, i) in a desire to examine first and second path effects.

The "triadic" cliques pertain to a variety of triadic configurations, the various forms of which are depicted in Figure 10.3.2 (readers will recognize that these are simply the various nonempty configurations from the triad census – see, for instance, Wasserman and Faust 1994). Note that the triadic forms include all three forms of two-stars because these cliques are in the intersection of the star maximal cliques and the various triadic cliques. If we impose homogeneity across isomorphic configurations, then there are parameters for each of the triadic configurations and every higher-order star (i.e., of higher order than 2). Typically, such a large number of parameters will still lead to unidentifiable models despite the homogeneity constraints. There are various suggestions in the literature to restrict the order of parameters. Until more recently, practice has been to ignore the effects of higher-order stars (see Robins, Pattison, and Elliott 2001b) and to fit models with just the triadic configurations of Figure 10.3.2. The model then becomes:

$$Pr(\mathbf{X} = \mathbf{x}) = \frac{1}{\kappa} \exp \sum_{p=1}^{15} \tau_p N(T_p),$$

where τ_p is the parameter pertaining to configuration T_p and $N(T_p)$ is the number of such configurations observed in the graph. There may still be insufficient data to fit models with the higher-order configurations so models with only density, mutuality, two-star, transitive triad (T_9), and cyclic (T_{10}) effects have been popular.

An alternative, discussed in a slightly different context here, is to fit configurations of a given order or less, for instance, configurations of order three. The relevant configurations are those in the bottom three rows of Figure 10.3.2, plus three-in-star, three-out-star, and various three-mixed-star configurations. See Lazega and Pattison (1999) for an example of a hierarchy of models based on a maximum order of configurations. The relevance of including higher-order stars (e.g., three-stars) in the model arises from simulation studies, which suggest that models may exhibit more stable and less degenerate behavior if they include at least three stars (Chapter 8, this volume).

The Markov random graph dependence structure can also be generalized to deal with multiple networks (Pattison and Wasserman 1999), valued networks (Robins, Pattison, and Wasserman 1999) and bipartite networks (Skvoretz and Faust 1999).

10.4 Higher-Order Dependence Structures

Markov dependence structures have a sensible intuitive basis in regard to many triads of individuals, and since being introduced by Frank and Strauss in 1986, the Markov dependence structure has become a mainstay of exponential random graph (p^*) modeling. Network analysts have adopted it with enthusiasm because it allows progress beyond the restrictive assumptions of dyadic independence.

In fact, there is little evidence to indicate one way or the other whether Markov dependence structures are an adequate representation of social processes in general. However, as Pattison and Robins (2002) argued, it is simple to conceive of hypothetical situations where Markov dependence is either too broadly or too narrowly specified. Pattison and Robins postulated that social processes arise within particular social locales or *social settings*. Their theoretical development here is sympathetic to the notion of *network domain* of White (see Mische and White 1998, and White 1995) and the notion of *focus* of Feld (1981). Accepting that social processes take place within social locales, as Pattison and Robins argued, it is quite possible that ties X_{ij} and X_{kl} could arise within a common locale – even though couples (i, j) and (k, l) contain distinct actors – and these couples might be appropriately modeled as conditionally dependent. In contrast, the couples (i, j) and (i, k) may never occupy the same settings, even though individual i is common to the two possible ties, in which case the couples might appropriately be modeled as conditionally independent of one another.

The possibility that couples involving the same actor could occupy different settings presents particular problems for Markov dependence structures in large networks. Actors i and j may not even be aware of each other's presence in the network and may have no common locale through which they could possibly meet, yet the standard Markov graph assumption gives as much weight in conditional dependence structure to the couple (i, j) as to any other couple.

Accordingly, there are two variations on Markov dependence structures that Pattison and Robins (2002) examined: how to limit Markov dependencies within a given pattern of settings (or *setting structure*), and how to elaborate possible dependencies between couples that share no actor at all. In the second case, a simple generic extension of the Markov dependence is problematic for exponential random graph models. In particular, if we allow dependence between couples (i, j) and (k, l) when $\{i, j\} \cap \{k, l\} = \emptyset$ (as well as when $\{i, j\} \cap \{k, l\} \neq \emptyset$), then the dependence graph is complete. In this case, every subset of nodes in M corresponds to a clique, and even with a general homogeneity assumption, the resulting model is not identified.

(A) *Setting Structures*

The first approach of Pattison and Robins (2002) is to hypothesize a setting structure directly and to constrain a broader dependence structure to apply only within settings. Each setting is assumed to correspond to some subset of possible network ties. Pattison and Robins deliberately leave the notion of setting abstract and general. They suggest as possible examples settings based on a spatiotemporal context, such as a group of people gathered together at the same time and place; settings based on a more abstract sociocultural space, such as pairs of persons linked by their political commitments; and settings that reflect external "design" constraints, such as organizational structure, task requirements in organizational settings, or hardware capabilities in communication networks. In dependence graph terms, settings are proposed to create boundaries among couples. They may overlap, with couples occupying many settings simultaneously. However, conditional dependencies among a set of ties are assumed to be realized only within common settings. Pattison and Robins start with a *generic dependence structure* (for instance, a Markov dependence structure) and then *constrain* it, through a *setting structure*, by assuming that the generic dependence only applies within settings.

Formally, this can be described as follows. A *setting s* is defined as a subset of couples and a *setting structure S* as a collection of settings on N, such that if s is a setting in S, then so is any subset of s. Formally, a setting structure is a *closed hypergraph* on the set C of couples. Suppose that random network $\mathbf{X}$ has generic dependence structure $\mathbf{D}$ whose edge set is E. If H denotes the set of all cliques of $\mathbf{D}$, then H is also a closed hypergraph on E (Robins 1998). An exponential random graph model *confined* by the setting structure S has the *setting-restricted* clique set $H_S = H \cap S$; H_S is also a closed hypergraph on E. A setting structure hypothesis thus provides one approach to setting parameters in a model to zero: by restricting the clique set of the dependence graph to H_S, in equation 10.1, $\theta_T = 0$ for any $T \notin H_S$.

Pattison and Robins (2002) noted several different forms for possible setting structures. If S comprises a single setting corresponding to the set C of all couples, then it is termed *universal*. In this case, the setting-restricted clique set H_S is simply the clique set H associated with the generic dependence structure $\mathbf{D}$. Setting structures for disjoint groups can also be defined. Suppose that $N = \cup_g N_g$ is a disjoint union of the node set N, and let S_g be the universal setting structure defined on N_g. Then $S = \{S_g\}$ defines a disjoint subgroup structure and the factorization in (10.1) decomposes into the form $\Pi_g P(X_g = x_g)$, where X_g denotes the random network on the node set N_g, and x_g is its corresponding realization. (See Anderson, Wasserman, and Crouch 1999, for an example involving different school classes, with dependencies applying within but not between classes.)

More generally, Pattison and Robins (2002) proposed settings as grouplike in structure, but potentially overlapping. In particular, if a setting is conceptualized in terms of the potential links among a subset N_m of individuals, then settings take the form $s_m = \{(i, j) : i, j \in N_m \text{ and } i \neq j\}$ and a potentially *overlapping subgroup setting structure* results. Versions of overlapping subgroup setting structures can also be used to explore the interaction between the proposed generic dependence structure and proximity as defined by regions in physical space.

Pattison and Robins (2002) also noted that an overlapping structure arises if settings arc assumed to be restricted to a maximum of k individuals so each setting comprises ties among a subgroup of individuals of size no greater than k.[5]

(B) *Partial Dependence Structures*

The second approach of Pattison and Robins (2002) is to examine non-Markov dependencies so as to permit the interactive social processes that give rise to network ties

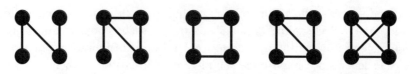

Figure 10.4.3. Some higher-order configurations in a three-path nondirected
random graph model.

themselves being a source of settings. In other words, new settings are created as network ties are generated: for instance, couples (i, j) and (k, l) may become conditionally
dependent if there is an observed tie between at least one of the actors in one couple
and at least one of the actors in the other couple. Such "longer-range" dependencies
might be incorporated into the dependence graph $\mathbf{D}$ by imposing such conditions as an
edge being present between (i, j) and (k, l), only if at least one tie is observed between
i or j and k or l. (For a similar approach in other statistical applications, see Baddeley
and Möller 1989.)

A Markov dependence assumption introduces conditional dependencies among couples comprising possible semipaths of length two. The condition in the previous paragraph extends the assumption of conditional dependence to couples comprising possible
semipaths of length 3 (or three-paths in nondirected networks). In general, Pattison and
Robins (2002) termed such a condition as *partial conditional independence*, whereby
network variables X_{ij} and X_{kl} are conditionally independent given certain observed
values of other variables (e.g., in nondirected networks if $x_{ik} = x_{il} = x_{jk} = x_{jl} = 0$),
but conditionally dependent for certain other observed values (e.g., if one of x_{ik}, x_{il},
x_{jk}, or x_{jl} is nonzero).

Formally, Pattison and Robins (2002) defined a *partial dependence structure* $\mathbf{D}_B$ for
a subset $B \subset C$ of couples. The node set of $\mathbf{D}_B$ is the set $C \backslash B$ of couples not in B and
the edge set of $\mathbf{D}_B$ is given by $\{((i, j), (k, l)): X_{ij}$ and X_{kl} are conditionally dependent,
given that $X_{mh} = x_{mh}$ for $(m, h) \in C \backslash B$ and $X_{mh} = 0$ for $(m, h) \in B\}$. In other words,
two possible ties are linked by an edge in $\mathbf{D}_B$ if they are assumed to be conditionally
dependent even when all the possible ties in the set B have observed values of 0. Note
that if $((i, j), (k, l)) \in \mathbf{D}_B$, then $((i, j), (k, l)) \in \mathbf{D}$; thus, $\mathbf{D}_B$ is a subgraph of $\mathbf{D}$ for
all $B \subset C$. It is possible though that $((i, j), (k, l))$ may be an edge in $\mathbf{D}$ but not in
$\mathbf{D}_B$, signifying that X_{ij} and X_{kl} are conditionally independent when $x_{mh} = 0$ for all
$(m, h) \in$ B. With these dependence structures defined, Pattison and Robins go on to
show that in equation 10.1 the parameter λ_T is nonzero if and only if T is a clique in $\mathbf{D}$
and in all $\mathbf{D}_B$ for which $T \cap B = \emptyset$.

One innovation arising from partial dependence structures is the development of
models investigating the presence of configurations of higher order than the stars and
triads of Markov random graphs. For instance, the three-path condition expressed previously permits connected configurations comprising four or more nodes that satisfy the
condition that every pair of edges lie on a path of length 3. Pattison and Robins (2002)
referred to this model as the *three-path* random graph model. For nondirected graphs,
configurations on four nodes satisfying this condition are shown in Figure 10.4.3.
For directed graphs, the full set of such configurations include all possible combinations of arrows in the configurations in Figure 10.4.3. As is seen in Section 10.5,

partial conditional independence is also important in developing meaningful models that incorporate actor attributes.

The partial dependence step allows the embedding of Markov random graph models in classes of models with more complex dependence structures. It thereby becomes possible to examine the sufficiency of Markov models by comparing them with models that make plausible but more complex assumptions. Moreover, complex dependency structures are postulated in several theoretical claims, for instance, the presence of *generalized exchange* instantiated in *cyclic* patterns of network ties (e.g., Bearman 1997); arguments about the nature of strategic activity in networks, including brokering and mediating behaviors; and arguments for indirect social influence and social selection effects. We now turn to social influence and social selection models, which involve actor attribute variables, to illustrate such theoretical claims.

10.5   Attribute Variables in Dependence Graphs for Networks

There are two important processes that have often been hypothesized to relate attribute and network variables. First, in social selection processes, actors create or alter ties on the basis of the attributes of other actors; that is, actor attributes may contribute to the formation or change of network ties. Second, in social influence processes, network ties may help to shape actor characteristics, in that individuals may be influenced by others with whom they have network ties. Clearly the two processes are not necessarily mutually exclusive, but the two classes of models described here ignore the effects of one process while examining the other.

In social selection models, we examine network ties as depending in part on the distribution of actor attributes. For social influence models, however, we examine the distribution of actor attributes as an outcome of a given set of network ties. In either case, we have a dependence structure that goes beyond what has been hitherto discussed: we have two types of variables and the dependence structure is directed from one type to another, in the sense that one set of variables is explanatory and the other set comprises outcome variables. (Outcome variables may still be interdependent, just as in the earlier cases.) To manage dependence structures of this nature, we need to return to the graphical modeling literature, in particular to dependence structures that are known as *two-block chain graphs*.

(A) *Two-Block Chain Graph*

Our exposition here follows Robins et al. (2001b), which first adapted the chain graph approach to the network literature in developing exponential random graph social influence models.

Directed edges in a dependence graph, represented by arrows, relate explanatory to response variables (Cox and Wermuth 1996). So, a directed edge from a to b in the graph can be used to represent the situation where Z_b is assumed to be a variable in response to explanatory variable Z_a. Here, Z_a is referred to as a *parent* of Z_b and Z_b as a *child* of Z_a (Lauritzen and Spiegelhalter 1988). The particular dependence graph of interest here is a directed graph to model the distribution of one set of variables (the *child* block of variables), given the values of another set of variables (the *parent* variables). There may well also be nondirected dependencies (e.g., of the various types discussed previously) within the two blocks. The dependence graph has the set of vertices partitioned into the two blocks; there are directed dependencies only from parent variables to child variables, and the only nondirected dependencies are within blocks. This type of graph is known as a two-block *chain graph* (Wermuth and Lauritzen 1990). Not all graphs with directed and nondirected edges can represent a coherent probability structure and so function as dependence graphs. However, any chain graph can represent coherent dependence relationships among the variables.

For the nondirected dependence graphs discussed earlier, the Hammersley-Clifford theorem provides the necessary link from the dependence graph structure to model parameterization. It is not immediately clear how to apply the Hammersley-Clifford theorem in the case where some of the edges in the dependence graph are directed. However, the graphical modeling literature provides some valuable results about converting directed to nondirected dependence graphs in such a way as to preserve the Markov properties of the original directed dependence graph. The resulting nondirected graph is often referred to as a *moral graph* (Lauritzen and Spiegelhalter 1988) because it involves introducing edges between parents of the same child (the so-called *marrying of the parents*). For the two-block chain graphs, where the interest is in the distribution of one set of variables given the distribution of another set of variables, the moral graph of a directed dependence graph can be defined as the nondirected graph with the same vertex set, but with edges between two vertices *a* and *b* in the moral graph if they are connected by an edge or an arrow in the original graph, or if they are both parents of the same child. The Hammersley-Clifford theorem can then be applied to the moral graph just as before.

(B) *Social Influence Models*

For social influence models, Robins et al. (2001b) presented a two-block chain graph, with attribute variables $\mathbf{Y} = (Y_i)$, $i \in N$ in the child block (response variables) and network variables $\mathbf{X}$ in the parent block (explanatory variables), with the interest in a conditional probability description $P(\mathbf{Y} = \mathbf{y} \mid \mathbf{X} = \mathbf{x})$, modeling the probabilities of observing particular attributes as a function of the network ties. In the first instance, they assume binary attribute variables and binary network variables. They show that the analogue of equation 10.1 for this dependence structure is:

$$Pr(\mathbf{Y} = \mathbf{y}|\mathbf{X} = \mathbf{x}) = \frac{1}{\kappa} \exp \sum_{R \subseteq \zeta} \sum_{Q \subseteq \mathrm{pa}(R)} \gamma_{R \cup Q} \prod_{k \in R} y_k \prod_{st \in Q} x_{st} \qquad (10.2)$$

where ζ is the set of maximal cliques among the attribute variables, pa(R) denotes the particular network variables that are parents of the attribute variables in R, and the parameters $\gamma_{R \cup Q}$ are nonzero only when $R \cup Q$ is a clique in the moral graph. As before, κ is a normalizing quantity.

Because the parameters relate to both attribute and network variables, they represent network configurations with "colors" on the nodes. Consider a clique $R \cup Q$ in the

Chain graph   Moral graph

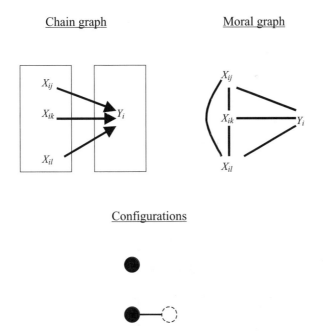

Configurations

Figure 10.5.4. Two-block chain graph and moral graph for a
simple social influence model, together with configurations for a
model of order 2. (Note: For configurations, filled circle
indicates actor with the attribute, whereas dotted empty circle
indicates actor who may or may not have the attribute.)

moral graph. Social influence arises because the distribution of attributes among the actors in R is affected in some way (depending on the parameter value and sign) by the network ties in Q.

A simple starting model that Robins et al. (2001b) considered assumes that there are no conditional dependencies among the attribute variables and that an attribute for actor i has network variables involving i as parents. They consider directed networks, but for the sake of a simple exposition, we only consider nondirected networks. The directed dependence graph and the moral graph are presented in Figure 10.5.4. Cliques of the moral graph have the form $\{Y_i\}$, $\{Y_i, X_{ij}\}$, $\{Y_i, X_{ij}, X_{ik}\}$, and so on. Each clique pertains to an actor i "having" the binary attribute Y_i as well as being involved in a certain number of ties (i.e., i is the focal point of stars of various order.) As there is one parameter for each clique, the resulting parameter-related configurations for a homogeneous model of order 2 are represented in Figure 10.5.4. The result is a simple three-parameter model. Here, the colored circles represent actors who "have" the binary attribute.

The top configuration in Figure 10.5.4 represents an actor without ties; the second configuration, an actor with one tie; and the third configuration, an actor with two

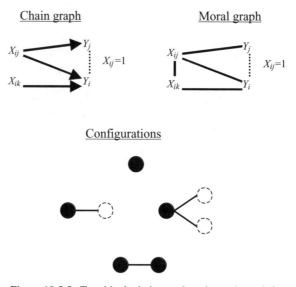

Figure 10.5.5. Two-block chain graph and moral graph for
a partial dependence social influence model, together with
configurations for a model of order 2. (Note: Dotted line
indicates partial conditional dependence.)

ties (because there are no stars of higher order than 2 in the model, the parameter
pertaining to this last configuration should be interpreted as a parameter pertaining to
actors with the attribute and with two or more ties). Examination of parameter estimates
allow interpretation of the relative importance of these configurations in the network.
Accordingly, judgments can be made about the importance of having a tie (or several
ties) with others to possession of the attribute. For instance, such a simple model could
investigate the hypothesis that an individual has high self-esteem if he or she has one
or more close friends.

Robins et al. (2001b) proceeded to examine models with dependencies among attributes that allow for particular social influence effects. They develop models for
attributes that are trichotomous, rather than binary, and for attributes that are measured
by a multiple item scale.

In contrast, here we present a simple model for dependent attributes based on a
partial dependence assumption. In addition to the dependencies in Figure 10.5.4, we
assume a partial conditional dependence between attribute variables Y_i and Y_j if there
is an observed network tie between i and j. The dependence graph and moral graph,
with the partial conditional dependency represented, is presented in Figure 10.5.5. The
cliques of the moral graph are as before, with the addition of cliques of the form $\{Y_i, Y_j\}$
when $X_{ij} = 1$. Figure 10.5.5 also presents the resulting configurations for a model that
again restricts parameters to those containing at most two ties.

There is an additional configuration, and hence an additional parameter in this model,
depicted at the bottom of the configurations in Figure 10.5.5. It represents the situation
where two actors both possess the attribute and have a tie between them. Robins et
al. (2001b) argued that this parameter represents social influence: if the estimate for

Chain graph   Moral graph

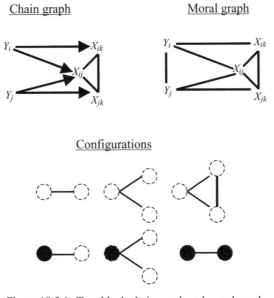

Configurations

Figure 10.5.6. Two-block chain graph and moral graph
for Markov attribute/Markov network dependencies
social selection model for a nondirected network,
together with configurations for a model of order 3.

this parameter is large and positive, then network partners are more likely to share the attribute, from which might be inferred that network partners influence one another toward possession of the attribute.

(C) *Social Selection Models*

Social selection models investigate claims that people construct social ties, in part, on the basis of certain attribute matches. For both social selection and social influence models, the dependence among ties interacts with attributes. In the case of social selection, we have a shaping of ties not just by the presence of other ties, but also by the distribution of the attributes of actors involved.

Technically, the approach to social selection models is similar to social influence models, but here the network variables are in the child block and the attribute variables in the parent block. Using this basic dependence structure, Robins et al. (2001a) developed a series of increasingly complex social selection models for binary attributes. For the most part, they adopt a *Markov attribute assumption* where a network variable X_{ij} is a child to a parent attribute variable Y_k if and only if $k \in \{i, j\}$. They discuss directed networks, but for ease of exposition we concentrate on nondirected graphs here. With Markov attributes and Markov graph dependencies among the network variables, Figure 10.5.6 provides a representation of that part of the dependence graph and moral graph that contains X_{ij}, as well as a resulting set of configurations. In a model limiting configurations to order 3, there are six configurations and hence six parameters in the model. The top three parameters in Figure 10.5.6 relate to standard Markov graph

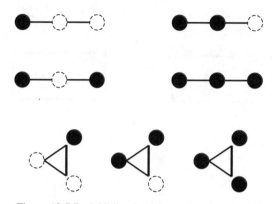

Figure 10.5.7. Additional configurations in a partial
dependent attribute model.

parameters. The bottom three configurations (reading, respectively, from left to right in Figure 10.5.6) pertain to an actor with the attribute expressing a tie to another actor (possibly without the attribute); an actor with the attribute expressing ties to two other actors; and two actors, each with the attribute, forming a tie between them. The last parameter can be used to test a *similarity* or *homophily* hypothesis, that actors with similar attributes form social ties.

The limitation of the Markov attribute assumption is apparent here. The model contains a parameter for a triad, but not for triadic configurations that include attributes. For such parameters, we need to invoke a *partial dependence attribute assumption*, whereby attribute variable X_k is a parent of network variable Y_{ij} if a tie is observed on either the couple (i, k) or (i, j). As Robins et al. (2001a) explained, this step results in additional parameters that incorporate attributes in triadic configurations. The additional parameters are represented in Figure 10.5.7.

An interesting technical difference between social influence and social selection models is that social influence models require at best ordered polytomous attribute measures, whereas social selection models can accommodate continuous attribute measures. Also, social selection models can incorporate a variety of additional functional forms. Robins et al. (2001a) fit both binary and continuous attribute measures in different illustrations of social selection models.

(D) *Temporal Models*

The two-block chain graph approach may also be applied to discrete time models for network change. Robins and Pattison (2001) developed a variety of models along these lines, including models that incorporate partial dependence assumptions. For instance, Robins and Pattison suggested that for certain temporal processes, network substructures might be created based on *constant ties*, ties that remain in place across time and from which new ties may develop into more complex patterning. They assume a cross-time dependence structure based on the *constant tie assumption*, whereby dependencies arise from constant but not transitory ties. This assumption is another example of a partial dependence approach, whereby a time 2 dependency is assumed when certain time 1 ties are observed.

In general, the complexity of network temporal models illustrates clearly that theoretical thought needs to be given to dependence assumptions. To a degree, a hierarchy of models – from Bernoulli-type models, through dyadic independence and Markov models, and then partial dependence models – can be usefully fitted to gain insight into the network data. However, the partial dependence approach allows new classes of models, usually with a complex parameterization. In this circumstance, perhaps the most powerful way to proceed is to develop particular dependence assumptions from theoretical claims and then examine the resulting models.

10.6 Social Space: An Interpretation of Social Dependence

We started this chapter with a description of dependence as a fundamental feature of sociality, not just as a statistical phenomenon. We conclude with an interpretation of the dependence hypotheses of Pattison and Robins (2002) in terms of "social space." Intuitively, the notions of *social proximity* and *social space* are appealing. Individuals occupy locations in geographic space in a way that often shapes social behavior: an extension to more generalized notions of proximity in social space is not unreasonable. In a social network, a tie represents a form of social proximity. For instance, we might use the term *proximity* to refer to a tie between two social elements; for instance, two individuals are socially *proximate* if they have a relationship.

Yet, abstractly, what is to count as an *element* in a social space? As social scientists, we are often accustomed to considering individuals as elements, or perhaps depending on context, groups, or organizations may be the elements represented by the nodes in the graph of our network. However, as we have noted previously, the variables of interest for us typically pertain not just to the individuals, but also to the ties between them. A more abstract construal of sociality, then, would consider possible ties (what we called *couples* previously) as elements. Frank and Strauss (1986) implicitly did so when they developed Markov random graph models. Yet, to use couples as elements requires a notion of proximity, not just for individuals, but also for ordered pair of individuals (i.e., couples).

This conceptual step permits an interpretation of dependence graphs as representing a form of social proximity. We propose that two possible ties are proximate when they are mutually contingent. This contingency can be represented as conditional dependence in a dependence graph. To consider couples as elements in social space does not supplant the notion of individuals as elements. The two representations coexist. The social space of individuals is represented by the network. The social space of ties is represented by the dependence graph. As we have seen, the two representations are not mutually exclusive, and attribute-based models give us a means to develop representations of social space in which proximity interpretations pertain to both individuals and couples simultaneously.

Nevertheless, it is the set of individuals that constitute *actors* within the system and we propose that proximity can only be instantiated through actors. Accordingly, we propose a hierarchy of possible hypotheses about tie proximities, based on various relations between the individuals who constitute the nodes of those particular ties. Different assumptions here have different modeling implications:

1. Tie proximities do not exist at all. This results in the class of Bernoulli random graph models.
2. Two couples are proximate if they share the same actors. This assumption results in the class of dyadic independence models.
3. Two couples are proximate if they share one actor. This assumption results in Markov random graph models.
4. Two couples are proximate if they have at least one pair of actors that in turn are proximate (i.e., are tied). This assumption results in partial conditional dependence models.

This interpretation of conditional dependence as proximity among ordered pairs of individuals in social space suggests further possible elaborations. For instance, it may be useful in certain contexts to develop notions of proximities among triples of individuals, perhaps to differentiate circumstances when three people meet simultaneously, rather than a series of dyadic transactions. Setting structures may be seen as such multiperson proximities.

An interpretation of dependence structures in terms of abstract social proximity certainly highlights the importance of theoretical considerations in proposing dependencies in particular contexts. We now have techniques to assess the effects of complex dependence structures, but there is often limited theoretical guidance as to which dependencies should best be examined. For instance, in what circumstances do we need to collect settings information in addition to network data? In other words, when do multiperson proximities count? To be able to raise such clearly pertinent questions suggests that the abstract notion of social space presented here, together with its potential for further generalization, may have value beyond a construal of some of the results in this chapter.

As network analysts, in our more ambitious moments we might cast ourselves as the geometers of social space. Dependence structures are central to whatever we construe social space to be, and we need to be explicit in the theoretical claims that we make for the dependencies that underpin networks and drive the behaviors of their actors.

Endnotes

1. Throughout this chapter, our intent is to summarize the modeling implications of particular dependence structures, so we do not provide fully elaborated detail on each of the models or describe methods of fitting them. Readers interested in this level of detail are referred to the various cited articles, or to Chapter 8 of this volume, for general information on model estimation techniques.
2. In this chapter, we introduce network variables to indicate the presence or absence of a tie. For each couple, there is one network tie variable, so the two may be loosely thought of as interchangeable.
3. These Markov properties should not be confused with Markov random graphs, discussed later in this chapter.

4. A clique is a single vertex or a subset of vertices adjacent to each other in the dependence graph.
5. One substantive interpretation for such a setting structure might be the hypothesis that persons can cognitively represent their relationships with no more than k individuals simultaneously, so people respond to their social world in terms of overlapping settings involving k others.

References

Anderson, C., Wasserman, S., and Crouch, B. (1999). A p^* primer: Logit models for social networks. *Social Networks, 21*, 37–66.

Asch, S. E. (1952). *Social Psychology*. Englewood Cliffs, NJ: Prentice Hall.

Baddeley, A., and Möller, J. (1989). Nearest-neighbour Markov point processes and random sets. *International Statistical Review, 57*, 89–121.

Baron, R. M., and Kenny, D. A. (1986). The moderator-mediator variable distinction in social psychological research: Conceptual, strategic and statistical considerations. *Journal of Personality and Social Psychology, 51*, 1173–1182.

Bearman, P. (1997). Generalized exchange. *American Journal of Sociology, 102*, 1383–1415.

Besag, J. (1974). Spatial interaction and the statistical analysis of lattice systems. *Journal of the Royal Statistical Society, Series B, 36*, 96–127.

Bryk, A. S., and Raudenbush, S. W. (1992). *Hierarchical Linear Models: Applications and Data Analysis Methods*. Newbury Park, CA: Sage.

Cox, D. R., and Wermuth, N. (1996). *Multivariate Dependencies – Models, Analysis and Interpretation*. London: Chapman and Hall.

Dawid, A. P. (1979). Conditional independence in statistical theory (with discussion). *Journal of the Royal Statistical Society, Series B, 41*, 1–31.

Doreian, P. (1982). Maximum likelihood methods for linear models. *Sociological Methods and Research, 10*, 243–269.

Edwards, D. (1995). *Introduction to Graphical Modelling*. New York: Springer-Verlag.

Erbring, L., and Young, A. A. (1979). Individuals and social structure: Contextual effects as endogenous feedback. *Sociological Methods and Research, 7*, 396–430.

Erdös, P., and Renyi, A. (1959). On random graphs. I. *Publicationes Mathematicae (Debrecen), 6*, 290–297.

Feld, S. (1981). The focused organization of social ties. *American Journal of Sociology, 86*, 1015–1035.

Frank, O., and Nowicki, K. (1993). Exploratory statistical analysis of networks. In J. Gimbel, J. W. Kennedy, and L. V. Quintas (Eds.), *Quo Vadis, Graph Theory? Annals of Discrete Mathematics, 55*, 349–366.

Frank, O., and Strauss, D. (1986). Markov graphs. *Journal of the American Statistical Association, 81*, 832–842.

Friedkin, N. E. (1993). Structural bases of interpersonal influence in groups: A longitudinal case study. *American Sociological Review, 58*, 861–872.

Friedkin, N. E. (1998). *A Structural Theory of Social Influence*. New York: Cambridge University Press.

Friedkin, N. E., and Johnsen, E. C. (1990). Social influence and opinions. *Journal of Mathematical Sociology, 15*, 193–205.

Friedkin, N. E., and Johnsen, E. C. (1997). Social positions in influence networks. *Social Networks, 19*, 210–222.

Holland, P. W., and Leinhardt, S. (1981). An exponential family of probability distributions for directed graphs (with discussion). *Journal of the American Statistical Association, 76*, 33–65.

Lauritzen, S. L. (1996). *Graphical Models*. Oxford, UK: Oxford University Press.

Lauritzen, S. L., and Spiegelhalter, D. J. (1988). Local computations with probabilities on graphical structures and their application to expert systems. *Journal of the Royal Statistical Society, Series B, 50*, 157–224.

Lazega, E., and Pattison, P. (1999). Multiplexity, generalized exchange and cooperation in organizations. *Social Networks, 21*, 67–90.

Mische, A., and White, H. C. (1998). Between conversation and situation: Public switching dynamics across network domains. *Social Research, 65*, 695–724.

Pattison, P. E., and Robins, G. L. (2002). Neighbourhood-based models for social networks. *Sociological Methodology, 32*, 301–337.

Pattison, P. E., and Wasserman, S. (1999). Logit models and logistic regressions for social networks, II. Multivariate relations. *British Journal of Mathematical and Statistical Psychology, 52*, 169–194.

Pearl, J., and Paz, A. (1987). Graphoids: A graph based logic for reasoning about relevancy relations. In B. D. Boulay, D. Hogg, and L. Steel (Eds.), *Advances in Artificial Intelligence – II* (pp. 357–363). Amsterdam: North-Holland.

Robins, G. L. (1998). *Personal Attributes in Interpersonal Contexts: Statistical Models for Individual Characteristics and Social Relationships.* Unpublished Ph.D. Thesis, University of Melbourne, Department of Psychology, Melbourne, Australia.

Robins, G. L., Elliott, P. E., and Pattison, P. (2001a). Network models for social selection processes. *Social Networks, 23*, 1–30.

Robins, G. L., and Pattison, P. E. (2001). Random graph models for temporal processes in social networks. *Journal of Mathematical Sociology, 25*, 5–41.

Robins, G. L., Pattison, P. E., and Elliott, P. (2001b). Network models for social influence processes. *Psychometrika, 66*, 161–190.

Robins, G. L., Pattison, P. E., and Wasserman, S. (1999). Logit models and logistic regressions for social networks, III. Valued relations. *Psychometrika, 64*, 371–394.

Skvoretz, J., and Faust, K. (1999). Logit models for affiliation networks. In M. Sobel and M. Becker (Eds.), *Sociological Methodology 1999* (pp. 253–280). New York: Blackwell.

Snijders, T. A. B., and Bosker, R. (1999). *Multilevel Analysis: An Introduction to Basic and Advanced Multilevel Modeling.* London: Sage.

van Duijn, M. A. J., van Busschbach, J. T., and Snijders, T. A. B. (1999). Multilevel analysis of personal networks as dependent variables. *Social Networks, 21*, 187–209.

Wasserman, S., and Faust, K. (1994). *Social Network Analysis: Methods and Applications.* Cambridge, UK: Cambridge University Press.

Wasserman, S., and Pattison, P. (1996). Logit models and logistic regressions for social networks: I. An introduction to Markov graphs and p^*. *Psychometrika, 61*, 401–425.

Weick, K. E., and Roberts, K. H. (1993). Collective mind in organizations: Heedful interrelating on flight decks. *Administrative Science Quarterly, 38*, 357–381.

Wermuth, N., and Lauritzen, S. L. (1990). On substantive research hypotheses, conditional independence graphs and graphical chain models. *Journal of the Royal Statistical Society, Series B, 52*, 21–50.

White, H. C. (1995). Network switchings and Bayesian forks: Reconstructing the social and behavioral sciences. *Social Research, 62*, 1035–1063.

Whittaker, J. (1990). *Graphical Models in Applied Multivariate Statistics.* Chichester, UK: John Wiley and Sons.

11

Models for Longitudinal Network Data

Tom A. B. Snijders

University of Groningen

This chapter treats statistical methods for network evolution. It is argued that it is most fruitful to consider models where network evolution is represented as the result of many (usually nonobserved) small changes occurring between the consecutively observed networks. Accordingly, the focus is on models where a continuous-time network evolution is assumed, although the observations are made at discrete time points (two or more).

Three models are considered in detail, all based on the assumption that the observed networks are outcomes of a Markov process evolving in continuous time. The independent arcs model is a trivial baseline model. The reciprocity model expresses effects of reciprocity, but lacks other structural effects. The actor-oriented model is based on a model of actors changing their outgoing ties as a consequence of myopic stochastic optimization of an objective function. This framework offers the flexibility to represent a variety of network effects. An estimation algorithm is treated, based on a Markov chain Monte Carlo (MCMC) implementation of the method of moments.

11.1   Some Basic Ideas About Longitudinal Social Network Data

The statistical modeling of social networks is difficult because of the complicated dependence structures of the processes underlying their genesis and development. One might think that the statistical modeling of longitudinal data on social networks is more difficult than modeling single observations of social networks. It is plausible, however, that in many cases, the rules defining the dynamics of network evolution are simpler than the rules required to describe a single network because a network is usually the result of a complex and untraceable history. This chapter on the statistical modeling of network dynamics focuses on models assuming that the network is observed at a number of discrete time points, but there is an unobserved network evolution going on between these time points. The first observation of the network is not modeled but regarded as given, so the history leading to this network is disregarded in the model construction. Hopefully, this will provide a better insight into the rules of network evolution than modeling the first network observation. Further, it is not assumed that the network process is in a steady state. Equilibrium assumptions are mostly unwarranted for observations on network processes, and making such assumptions could lead to biased conclusions.

The treatment of methods for analyzing longitudinal network data presupposes that such data are available. It is evident that the collection of such data requires even more effort than the collection of network data on a single moment because, in most types of network data collection, the researcher will have to retain the collaboration of the network members.

As data, we suppose that we have M repeated observations on a network with the same set of g actors. The observed networks are represented as digraphs with adjacency matrices $\mathbf{X}(t_m) = \big(X_{ij}(t_m)\big)$ for $m = 1, \ldots, M$, where i and j range from 1 to g. The variable $X_{ij}(t)$ indicates whether at time t there is a tie from i to j (value 1) or not (value 0). The diagonal of the adjacency matrix is defined to be 0, $X_{ii}(t) = 0$ for all i. The number M of repeated observations must be at least 2.

Various models have been proposed for the statistical analysis of longitudinal social network data. Earlier reviews were given by Wasserman (1978), Frank (1991), and Snijders (1995). This chapter does not provide a general review of this literature, but focuses on models based on the assumption of continuous-time network evolution. The motivation for this choice is the following.

When thinking of how to construct a statistical model for the network dynamics that lead to the change from $\mathbf{X}(t_1)$ to $\mathbf{X}(t_2)$, then on to $\mathbf{X}(t_3)$, and so on, a first question is whether these changes are represented by one "jump," or are the result of a series of small changes. It is a natural idea to conceive of network dynamics as not being bound in a special way to the observation moments, but as a more or less continuous process that feeds back on itself because at each moment the current network structure is an important determinant of the likelihood of the changes that might occur next. The idea of regarding the dynamics of social phenomena as being the result of a continuous-time process, even though observations are made at discrete time points, was already proposed by Coleman (1964). Several methods have been proposed for analyzing repeated observations on social networks using models where changes are made in discrete steps from one observation moment to the next (Katz and Proctor 1959; Wasserman 1987; Wasserman and Iacobucci 1988; Sanil, Banks, and Carley 1994; Banks and Carley 1996; Robins and Pattison 2001). This chapter does not treat these models, but focuses on models that assume that the network $\mathbf{X}(t)$ is evolving in continuous time, although being observed only at the discrete moments $t_m, m = 1, \ldots, M$.

In this class of models, the ones most directly amenable to statistical analysis are those postulating that the network $\mathbf{X}(t)$ is a continuous-time Markov chain. For categorical nonnetwork data, such models were proposed by Coleman (1964) and the statistical treatment was elaborated by Kalbfleisch and Lawless (1985). Modeling the evolution of network data using continuous-time Markov chains was proposed by Holland and Leinhardt (1977a, 1977b) and Wasserman (1977). The first authors proposed the principle, but did not work it out in practical detail. Wasserman (1977, 1979, 1980), followed by Leenders (1995a), elaborated the so-called *reciprocity model*, which is a continuous-time Markov model that represents only reciprocity as a network effect. Leenders (1995a, 1996) also included similarity effects (as a function of covariates) in this model. Snijders and van Duijn (1997) and Snijders (2001) elaborated the so-called stochastic actor-oriented model, which is a model for network dynamics that can include arbitrary network effects. This chapter treats some earlier models, such as the reciprocity model, and focuses on the actor-oriented model.

11.2 Descriptive Statistics

Any empirical analysis of longitudinal network data should start by making a basic data description in the form of making graphs of the networks or plotting some basic network statistics over time. These can include the density or average degree, degree variance, number of isolates, number of components of given sizes, parameters for reciprocity, transitivity, segmentation, and so on.

Next to sequences of statistics for the M observed networks, it is instructive to give a description of the number and types of changes that occurred. This can be done in increasing stages of structural complexity. The simplest stage is given by the change counts, indicating how many tie variables changed from h to k from observation moment t_m to t_{m+1},

$$N_{hk}(m) = \sharp\{(i, j) \mid X_{ij}(t_m) = h, X_{ij}(t_{m+1}) = k\} \qquad (11.1)$$

for $h, k = 0, 1$, where $\sharp A$ denotes the number of elements of the set A, and the corresponding change rates

$$r_h(m) = \frac{N_{h1}(m)}{N_{h0}(m) + N_{h1}(m)}. \qquad (11.2)$$

This idea can also be applied at the dyadic level (see Wasserman 1980, Table 5). The added complication here is that there are two ways in which a dyad can be asymmetric at two consecutive observation moments: it can remain the same, or the two tie variables can interchange their values. Triadic extensions are also possible.

11.3 Example

As an example, the network of thirty-two freshmen students is used that was studied by Van de Bunt (1999) and also by van de Bunt, van Duijn, and Snijders (1999). These references give more detailed background information on this data set. It was collected in 1994 to 1995. The network consists of thirty-two freshmen students in the same discipline at a university in The Netherlands, who answered a questionnaire with sociometric (and other) questions at seven times points during the academic year, coded t_0 to t_6. Times t_0 to t_4 are spaced 3 weeks apart, t_4 to t_6 6 weeks. This data set is distributed with the SIENA program (Snijders and Huisman 2003). The set of all students majoring in this discipline started with fifty-six persons. A number of them stopped with the university studies during the freshmen year and were deleted from this data set. Of the remaining persons, there were thirty-two who responded to most of the questionnaires; they form the network analyzed here. The relation studied here

Table 11.3.1. *Basic Descriptives*

Time	t_0	t_1	t_2	t_3	t_4	t_5	t_6
Average degree	0.19	3.78	4.63	5.60	6.95	7.73	6.96
Mutuality index	0.67	0.66	0.67	0.64	0.66	0.74	0.71
Transitivity index	–	0.44	0.51	0.44	0.45	0.56	0.46
Fraction missing	0.00	0.06	0.09	0.16	0.19	0.04	0.22

is defined as a "friendly relation"; the precise definition can be found in van de Bunt (1999).

Figures of the changing network are not presented because these are not very illuminating due to the large numbers of arcs. Table 11.3.1 presents some descriptive statistics. Each statistic is calculated on the basis of all available data required for calculating this statistic.

The average degree, starting at virtually nil, rises rapidly to a value of about 7. The mutuality index (defined as the fraction of ties reciprocated) is remarkably constant at almost 0.7. The transitivity index (defined as the number of transitive triplets divided by the number of potentially transitive triplets) is also rather constant at almost 0.5.

The change counts (11.1) are indicated in Table 11.3.2. The total number of changes between consecutive observation moments is 104 in the first period, and 51 to 80 in all further periods.

11.4   Continuous-Time Markov Chains

This section introduces the basics of continous-time Markov chains. These stochastic processes are treated extensively in textbooks such as Taylor and Karlin (1998) and Norris (1997). Introductions aiming specifically at social networks are given by Leenders (1995b) and Wasserman (1979, 1980).

This section is phrased in terms of an arbitrary finite outcome space $\mathcal{X}$, which in the case of network dynamics is the set of all directed graphs – equivalently, all adjacency matrices. The observation times t_1 to t_M are embedded in an interval of time

Table 11.3.2. *Change Frequencies $N_{hk}(m)$ for the Periods $t_m - t_{m+1}$ (Only for Arc Variables Available at t_m and t_{m+1})*

	m					
h, k	0	1	2	3	4	5
0 to 0	820	716	590	530	546	546
0 to 1	104	43	47	31	50	35
1 to 0	0	22	13	20	30	30
1 to 1	6	87	94	98	140	130

points $T = [t_1, t_M] = \{t \in \mathbb{R} \mid t_1 \leq t \leq t_M\}$. It is assumed that changes can take place unobserved between the observation moments.

Consider a stochastic process $\{X(t) \mid t \in T\}$ with a finite outcome space $\mathcal{X}$, where the time parameter t assumes values in a bounded or unbounded interval $T \subset \mathbb{R}$. Such a stochastic process is a Markov process or Markov chain if for any time $t_a \in T$, the conditional distribution of the future, $\{X(t)|t > t_a\}$ given the present and the past, $\{X(t)|t \leq t_a\}$, is a function only of the present, $X(t_a)$. This implies that for any possible outcome $\tilde{x} \in \mathcal{X}$, and for any pair of time points $t_a < t_b$,

$$P\{X(t_b) = \tilde{x} \mid X(t) = x(t) \text{ for all } t \leq t_a\}$$
$$= P\{X(t_b) = \tilde{x} \mid X(t_a) = x(t_a)\}. \tag{11.3}$$

The Markov chain is said to have a stationary transition distribution if the probability (11.3) depends on the time points t_a and t_b only as a function of the time elapsed in between, $t_b - t_a$. It can be proven that if $\{X(t) \mid t \in T\}$ is a continuous-time Markov chain with stationary transition distribution, then there exists a function $q : \mathcal{X}^2 \to \mathbb{R}$ such that

$$q(x, \tilde{x}) = \lim_{dt \downarrow 0} \frac{P\{X(t + dt) = \tilde{x} \mid X(t) = x\}}{dt} \quad \text{for } \tilde{x} \neq x$$
$$q(x, x) = \lim_{dt \downarrow 0} \frac{P\{X(t + dt) = x \mid X(t) = x\} - 1}{dt}. \tag{11.4}$$

This function q is called the intensity matrix or the infinitesimal generator. The interpretation is that for any given value x, if $X(t) = x$ at some moment t, then the probability that the process changes to the new value $\tilde{x}$ in the short time interval from t to $t + dt$ is approximately $q(x, \tilde{x}) dt$. The element $q(x, \tilde{x})$ is referred to as the *rate* at which x tends to change into $\tilde{x}$ (for $x \neq \tilde{x}$). More generally, an event is said to happen at a rate r, if the probability that it happens in a very short time interval $(t, t + dt)$ is approximately equal to $r dt$. Note that the diagonal elements $q(x, x)$ are negative and are defined such that the row sums of the matrix Q are 0.

More understanding of what the intensity matrix means for the distribution of $X(t)$ can be obtained by considering how the distribution could be simulated. A process $X(t)$ for $t \geq t_0$ with this distribution can be simulated as follows, given the current value $X(t_0) = x$:

1. Generate a random variable D with the exponential distribution with parameter $-q(x, x)$ (it may be noted that the expected value of this distribution is $-1/q(x, x)$).
2. Choose a random value $Y \in \mathcal{X}$, with probabilities

$$P\{Y = \tilde{x}\} = \frac{q(x, \tilde{x})}{-q(x, x)} \quad \text{for } \tilde{x} \neq x; \ P\{Y = x\} = 0.$$

3. Define $X(t) = x$ for $t_0 < t < t_0 + D$ and $X(t_0 + D) = Y$.
4. Set $t_0 := t_0 + D$ and $x := Y$ and continue with step 1.

The simultaneous distribution of the Markov chain $\{X(t) \mid t \geq t_a\}$ with stationary transition distribution is determined completely by the probability distribution of the initial value $X(t_a)$, together with the intensity matrix. The transition matrix

$$P(t_b - t_a) = (P\{X(t_b) = \tilde{x} \mid X(t_a) = x\})_{x,\tilde{x} \in \mathcal{X}} \tag{11.5}$$

must satisfy

$$\frac{d}{dt}P(t) = Q P(t). \tag{11.6}$$

The solution to this system of differential equations is given by

$$P(t) = e^{t Q}, \tag{11.7}$$

where Q is the matrix with elements $q(x, \tilde{x})$ and the matrix exponential is defined by

$$e^{tQ} = \sum_{h=0}^{\infty} \frac{t^h Q^h}{h!}.$$

If the Markov chain has a stationary transition distribution, and starting from each state x it is possible (with a positive probability) to reach each other state $\tilde{x}$, then the random process $X(t)$ has a unique limiting distribution. Representing this distribution by the probability vector π with elements $\pi_x = P\{X = x\}$, this means that

$$\lim_{t \to \infty} P\{X(t) = \tilde{x} \mid X(0) = x\} = \pi_{\tilde{x}} \quad \text{for all } \tilde{x}, x \in \mathcal{X}.$$

This is also the stationary distribution in the sense that

$$\pi' P(t) = \pi' \quad \text{for all } t$$

[i.e., if the initial probability distribution is π, then this is the distribution of $X(t)$ for all t]. It can be shown that the stationary distribution also satisfies

$$\pi' Q = 0.$$

It can be hard to find this limiting distribution for a given intensity matrix. Sometimes, it can be found by checking a convenient sufficient condition for stationarity, the so-called *detailed balance condition*. The probability vector π and the intensity matrix Q are said to be in detailed balance if

$$\pi_x q(x, \tilde{x}) = \pi_{\tilde{x}} q(\tilde{x}, x) \quad \text{for all } \tilde{x} \neq x. \tag{11.8}$$

This can be understood as follows: assume a mass distribution over the vertex set $\mathcal{X}$ and a flow of this mass between the vertices; if there is a mass π_x at vertex x, then the rate of flow is $\pi_x q(x, \tilde{x})$ from x to any $\tilde{x} \neq x$. Then (11.8) indicates that as much mass flows directly from $\tilde{x}$ to x as directly from x to $\tilde{x}$, so the flow keeps the mass distribution unchanged. If each state $\tilde{x}$ is (directly or indirectly) reachable from each other state x and the detailed balance equation holds, then indeed π is the unique stationary distribution.

In this chapter, this theory is applied to stochastic processes where $\mathcal{X}$ is the set of all digraphs, or adjacency matrices, with elements denoted by **x**. The models discussed here have the property that, at most, one tie changes at any time point (a model where several ties can change simultaneously is the party model of Mayer 1984). All transition

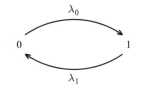

Figure 11.5.1. Transition rates in the independent
arcs model.

rates $q(\mathbf{x}, \tilde{\mathbf{x}})$ for adjacency matrices $\mathbf{x}$ and $\tilde{\mathbf{x}}$ differing in two or more elements then are
0. A more convenient notation for such models is obtained by working with the rate at
which $X_{ij}(t)$ changes to its opposite (0 to 1, or 1 to 0), defined by

$$q_{ij}(\mathbf{x}) = q(\mathbf{x}, \tilde{\mathbf{x}}) \tag{11.9}$$

where

$$\tilde{x}_{hk} = \begin{cases} x_{hk} & \text{if } (h, k) \neq (i, j) \\ 1 - x_{ij} & \text{if } (h, k) = (i, j) \end{cases}.$$

The value $q_{ij}(\mathbf{x})$ can be interpreted as the propensity for the arc variable X_{ij} to change
into its opposite $(1 - X_{ij})$, given that the current state of the network is $\mathbf{X} = \mathbf{x}$.

11.5   A Simple Model: Independent Arcs

The simplest network model of this kind is the total independence model, in which all
arc variables $X_{ij}(t)$ follow independent Markov processes (Figure 11.5.1). This may
be an uninteresting model for practical purposes, but it sometimes provides a useful
baseline because it allows explicit calculations. It is also a simple illustration of the
theory of the preceding section. For each arc variable separately, the model applies with
$\mathcal{X} = \{0, 1\}$, and the rates at which the two states change into each other are denoted
λ_0 and λ_1.

The value $X_{ij} = 0$ changes into 1 at a rate λ_0, whereas the value 1 changes into 0 at
a rate λ_1. The intensity matrix for the tie variables is equal to

$$Q = \begin{pmatrix} -\lambda_0 & \lambda_0 \\ \lambda_1 & -\lambda_1 \end{pmatrix}.$$

This means that the intensity matrix (11.9) for the entire adjacency matrix is given by

$$q_{ij}(\mathbf{x}) = \lambda_{x_{ij}}. \tag{11.10}$$

The transition probabilities can be derived from (11.6) as follows. (These results are
also given in Taylor and Karlin 1998, pp. 362–364.)

Denote $\xi_h(t) = \mathrm{P}\{X_{ij}(t) = 1 \mid X_{ij}(0) = h\}$ for $h = 0, 1$. The transition matrix (11.5)
is equal to

$$P(t) = \begin{pmatrix} 1 - \xi_0(t) & \xi_0(t) \\ 1 - \xi_1(t) & \xi_1(t) \end{pmatrix}.$$

This implies that (11.6) can be written as

$$\xi_h'(t) = \lambda_0 - (\lambda_0 + \lambda_1)\xi_h(t) \qquad (h = 0, 1).$$

This differential equation has the solution

$$\xi_h(t) = \frac{1}{\lambda_0 + \lambda_1} \{\lambda_0 - \exp(-\lambda_0 + \lambda_1(t + c))\},$$

where c depends on the initial condition $X_{ij}(0)$. With the initial conditions $\xi_h(0) = h$, we obtain the solutions

$$\xi_0(t) = \frac{\lambda_0}{\lambda_+} \{1 - \exp(-\lambda_+ t)\},$$

$$\xi_1(t) = \frac{1}{\lambda_+} \{\lambda_0 + \lambda_1 \exp(-\lambda_+ t)\},$$

where $\lambda_+ = \lambda_0 + \lambda_1$. Note that this implies $0 < \xi_0(t) < \lambda_0/\lambda_+ < \xi_1(t) < 1$. These equations imply that, for all t,

$$\frac{P\{X_{ij}(t) = 1 \mid X_{ij}(0) = 0\}}{P\{X_{ij}(t) = 0 \mid X_{ij}(0) = 1\}} = \frac{\xi_0(t)}{1 - \xi_1(t)} = \frac{\lambda_0}{\lambda_1}. \qquad (11.11)$$

For $t \to \infty$, the probability that $X_{ij}(t) = 1$ approaches the limit λ_0/λ_+ irrespective of the initial condition. The stationary probability vector $\pi = (\lambda_1/\lambda_+, \lambda_0/\lambda_+)$ satisfies the detailed balance equations (11.8), given here by

$$\pi_0 \lambda_0 = \pi_1 \lambda_1.$$

Maximum likelihood estimators for the parameters in this model are discussed by Snijders and van Duijn (1997).

11.6 The Reciprocity Model

The reciprocity model (Wasserman 1977, 1979, 1980) is a continuous-time Markov chain model for directed graphs where all dyads $(X_{ij}(t), X_{ji}(t))$ are independent and have the same transition distribution, but the arc variables within the dyad are dependent. This model can be regarded as a Markov chain for the dyads, with outcome space $\mathcal{X} = \{00, 01, 10, 11\}$. The transition rates can be expressed by

$$q_{ij}(\mathbf{x}) = \lambda_h + \mu_h x_{ji} \quad \text{for } h = x_{ij}. \qquad (11.12)$$

These transition rates are summarized in Figure 11.6.2.

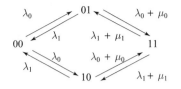

Figure 11.6.2. Transition rates between dyads.

The stationary distribution for the dyads can be derived by solving the detailed balance equations. It is given by

$$\pi_{00} = \frac{\lambda_1(\lambda_1 + \mu_1)}{\lambda_0(\lambda_0 + \mu_0) + (\lambda_1 + \mu_1)(2\lambda_0 + \lambda_1)},$$

$$\pi_{11} = \frac{\lambda_0(\lambda_0 + \mu_0)}{\lambda_0(\lambda_0 + \mu_0) + (\lambda_1 + \mu_1)(2\lambda_0 + \lambda_1)}, \tag{11.13}$$

$$\pi_{01} = \pi_{10} = \tfrac{1}{2}(1 - \pi_{00} - \pi_{11}) \tag{11.14}$$

$$= \frac{\lambda_0(\lambda_1 + \mu_1)}{\lambda_0(\lambda_0 + \mu_0) + (\lambda_1 + \mu_1)(2\lambda_0 + \lambda_1)}$$

(cf. Wasserman 1979; Snijders 1999).

The transition matrix $P(t)$ has a rather complicated form. It was derived by Wasserman (1977) (whose result contains a minor error) and Leenders (1995a) from (11.7) by an eigenvalue decomposition of Q, and by Snijders (1999) by solving the differential equation system (11.6). The reader is referred to the latter two publications for the precise expressions.

This model can be extended by making the change rates (11.12) dependent on covariates. This was done by Leenders (1995a, 1996), who combined the effects of reciprocity and covariate-dependent similarity. However, such extensions are limited by the fact that the reciprocity model postulates that all dyads are independent, which is a severe restriction that runs counter to many basic ideas of social network analysis.

11.7 The Popularity Model

A model in which transition rates depend on in-degrees was proposed by Wasserman (1977, 1980). He called this the *popularity model* because it expresses that the popularity of actors, as measured by their in-degrees, is determined endogenously by the network evolution. The transition rates of this popularity model are given by

$$q_{ij}(\mathbf{x}) = \lambda_h + \pi_h x_{+j} \quad \text{for } h = x_{ij}. \tag{11.15}$$

A mathematical equivalent model is the expansiveness model, in which the transition rates depend on the out-degrees (see Wasserman 1977). Under the popularity model, the columns of the adjacency matrix follow independent stochastic processes. The in-degrees $X_{+j}(t)$ themselves follow so-called birth-and-death processes, which property was exploited by Wasserman (1980) to derive the stationary distribution.

11.8   Actor-Oriented Models

In models for network dynamics that represent the effects of current network structure on the ongoing changes in the network, the probabilities of relational changes must depend on potentially the entire network structure. This generalizes the models presented in the preceding two sections, where only one effect (reciprocity or popularity, respectively) is considered, isolated from other effects. This more encompassing approach may be regarded as a kind of macro-to-micro modeling, where the entire network is the macro level and where the micro level is the single tie, or the collection of ties of a single actor. The model will be a stochastic process on the set of all digraphs, which from now on will be the set denoted by $\mathcal{X}$.

An actor-oriented approach to this type of modeling was proposed by Snijders (1995, 1996), Snijders and van Duijn (1997), and Snijders (2001). The elements of the actor-oriented approach are listed in Snijders (1996, Section 2). Some applications were presented by van de Bunt et al. (1999), de Nooy (2002), and van Duijn et al. (2003). This actor orientation means that, for each change in the network, the perspective is taken of the actor whose tie is changing. It is assumed that actor i controls the set of outgoing tie variables $(X_{i1}, \ldots, X_{ig})$, collected in the ith row of the adjacency matrix. The network changes only by one tie at a time. Such a change is called a *ministep*. The moment when actor i changes one of his ties, and the particular change that he makes, can depend on the network structure and on attributes represented by observed covariates. The "moment when" is stochastically determined in the model by the *rate function*, and "the particular change to make" by the *objective function* and the *gratification function*. First, we discuss the roles of these three ingredients of the model; second, we discuss how they can be specified.

(A)   *Rate Function*

The rate function indicates how frequently the actors make ministeps:

> The ***Rate Function*** $\lambda_i(\mathbf{x})$ for actor i is the rate at which changes occur in this actor's outgoing ties.

The rate function can be formally defined by

$$\lambda_i(\mathbf{x}) = \lim_{dt \downarrow 0} \frac{1}{dt} \, \mathrm{P}\{X_{ij}(t + dt) \neq X_{ij}(t) \text{ for some } j \in \{1, \ldots, g\} \mid \mathbf{X}(t) = \mathbf{x}\}.$$

$$(11.16)$$

The simplest specification of the rate of change of the network is that all actors have the same rate of change ρ of their ties. This means that for each actor, the probability that this actor makes a ministep in the short time interval $(t, t + dt)$ is approximately $\rho \, dt$, and in a short time interval there is independence between the actors in whether they take a ministep. Then $\lambda_i(\mathbf{x}) = \rho$ for all i. The waiting times D between successive ministeps of each given actor then have the exponential distribution with probability density function $\rho e^{-\rho d}$ for $d > 0$, and the expected total number of ministeps made by all actors between time points t_a and t_b is $g\rho(t_b - t_a)$. As is intuitively clear, this expected number is proportional to the total number of actors g, proportional to the rate of change ρ, and proportional to the time length $t_b - t_a$.

Sometimes it can be theoretically or empirically plausible to let these change rates differ between actors as a function of covariates, or to let them depend dynamically on network structure. This is elaborated in Section 11.9(B).

(B) *Objective Function*

The basic idea of the actor-oriented model is that, when actor i has the occasion to make a change in his or her outgoing tie variables $(X_{i1}, \ldots, X_{ig})$, this actor selects the change that gives the greatest increase in the so-called objective function plus a random term.

The ***Objective Function*** $f_i(\mathbf{x})$ of actor i is the value attached by this actor to the network configuration $\mathbf{x}$.

Thus, the objective function represents the preference distribution of the actor over the set $\mathcal{X}$ of all possible networks. It will be assumed that if there are differences between actors in their objective functions, these can be identified on the basis of covariates; in other words, the objective function does not contain unknown actor-specific parameters, but it can contain known actor-specific covariates.

When actor i makes a change in $(X_{i1}, \ldots, X_{ig})$ (i.e., makes a ministep), he or she changes how he or she is tied to exactly one of the $g - 1$ other actors. From one of the $X_{i+} = \sum_j X_{ij}$ other actors to whom i is tied, he or she could withdraw the tie; or to one of the $g - 1 - X_{i+}$ others to whom he or she is not tied, he or she could extend a tie. Given that the present network is denoted by $\mathbf{x} = \mathbf{X}(t)$, the new network that would result by changing the single tie variable x_{ij} into its opposite $1 - x_{ij}$ is denoted $\mathbf{x}(i \leadsto j)$ (to be interpreted as "the digraph obtained from $\mathbf{x}$ when i changes the tie variable to j"). The choice is modeled as follows. Denote by $U(j)$ a random variable that indicates the unexplained, or residual, part of the attraction for i to j. These $U(j)$ are assumed to be random variables distributed symmetrically about 0 and independently generated for each new ministep (this is left implicit in the notation). The actor chooses to change his or her tie variable with that other actor j ($j \neq i$) for whom the value of

$$f_i(\mathbf{x}(i \leadsto j)) + U(j)$$

is highest. This can be regarded as a myopic stochastic optimization rule: myopic because only the situation obtained immediately after the ministep is considered, stochastic because the unexplained part is modeled by means of a random variable.

A convenient and traditional choice for the distribution of $U(j)$ is the type 1 extreme value distribution or Gumbel distribution with mean 0 and scale parameter 1 (Maddala 1983). Under this assumption, the probability that i chooses to change x_{ij} for any particular j, given that i makes some change, is given by

$$p_{ij}(\mathbf{x}) = \frac{\exp(f_i(\mathbf{x}(i \rightsquigarrow j)))}{\sum_{h=1, h \neq i}^{g} \exp(f_i(\mathbf{x}(i \rightsquigarrow h)))} \quad (j \neq i), \tag{11.17}$$

which can also be written as

$$p_{ij}(\mathbf{x}) = \frac{\exp(f_i(\mathbf{x}(i \rightsquigarrow j)) - f_i(\mathbf{x}))}{\sum_{h=1, h \neq i}^{g} \exp(f_i(\mathbf{x}(i \rightsquigarrow h)) - f_i(\mathbf{x}))}. \tag{11.18}$$

This probability is also used in multinomial logistic regression, cf. Maddala (1983: p. 60).

(C) *Gratification Function*

Sometimes the order in which changes could occur makes a difference for the desirability of the states of the network. For example, if reciprocated ties are generally preferred over nonreciprocated ties, it is possible that the difference in attractiveness between a reciprocated and a nonreciprocated tie is greater for canceling an existing tie than for extending a new tie (i.e., for actor i the existence of the tie from j to i will make it more attractive to extend the reciprocating tie from i to j if it did not already exist, but if the latter tie does exist, the reciprocation will have an even stronger effect, making it very unattractive to withdraw the reciprocated tie from i to j). Such a difference between creating and canceling ties cannot be represented by the objective function. For this purpose, the gratification function can be used as another model ingredient.

> The **Gratification Function** $g_i(\mathbf{x}, j)$ of actor i is the value attached by this actor (in addition to what follows from the objective function) to the act of changing the tie variable x_{ij} from i to j, given the current network configuration $\mathbf{x}$.

Thus, the gratification function represents the gratification to i obtained – in addition to the change in objective function – when changing the current network $\mathbf{x}$ into $\mathbf{x}(i \rightsquigarrow j)$.

When a gratification function is included in the model, actor i chooses to change x_{ij} for that other actor j for whom

$$f_i(\mathbf{x}(i \rightsquigarrow j)) + g_i(\mathbf{x}, j) + U(j)$$

is largest. Under the assumption of the Gumbel distribution for the residuals $U(j)$, this leads to the conditional choice probabilities

$$p_{ij}(\mathbf{x}) = \frac{\exp(f_i(\mathbf{x}(i \rightsquigarrow j)) + g_i(\mathbf{x}, j))}{\sum_{h=1, h \neq i}^{g} \exp(f_i(\mathbf{x}(i \rightsquigarrow h)) + g_i(\mathbf{x}, h))} \quad (j \neq i). \tag{11.19}$$

Again, it can be convenient to subtract $f_i(\mathbf{x})$ within the exponential function, cf. the difference between (11.18) and (11.17).

The dissolution and creation of ties work in precisely opposite ways if

$$g_i(\mathbf{x}(i \rightsquigarrow j), j) = -g_i(\mathbf{x}, j);$$

note that $g_i(\mathbf{x}(i \rightsquigarrow j), j)$ is the gratification obtained for changing $\mathbf{x}(i \rightsquigarrow j)$ back into $\mathbf{x}$. If this condition holds there is no need for a gratification function, because its effects could be represented equally well by the objective function. The gratification function will usually be a sum of terms, some of which contain the factor $(1 - x_{ij})$, whereas the others contain the factor x_{ij}. The first-mentioned terms are active for creating a tie (where initially $x_{ij} = 0$), whereas the others are active for dissolution of a tie (where initially $x_{ij} = 1$). Such effects cannot be represented by the objective function. The specification is discussed further in Section 11.9(c).

(D) *Intensity Matrix*

The ingredients of the actor-oriented model, described previously, define a continuous-time Markov chain on the space $\mathcal{X}$ of all digraphs on this set of g actors.

The intensity matrix in the representation (11.9) is given by

$$q_{ij}(\mathbf{x}) = \lim_{dt \downarrow 0} \frac{1}{dt} P\{\mathbf{X}(t + dt) = \mathbf{x}(i \rightsquigarrow j) \mid \mathbf{X}(t) = \mathbf{x}\}$$
$$= \lambda_i(\mathbf{x}) \, p_{ij}(\mathbf{x}), \tag{11.20}$$

where $p_{ij}(\mathbf{x})$ is given by (11.19), or by (11.17) if there is no gratification function. Expression (11.20) is the rate at which actor i makes ministeps, multiplied by the probability that, *if* he or she makes a ministep, he or she changes the arc variable X_{ij}.

This Markov chain can be simulated by repeating the following procedure. Start at time t with digraph $\mathbf{x}$.

1. Define

$$\lambda_+(\mathbf{x}) = \sum_{i=1}^{g} \lambda_i(\mathbf{x})$$

   and let Δt be a random variable with the exponential distribution with parameter $\lambda_+(\mathbf{x})$.
2. The actor i who makes the ministep is chosen randomly with probabilities $\lambda_i(\mathbf{x})/\lambda_+(\mathbf{x})$.
3. Given this i, choose actor j randomly with probabilities (11.19).
4. Now change t to $t + \Delta t$ and change x_{ij} to $(1 - x_{ij})$.

11.9   Specification of the Actor-Oriented Model

The principles explained previously have to be filled in with a specific model for the objective, rate, and gratification functions. These functions will depend on unknown parameters like in any statistical model, which are to be estimated from the data. When modeling longitudinal network data by actor-oriented models, it will often be useful to start by fitting models with only an objective function (i.e., where the rate function is constant and the gratification function is nil). In a later stage, nonconstant rate and gratification functions may be brought into play. At the end of Section 11.9(B), some instances are discussed where it may be advisable to specify a nonconstant rate function

Figure 11.9.3. Transitive triplet.

right from the start of modeling. A wide range of specifications could be given for the three functions. In the next section, specifications are given – most of which were proposed in Snijders (2001) and that are implemented in the SIENA software (Snijders and Huisman 2003).

(A) *Objective Function*

The objective function is represented as a weighted sum dependent on a parameter $\beta = (\beta_1, \ldots, \beta_L)$,

$$f_i(\beta, \mathbf{x}) = \sum_{k=1}^{L} \beta_k s_{ik}(\mathbf{x}). \tag{11.21}$$

The functions $s_{ik}(\mathbf{x})$ represent meaningful aspects of the network, as seen from the viewpoint of actor i. Some potential functions $s_{ik}(\mathbf{x})$ are the following:

1. *Density effect*, defined by the out-degree

$$s_{i1}(\mathbf{x}) = x_{i+} = \sum_{j} x_{ij}.$$

2. *Reciprocity effect*, defined by the number of reciprocated ties

$$s_{i2}(\mathbf{x}) = x_{i(r)} = \sum_{j} x_{ij} x_{ji}.$$

3. *Transitivity effect*, defined by the number of transitive patterns in i's ties, as indicated in Figure 11.9.3. A transitive triplet for actor i is an ordered pairs of actors (j, h) to both of whom i is tied, and j is also tied to h. The transitivity effect is given by

$$s_{i3}(\mathbf{x}) = \sum_{j,h} x_{ij} x_{ih} x_{jh}.$$

4. *Balance*, defined by the similarity between the outgoing ties of actor i and the outgoing ties of the other actors j to whom i is tied,

$$s_{i4}(\mathbf{x}) = \sum_{j=1}^{g} x_{ij} \sum_{\substack{h=1 \\ h \neq i,j}}^{g} (b_0 - \mid x_{ih} - x_{jh} \mid), \tag{11.22}$$

where b_0 is a constant included to reduce the correlation between this effect and the density effect. Given that the density effect is included in the model, the value of b_0 only amounts to a reparametrization of the model (viz., a different value for the parameter of the density effect). The proposed value is such that it yields a zero average for (11.22) over the first $M - 1$ observed networks $\mathbf{x}(t_m)(m = 1, \ldots, M - 1)$ and over all actors, and is given by

$$b_0 = \frac{1}{(M - 1)g(g - 1)(g - 2)} \sum_{m=1}^{M-1} \sum_{i,j=1}^{g} \sum_{\substack{h=1 \\ h \neq i,j}}^{g} |x_{ih}(t_m) - x_{jh}(t_m)| \, .$$

5. *Number of geodesic distances two effect*, or indirect relations effect, defined by the number of actors to whom i is indirectly tied (through one intermediary, i.e., at geodesic distance 2),

$$s_{i5}(\mathbf{x}) = \sharp\{j \mid x_{ij} = 0, \max_h(x_{ih} x_{hj}) > 0\}.$$

6. *Popularity effect*, defined by the sum of the in-degrees of the others to whom i is tied,

$$s_{i6}(\mathbf{x}) = \sum_j x_{ij} x_{+j} = \sum_j x_{ij} \sum_h x_{hj}.$$

7. *Activity effect*, defined by the sum of the out-degrees of the others to whom i is tied, which is equal to the number of actors h who can be reached from i by a path $i \to j \to h$ of length two,

$$s_{i7}(\mathbf{x}) = \sum_j x_{ij} x_{j+} = \sum_j x_{ij} \sum_h x_{jh}.$$

The conceptual interpretations of effects 3 to 5 are closely related, and some further discussion may be helpful for their explanation. The formula for balance is motivated by writing it as the sum of centered similarities between i and those to whom he or she is tied. The similarity between the ties of actors i and j to the same third actor h can be expressed as $(1- |x_{ih} - x_{jh}|)$, which is 1 if $x_{ih} = x_{jh}$ and 0 otherwise. Formula (11.22) can be written as

$$\sum_{j=1}^{g} x_{ij} (r_{ij}(\mathbf{x}) - \bar{r}),$$

where r_{ij} is the number of equal outgoing tie variables of i and j,

$$r_{ij}(\mathbf{x}) = \sum_{\substack{h=1 \\ h \neq i,j}}^{g} (1 - |x_{ih} - x_{jh}|) \tag{11.23}$$

$$\bar{r} = \frac{1}{(M - 1)g(g - 1)(g - 2)} \sum_{m=1}^{M-1} \sum_{i,j=1}^{g} \sum_{\substack{h=1 \\ h \neq i,j}}^{g} r_{ij}(\mathbf{x}(t_m)).$$

[The average $\bar{r}$ is not calculated for the current network $\mathbf{x}$, but over all $M - 1$ networks that figure as initial observations for time periods (t_m, t_{m+1}).]

It is more customary in network analysis to base balance on a similarity measure defined by the correlation or Euclidean distance between rows and columns of the adjacency matrix (cf. Wasserman and Faust 1994). This would be possible here, too, but the number of matches is used because correlations or Euclidean distances are not very appropriate measures for vectors with only 0 and 1 entries.

Positive transitivity and balance effects, and negative number of distances two effects, all represent some form of network closure. This can be seen from the fact that local maxima for these effects are achieved by networks consisting of several disconnected complete subgraphs, which are maximally closed networks, where a local maximum is defined as a digraph for which the said function decreases whenever one arc is shifted to another location (which keeps the density constant). These three effects differ in the precise representation of network closure. To glean some more insight into their differences, it may be instructive to write them in ways that exhibit their similarities. The number of transitive triplets can be written as

$$s_{i3}(\mathbf{x}) = \sum_j x_{ij} \sum_h x_{ih} x_{hj},$$

and the number of distances two as

$$s_{i5}(\mathbf{x}) = \sum_j (1 - x_{ij}) \max_h (x_{ih} x_{hj}).$$

The structure of these two functions is similar, a sum over other actors j of a variable involving third actors h, with the following differences. First, the factor x_{ij} in the definition of $s_{i3}(\mathbf{x})$ implies that the summation over other actors j is made only over those to whom i has a tie, whereas the factor $(1 - x_{ij})$ in the definition of $s_{i5}(\mathbf{x})$ means that values are summed over those j to whom i does *not* have a tie – this accounts for the fact that $s_{i3}(\mathbf{x})$ indicates a positive and $s_{i5}(\mathbf{x})$ a negative network closure effect. Second, for the third actors h in $s_{i3}(\mathbf{x})$, the *number* of actors h is counted through whom there is a two-path $\{i \rightarrow h, h \rightarrow j\}$, whereas in $s_{i5}(\mathbf{x})$ only the existence of *at least one* such two-path counts.

The basic component of the balance function is

$$\sum_j x_{ij} r_{ij}(\mathbf{x}) = \sum_{\substack{j,h=1 \\ j \neq h}}^{g} x_{ij}(1 + 2x_{ih} x_{jh} - x_{ih} - x_{jh});$$

some calculations show that this is equal to

$$2s_{i3}(\mathbf{x}) + s_{i1}(\mathbf{x})(g - 1 - s_{i1}(\mathbf{x})) - s_{i7}(\mathbf{x}).$$

This demonstrates that the balance effect includes the number of transitive triplets and, in addition, a quadratic function of the out-degree $s_{i1}(\mathbf{x})$, which is maximal if the out-degree is equal to $(g - 1)/2$, and the negative activity effect.

Nonlinear functions of the effects $s_{ik}(\mathbf{x})$ could also be included. For example, to represent more complicated effects of the out-degrees, one or more of the following could be used in addition to the density effect.

8. *Out-degree truncated at c*, where c is some constant, defined by

$$s_{i8}(\mathbf{x}) = \max(x_{i+}, c).$$

9. *Square root out-degree* $- c \times$ out-degree, defined by

$$s_{i9}(\mathbf{x}) = \sqrt{x_{i+}} - cx_{i+},$$

where c is a constant chosen by convenience to diminish the collinearity between this and the density effect.

10. *Squared (out-degree $- c$)*, defined by

$$s_{i10}(\mathbf{x}) = (x_{i+} - c)^2,$$

where again c is a constant chosen to diminish the collinearity between this and the density effect.

The squared out-degree has a graph-theoretic interpretation, which can be seen as follows. The number of two-stars outgoing from vertex i is

$$\frac{1}{2} \sum_{\substack{j,h=1 \\ j \neq h}}^{g} x_{ij} x_{ih} = \binom{x_{i+}}{2},$$

a quadratic function of the out-degree x_{i+}. Therefore, including as effects the out-degree and the squared out-degree of actor i is equivalent to including as effects the out-degree and the number of outgoing two-stars of this actor.

When covariates are available, the functions $s_{ik}(\mathbf{x})$ can be dependent on them. For network data, a distinction should be made between actor-bound covariates v_i and dyadic covariates w_{ij}. The main effect for a dyadic covariate w_{ij} is defined as follows.

11. *Main effect of W (centered)*, defined by the sum of the values of w_{ij} for all others to whom i is tied,

$$s_{i11}(\mathbf{x}) = \sum_j x_{ij} (w_{ij} - \bar{w}),$$

where $\bar{w}$ is the mean value of w_{ij}.

For each actor-dependent covariate V the following three effects can be considered:

12. *V-related popularity*, defined by the sum of the covariate over all actors to whom i is tied,

$$s_{i12}(\mathbf{x}) = \sum_j x_{ij} v_j.$$

13. *V-related activity*, defined by i's out-degree weighted by his or her covariate value,

$$s_{i13}(\mathbf{x}) = v_i x_{i+}.$$

14. *V-related dissimilarity*, defined by the sum of absolute covariate differences between i and the others to whom he or she is tied,

$$s_{i14}(\mathbf{x}) = \sum_j x_{ij} \mid v_i - v_j \mid.$$

Of course actor-dependent covariates can be represented by dyadic covariates (e.g., the three preceding effects can be represented, respectively, by main effects of the dyadic covariates $w_{ij} = v_i$, $w_{ij} = v_j$, and $w_{ij} = \mid v_i - v_j \mid$).

(B) *Rate Function*

The time scale at which networks change may well be quite different from the physical time scale of clocks. Therefore, physical time elapsed between observations will usually have a tenuous relation with the amount of change between observed networks. If there are more than two observation moments, a natural first specification is to treat the rate of change within each period (t_m, t_{m+1}) as a free parameter ρ_m, without an *a priori* relation to the time difference $(t_{m+1} - t_m)$.

When actor-bound covariates are available, they could have an effect on the rate of change. An important class of examples is the following. In some cases, there are size differences between actors associated with differences in change rate of their networks. For example, in studies of relations between companies, big companies may have more ties but also change ties more quickly than small companies. Another example is that individuals who are socially very active may have many outgoing ties and may also change these more quickly than those who are less active. Therefore, if some measure of size or activity is available, this could be used as an explanatory variable both in the objective function (as an activity effect) and in the rate function.

Because the rate of change is necessarily positive, a covariate must be related to the rate function in such a way that the rate function will always stay positive. Often, it will be suitable for this purpose to use an exponential link function (where this term is used as in generalized nonlinear modeling; cf. McCullagh and Nelder 1989). The rate function then can be defined as

$$\rho_i(\alpha, \mathbf{x}) = \rho_m \exp \left(\sum_h \alpha_h v_{hi} \right),$$

where the sum extends over one or more covariates V_h.

The rate of change can also depend on positional characteristics of the actors. A primary positional characteristic is the degree, which can be distinguished in the out-degree, the in-degree, and the number of reciprocated ties

$$x_{i(r)} = \sum_j x_{ij} x_{ji}.$$

The latter statistic is called the *reciprocated degree* of actor i. The dependence of the rate function on the degrees can be defined in such a way that the reciprocity model is obtained as a special case of the actor-oriented model.

As the simplest case, consider the independent arcs model, where the intensity matrix is defined by

$$q_{ij}(\mathbf{x}) = \lambda_{x_{ij}}.$$

This model can be obtained as an actor-oriented model with the objective function defined by only the density effect,

$$f_i(\beta, \mathbf{x}) = \beta_1 x_{i+}$$

for which

$$f_i(\beta, \mathbf{x}(i \rightsquigarrow j)) - f_i(\beta, \mathbf{x}) = \beta_1(1 - 2x_{ij}).$$

When the rate function is defined by

$$\rho\{(g - 1 - x_{i+})e^{\beta_1} + x_{i+}e^{-\beta_1}\}, \qquad (11.24)$$

formulae (11.18) and (11.20) show that the intensity matrix is given by

$$q_{ij}(\mathbf{x}) = \rho e^{\beta_1 (1 - 2x_{ij})},$$

which can be reformulated to expression (11.10) by defining $\lambda_0 = \rho e^{\beta_1}$, $\lambda_1 = \rho e^{-\beta_1}$. This shows that this simple actor-oriented model is the same as the independent arcs model.

More generally, Snijders and van Duijn (1997) demonstrated that the reciprocity model is obtained as a special case of the actor-oriented model when the rate function is a linear combination of the in-degree, out-degree, and reciprocated degree. This is a motivation for letting the rate function depend on the degrees by a function of the form (11.24) if only one of the three degree types is implicated, and by averages of such functions in the case of dependence on two or three of the degree types. An alternative would be, of course, to also use the exponential link function for the degrees.

Summarizing, it is proposed to define the rate function as a product of three factors

$$\lambda_i(\rho, \alpha, \mathbf{x}, m) = \rho_m \left\{ \exp\left(\sum_h \alpha_h v_{hi} \right) \right\} \lambda_{i3} \qquad (11.25)$$

where the first factor represents the effect of the period, the second the effect of actor-bound covariates, and the third the effect of actor position. This latter effect has the form

$$\lambda_{i3} = \left\{ \frac{x_{i+}}{g - 1} e^{\alpha_1} + \frac{g - 1 - x_{i+}}{g - 1} e^{-\alpha_1} \right\} \qquad (11.26)$$

if the rate depends on the out-degrees, which can be replaced by the same function of the in-degrees or reciprocated degrees. If the rate function depends on two or all three types of degree, λ_{i3} is defined as an average of such functions (cf. Snijders and van Duijn 1997).

The discussion motivating formula (11.24) implies that the actor-oriented model specified by the rate function (11.26) – a reparametrization of (11.24) – and an objective function (11.21), including the density effect $\beta_1 x_{i+}$, subsumes as a special case the independent arcs model (viz., for $\alpha_1 = -\beta_1$, and $\beta_k = 0$ for all $k \geq 2$). Because the independent arcs model is suitable as an "empty" reference model, this gives a special theoretical role to the rate function (11.26).

A model with a constant rate function (i.e., a rate function not depending on covariates or positional characteristics) is usually easier to explain and can be simulated in a simpler and therefore quicker way. The latter is an advantage given the time-consuming algorithm for estimation. Therefore, in many cases it is advisable to start modeling using a constant rate function and to add the complexity of a nonconstant rate function at a later stage. However, exceptions can occur, for example, if there are important size differences between the actors in the network – which can be reflected by exogenously given covariates but also by, for example, the out-degrees as an endogenous network characteristic. The effect of such a size measure on the rate of change can be so predominant that modeling can be biased, and even the convergence of the estimation algorithm can be jeopardized, if such an indicator of size is not included as an effect on the rate function.

(C) *Gratification Function*

The gratification function can also be defined conveniently as a weighted sum

$$g_i(\gamma, \mathbf{x}, j) = \sum_{h=1}^{H} \gamma_h \, r_{ijh}(\mathbf{x}). \tag{11.27}$$

Some possible functions $r_{ijh}(\mathbf{x})$ are the following. Recall that when $r_{ijh}(\mathbf{x})$ includes a factor x_{ij} it refers to the gratification experienced for breaking a tie, whereas the inclusion of a factor $(1 - x_{ij})$ refers to gratification for creating a tie.

1. *Breaking off a reciprocated tie*:

$$r_{ij1}(\mathbf{x}) = x_{ij} \, x_{ji}.$$

2. *Number of indirect links for creating a new tie*, representing the fact that indirect links (at geodesic distance 2) to another actor may facilitate the creation of a new tie:

$$r_{ij2}(\mathbf{x}) = (1 - x_{ij}) \sum_h x_{ih} x_{hj}.$$

3. *Effect of dyadic covariate W on breaking off a tie*:

$$r_{ij3}(\mathbf{x}) = x_{ij} \, w_{ij}.$$

11.10   MCMC Estimation

The network evolution model is too complicated for explicit calculation of probabilities or expected values, but it can be simulated in a rather straighforward way. This is exploited in the method for parameter estimation that was first proposed in Snijders (1996) and elaborated for the present model in Snijders (2001). Here, we sketch only the estimation method for the actor-oriented model with a constant rate function ρ_m between t_m and t_{m+1}, and without a gratification function. This sketch is restricted to the so-called conditional estimation method. A more precise and general treatment, background references, and a motivation of the estimation method are presented in Snijders (2001).

(A) *Method of Moments*

The observed networks are denoted $\mathbf{x}^{\text{obs}}(t_m)$, $m = 1, \ldots, M$. Suppose that the objective function is given by (11.21),

$$f_i(\beta, \mathbf{x}) = \sum_{k=1}^{L} \beta_k s_{ik}(\mathbf{x}).$$

Then greater values of β_k are expected to lead for all actors i to higher values of the statistics $s_{ik}(\mathbf{X}(t_{m+1}))$, when starting from a given preceding network $\mathbf{x}^{obs}(t_m)$. The principle of estimation is now to determine the parameters β_k in such a way that, summed over i and m, the expected values of these statistics are equal to the observed values. These observed target values are denoted

$$s_k^{obs} = \sum_{m=1}^{M-1} \sum_{i=1}^{g} s_{ik}(\mathbf{x}^{obs}(t_{m+1})) \quad (k = 1, \ldots, L) \tag{11.28}$$

and collected in the vector s^{obs}. For historical reasons, this approach to estimation by fitting "observed" to "expected" has in statistical theory the name of *method of moments* (Bowman and Shenton 1985). Because in our case the expected values cannot be calculated explicitly, they are estimated from simulations.

The simulations in the conditional estimation method run as follows.

1. For two digraphs $\mathbf{x}$ and $\mathbf{y}$ define their distance by

$$\|\mathbf{x} - \mathbf{y}\| = \sum_{i,j} |x_{ij} - y_{ij}|, \tag{11.29}$$

   and for $m = 1, \ldots, M - 1$ let c_m be the observed distances

$$c_m = \|\mathbf{x}^{obs}(t_{m+1}) - \mathbf{x}^{obs}(t_m)\|. \tag{11.30}$$

   This method of estimation is called "conditional" because it conditions on these values c_m.
2. Use the given parameter vector $\beta = (\beta_1, \ldots, \beta_L)$ and the fixed rate of change $\lambda_i(\mathbf{x}) = 1$.
3. Make the following steps independently for $m = 1, \ldots, M - 1$.
   (a) Define the time (arbitrarily) as 0 and start with the initial network

$$\mathbf{X}_m(0) = \mathbf{x}^{obs}(t_m). \tag{11.31}$$

   (b) Simulate, as described in Section 11.8(D), the actor-oriented model $\mathbf{X}_m(t)$ until the first time point, denoted R_m, where

$$\|\mathbf{X}_m(R_m) - \mathbf{x}^{obs}(t_m)\| = c_m.$$

4. Calculate for $k = 1, \ldots, L$ the generated statistics

$$S_k = \sum_{m=1}^{M-1} \sum_{i=1}^{g} s_{ik}(\mathbf{X}_m(R_m)). \tag{11.32}$$

This simulation yields, for the input parameter vector β, as output the random variables $(S, R) = (S_1, \ldots, S_L, R_1, \ldots, R_{M-1})$. Note that the time parameter within the mth simulation runs from 0 to R_m.

For the estimation procedure, it is desired to find the vector $\hat{\beta}$ for which the expected and observed vectors are the same,

$$\mathcal{E}_{\hat{\beta}} S = s^{\text{obs}}. \tag{11.33}$$

This is called the *moment equation*.

(B) *Robbins-Monro Procedure*

The procedure of Snijders (2001) for approximating the solution to the moment equation is a variation of the Robbins-Monro (1951) algorithm. Textbooks on stochastic approximation contain further explanations and particulars about such algorithms (e.g., Pflug 1996; Chen 2002). It is a stochastic iteration method. Denote the initial value by $\beta^{(0)}$. This could be a value obtained from fitting an earlier, possibly simpler, model, or the initial estimate mentioned in Section 11.13(B). This procedure consists of three phases. The first phase is of a preliminary nature, with the purpose of roughly estimating the sensitivity of the expected value of S_k to variations in β_k; in the second phase, the estimate is determined; and the third phase is for checking the resulting estimate and calculating the standard errors.

1. From a relatively small number (we use $n_1 = 7 + 3L$) of simulations, estimate the derivatives

    $$\frac{\partial}{\partial \beta_k} \mathcal{E}_{\beta} S_k$$

    in $\beta = \beta^{(0)}$ by the averages of the corresponding difference quotients, using common random numbers. Denote by D_0 the diagonal matrix with these estimates as diagonal elements.
2. Set $\beta^{(1)} = \beta^{(0)}$, $a = 0.5$, $n_2 = L + 207$. Repeat a few times (advice: four times) the following procedure.
    (a) Repeat for $n = 1, \ldots, n_2$:
    for the current $\beta^{(n)}$ simulate the model in the way indicated previously, and denote the resulting value of S by $S^{(n)}$. Update β by

    $$\beta^{(n+1)} = \beta^{(n)} - a D_0^{-1} \left(S^{(n)} - s^{\text{obs}} \right).$$

    (b) Update β by

    $$\beta^{(1)} = \frac{1}{n_2} \sum_{n=1}^{n_2} \beta^{(n)}.$$

    (c) Redefine $a = a/2$, $n_2 = 2^{4/3}(n_2 - 200) + 200$.
3. Define the estimate $\hat{\beta}$ as the last calculated value $\beta^{(1)}$. From a rather large (e.g., $n_3 = 500$ or $1,000$) number of simulations with $\beta = \hat{\beta}$, estimate the covariance matrix $\hat{\Sigma}$ of S and, using common random numbers, the partial derivative

matrix D with elements

$$d_{hk} = \frac{\partial}{\partial \beta_k} \mathcal{E}_\beta S_h.$$

Finally, calculate the estimation covariance matrix by

$$\text{cov}(\hat{\beta}) = \hat{D}^{-1} \hat{\Sigma} (\hat{D}^{-1})'. \tag{11.34}$$

Step 2(a) is called a subphase of phase 2. Note that from one subphase to the next the initial value $\beta^{(1)}$ changes, the updating factor a decreases, and the number of simulations n_2 increases.

The standard errors of the elements of $\hat{\beta}$ are the square roots of the diagonal elements of $\text{cov}(\hat{\beta})$ in (11.34). The simulations of phase 3 can also be used to check if, for this value $\hat{\beta}$, the moment equation (11.33) is indeed approximately satisfied. The procedure is an instance of MCMC estimation because it is based on Monte Carlo simulations and the provisional estimates $\beta^{(n)}$ in each subphase are a Markov chain.

The parameter a is called the gain parameter and can initially have any value between 0 and 1. Values closer to 0 will lead to a less mobile value for $\beta^{(n)}$ and consequently may require more steps for going from the starting value to a good final estimate, but will lead to a more stable procedure. When the algorithm has come close to the solution of the moment equation (which often happens rather quickly), the provisional values $\beta^{(n)}$ during the steps in 2(a) carry out a random dance about this solution. The reason for taking the average in step 2(b) is that the average of such a collection of random positions is a better estimate than the last value.

The parameters ρ_m are usually of minor substantive importance. They can be estimated by

$$\hat{\rho}_m = \frac{\bar{R}_m}{t_{m+1} - t_m} \tag{11.35}$$

where $\bar{R}_m$ is the average of the simulated time lengths for period m during phase 3.

(C) *Missing Data*

It is hard to collect complete network data at multiple repeated occasions, and therefore it is of practical importance to have a reasonable procedure for dealing with missing data. There can be several reasons why data are missing.

If the composition of the set of actors in the network has changed during the observation period, with some actors joining and/or some actors leaving the group, this can be dealt with by reflecting this changing composition in an appropriate specification of the network evolution model, where only the actors present at the given moment can be involved in tie changes. This is elaborated by Huisman and Snijders (2003).

For other cases, when the composition of the network is constant and it is reasonable to assume that the missing data are due to random nonresponse, the following procedure is proposed. The procedure is designed to be simple and to minimize the influence of the missing data on the results.

1. For the initial networks (11.31) used in the simulations, missing arc variables $x_{ij}^{\text{obs}}(t_m)$ are replaced by the value.
2. For the observed statistics s^{obs} in (11.28), as well as for the simulated statistics S in (11.32) used in the estimation algorithm, an arc variable x_{ij} is replaced by 0 if it is missing for at least one of the observations $\mathbf{x}^{\text{obs}}(t_m)$ or $\mathbf{x}^{\text{obs}}(t_{m+1})$.

This procedure is implemented in SIENA (Snijders and Huisman 2003) and used in the example of Section 11.12.

11.11 Testing

Standard statistical theory about estimation by the method of moments (e.g., Bowman and Shenton 1985) yields the expression given in (11.34) for the estimation covariance matrix,

$$\text{cov}(\hat{\beta}) = \hat{D}^{-1} \hat{\Sigma} (\hat{D}^{-1})'.$$

If the parameter estimates $\hat{\beta}_k$ are approximately normally distributed, the null hypothesis that a single element of the parameter vector is zero,

$$H_0 : \beta_k = 0,$$

can be tested by the t-statistic

$$t_k = \frac{\hat{\beta}_k}{\text{s.e.} (\hat{\beta}_k)} \tag{11.36}$$

in the standard normal distribution. The same procedure can be followed for the parameters α_k of the rate function and γ_k of the gratification function.

It is plausible that the parameter estimates are indeed approximately normally distributed, but at this moment a proof is not available. It would be useful to conduct simulation studies supporting the validity of this t-test.

11.12 Actor-Oriented Model Results for the Example

The example introduced in Section 11.3 was analyzed using SIENA version 1.92 (Snijders and Huisman 2003).

In addition to the structural effects, effects of three covariates were considered: gender, program, and smoking. Gender and smoking are dummy variables coded 1 for female and 2 for male and, respectively, 1 for smoking and 2 for nonsmoking. Program is a numerical variable coded 2, 3, and 4 for the length in years of the program followed by the students. Greater similarity on this variable indicates a greater opportunity for interaction. All covariates are centered by SIENA (i.e., the mean is subtracted), including the dissimilarity variables defined as $(\mid v_i - v_j \mid - c)$, where c is the average of all $\mid v_i - v_j \mid$ values.

Table 11.12.3. *Parameter Estimates for Model with (Except Rate
Parameters) Constant Parameters Throughout Period t_1–t_6*

Effect		Estimate	Standard error
Rate function			
ρ_0	Rate parameter t_0–t_1	24.84	4.57
ρ_1	Rate parameter t_1–t_2	5.43	0.93
ρ_2	Rate parameter t_2–t_3	5.82	0.99
ρ_3	Rate parameter t_3–t_4	4.01	0.67
ρ_4	Rate parameter t_4–t_5	4.62	0.59
ρ_5	Rate parameter t_5–t_6	3.77	0.53
α_1	Out-degree effect on rate	1.15	0.44
Objective function			
β_1	Density	−1.26	0.09
β_2	Reciprocity	2.42	0.25
β_3	Number of distances 2	−0.85	0.08
β_4	Gender popularity	0.45	0.13
β_5	Gender activity	−0.02	0.15
β_6	Gender dissimilarity	−0.36	0.14
β_7	Program dissimilarity	−0.35	0.07
β_8	Smoking dissimilarity	−0.33	0.09

Several models were fitted provisionally to explore which are the most important effects. Next to the reciprocity effect, the distance two effect appeared to be the main structural effect. Of the covariate effects, all three similarity effects and the gender activity effect seemed important. To avoid misspecifying the gender effect in the objective function, the gender popularity effect was also retained. The rate function seemed dependent on the out-degrees. There seemed to be no strong gratification function effects. Therefore, Table 11.12.3 presents the results for a model including these effects; for the sake of simplicity, this model further assumes that – except for the constant factors in the rate function – all parameters are constant throughout the period from t_0 to t_6. For the definition of the rate parameters, the numerical values of the time lengths $t_{m+1} - t_m$ are arbitrarily set equal to 1.0.

As a check on the assumption of constant parameters, Figure 11.12.4 gives the parameter estimates obtained for each period separately, with approximate confidence intervals extending two standard errors to either side of the parameter estimate. For the period t_0–t_1–t_2, a common vector of parameters was estimated because the period t_0–t_1, due to the very sparse network at t_0 (average degree 0.2), led to unstable results. In view of the widths of the error bars, the graphs in this figure show that there is no strong evidence for parameter differences. Adding to the model of Table 11.12.3 the other two network closure effects, transitivity and balance, led to nonsignificant t-tests for these parameters, while this did not make the number of distances two effect disappear. Also, the other effects mentioned in Section 11.9 were not significant. It can be concluded that Table 11.12.3 may be regarded as a reasonable representation of the network evolution in the whole observation period.

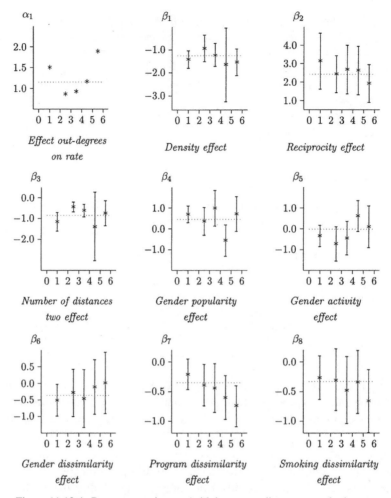

Figure 11.12.4. Parameter estimates (with bars extending two standard errors to either side) separately for periods t_0–t_2, t_2–t_3, t_3–t_4, t_4–t_5, and t_5–t_6. The dotted lines indicate the corresponding parameter estimates from Table 11.12.3. The upper left figure does not show bars because these would all extend outside the figure.

The table shows, judging by the t-ratios of parameter estimate divided by standard error, that there is strong evidence for the reciprocity effect and the network closure effect expressed by a relatively low number of distances two. The fact that the latter effect is significant and not the transitive triplets effect (see Figure 11.3) indicates that what drives the network closure is not an extra attraction for individual i to other individuals j based on the *number* of indirect connections $i \rightarrow h \rightarrow j$, but rather the attraction to others j to whom i has *at least one* such indirect tie. The covariate effects show that male students tend to attract more choices than females, and similarity on gender, program, and smoking behavior leads to a higher likelihood of a tie; male and female students do not differ in the propensity to make choices. An interpretation of the numerical values of the parameter estimates is given in Section 11.13(C).

11.13 Parameter Interpretation in the Actor-Oriented Model

The interpretation of the quantitative values of the parameters in the actor-oriented model is given here with the help of some rough approximations. This section only treats the model where the change rates are constant.

(A) *Rate of Change Parameter*

The expected number of changes per time unit during the period (t_m, t_{m+1}) is ρ_m for each actor. However, two subsequent changes in the same arc variable X_{ij} will cancel each other. In the unobserved interval between t_m and t_{m+1}, some of the changes will therefore be reversals to the situation observed at t_m. This implies that for each actor, the expected number of observed tie differences between the two observations will be a bit less than $\rho_m(t_{m+1} - t_m)$. The extent to which it falls below the latter value will be considerable when ρ_m is so large that the stochastic process is getting near to the equilibrium distribution. Therefore, if $\rho_m(t_{m+1} - t_m)$ is small compared with $g - 1$, the expected value of the average number of changes observed per actor per unit of time,

$$\frac{1}{g\,(t_{m+1} - t_m)} \|\mathbf{X}(t_{m+1}) - \mathbf{X}(t_m)\|, \tag{11.37}$$

where $\|.\|$ is defined in (11.29), will be close to ρ_m. As $\rho_m(t_{m+1} - t_m)$ increases, this expected value will increase less than proportionately. The consequence is that $\hat{\rho}_m$ will be close to (11.37) if this results in a small value of $\rho_m(t_{m+1} - t_m)$, and the ratio of $\hat{\rho}_m$ to (11.37) will increase as a function of the observed number of changes.

(B) *Density Parameter*

As a prologue to the interpretation of the other parameters, note that if all parameters of the objective and gratification functions are zero and the rate of change is ρ, then the variables $X_{ij}(t)$ follow independent arc processes and (11.20) implies that the parameters are $\lambda_0 = \lambda_1 = \rho/(g - 1)$. The limiting digraph distribution of this process is the random graph with density 0.5. This is the "null process" of the actor-oriented model.

For the interpretation of the parameter β_1 for the density effect $s_{i1}(\mathbf{x}) = \sum_j x_{ij}$, consider the actor-oriented model that contains just this effect, with constant change rate ρ and without a gratification function. In this model, the rows $(X_{i1}(t), \ldots, X_{ig}(t))$ follow independent stochastic processes. The intensity matrix (11.20) is given by

$$q_{ij}(\mathbf{x}) = \frac{\rho e^{\beta_1(1-2x_{ij})}}{(g - 1 - x_{i+})e^{\beta_1} + x_{i+}e^{-\beta_1}}.$$

If the number g of actors is large and the out-degrees are small relative to the number of actors, this can be roughly approximated by

$$q_{ij}(\mathbf{x}) \approx \frac{\rho e^{-2\beta_1 x_{ij}}}{g - 1},$$

which is the intensity matrix of the independent arcs model for

$$\lambda_0 = \frac{\rho}{g-1}, \quad \lambda_1 = \frac{\rho e^{-2\beta_1}}{g-1}.$$

Using the results of Section 11.5, this implies that, for each actor i, the log-odds will tend to $2\beta_1$ and the out-degree will for $t \to \infty$ fluctuate about the asymptotic value

$$\frac{(g-1)\lambda_0}{\lambda_0 + \lambda_1} = \frac{(g-1)e^{2\beta_1}}{1 + e^{2\beta_1}}. \tag{11.38}$$

For example, if $\beta_1 = 0$, the out-degrees will tend to be $(g-1)/2$ on average. (Symmetry considerations imply that the latter result is true, even though in this case the out-degrees are not small relative to g.) An exact analysis (not further discussed here) shows that for $t \to \infty$ and fixed g, the asymptotic expected value of X_{i+} is

$$\frac{(2g-3)e^{2\beta_1} + 1}{2 + 2e^{2\beta_1}}, \tag{11.39}$$

which is quite close to (11.38). All this suggests that, for the usual cases where network densities are much lower than 0.5, a negative density parameter is expected.

Now suppose that this process is observed at times t_1 and t_2. Then (11.2) and (11.11) imply that

$$\frac{r_1}{1 - r_0}, \tag{11.40}$$

the fraction of $X_{ij} = 0$, which turned into 1, divided by the fraction of $X_{ij} = 1$, which turned into 0, is expected to be $\lambda_0/\lambda_1 = e^{2\beta_1}$. Therefore, an estimate for β_1 is one-half the corresponding log odds,

$$\frac{1}{2} \log \left(\frac{N_{01}}{(N_{01} + N_{00})} \frac{(N_{10} + N_{11})}{N_{10}} \right),$$

where N_{hk} is defined as in (11.1).

This can be used for an initial estimate for the estimation method of Section 11.10(B) in the case where M observations are available, even when more effects than just the density are included. This initial estimate is given by

$$\hat{\beta}_1 = \frac{1}{2} \log \left(\frac{\sum_{m=1}^{M-1} N_{01}(m)}{\sum_{m=1}^{M-1} (N_{01}(m) + N_{00}(m))} \frac{\sum_{m=1}^{M-1} (N_{10}(m) + N_{11}(m))}{\sum_{m=1}^{M-1} N_{10}(m)} \right) \tag{11.41}$$

for the density effect and $\hat{\beta}_k = 0$ for all $k \geq 2$ (the other effects).

The interpretation of β_1 as approximately one-half the log-odds for the set of arc variables X_{ij} in an equilibrium situation, and the interpretation based on (11.40), do not hold any more for models that include other effects in addition to the density effect. The difference in interpretation will depend on the extent to which the parameters for the other included effects lead to lower or higher overall densities of the network. However, in many practical applications, we still observe negative estimates for β_1 as a reflection of the fact that the network density in a hypothetical equilibrium situation would be clearly less than 0.5.

Network Boundary Effects

What happens with these models if they are applied to networks for which the network boundary has been defined in a rather generous way – so the number g of actors is large and only a small fraction of the network members would be candidate relational partners for any actor? Such a situation can be modeled by letting g tend to infinity, while keeping the out-degrees X_{i+} finite. This is just the assumption made previously for the approximation of the actor-oriented model by the independent arcs model. In the approximating limiting distribution, the log-odds was found to tend to $2\beta_1$, which corresponds for the out-degrees to a binomial distribution with a mean of

$$\frac{(g-1)e^{2\beta_1}}{1+e^{2\beta_1}},$$

which tends to infinity with g. This is at odds with the assumption that the out-degrees X_{i+} remain finite. However, if we let

$$\beta_1 = \eta - \frac{1}{2}\log(g-1),$$

for some fixed number η, the limiting distribution tends to the Poisson distribution with mean $e^{2\eta}$, which does remain finite and is independent of g.

This suggests that if we first consider a certain network with g_0 actors, and then add further actors, most of which are not relevant to the actors present earlier, so the number of ties from the earlier present actors to the new actors is quite small, we should expect the density parameter slowly to decrease, by a term slightly less than $\frac{1}{2}\log\big((g-1)/(g_0-1)\big)$.

(C) Other Parameters

Section 11.13(B) shows that, already for an objective function consisting only of the density effect, quite crude approximations are required to make descriptive statements about the probability distributions corresponding to certain parameter values, and these descriptions do not take us very far.

Another way to obtain insight into the parameter values is to consider the implied objective function, which indicates the preferences of the actors. For the example as presented in Table 11.12.3, this function is

$$f_i(\mathbf{x}) = \sum_j \Big\{ -1.26 + 2.42x_{ji} + 0.45v_{1j} - 0.36\mid v_{1i} - v_{1j}\mid$$
$$-0.35\mid v_{2i} - v_{2j}\mid - 0.33\mid v_{3i} - v_{3j}\mid \Big\}x_{ij}$$
$$-0.85\sum_j(1-x_{ij})\max_h(x_{ih}\,x_{hj}),$$

where (due to the centering applied) $v_{1i} = -0.25$ for female and 0.75 for male students; the program variable v_{2i} has values -1.3, -0.3, and 0.7; and $v_{3i} = -0.6$ for smokers and 0.4 for nonsmokers. The contribution of the gender activity effect was set to 0.

This expression can be brought into clearer shape by some recoding. Denote $z_{1i} = 1$ for male and 0 for female students, $s_{1ij} = 1$ if students i and j have the same gender and 0 otherwise, the program similarity variable $s_{2ij} = 2 - |v_{2i} - v_{2j}|$, and $s_{3ij} = 1$ if students i and j have the same smoking behavior and 0 otherwise. Then the s_{hij} are similarity variables, equal to 0 in the case of the greatest dissimilarity. The objective function then is

$$f_i(\mathbf{x}) = \sum_j \Big\{ -2.78 + 2.42x_{ji} + 0.85 \max_h(x_{ih}\,x_{hj}) + 0.45z_{1j} + 0.36s_{1ij}$$

$$+ 0.35s_{2ij} + 0.33s_{3ij} \Big\} x_{ij} - 0.85 \sum_j \max_h(x_{ih}\,x_{hj}).$$

The first two lines show that, for example, for a male actor i in program $v_{2i} = 2$, creating a new tie to a female student who did not already choose i as a friend, of different smoking behavior and in program $v_{2j} = 4$, to whom no length two path exists, leads to an objective function loss of 2.78. The third line implies that for each student h chosen by j who was not already chosen by any of i's present friends, creating the new tie from i to j leads to an additional loss for i of 0.85. Such students h would point to a lack of embeddedness of j in i's current network. However, if j already chose i as a friend, while the other characteristics are as mentioned, the first two lines imply a loss of only $2.78 - 2.42 = 0.36$. This loss is approximately nullified if the potential friend j has the same smoking behavior or is in program $v_{2j} = 3$. A very crude summary of the preceding is that a tie to another student is worthwhile only if the tie is reciprocated and there also is similarity on at least one variable.

The total contribution of gender for male students is nil for choosing a female friend and $0.45 + 0.36 = 0.81$ for choosing a male friend; for female students, it is 0.36 for choosing a female and 0.45 for choosing a male friend. Thus, for female students the value of a friendship with a male or a female other student is about the same, whereas male students have a clear preference for friendships to other males.

The value of already being chosen by the other (equal to 2.42) is about thrice as large as the value of already having at least one indirect tie to the other (0.85); the latter value is about the same as the advantage, for males, that males have over females (0.81) and slightly larger than the advantage of following the same program compared with following the most different programs ($2 \times 0.35 = 0.70$); and about two and a half times the value of having the same smoking behavior (0.33).

11.14 Discussion

Longitudinal network data can yield important insights into social processes, but these insights can be obtained only when using adequate models for data analysis. There exist many models for network evolution that are not accompanied by methods for statistical data analysis, and recently there has been quite a surge in publications about such models stimulated, for example, by applications to the growth of the World Wide

Web. However, to know how strong and how uncertain the conclusions are that we may draw from empirical data, and to know the extent to which our models are, or are not, supported by the empirical data – which will steer the development of extended or new models in directions that are empirically fruitful – it is desirable to have a statistical component in models for network evolution. The requirement of statistical evaluation leads to parsimony and modesty in model building. The complexity of network dynamics, in which everything seems to depend on everything else, implies that even modest models are mathematically quite complex, as is demonstrated by the models of this chapter. These models are (as far as I know) the first statistical models for network evolution that allow a variety of endogenous network effects, of which the various types of network closure effects (transitive triplets, number of pairs at a geodesic distance equal to 2, balance, as presented in Section 11.9(A)) are primary examples. I hope that the availability of these models and of the software to analyze data according to these models (the SIENA program that is included in the StOCNET system, which can be downloaded from `http://stat.gamma.rug.nl/stocnet/`; see Snijders and Huisman 2003; and see also Chapter 13 in this volume) will be a stimulus for the collection and statistical evaluation of longitudinal network data.

One of the assumptions in the actor-oriented model is that actors optimize myopically, considering only the situation to be obtained immediately after the next change they are going to make. It would be theoretically interesting to elaborate models with more farsighted actors, but the risk is that such models would be less robust and more limited to specific applications than the simpler myopic models. The interpretation of the myopic models is that the effects in the objective and gratification functions represent what the actors try to achieve in the short run, and do not directly reflect their goals in the long run.

The further application of these models should also indicate the points where they must be further extended and modified to provide a better fit to empirical data and to be better aligned with the theoretical questions that researchers may have. The actor-oriented approach explained here, and its implementation using the rate, objective, and gratification functions, is quite flexible and open for extension by a variety of effects in addition to those mentioned here, but other models can also be proposed. One example is the alternative actor-oriented model of Snijders (2003) in which the focus is on giving a good fit to the observed out-degrees. Another example would be a tie-oriented or dyad-oriented model, driven not by changes made by optimizing actors, but by changes in tie variables, which would be closely compatible with the exponential random graph models proposed by Frank and Strauss (1986) and Wasserman and Pattison (1996) and treated in Chapters 8 to 10 of this volume; these tie changes could be according to Gibbs or Metropolis-Hastings steps as described in Snijders (2002). Testing goodness-of-fit of network evolution models, which will give empirical indications for model modifications and extensions, is the topic of Schweinberger (2004).

The approach presented here can also be extended by considering more complex data sets. A multilevel approach to network evolution, in which the data is composed of multiple parallel networks that evolve according to a similar model, but with different parameters, was initiated by Snijders and Baerveldt (2003), and may be further extended. As the mutual influence between networks and behavior is theoretically and practically important, research is also under way about modeling the simultaneous evolution of networks and individual behavior. The models presented in this chapter have a rich potential for applications, but perhaps an even richer potential for further extensions.

References

Banks, D. L., and K. M. Carley. 1996. Models for network evolution. *Journal of Mathematical Sociology, 21*: 173–196.

Bowman, K. O., and L. R. Shenton. 1985. Method of moments, pp. 467–473 in *Encyclopedia of Statistical Sciences, vol. 5*, edited by S. Kotz, N. L. Johnson, and C. B. Read. New York: Wiley.

Chen, H.-F. 2002. *Stochastic Approximation and Its Applications.* Dordrecht, The Netherlands: Kluwer.

Coleman, J. S. 1964. *Introduction to Mathematical Sociology.* New York: The Free Press of Glencoe.

de Nooy, W. 2002. The dynamics of artistic prestige. *Poetics*, 30: 147–167.

Doreian, P., and F. N. Stokman (eds.). 1997. *Evolution of Social Networks.* Amsterdam: Gordon and Breach.

Frank, O. 1991. Statistical analysis of change in networks. *Statistica Neerlandica*, 45: 283–293.

Frank, O., and D. Strauss. 1986. Markov graphs. *Journal of the American Statistical Association*, 81: 832–842.

Holland, P., and S. Leinhardt. 1977a. A dynamic model for social networks. *Journal of Mathematical Sociology*, 5: 5–20.

Holland, P., and S. Leinhardt. 1977b. Social structure as a network process. *Zeitschrift für Soziologie*, 6: 386–402.

Huisman, M., and T. A. B. Snijders. 2003. Statistical analysis of longitudinal network data with changing composition. *Sociological Methods and Research*, 32: 253–287.

Kalbfleisch, J. D., and J. F. Lawless. 1985. The analysis of panel data under a Markov assumption. *Journal of the American Statistical Association*, 80: 863–871.

Katz, L., and C. H. Proctor. 1959. The configuration of interpersonal relations in a group as a time-dependent stochastic process. *Psychometrika*, 24: 317–327.

Leenders, R. Th. A. J. 1995a. Models for network dynamics: a Markovian framework. *Journal of Mathematical Sociology*, 20: 1–21.

Leenders, R. Th. A. J. 1995b. *Structure and Influence. Statistical Models for the Dynamics of Actor Attributes, Network Structure and Their Interdependence.* Amsterdam: Thesis Publishers.

Leenders, R. Th. A. J. 1996. Evolution of friendship and best friendship choices. *Journal of Mathematical Sociology*, 21: 133–148.

Maddala, G. S. 1983. *Limited-Dependent and Qualitative Variables in Econometrics.* Cambridge: Cambridge University Press.

Mayer, T. F. 1984. Parties and networks: stochastic models for relationship networks. *Journal of Mathematical Sociology*, 10: 51–103.

McCullagh, P., and J. A. Nelder. 1989. *Generalized Linear Models,* 2nd ed. London: Chapman & Hall.

Norris, J. R. 1997. *Markov Chains.* Cambridge: Cambridge University Press.

Pflug, G. Ch. 1996. *Optimization of Stochastic Models.* Boston: Kluwer.

Robins, G., and P. Pattison. 2001. Random graph models for temporal processes in social networks. *Journal of Mathematical Sociology*, 25: 5–41.

Robbins, H., and S. Monro. 1951. A stochastic approximation method. *Annals of Mathematical Statistics*, 22: 400–407.

Sanil, A., D. L. Banks, and K. M. Carley. 1994. Models for evolving fixed-node networks: model fitting and model testing. *Social Networks*, 17, 1–26.

Schweinberger, M. 2004. Testing goodness of fit of network evolution models. *Submitted.*

Snijders, T. A. B. 1995. Methods for longitudinal social network data, pp. 211–227 in *New Trends in Probability and Statistics, Vol. 3: Multivariate Statistics and Matrices in Statistics*, edited by E.-M. Tiit, T. Kollo, and H. Niemi. Vilnius, Lithuania: TEV and Utrecht, The Netherlands: VSP.

Snijders, T. A. B. 1996. Stochastic actor-oriented models for network change. *Journal of Mathematical Sociology, 21:* 149–172.

Snijders, T. A. B. 1999. The transition probabilities of the reciprocity model. *Journal of Mathematical Sociology,* 23: 241–253.

Snijders, T. A. B. 2001. The statistical evaluation of social network dynamics, pp. 361–395 in *Sociological Methodology – 2001*, edited by M. E. Sobel and M. P. Becker. Boston: Basil Blackwell.

Snijders, T. A. B. 2002. Markov chain Monte Carlo estimation of exponential random graph models. *Journal of Social Structure*, 3 (2).

Snijders, T. A. B. 2003. Accounting for degree distributions in empirical analysis of network dynamics, pp. 146–161 in *Dynamic Social Network Modeling and Analysis: Workshop Summary and Papers*, edited by R. Breiger, K. Carley, and P. Pattison. National Research Council of the National Academies. Washington, DC: The National Academies Press.

Snijders, T. A. B., and C. Baerveldt. 2003. A multilevel network study of the effects of delinquent behavior on friendship evolution. *Journal of Mathematical Sociology*, 27: 123–151.

Snijders, T. A. B., and J. M. Huisman. 2003. *Manual for SIENA Version 1.98*. Groningen: ICS, University of Groningen. Available from: http://stat.gamma.rug.nl/stocnet/.

Snijders, T. A. B., and M. A. J. van Duijn. 1997. Simulation for statistical inference in dynamic network models, pp. 493–512 in *Simulating Social Phenomena*, edited by Conte, R., R. Hegselmann, and P. Terna. Berlin: Springer.

Taylor, H. M., and S. Karlin. 1998. *An Introduction to Stochastic Modeling*, 3rd ed. New York: Academic Press.

van de Bunt, G. G. 1999. *Friends by Choice. An Actor-Oriented Statistical Network Model for Friendship Networks Through Time*. Amsterdam: Thesis Publishers.

van de Bunt, G. G., M. A. J. van Duijn, and T. A. B. Snijders. 1999. Friendship networks through time: An actor-oriented statistical network model. *Computational and Mathematical Organization Theory*, 5: 167–192.

van Duijn, M. A. J., E. P. H. Zeggelink, J. M. Huisman, F. N. Stokman, and F. W. Wasseur. 2003. Evolution of sociology freshmen into a friendship network. *Journal of Mathematical Sociology*, 27: 153–191.

Wasserman, S. 1977. *Stochastic Models for Directed Graphs*. Ph.D. dissertation, Harvard University, Department of Statistics, Cambridge, MA.

Wasserman, S. 1978. Models for binary directed graphs and their applications. *Advances in Applied Probability*, 10: 803–818.

Wasserman, S. 1979. A stochastic model for directed graphs with transition rates determined by reciprocity, pp. 392–412 in *Sociological Methodology 1980*, edited by K. F. Schuessler. San Francisco: Jossey-Bass.

Wasserman, S. 1980. Analyzing social networks as stochastic processes. *Journal of the American Statistical Association*, 75: 280–294.

Wasserman, S. 1987. The conformity of two sociometric relations. *Psychometrika*, 53: 261–282.

Wasserman, S., and K. Faust. 1994. *Social Network Analysis: Methods and Applications*. New York: Cambridge University Press.

Wasserman, S., and D. Iacobucci. 1988. Sequential social network data. *Psychometrika*, 53: 261–282.

Wasserman, S., and P. Pattison. 1996. Logit models and logistic regression for social networks: I. An introduction to Markov graphs and p^*. *Psychometrika*, 61: 401–425.

12

Graphic Techniques for Exploring Social Network Data

Linton C. Freeman

University of California, Irvine

Social network analysts study the structural patterning of the ties that link social actors. For the most part, they seek to uncover two kinds of patterns: (1) those that reveal subsets of actors that are organized into cohesive social groups, and (2) those that reveal subsets of actors that occupy equivalent social positions, or roles.

To uncover patterns of those kinds, network analysts collect and examine data on actor-to-actor ties. Such data record who is connected to whom and/or how closely they are connected. Typically, the data are organized into square, N-dimensional, N-by-N matrices, where the N rows and the N columns both refer to the social actors being studied. Cell entries in these matrices indicate either the presence/absence or the strength of some social relationship linking the row actor to the column actor. In this chapter, we deal only with symmetric relationships where, given a connection from actor i to actor j, actor j is also connected to i in the same way.

Network analysts sometimes use standard statistical procedures in examining their actor-by-actor matrices. Although there are several statistical modeling tools that have been developed specifically for network data (Holland and Leinhardt 1981; Wasserman and Pattison 1996), these tools were designed primarily for testing hypotheses. They do not provide a simple direct way to explore the patterning of network data – one that will permit an investigator to "see" groups and positions.

Visual images can be used to examine the patterning of network data. In an earlier paper (Freeman 2000), I reviewed the history of the use of visual images in social network analysis. In this chapter, I show how to use images in an exploratory way to learn something about the properties of a network data set. The next section introduces some ways to create visual images that can be used to display the kinds of structure of interest to network analysts. Then the following section will show how those images can be adapted to help to uncover both the antecedents and the consequences of observed network structure.

12.1 Visual Images

Moreno (1932, 1934) was the first to use visual images to display the patterning of linkages among social actors.[1] In Moreno's images, each actor was represented by a point, and each link was shown by a line connecting a pair of points. One of his earliest

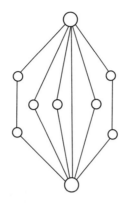

Figure 12.1.1. Moreno's early image.

images (Moreno 1932: p. 101) is reproduced as Figure 12.1.1. He characterized that image as showing "a group in which two dominating individuals are strongly united both directly and indirectly through other individuals." Thus, Moreno viewed that picture as a display of both cohesiveness ("strongly united") and social roles ("dominating individuals").

In this early work, Moreno demonstrated "that variations in the locations of points could be used to stress important structural patterns in the data" (Freeman 2000). Figure 12.1.2, for example, shows his image of friendship choices among fourth graders (Moreno 1934: p. 38). He used triangles to designate boys and circles to designate girls. He also used directed lines with arrowheads to show which child was the chooser and which the chosen. The important point, however, is that in order to stress the enormous tendency for children of that age to generate same-gender choices, Moreno located all the boys on the left of the picture and all the girls on the right.

Moreno developed many procedures for arranging points that succeeded in emphasizing the structural features of the data that he wanted to stress. However, those procedures were all essentially *ad hoc*. Moreno did not introduce any systematic general procedure for locating points in images. Instead, he developed different procedures – each tailored to the demands of each new data set. In any particular image, the placement of points depended on the idea Moreno wanted to communicate about the particular data set being examined.

Later analysts continue to use visual images and to develop procedures for placing points in ways designed to reveal structural patterning. However, a central aim of this newer work has been to develop *principled* procedures – procedures that are specified in exact terms and that will produce the same results when they are applied repeatedly or by different investigators.

Most of this newer work embodies a fundamental assumption. It assumes that a display of a social pattern should preserve the pattern. Thus, the points in a visual image should be located so the observed strengths of the inter-actor ties are preserved. Those pairs that are socially closest in the observed data should be spatially closest in the graphic image. Those pairs that are the most socially remote in the data should be the farthest apart in the image.

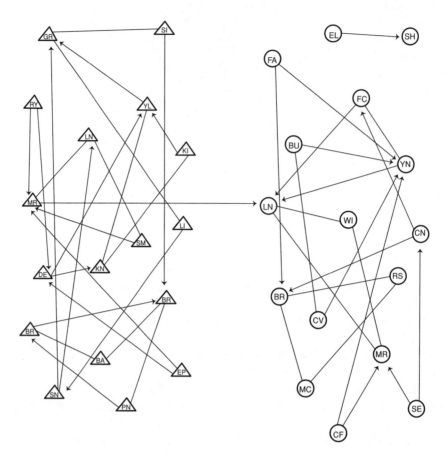

Figure 12.1.2. Moreno's image of fourth-grade friendship choices.

This aim raises a nontrivial problem. I indicated previously that network data come in the form an N-by-N matrix of observed social proximities. Such a matrix is N-dimensional. That is, each social actor in the data set is at some specified closeness or social proximity to every actor in the set. We can assume that the actors are all closest to themselves. An actor's proximity to each of the $N-1$ other actors will take some smaller numeric value, based on reports or observations. Thus, it is clear that each actor is assigned a score on each of N variables, and each of these scores specifies an inter- or intra-actor social proximity.

In general, then, to specify all these proximities exactly, we need to use N dimensions – as many as there are actors. However, if we are dealing with more than three actors, this might raise a problem. We can actually view a picture of spatial prox- imities in a collection of points only if they are arrayed in one, two, or three dimensions. Thus, to create a visual display, we need a way of simplifying the social proximities recorded in the data – a way of reducing its dimensionality. What we are seeking, therefore, is some systematic procedure that will specify a location for each point in a picture with no more than three dimensions. Moreover, the pattern of spatial proximities of the points in that picture must reflect, as closely as possible, the pattern of social proximities of the actors in the original N-dimensional data matrix.

Two main approaches are used to construct such images. The first is based in a search algorithm. It is called *multidimensional scaling, smallest space analysis*, or *spring embedding*. These are simply variations on a common approach. They all involve the search for an optimal location for points. So, here I will lump them all together and refer to them simply as multidimensional scaling (MDS).

MDS requires that the investigator specify a desired dimensionality – typically, one, two, or three. Then, given that specified number of dimensions, MDS uses a search procedure to try to find optimal locations at which to place the points. Optimal locations are either (1) those that come closest to reproducing the pattern of the original N-dimensional social proximities contained in the data matrix (metric MDS), or (2) those that come closest to reproducing the order, but not necessarily the exact magnitudes, of the original proximities (nonmetric MDS).

A number of different procedures have been developed to search for optimal locations for points (Krempel 1999). There are several ways to evaluate how closely the pattern of a given set of MDS proximities corresponds to the pattern of proximities in the original data matrix (Kruskal and Wish 1978).[2] However, all the MDS procedures share a general approach; all involve a search for an optimal arrangement.

The second approach is determinate. It is based on an algebraic procedure, *singular value decomposition* (SVD).[3] SVD transforms the N original variables into N new variables, or dimensions. These new dimensions are ordered from largest to smallest in terms of how much of the variance, or patterning, in the original data is associated with each. The most variance is always associated with the first dimension. Each succeeding dimension is, in turn, associated with progressively less of the variance.

If a one-, two-, or three-dimensional visual image is going to be useful, the hope is that the first or the first two or three of these new dimensions will be associated with virtually all the variance contained in the original data (Weller and Romney 1990). If, in contrast, the first few dimensions are associated with very little of the original variance, SVD will not yield useful results.

As was the case with MDS, there are several ways of getting SVD solutions. SVD itself is always calculated the same way, but there are differences in the ways the data are preprocessed before SVD is run. One standard preprocessor removes the effects of differences in the sizes of the row and column totals. When that approach is taken, the results are said to be produced by *correspondence analysis*. Another preprocessor – perhaps the best-known one – removes the effects of differences in means and the variances in rows and columns. When that is done, the results are described as produced by *principal components analysis*.

12.2 The Search for Structure

In every case, whether we use MDS or SVD to explore data, the first problem will always be to determine whether the data embody any interesting patterning at all. To examine this question, I will draw upon a data set collected on a beach by Freeman, Freeman, and Michaelson (1988). We asked forty-three regular beach goers to sort cards naming beach people into piles in terms of who was socially close to whom. These sorts

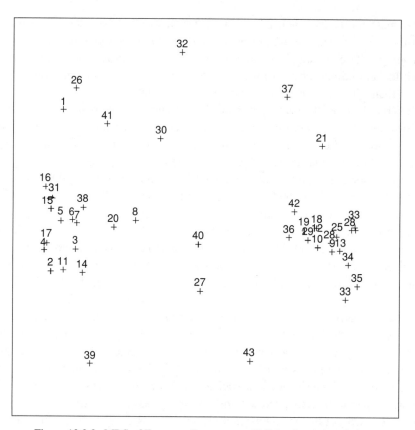

Figure 12.2.3. MDS of Freeman, Freeman, and Michaelson's beach data.

were used to produce a matrix in which each cell contained a tally of the number of times the row person had been grouped together with the column person. This matrix of judged social proximities was used as input to MDS, and the two-dimensional image in Figure 12.2.3 was produced.

The arrangement of points in Figure 12.2.3 divides most of them into two fairly dense clusters on the right and the left. Each cluster has core members located near the center of the cluster. Each has peripheral points that surround the core. In addition, several points (27, 30, 32, 40, and 43) fall in the center, between the two main clusters. Thus, this image seems to display social groups as clusters. Moreover, it places individuals in core and peripheral positions within each group, and it suggests that some actors occupy "bridging" positions between the two groups. This arrangement is completely consistent with the ethnographic data and the systematic observations originally reported by Freeman, Freeman, and Michaelson.

Beyond shape, another feature of this MDS output is important. Most MDS programs report an index of "stress." Higher values of stress indicate that the proximities calculated by MDS do not correspond very well to the original N-dimensional proximities. In this case, the stress = .17. This is reasonable for a 43-by-43 data matrix.

Now let us compare that image with one in which there is no systematic social patterning. We can construct such an image from the data that produced Figure 12.2.3.

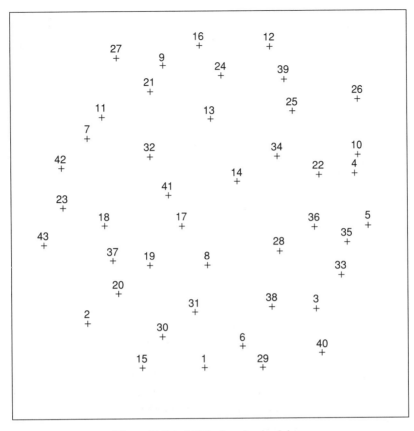

Figure 12.2.4. MDS of randomized data.

We first remove all the entries from the 43-by-43 data matrix and save them. Then we return each frequency to a randomly chosen cell, preserving symmetry. The result is a new matrix in which the overall distribution of cell entries is identical to that of the original data. However, in this new matrix actors are paired at random.

The result of applying MDS to this new matrix is shown in Figure 12.2.4. There, the points form into an almost circular disk. This shape is critical. Generally, any MDS image that is shaped like a disk in two dimensions or a sphere in three, suggests that the links are unpatterned. Moreover, the stress index is .36. This high value confirms that there is little patterning here.

SVD can be applied to the same data with similar results. See, for example, the image in Figure 12.2.5. The same beach data that produced Figure 12.2.3 were used to produce Figure 12.2.5. They were preprocessed (using correlations) to remove the effects of differences in means and variances. Then they were processed using SVD. The result is called *principal components analysis.*

This SVD image of the beach data yields an even more dramatic display of the two main groups of beach goers. Core and peripheral group members are still shown, as are the bridging members. Note that, on the horizontal dimension, which actors are clustered together and which are pulled apart is consistent with the MDS image.

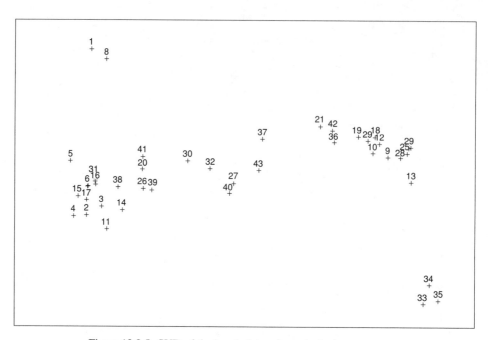

Figure 12.2.5. SVD of the beach data using principal components.

The proportion of variance associated with the first two dimensions here provides further evidence that structure is present. For these data, the first two dimensions are associated with 36% of the variance. This is a substantial proportion. Clearly, SVD has captured the structure in these data.

When the random data are entered into SVD we again see a disklike pattern. This time the pattern is somewhat more irregular than the one produced by MDS, but it is still essentially an amorphous disk. In the present case, somewhat less than 11% of the total variance is displayed in the two dimensions shown in the figure. This is a relatively small proportion and, because it is so small, it provides further evidence that the image contains little important structural information.

Thus, in the general case – using either MDS or SVD – it is relatively simple to determine whether a data set has, or does not have, interesting structural properties. If the plot produces an image that is shaped like a disk or a globe, it is generally not interesting from a structural perspective. However, to the degree that it departs from these forms, it displays important structural properties. This approach, then, can be used for the first step in the exploratory analysis of network data.

12.3 Finding Correlates of Structural Patterns

When we uncover a data set that has an interesting structural form, we are just beginning. We are simply ready for the next step in exploratory analysis. The really interesting questions involve finding the antecedents and the consequences of observed structural patterns.

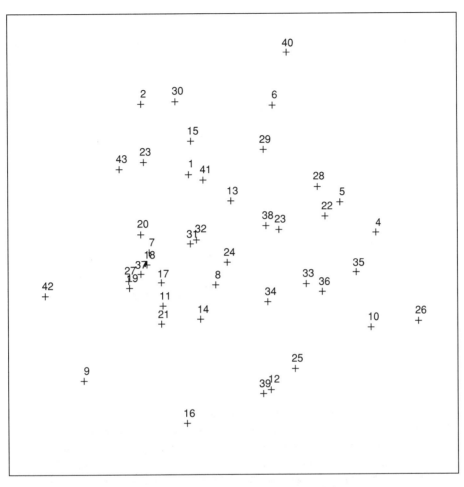

Figure 12.2.6. SVD of the randomized beach data.

The basic approach I will use to finding these features is not new. Bock and Husain (1952) used it to show how a class of ninth graders chose partners for an assignment. They asked each of the sixteen members of a ninth-grade class to rank all of the others in terms of their desirability as collaborators on a joint research project. Then they calculated principal components and produced the image shown in Figure 12.3.7.

Bock and Husain plotted the student's partner choices in two dimensions. Moreover, they used gender symbols to emphasize the differences between the choices made by females and those made by males. In this case, the males and females formed distinct clusters in which males chose other males and females chose other females. The point of the labeling was to call attention to the fact that the main basis for partner choice was gender.

In the 1950s, this device of identifying subsets of points in a structural display according to the various characteristics of the actors involved was difficult. It involved manually specifying the locations of points, hiring a draftsman, and photographically reproducing the final drawing for printing.

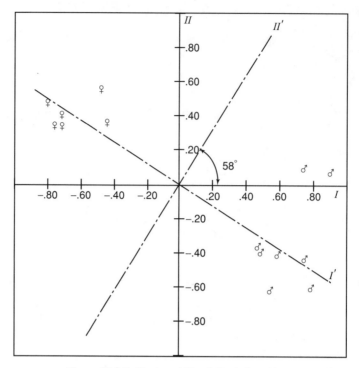

Figure 12.3.7. Bock and Husain's ninth graders.

Today, the whole process has been simplified with the use of personal computers. Using standard computer programs, we can automatically produce images that call attention to particular subsets of points by assigning distinct symbols or colors to identify them. In the work described here, I have used a program called MAGE (Richardson and Richardson 1992).[4] It is excellent for exploratory work in social network analysis (Freeman, Webster, and Kirke 1998). Like the picture produced by Bock and Husain, images produced by MAGE can be used to communicate findings in published reports.[5] However, more important, they can be generated with such ease that investigators can use them for exploratory work. Images in which subsets of points are identified can be used to explore the impact of any number of external variables on a structural pattern.

In the next three sections, I show how MAGE has been used to explore these questions. These sections illustrate three applications of visual analysis. They show how graphic techniques can help in (1) pure exploratory research, (2) examining an *a priori* hunch, and (3) validating a model. Finally, in the last section, I illustrate another approach. There I will show how animation can be used to generate new *post hoc* structural insights.

12.4   Exploratory Research

One of my students, Marbella Canales, worked in the cosmetics department of an upscale department store. She asked each of her fellow employees to list any of the

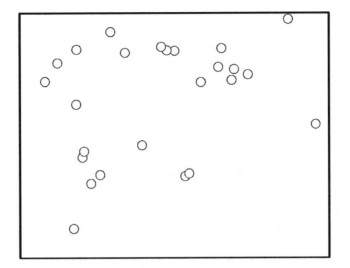

Figure 12.4.8. MDS of department store data.

others with whom he or she spent leisure time. This produced a binary, on/off, matrix of social links. That matrix was used to calculate the lengths of the shortest paths – from actor, through social link, to actor, through link, and so on – linking each pair of employees. Those distances were entered into the MDS program. A three-dimensional MDS produced the arrangement shown in Figure 12.4.8.

Figure 12.4.8 is not a disk. It shows that patterning is present in these data. That patterning is even more evident when we add the actor-to-actor ties reported by the employees (Figure 12.4.9). The pattern of linkages forms a horseshoe shape. This is commonly seen in MDS; it indicates that the actors are laid out into an almost linear string.

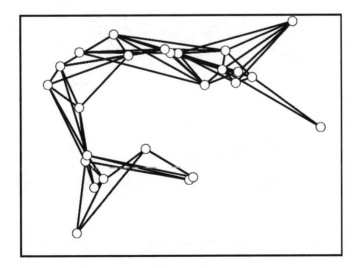

Figure 12.4.9. MDS of department store data showing ties.

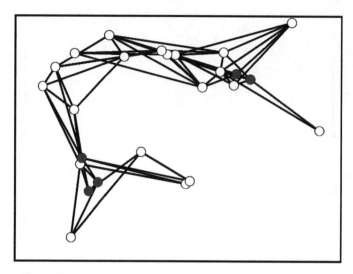

Figure 12.4.10. MDS of department store data showing actors with
Middle-Eastern ethnic backgrounds.

Canales had collected the usual sociological "face sheet" data from her coworkers. She was interested in the degree to which age, gender, ethnicity, and so on might be entailed in the choices of partners for leisure time interaction. To answer these questions, she colored points in the display so she could pinpoint the locations of actors who possessed particular attributes. In Figure 12.4.10, for example, all the actors who had Middle-Eastern ethnic backgrounds were shaded gray. Clearly, the gray points are distributed all over the figure, and partner choices are not based on that ethnic factor.

The same was true for other ethnicities. In Figure 12.4.11, the two employees with Asian backgrounds are shaded gray. They are widely separated. Marital status seems

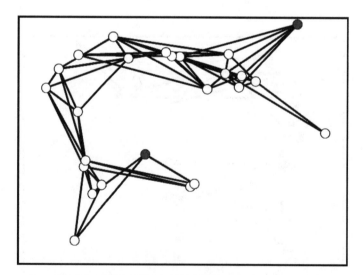

Figure 12.4.11. MDS of department store data showing actors with
Asian backgrounds.

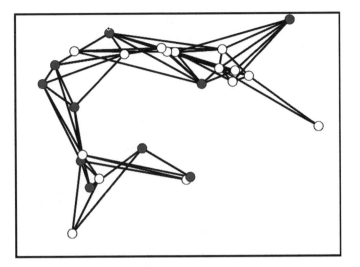

Figure 12.4.12. MDS of department store data showing married
actors.

also to have had very little effect. In Figure 12.4.12, married actors are shaded yellow.
They may be slightly clustered on the left side of the figure, but they are still found all
over the image. Similarly, the single actors cluster slightly on the right, but they too are
found everywhere in the image.

Age, however, turned out to be important. In Figure 12.4.13, those actors who were
age 30 or younger are dark gray, those older than 30 but 40 or less are white, and
those older than 40 are light gray. These three categories are distinctly separated in the
image. Thus, age turns out to be one characteristic that is important to these individuals

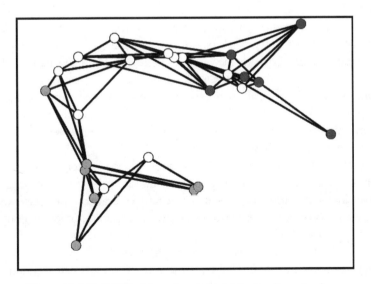

Figure 12.4.13. MDS of department store data showing actors' age
grades.

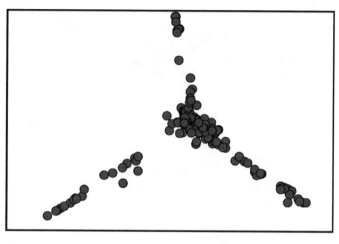

Figure 12.5.14. SVD of athletes.

when it comes to choosing partners for interaction. It was the only face sheet variable to display a systematic patterning. Using strictly visual techniques, then, Canales was able to discover an important correlate of interaction among her coworkers.

12.5   Examining an *a priori* Hunch

Another of my students, Laticia Oseguera, was a collegiate basketball star. She had an intuitive idea that athletes would confide in their teammates more or less according to whether theirs was a team sport like basketball or an individual sport like tennis. Coparticipants in individual sports, she believed, would be more willing to confide in teammates.

Oseguera collected data from 191 athletes in thirteen sports at her university. All members of the men's and women's basketball teams, the men's and women's soccer teams, the men's water polo team, the women's volleyball team, the men's and women's tennis teams, the men's and women's track teams, the men's and women's swimming teams, and the men's golf team were surveyed. Each was asked to name any other athletes with whom he or she had discussed important personal problems. Then the resulting matrix was used as input for the principal components version of SVD. The two-dimensional result is shown in Figure 12.5.14.

Although there is a somewhat globelike clump in the center, the three long arms show a dramatic structural patterning in this data set. Athletes on these arms chose one another along the arm; those near the center were apparently less exclusive. If Oseguera's idea is correct, athletes from all individual sports should fall along the arms and the team sport athletes should cluster near the middle of the image. She explored this notion by coloring individuals in terms of their sport.

In Figure 12.5.15, members of the men's tennis team are white. Tennis is an individual sport and their position at the extreme periphery suggests that Oseguera's

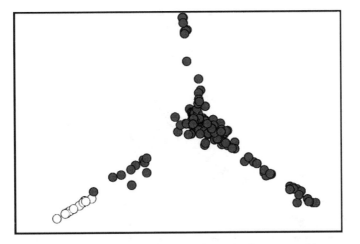

Figure 12.5.15. SVD of athletes; male tennis players are white.

idea was correct for them. Most of their confidants are fellow tennis players, but they are also adjacent to another cluster of athletes with whom they apparently sometimes communicate.

That other collection is shaded light gray in Figure 12.5.16. They turn out to be members of the female tennis team. Like their male counterparts, they are involved in an individual sport and are peripheral. Among the tennis players, the women are not as peripheral as the men, but they are still distinctly separated from the main body of athletes. This provides further support for Oseguera's idea.

However, the really interesting feature here is that the female tennis players are in a position where they bridge between their male tennis counterparts and the rest of the athletes. Certainly their bridging position is consistent with the common observation that women often provide the links between otherwise unconnected social networks.

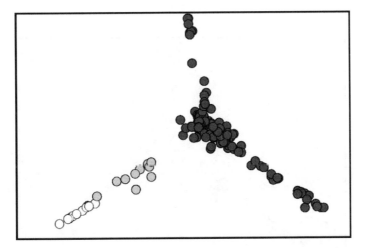

Figure 12.5.16. SVD of athletes; female tennis players are light gray.

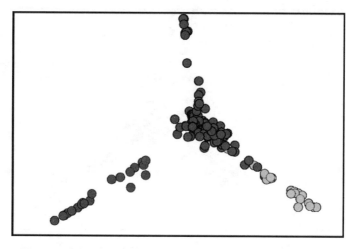

Figure 12.5.17. SVD of athletes; male soccer players are light gray.

In Figure 12.5.17, the light gray points are the male soccer players. They are involved in a team sport and their position, at the end of an arm, contradicts Oseguera's idea. Apparently, they confide in one another.

The white points in Figure 12.5.18 are the members of the women's soccer team. Like the male soccer players, they contradict Oseguera's idea by being both involved in a team sport and confiding in their fellow team members. However, like the female tennis players, they occupy an intermediate position on the same arm as their male counterparts and they are a bridge between the members of the men's soccer team and the center.

The light gray points in Figure 12.5.19 are members of the men's golf team. They are involved in an individual sport and their peripheral position is, again, consistent with Oseguera's original idea.

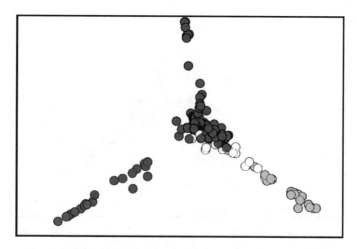

Figure 12.5.18. SVD of athletes; female soccer players are white.

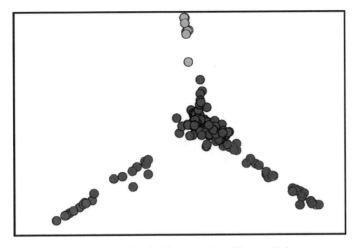

Figure 12.5.19. SVD of athletes; male golfers are light gray.

Finally, the white points in Figure 12.5.20 are members of the men's water polo team. This is another team sport and its position contradicts Oseguera's original idea. Moreover, because there is no female golf team, the bridging position with respect to the golfers is occupied by the water polo players.

The remaining athletes, male and female basketball players, members of the men's and women's swimming team, the male and female track team members, and the women's volleyball team are all clustered closely together in the center. Because some of these athletes are involved in team sports and some in individual sports, and because the athletes found in peripheral positions also represent each category, Oseguera ended up rejecting her intuitive idea.

However, after a look at the data, she was able to come up with a new *post hoc* idea. She was able to demonstrate a tendency for female athletes to bridge between the male

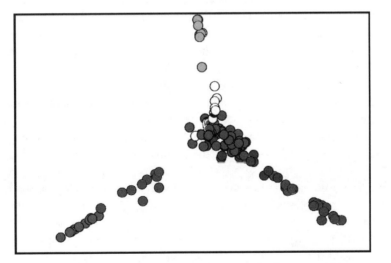

Figure 12.5.20. SVD of athletes; male water polo players are white.

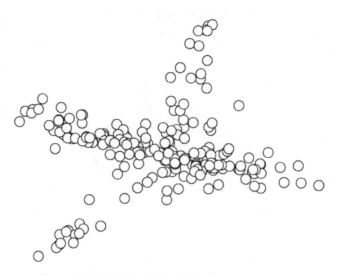

Figure 12.6.21. SVD of friendships in a residence hall.

athletes who were involved in the same sport and the main body of athletes from other sports.

12.6   Validating a Model

Cynthia Webster had been working on the development of a new procedure for uncovering small close-knit cliquelike groups in social network data. She wanted to determine how well it worked when applied to data. She had already collected a large data set on friendship in an Australian residential college. In that study, she had interviewed all 217 residents individually and asked them to name their friends within the college. The residents had also indicated the strength of each friendship tie. In all, five levels of friendship were designated (5 = best friend, 4 = close friend, 3 = friend, 2 = friendly acquaintance, 1 = acquaintance).

Webster symmetrized that original matrix and then applied her new method to uncover all the tightly connected subsets of residents. She assigned each group a name based on her ethnographic experience in the setting.

Webster reasoned that in order to validate her new procedure she had to demonstrate that her groups were tightly knit when the data were analyzed using an independent procedure. She set about, then, to determine the relation between the proximity structure of her data as displayed by SVD and the groups she had uncovered using her new method.

She preprocessed the data to remove the effects of means and variances, and calculated a three-dimensional SVD (Freeman et al. 1998). The first two axes are shown in Figure 12.6.21.

The points in the image are clearly arranged into a four-pronged propeller-like object. Webster reasoned that if her method agreed with the SVD result, each of her groups would be found together in a tight cluster of points in the image. In particular, the four

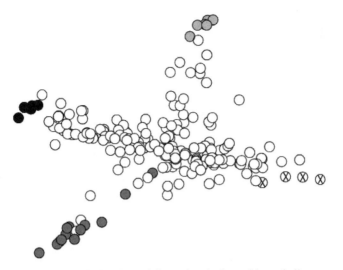

Figure 12.6.22. The outlying points in the residence hall.

outlying clusters in the image would correspond to distinct groups she had uncovered with her new method.

So she marked points according to group memberships and discovered that the outlying clusters were easily identifiable in terms of her groups. In Figure 12.6.22 in light gray at the top are the points included in a group she named "the grunges." They were a collection of rebellious "hippie" students. A group of students who were preoccupied with religion are shaded dark gray at the bottom of the figure. The interesting feature is that they are bipolar to the grunges. This polarity makes a certain amount of sense. A group on the left shaded black identifies a third extreme in the image. Webster called these students "the women." They were the somewhat proper female social leaders in the community. Finally, the fourth extreme in the image is occupied by the students Webster called "math heads." They are marked with an **X**. These were the nonsocial "nerds" in this student residence. Again, it makes sense that these "math heads" would fall at the opposite pole from "the women."

All in all, then, this exercise shows that, at least so far as the extremes are concerned, Webster's grouping method produces groups that are consistent with the spatial patterns displayed by SVD.

12.7 A *Post hoc* Analysis

The final example involves a network study by Freeman and Freeman (1980). In the late 1970s, we examined the impacts of EIES, a computer communication system that worked much as the Internet does today. It facilitated an e-mail-like message transmission and the development of conferences, or discussion groups. Subjects were from the United States and Canada, and all were involved in the study of social networks.

Before the computer hookup was inaugurated, the participants were given a questionnaire in which they identified those others whom they knew about, those they had

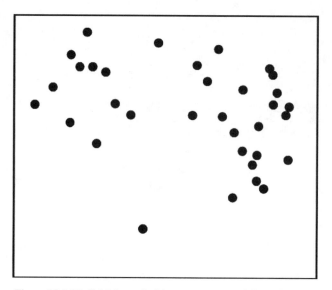

Figure 12.7.23. Initial proximities among network investigators.

met, those who were friends, and those they considered to be close personal friends. Then, after eight months of computer connection, they were queried again.

The fact that we had two waves of data permitted us to study the changes in interpersonal ties during the eight months of computer communication. So we stacked the two matrices – before and after, normalized to remove the effects of differences in row and column totals, and entered the combined data into SVD. The resulting image showed the changes in the proximities between pairs of network analysts that occurred during the eight-month period.

To examine these changes, I used an animation program, MOVIEMOL.[6] The initial proximities are shown in Figure 12.7.23. They are patterned in a way that suggests the presence of two main clusters.

However, in this case, I was primarily concerned with change. So I examined the before–after transition using MOVIEMOL animation. I began to see a pattern; the points could be divided into four distinct categories according to the direction of their movement. Some moved greater distances and some smaller distances, but the directions were patterned. These directions are shown in Figure 12.7.24.

So I shaded those points according to their directions of movement. Those that moved up and to the left were shaded light gray. Those that moved down and to the right were dark gray. Those that dropped toward the lower left were made white. The remaining two points that did not move were made black. You can see their final locations in Figure 12.7.25.

After identifying the points of various colors, it was clear what the various directions of movement implied. The white points were individuals who did not participate and who dropped out of network research during the experimental period. The black pair did not participate in the Internet at all, but they did remain in the network research area. The light gray points represented individuals from several fields who at that time were in the process of organizing an interdisciplinary social networks specialty. And

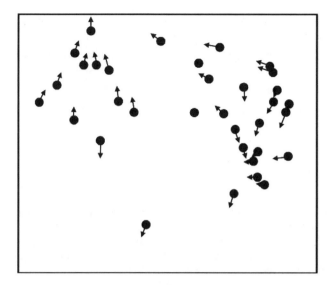

Figure 12.7.24. Directions of movement among network
investigators.

the dark gray points were sociologists who objected to forming a new specialty and who were anxious to define network research simply as a subarea of sociology. In this case, then, watching the animation yielded a new *post* hoc insight that helped to make sense of a data set.

12.8 Conclusion

In this chapter, I demonstrate a simple and straightforward approach to exploratory analysis of social network data. This approach uses a search procedure (MDS) and/or an

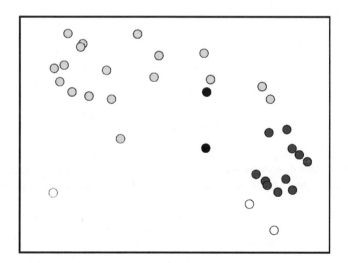

Figure 12.7.25. Movement classes among network investigators.

algebraic data reduction scheme (SVD) along with easily available programs for graphic display (MAGE and MOVIEMOL). With these tools, an investigator can determine whether a given data set contains any interesting structural features. These features are revealed simply by looking at visual images. This approach makes it simple to develop new insights based on characteristics of the data. In addition, it can be used to conduct preliminary tests of *a priori* ideas, to explore the fit of models to data and, using animation, to examine dynamic processes.

Endnotes

1. Similar graphic images were produced earlier by investigators working on problems of genealogy. However, these early images were oriented from top to bottom to represent descent, so they were not the nonoriented images used by contemporary social network analysts.
2. In this chapter, I used the procedures built in to the MDS program that is part of the UCINET 5 package (Borgatti, Everett, and Freeman 1999). Similar MDS programs are included in many standard statistical packages.
3. I have used the SVD program in UCINET 5 (Borgatti et al. 1999). However, any other standard statistical package might just as well have been used.
4. This program can be downloaded at no cost from: ftp://kinemage.biochem.duke.edu/.
5. MAGE is designed to make it easy to construct and manipulate network images on a computer screen, but it is limited in its ability to produce images for the printed page. Therefore, although the work described here was done using MAGE, it is presented here using bitmap images produced another program that generates XML.
6. MOVIEMOL can be downloaded at no cost from: http://www.fos.su.se/moviemol.html.

References

Bock, R. D., and S. Z. Husain. 1952. Factors of the tele: a preliminary report. *Sociometry*, 15:206–219.

Borgatti, S. P., M. G. Everett, and L. C. Freeman, 1999. *Ucinet 5 for Windows: Software for Social Network Analysis*. Natick, MA: Analytic Technologies.

Freeman, L. C. 2000. Visualizing social networks. *Journal of Social Structure*, 1.

Freeman, L. C., and S. C. Freeman. 1980. A semi-visible college: structural effects on a social networks group. *Electronic Communication: Technology and Impacts*. In M. M. Henderson and M. J. MacNaughton, eds. (pp. 77–85). Boulder, CO: Westview Press.

Freeman, L. C., S. C. Freeman, and A. G. Michaelson. 1988. On human social intelligence. *Journal of Social and Biological Structures*, 11:415–425.

Freeman, L. C., C. M. Webster, and D. M. Kirke. 1998. Exploring social structure using dynamic three-dimensional color images. *Social Networks*, 20:109–118.

Holland, P. W., and S. Leinhardt. 1981. An exponential family of probability distributions for directed graphs. *Journal of the American Statistical Association*, 76:33–50.

Krempel, L. 1999. Visualizing networks with spring embedders: two-mode and valued data. In *Proceedings of the Section on Statistical Graphics* (pp. 36–45). Alexandria, VA: American Statistical Association.

Kruskal, J. B., and M. Wish. 1978. *Multidimensional Scaling*. Beverly Hills, CA: Sage.

Moreno, J. L. 1932. *Application of the Group Method to Classification*. New York: National Committee on Prisons and Prison Labor.

Moreno, J. L. 1934. *Who Shall Survive?* Washington, DC: Nervous and Mental Disease Publishing Company.

Richardson, D. C., and J. S. Richardson. 1992. The kinmage – a tool for scientific communication. *Protein Science* 1:3–9.

Wasserman, S., and P. Pattison. 1996. Logit models and logistic regressions for social networks I. An introduction to Markov random graphs and p^*. *Psychometrika*, 60:401–426.

Weller, S. C., and A. K. Romney. 1990. *Metric Scaling: Correspondence Analysis*. Beverly Hills, CA: Sage.

13

Software for Social Network Analysis

Mark Huisman

Heymans Institute/DPMG
University of Groningen

Marijtje A. J. van Duijn

ICS/Statistics & Measurement Theory
University of Groningen

13.1 Introduction

This chapter reviews software for the analysis of social networks. Both commercial and freely available packages are considered. Based on the software page on the INSNA website (http:// www. insna.org/INSNA/soft_inf.html), and using the main topics in the book on network analysis by Wasserman and Faust (1994), which we regard as the standard text, we selected twenty-seven software packages: twenty-three stand-alone programs, listed in Table 13.1.1, and five utility toolkits given in Table 13.1.2.

Software merely aimed at visualization of networks was not admitted to the list because this is the topic of Chapter 12 of this book (Freeman 2004). We do review a few programs with strong visualization properties. Some were originally developed for network visualization, and now contain analysis procedures (e.g., NetDraw; Borgatti 2002). Other programs were specifically developed to integrate network analysis and visualization (e.g., NetMiner, Cyram 2004, and visone; Brandes and Wagner 2003). Two other programs for network visualization are worth mentioning here because some of the reviewed software packages have export functions to these graph drawing programs, or they are freely distributed together with the social analysis software: KrackPlot (Krackhardt, Blythe, and McGrath 1994) and Mage (Richardson 2001).

The age of the software was not a criterion for selection, although the release dates of the last versions of the majority of the reviewed software were within the last one or two years.

Tables 13.1.1 and 13.1.2 describe the main objective or characteristic of each program. The data format distinguishes three aspects: (1) type of data the program can handle, (2) input format, and (3) whether there is an option to indicate missing value codes for network relations. Next, the functionality is described. For each program, we indicate whether the software contains (network) visualization options; for a toolkit, its environment (software package or operating system other than Windows); and for both groups of software, the kind of analyses it can perform. We use the network terminology and categorization of Wasserman and Faust (1994) for the different types of analysis: structural and locational properties, roles and positions, dyadic and triadic

Table 13.1.1. *Overview of Selected Programs for Social Network Analysis, with the Number of the Version That Was Reviewed, Their Objectives, Data Format (Type, Input Format, Missing Values), Functionality (Visualization Techniques, Analysis Methods), and Support (Availability of the Program, Manual, and Online Help)*

	Program	Version	Objective	Data Type[a]	Data Input[b]	Data Miss.	Funct. Visual.	Funct. Analyses[c]	Funct. Avail.[d]	Support Manual	Support Help
	Agna	2.1.1	General	c	m	No	Yes	d, sl, Sequential	Free	Yes	Yes
	Blanche	4.6.5	Network dynamics	c	m	No	Yes	Simulation	Free	Yes	Yes
	FATCAT	4.2[e]	Contextual analysis	c	ln	Yes	Yes	d, s	Free[e]	No	Yes
	GRADAP	2.0[e]	Graph analysis	c	ln	Yes	No	d, sl, dt	Com[e]	Yes	No
	Iknow	—	Knowledge networks	e	n	—	Yes	d, sl	Free	Yes	Yes
	InFlow	3.0	Network mapping	c, e	ln	No	Yes	d, sl, rp	Com	Yes	Yes
	KliqFinder	0.05	Cohesive subgroups	c	m, ln	No	No	sl, s	—	Yes	No
*	MultiNet	4.38	Contextual analysis	c, l	ln	Yes	Yes	d, rp, s	Free	No[k]	Yes
	NEGOPY	4.30[e]	Cohesive subgroups	c	ln	Yes	Yes	d, sl, rp	Com[e]	Yes	Yes
	NetDraw	1.0	Visualization	c, e, a	m, ln	Yes	Yes	d, sl	Free	Yes	No
*	NetMiner II	2.4.0	Visual analysis	c, e, a	m, ln	No	Yes	d, sl, rp, dt, s	Com[i, j]	Yes	Yes
	NetVis	2.0	Visual exploration[f]	c, e, a	m, ln	No	Yes	d, sl	Free[f, i]	No	Yes
*	Pajek	1.00	Large data visualization	c, a, l	m, ln	Yes[g]	Yes	d, sl, rp, dt	Free	No	No
	PermNet	0.94	Permutation tests	c	m	Yes	No	dt, s	Free	No	Yes
	PGRAPH	2.7	Kinship networks	c	ln	—	No	d, rp	Free	No[l]	Yes

(continued)

271

Table 13.1.1 (continued)

	Program	Version	Data			Functionality			Support	
			Type[a]	Input[b]	Miss.	Visual.	Analyses[c]	Avail.[d]	Manual	Help
	ReferralWeb	2.0	e	ln	—	Yes	d	—[i]	Yes	Yes
	SM LinkAlyzer	2.1	e	ln	—	Yes	d	Com[j]	Yes	Yes
	SNAFU	2.0	c	m, ln	No	Yes	d, sl	Free[f]	No	No
	Snowball	—[e]	e	ln	—	No	s	Free[e]	Yes	No
*	StOCNET	1.5	c	m	Yes	No	d, dt, s	Free	Yes	Yes
*	STRUCTURE	4.2[e]	c, a	m	Yes[g]	No	sl, rp	Free[e]	Yes	No
*	UCINET	6.55	c, e, a	m, ln	Yes	Yes[h]	d, sl, rp, dt, s	Com[j]	Yes	Yes
*	visone	1.1	c, e	m, ln	No	Yes	d, sl	Free	No	No

[a] c=complete, e=ego centered, a=affiliation, l=large networks.

[b] m=matrix, ln=link/node, n=node.

[c] d=descriptive, sl=structure and location, rp=roles and positions, dt=dyadic and triadic methods, s=statistical.

[d] com=commercial product, free=freeware/shareware.

[e] DOS program which is no longer updated.

[f] Open source software.

[g] Only missing value codes for attributes.

[h] No graph drawing routines.

[i] Freely accessible on the Internet (some with reduced functionality).

[j] An evaluation/demonstration version is available.

[k] The manual of some modules is available.

[l] The manual is available after registration.

Table 13.1.2. *Overview Of Selected Software Toolkits For Social Network Analysis, The Number Of The Version That Was Reviewed, Their Objectives, Data Format (Type, Input Format, Missing Values), Functionality (Hardware/Software Environment, Analysis Methods), And Support (Availability Of The Program, Manual, And Online Help)*

Program	Version	Objective	Data			Functionality		Support		
			Type[a]	Input[b]	Miss.	Envir.	Analyses[c]	Avail.[d]	Manual	Help
JUNG	1.4.3	Modeling graphs	c	ln	—	Java	d, sl, vis	Free	Yes	—
MatMan	1.1	Structural analysis	c, a	m	No	Excel	d, sl, Ethological	Com	Yes	Yes
SNA	0.44	General	c	m	No	R/S	d, sl, rp, dt, s, vis	Free	Yes	—
SNAP	2.5	General	c	m	No	Gauss	d, sl, rp, dt, s	Com	Yes	—
yFiles	2.2.1	Visual exploration	c	ln	—	Java	d, sl, vis	Com	Yes	—

[a] c=complete, e=ego centered, a=affiliation, l=large networks.

[b] m=matrix, ln=link/node, n=node.

[c] d=descriptive, sl=structure and location, rp=roles and positions, dt=dyadic and triadic methods, s=statistical, vis=visualization.

[d] com=commercial product, free=freeware/shareware.

methods, and statistical dyadic interaction models. The theoretical background of almost all the obtainable output can also be found there. Where necessary, additional references are given. The amount of support is the final characteristic mentioned in the table, distinguishing availability of the program (free or commercial, not listing prices), presence and availability of a manual, and presence of online help during execution of the program.

Section 13.2 provides an extensive review of six programs (indicated by an asterisk in Table 13.1.1). These programs are either regarded as general and well-known (UCINET, Pajek, NetMiner) or as having specific features worth mentioning and illustrating (MultiNet, STRUCTURE, StOCNET). We examine the properties of these packages with respect to data entry and manipulation, visualization, and social network analysis. The software is illustrated by applying a selection of routines to an example data set. A complete reference to a program is given only once, either at the start of the section in which it is reviewed or, for nonreviewed software, at the first mention.

We consider the remaining software to be more specialized and discuss their objectives and properties to a limited extent in Section 13.3.[1] In this section, we also review some routines that were developed to perform social network analysis in general software or on operating systems other than Windows.

The chapter concludes with a section comparing the routines and support offered by the various programs discussed in Section 13.2, and some general recommendations. This section is by no means final because by definition a chapter like this becomes outdated with publication.

13.2   Social Network Software – A Closer Look

In this section, the programs UCINET, Pajek, NetMiner II, STRUCTURE, MultiNet, and StOCNET are investigated in more detail with the help of an example data set. The order in which the packages are presented is based on age, as well as on generality. We start with three general packages, covering a wide range of analysis methods. They are presented according to age: UCINET, Pajek, and NetMiner II. Next, the program STRUCTURE is presented. We consider STRUCTURE as a general program featuring a limited number of methods. Although it has become somewhat outdated, STRUCTURE has some unique features worth presenting. Finally, two more specialized packages are presented: MultiNet and StOCNET.

In the presentation, we focus on five groups of procedures the software does or does not possess:

1. Data entry and data manipulation
2. Visualization techniques
3. Social network analysis routines, divided into three types of methods:
    (a) Descriptive methods to calculate (simple) network statistics (e.g., centrality or transitivity)
    (b) Procedure-based analysis based on more complex (iterative) algorithms (e.g., cluster analysis or eigendecompositions)

(c) Statistical modeling based on probability distributions (e.g., exponential random graph models or Quadratic Assignment Procedure (QAP) correlation)

The choice of social network analysis routines that were inspected is based on the categorization of methods given by Wasserman and Faust (1994) explained in the introduction, and on the analysis methods presented in earlier chapters in this book.

- Structure and location: centrality (Everett and Borgatti 2004) and cohesive subgroups (cliques)
- Roles and positions: structural equivalence, blockmodeling (Doreian, Batagelj, and Ferligoj 2004), eigendecompositions
- Dyadic and triadic methods
- Statistical methods: exponential random graph models (Wasserman and Robins 2004), QAP correlation, statistical analysis of network evolution (Snijders 2004)

(A) *Example Data*

The example data used are Freeman's Electronic Information Exchange System (EIES) network (Freeman and Freeman 1979), three one-mode networks with two relations on a set of actors ($n = 32$) that is frequently used by social network researchers. The data come from a computer conference among social network researchers and were collected as part of a study of the impact of the EIES. Two relations were recorded: the number of messages sent and acquaintanceship. The acquaintanceship relation is longitudinal, measured at two time points, ranging from 0 (did not know the other) to 4 (close personal friend). For some analysis procedures, the data need to be binary (relation absent or present). The following dichotomization is used for the acquaintanceship networks: 1 for values larger than 2 (friend, close friend), 0 for other values (not knowing, not having met, having met). The data set contains two actor attribute variables: primary disciplinary affiliation (sociology, anthropology, statistics and mathematics, psychology), and the number of citations (social science citation index). The complete data set can be found in Wasserman and Faust (1994) and is one of the standard data sets distributed with UCINET.

(B) *UCINET*

UCINET 6 (Version 6.55; Borgatti, Everett, and Freeman 2004) is a comprehensive program for the analysis of social networks and other proximity data. It is probably the best-known and most frequently used software package for the analysis of social network data and contains a large number of network analytic routines. The program is a commercial product, but a free evaluation version is available, which can be run for 30 days without registering. The manual consists of two parts: a user's guide (data management and manipulation) and a reference guide (network analysis). It also available online through the help function.

UCINET is a menu-driven Windows program, and, as the developers say themselves, "is built for speed, not for comfort" (Borgatti et al. 1999). Choosing procedures from the

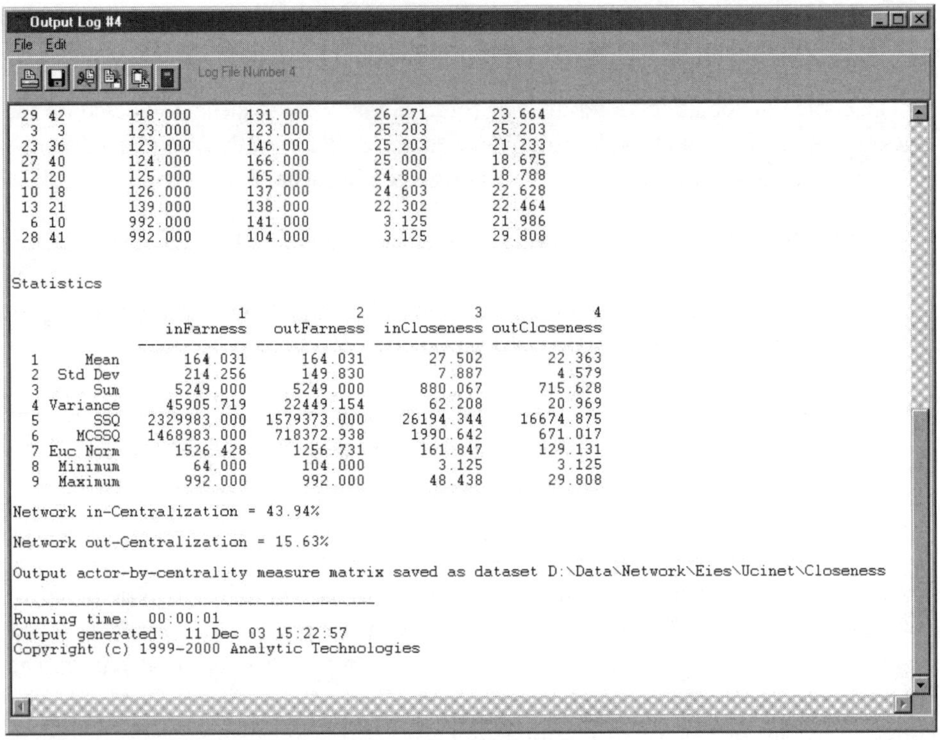

Figure 13.2.1. **UCINET** log file presenting the results of centrality analysis of the EIES acquaintanceship data (first observation).

menus usually results in opening a parameter form where the input for the algorithms is specified. Speedbuttons are available for data management, export to **Pajek** and **Mage**, and launching **NetDraw**; these three programs are distributed with **UCINET**. Two kinds of output are generated: textual output, saved in log files and displayed on the screen (see Figure 13.2.1 for an example), and data sets that can be used as input for other procedures.

Data Entry and Manipulation

UCINET is matrix oriented, that is, data sets are collections of one or more matrices. A single **UCINET** data set consists of two files: one containing the actual data (extension ##D) and one containing information about the data (##H). **UCINET** data sets can be created by importing data or by entering data directly via the built-in spreadsheet. The spreadsheet editor, containing the EIES data, is shown in Figure 13.2.2. The import function can process several types of network data: raw ASCII data, ASCII data saved in DL format, Excel data sets, and data formats from the programs **KrackPlot**, **NEGOPY**, and **Pajek**.

UCINET provides a large number of data management and transformation tools like selecting subsets, merging data sets, permuting, transposing, or recoding data. It has a full-featured matrix algebra language; it can handle two-mode (affiliation) data as well as derive one-mode data sets from two-mode data. There is an option to enter

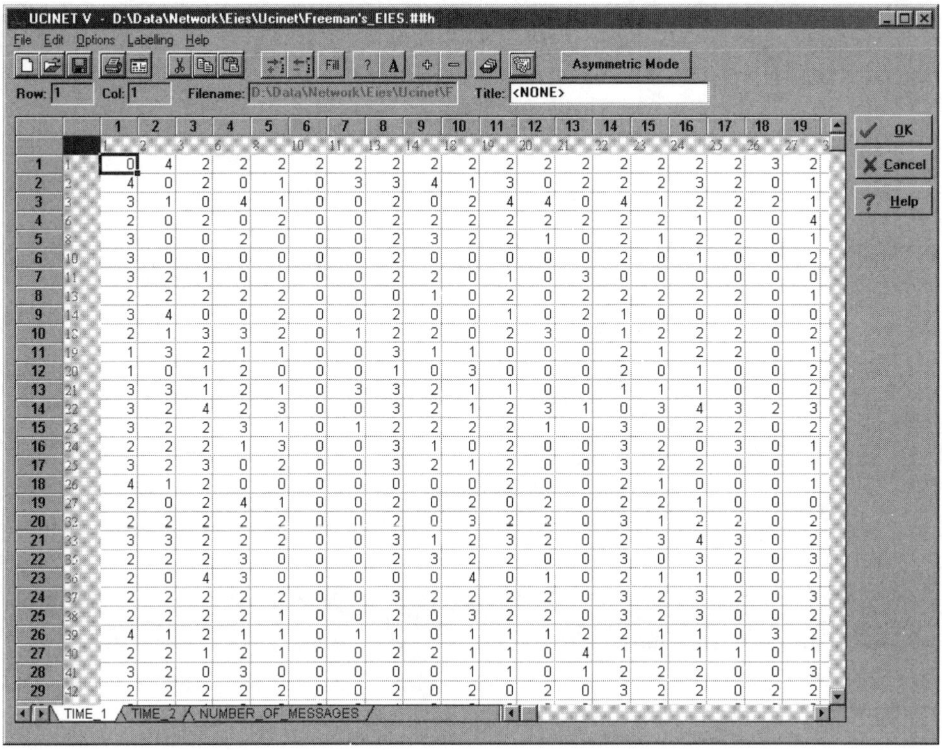

Figure 13.2.2. **UCINET** spreadsheet editor containing the EIES data.

attribute data and to specify missing values. It should be noted, however, that only a few procedures can handle missing values properly. **UCINET** is distributed with a large number of example data sets, including Freeman's EIES data.

Visualization Techniques

UCINET contains graphic tools to draw scatterplots, dendrograms, and tree diagrams (Figure 13.2.3), which can be saved as bitmap files (**BMP**). The program itself does not contain graphic procedures to visualize networks, but it has a speedbutton to execute the program **NetDraw** (Borgatti 2002), which reads **UCINET** files natively. **NetDraw**, developed for network visualization, has advanced graphic properties and is further discussed later in this chapter. In addition to export functions to **Pajek** and **Mage**, data can be exported for visualization in **KrackPlot**.

Descriptive Methods

The program contains a large number of network analytic routines for the detection of cohesive subgroups (cliques, clans, plexes) and regions (components, cores), for centrality analysis, for ego network analysis, and for structural holes analysis. As an example, the output of a centrality analysis is presented in Figure 13.2.1. For each node, it contains the in- and out-farness (the sum of the lengths of the geodesics to and from every other node), and the in- and out-closeness centrality (the reciprocal of farness times $g - 1$, with g the number of actors), some descriptive statistics, as well as Freeman's group

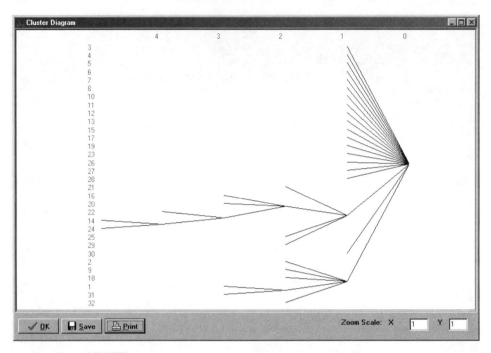

Figure 13.2.3. UCINET tree diagram for the single link hierarchical clustering of the clique overlap matrix (first observation of the EIES acquaintanceship data).

closeness index (Freeman 1979). The in-closeness for the EIES acquaintanceship data is 43.9% and 68.6%, and the out-closeness is 15.6% and 53.7% for time points 1 and 2, respectively. The data were dichotomized (see Section 13.2(A)) before the analysis. If the user does not dichotomize and symmetrize the network, default options are used (all entries larger than 0 are given value 1, and the data are symmetrized by using the maximum value in a dyad). The default symmetrization was used here.

Group centrality options have been added more recently (Everett and Borgatti 2004). The program finds the most central subgroup of fixed size or tests the (degree) centrality of a specified group. For the dichotomized and symmetrized EIES data (first observation), the most central subgroup of six actors consists of sociologists and anthropologists (centrality 87.5%). The degree centrality of the group of sociologists is twenty-four. These results differ from the results of Everett and Borgatti (2004), due to the different transformations applied. The mean, standard deviation, and p-values based on permutation tests are given: 27.6, 1.54, and 0.97, respectively.

Analyzing the dichotomized and symmetrized (reciprocal relations) EIES data to detect cohesive subgroups based on complete mutuality (i.e., cliques) results in finding eight and fifteen cliques in the EIES data at the first and second time point, respectively. The cliques are presented in Table 13.2.3 (the cohesion index is provided by NetMiner, see Section 13.2(D)). UCINET provides the opportunity to further inspect the cliques by calculating the clique overlap with a single link hierarchical cluster procedure (which is presented in the next paragraph as an example of a procedure-based technique). The cliques found at the second observation are the same or combinations of those found at the first observation.

Table 13.2.3. *Cliques in the EIES Acquaintanceship Data Obtained with* **UCINET**

First Observation			Second Observation		
Cline	Actors	Cohesion[a]	Clique	Actors	Cohesion[a]
1	14,20,22,24	7.000	1	1,2,31,32	6.222
2	14,16,22,24	7.467	2	1,11,31,32	6.588
3	14,22,24,29	8.000	3	1,13,31	5.118
4	14,20,24,25	9.333	4	1,18,31	5.800
5	2,9,32	14.500	5	1,29,31	4.143
6	1,2,31	10.875	6	1,8,11,32	10.182
7	1,18,31	29.000	7	1,2,9,32	8.615
8	16,21,22	7.909	8	3,14,23	9.667
			9	10,20,29	6.692
			10	14,20,22,24,29	8.438
			11	14,20,24,25	8.615
			12	14,16,22	6.214
			13	14,15,29	5.800
			14	15,29,31	6.214
			15	16,21,22	10.875

[a] Cohesion index of Bock and Husain (1950), provided by NetMiner.

Procedure-Based Analysis

UCINET contains a number of routines for procedure-based analysis. One procedure, cluster analysis, was already mentioned. Other procedures are multidimensional scaling (metric or nonmetric), two-mode scaling (singular value decompositions, factor analysis, and correspondence analysis), analysis of roles and positions (structural, role, and regular equivalence) and fitting core-periphery models.

There are hierarchical and nonhierarchical procedures to perform a cluster analysis of the relational data. Using the adjacency matrix as input, the actors are clustered on the basis of their relations. In the analysis of clique overlap mentioned previously, the so-called clique overlap matrix is used as input. This matrix indicates for each pair of actors the number of times they occur in the same clique. The result for the first observation of the EIES data – that is, a tree diagram showing the progress of the cluster analysis – is presented in Figure 13.2.3 (single link procedure; average and complete link are also available). It shows the level of overlap between the cliques (e.g., actors 14 and 24 are most often together in one clique, followed by the combination of actors 14, 22, and 24).

Several types of structural equivalence procedures can be performed based on the measurement of equivalence (Euclidean distances, correlations, cost functions). The equivalence of the actors is given in a so-called equivalence matrix, which is the input of a hierarchical cluster procedure to find clusters of actors. For example, using the procedure based on comparisons of actor profiles (rows or columns in the adjacency matrix) measured by Euclidean distances (Burt 1976), actors 12 and 23 are most equivalent, with the minimum distance of 5.8 between them (first observation of the acquaintanceship data). These actors are the first ones to be joined in one cluster. Actor

Table 13.2.4. *QAP Correlations Obtained with* **UCINET** *in the EIES Data*
(p-Values in Parentheses; 2,500 Permutations)

	Acquaintanceship			
	Time 1		Time 2	
Acquaintanceship time 2	0.809	(0.00)	—	—
Messages sent	0.240	(0.00)	0.347	(0.00)

1 joins this cluster at one of the last stages of the process, having an equivalence value of 16.3 and 15.9 with actors 12 and 23, respectively.

Statistical Modeling

Various statistical routines are available in **UCINET**, ranging from simple statistics to fitting the p_1 model (Holland and Leinhardt 1981). There are autocorrelation methods, QAP correlation and regression procedures, and univariate vector methods combined with permutation tests. An example of the latter group of methods is analysis of variance (ANOVA) with attribute vectors and/or rows or columns of the adjacency matrix, representing a sending or receiving actor, as variables. This is different from procedures where all incoming and outgoing links in an adjacency matrix are used as input for an ANOVA (e.g., **MultiNet**).

Fitting the p_1 model to the first observation of the dichotomized EIES acquaintanceship data gives estimates of the "density" and "reciprocity" parameters (-3.45 and 4.39), and for each actor the expansiveness and popularity parameters (not presented). Expected values and residuals to inspect the fit of the model are also given. Computation of QAP correlations between the three EIES matrices gives the correlations as presented in Table 13.2.4, with *p*-values indicating the percentage of random correlations that are as large as the observed correlation in 2,500 permutations (see Krackhardt 1987). Besides Spearman correlations, the simple matching coefficient, the Jaccard coefficient, and Goodman-Kruskal's gamma are calculated.

(C) *Pajek*

Pajek (Version 1.00; Batagelj and Mrvar 2004) is a network analysis and visualization program, specifically designed to handle large data sets. The main goals in the design of **Pajek** are (1) to facilitate the reduction of a large network into several smaller networks that can be treated further using more sophisticated methods, (2) to provide the user with powerful visualization tools, and (3) to implement a selection of efficient network algorithms (Batagelj and Mrvar 1998). The program can be downloaded free of charge, and its developers are continually updating it. There is no online help, however, and the available documentation is not sufficiently detailed for users who are not experts in network analysis.[2]

Pajek can handle multiple networks simultaneously, as well as two-mode networks and time event networks. Time event networks summarize the development or evolution of networks over time in a single network (using time indicators). In Pajek, very large networks can be analyzed, with more than 1 million nodes. (The available memory on the computer sets the actual limit. To save memory, names and labels of nodes are not kept for extremely large networks, but these can be attached later to smaller subnetworks.)

Large networks are hard to visualize in a single view. Therefore, meaningful substructures have to be identified, which can be visualized separately. The algorithms implemented in Pajek are especially designed for this purpose (see Batagelj and Mrvar 2003). Pajek uses six different data structures: (1) networks (nodes and arcs/edges), (2) partitions (classifications of nodes, where each node is assigned exclusively to one class), (3) permutations (reordering of nodes), (4) clusters (subsets of nodes), (5) hierarchies (hierarchically ordered clusters and nodes), and (6) vectors (properties of nodes). Partitions contain discrete attributes of nodes, whereas vectors contain continuous attributes.

The structure of the program is entirely based on these six data structures and on transitions among these structures. The main window presents six drop lists – one for each data object – as well as buttons to open, save, and edit the data objects in these lists. The program is menu driven, where the menu items are ordered according to the data objects to which they apply. The results generated by the procedures are usually presented using the data structures (instead of graphic or tabular output), and can be used as input in other procedures such as visualization methods.

Data Entry and Manipulation

Network data can be entered in four ways: (1) by defining a (small) network inside the program, (2) by importing ASCII network data from network files (extension NET), (3) by importing data from software packages with other formats (e.g., UCINET DL files and formats of some visualization programs), and (4) by opening a Pajek project file (PAJ), which combines all different data structures into a single file. The NET files consist of a node list and arcs/edges list, aimed at entering large networks more efficiently, specifying only the existing ties. For small networks, the link list can be replaced by an adjacency matrix. Other data objects can be imported from ASCII data files or generated inside the program. For example, attribute data have to be entered as partitions in ASCII data files (CLU) or as vectors in ASCII data files (VEC). All data objects together can be saved in a PAJ file.

Pajek contains manipulation options for all its data structures. For example, networks can be transposed, directed graphs changed into undirected graphs and vice versa, lines can be added or removed, or the network can be reduced by shrinking classes or extracting parts. The program also contains basic network operations such as recoding or dichotomization. There is no option to specify missing relations, whereas it is possible to specify missing values for attributes (partitions and vectors). Also, there are ample transformations for attributes and options to create other data objects on the basis of the attributes (hierarchies, clusters).

Pajek offers facilities for longitudinal network analysis. Time indicators for the actors' presence in the network at certain observations can be included in the data files, and the user can generate a series of cross-sectional networks. Analyses can be performed on these networks, and the evolution of the network can be examined (e.g., the evolution of balance in a network). These analyses are nonstatistical; for statistical analysis of network evolution, the module SIENA of the StOCNET package can be used (Section 13.2(G); see also Snijders 2004).

Visualization Techniques

The graphic properties of Pajek are advanced. The *Draw* window gives the user many options to manipulate the graphs (layout, size, color, spin, etc.). Moreover, graphic representations of partitions, vectors, and combinations of partitions and vectors can be obtained. The network drawing is based on the principle that distances between nodes should reveal the structural patterning of the network (see also Freeman 2004). Besides simple layouts (circle, random), Pajek has several automatic procedures to find optimal layouts: procedures using eigenvectors, special procedures for layer drawing of acyclical networks, and spring embedders. The latter procedures are so named because in those algorithms it is assumed that the nodes are connected by springs, whose stress is to be minimized.

Pajek uses two spring-embedding algorithms to visualize network data: the Kamada-Kawai and the Fruchterman-Reingold algorithms. The former one produces more stable results, but is slower and less suited for large networks. The latter algorithm is faster and can handle large networks. Both are optimization procedures that do not yield the same mapping each time they are run. The graphs, however, should resemble each other largely.

The Kamada-Kawai algorithm is used to draw a graph of the EIES acquaintanceship data at the first observation point, which is presented in Figure 13.2.4. In the network drawing, partitions (here actor's discipline) are depicted by colors and shapes: a blue diamond is sociology, a red circle is anthropology, a magenta circle is statistics, and a green box is psychology. Vector values (here number of citations) are represented by the size of the nodes, where larger nodes indicate higher citation rates. The nodes can be dragged and dropped to improve the graph, and right-clicking a node shows (textually) to which other nodes it is tied. The programs NetDraw, distributed with UCINET, and NetMiner have the same functionalities.

By creating a super matrix that combines the two acquaintanceship matrices (at the two time points), a visualization of the (dichotomized) EIES data over time can be created (see Everton 2002). Such a super matrix can be created in, for instance, UCINET, and can be exported to Pajek or opened in NetDraw. Using the Fruchterman-Reingold algorithm to draw the network results in a visualization of the evolution of the network, presented in Figure 13.2.5. Networks can also be drawn manually by dragging and dropping nodes with the mouse, as was done to improve the graph in Figure 13.2.5. Pajek also supports three-dimensional (3D) visualization. The visualizations can be saved using several formats, among others (encapsulated) postscript file (EPS), scalable vector graphics file (SVG), kinemages file (KIN), bitmap file (BMP), and virtual reality file (VRML).

Descriptive Methods

Each data object in Pajek has its own descriptive methods. The largest number of methods is available for networks, for instance, computation of degrees, depths, cores,

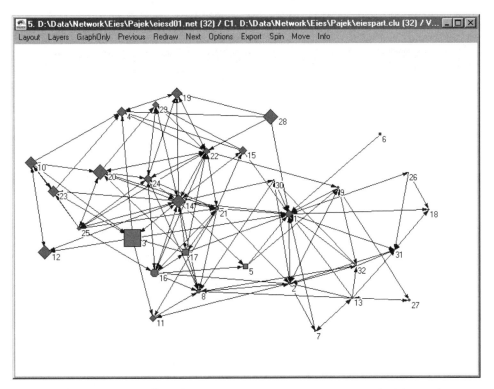

Figure 13.2.4. **Pajek** Draw window presenting the graph of the dichotomized EIES acquaintance-ship network (first observation) using the Kamada-Kawai spring embedder.

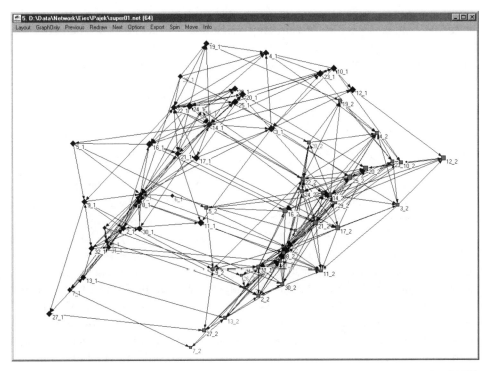

Figure 13.2.5. **Pajek** Draw window presenting the simultaneous drawing of the dichotomized EIES acquaintanceship networks (both observations) using the Fruchterman-Reingold spring embedder.

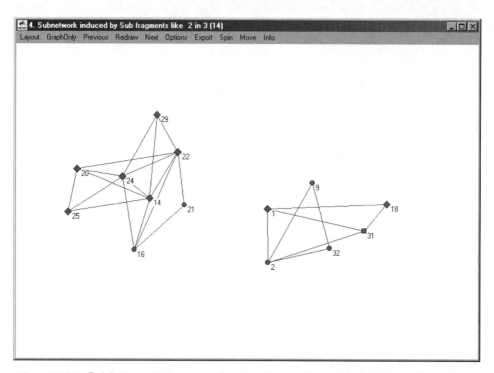

Figure 13.2.6. **Pajek** Draw window presenting the subnetwork consisting of triads (cliques) in the first observation of EIES acquaintanceship network.

or cliques (output is a partition), centrality (closeness, betweenness), detection of components (weak, strong, biconnected, symmetric), paths (or flows), structural holes, and some binary operations on two networks. The menu *Info* gives general characteristics of each data structure.

Computing closeness centrality with **Pajek** is straightforward. The network has to be dichotomized before calculating the closeness. For directed graphs, the in- or out-closeness can be calculated, as well as the closeness for the symmetrized network (default using the maximum of the two links), by choosing the command *All*. This latter option gives 0.390 and 0.515 for closeness for time points 1 and 2, respectively.

Identifying cliques in large networks is difficult because of the large number of cliques. Therefore, unlike **UCINET**, Pajek has no direct procedures for detecting cliques. There is, however, an indirect way of finding cliques by looking for complete triads (cliques of size 3) in a network (De Nooy, Mrvar, and Batagelj 2004). Using the option to search for particular fragments (in this case triads) in the first observation of the dichotomized and symmetrized (based on reciprocated relations) acquaintanceship network, cliques of size 3 are found. The output, presented in Figure 13.2.6, consists of several data objects, one of them being a subnetwork made of the desired cliques. Figure 13.2.6 shows the triads (cliques of size 3), as well as the cliques of size 4, which were also found with **UCINET** (see Table 13.2.3). In addition, a hierarchy is generated to inspect the overlap of triads, as well as a partition to identify the number of triads to which a node belongs (not shown here).

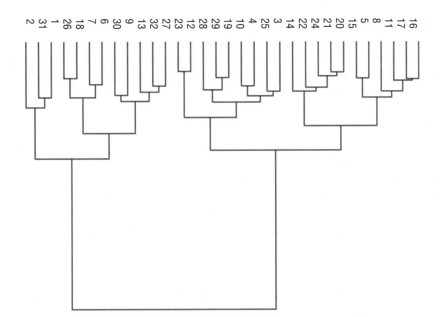

Figure 13.2.7. Dendrogram of the hierarchical cluster analysis (Ward linkage) of the EIES acquaintanceship data (first observation) obtained with **Pajek**.

Instead of a clique procedure, **Pajek** contains the procedure *p-cliques*. This procedure results in a partition of the network nodes into clusters such that the nodes within one cluster have at least a proportion of *p* neighbors inside the cluster (cf. **NEGOPY**). For large networks, it is preferable to use *k*-cores instead of cliques, because of the computing time. Dense parts of large networks can be found using *k*-cores.

Procedure-Based Analysis

Pajek contains several procedure-based methods, for instance, for detecting structural balance and clusterability, hierarchical decomposition, and blockmodeling (structural, regular equivalence). For the analysis of structural equivalent actors, dissimilarities between nodes can be computed in several ways. In its pull-down menu, **Pajek** indicates if the network is too large for calculating dissimilarities, in view of the computational complexity and the amount of time involved. For the first observation of the acquaintanceship data, dissimilarities between actors are calculated using Euclidean distances, and the resulting matrix is used in a hierarchical cluster analysis, using Ward's linking method to combine clusters (the default option out of six). The resulting clusters are presented as a hierarchy and the corresponding dendrogram is saved in an **EPS** file. The dendrogram, presented in Figure 13.2.7, shows two very dissimilar clusters: one containing the actors 1, 2, 6, 7, 9, 13, 18, 26, 27, 30, 31, and 32, that is, few sociologists, and actors with low citation rates, who were all positioned on the right side of the graph in Figure 13.2.4, the other containing the remaining actors. An almost identical solution was found with **UCINET** that employs the single linkage method.

Blockmodeling the dichotomized acquaintanceship data in which the block types are defined using structural equivalence does not yield statisfactory results. Starting from random partitions, the final, best-fitting partitions (in two, three, or four blocks) still had large associated error scores (125, 115, and 111, respectively). Besides blockmodeling based on structural and regular equivalence, Pajek can be used for generalized blockmodeling, where combinations of permitted block types can be defined by the user (see Doreian, Batagelj, and Ferligoj 2004).

Statistical Modeling

The program contains only a few basic statistical procedures. Attributes of nodes (including structural properties that can be expressed as attributes), which are available as partitions and vectors, can be included in statistical analyses: computation of correlations, linear regression, and cross-tabulation (including some measures of association). However, the statistical packages R and SPSS can be called with Pajek data structures (networks and vectors) and the statistical procedures available in these packages can be used (see Section 13.3(C)).

(D) *NetMiner II*

NetMiner II (Version 2.4.0; Cyram 2004) is a software tool that combines social network analysis and visual exploration techniques. It allows users to explore network data visually and interactively, and helps to detect underlying patterns and structures of the network. Two versions of the program are available for users: NetMiner II for Windows (commercial) and NetMiner II for Web (online freeware with reduced functionality compared with the commercial product). Both versions are Java-based applications. A free evaluation version is available, which can be used for 21 days without registering. NetMiner offers good support providing online help, and a user's manual that can be downloaded from the Cyram website.

The program is especially designed for the integration of exploratory network analysis and visualization. To facilitate this integration, the main window of the program contains a map frame in which the results of the analysis are graphically presented and a separate map control toolbar (apart from the main toolbar). Moreover, the *Explore* panel can be activated to inspect the results of the analysis. In Figure 13.2.8, the main NetMiner window and its features are presented.

Data Entry and Manipulation

NetMiner adopts a network data model that is optimized for integrating analysis and visualization. It combines three types of variables: adjacency matrices (called *layers*), affiliation variables, and actor attribute data. The data can be entered in three ways: (1) directly via the built-in matrix editor (a spreadsheet editor similar to the one that is available in UCINET; see Figure 13.2.2), (2) by importing Excel datasheets, comma-separated ASCII values files (CSV), or UCINET DL files, or (3) by opening a NetMiner data file (NTF), which contains the values of the three types of variables. Data sets are saved as NTF files or can be exported in Excel, CSV, or UCINET DL format.

The program contains ample data manipulation options (transformation, recoding, symmetrizing, dichotomizing, selection, normalization, etc.), facilitated by the data

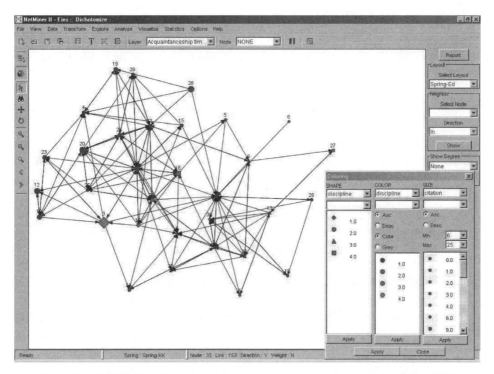

Figure 13.2.8. NetMiner II user interface presenting the graph for the dichotomized EIES acquaintanceship network (first observation) using the Kamada-Kawai spring embedder.

manager that contains the transformation history. It is possible to create random graphs (including scale-free networks) and to edit text files. A drawback, however, is that the program does not allow the specification of missing values.

Visualization Techniques

Like Pajek and NetDraw, NetMiner has advanced graphic properties. Moreover, almost all results are presented both textually and graphically, contrary to both other programs, where the user needs to request visualization of the results of a certain analysis. In NetMiner, graphic and textual results are directly obtained via the *Explore* function of the main menu. The other two functions of the main menu produce either textual results in report form (*Analyze*) or graphs (*Visualize*) with various options.

The *Analyze* function has reduced computing time in comparison to the *Explore* function and contains more analysis methods. Network drawing can be based on spring-embedding algorithms, multidimensional scaling, so-called applied procedures based on analysis procedures (e.g., centrality vectors or clustering combined with spring embedders), and simple procedures (circle, random).

The Kamada-Kawai and Fruchterman-Reingold algorithms are the spring embedders that are implemented in NetMiner, as well as two algorithms based on the spring embedder by Eades. In Figure 13.2.8, the user interface of NetMiner is presented, in which the map frame contains a graph of the first observation of the EIES acquaintanceship network obtained with spring embedding algorithm of Kamada-Kawai. The aim of the Kamada-Kawai algorithm is to find a set of coordinates in which, for each pair of nodes, the Euclidean distance is approximately proportional to the geodesic distance between two nodes (e.g., see Everton 2002; Freeman 2004). Although the procedure does not produce exactly the same mapping each time it is used, the graphs obtained with the Kamada-Kawai algorithm in Pajek (Figure 13.2.4) and NetMiner (Figure 13.2.8) largely resemble each other.

NetMiner has the functionality to set node shape, color, and size according to three attribute variables (both categorical and continuous), like Pajek and NetDraw. In Figure 13.2.8, the nodes are colored and shaped according to the attribute discipline: a blue diamond is sociology, a red circle is anthropology, a magenta triangle is statistics, and a green box is psychology. The size of the nodes reflects the value of the second attribute, the number of citations, where larger nodes reflect higher citation rates.

The multidimensional scaling algorithms for drawing graphs in NetMiner can be metric or nonmetric. For instance, Torgerson-Gower's classical metric multidimensional scaling (principal coordinate analysis), based on an eigenvalue decomposition of which only the first two positive eigenvalues and eigenvectors, can be applied.

NetMiner supports various 3D visualizations and contains a graph editor that can be used to generate new graphs (random placement of nodes or positioning by user) or edit existing graphs (adding new nodes or links). All visual displays can be saved in a wide variety of formats (including EPS, GIF, JPEG, PDF, PNG, EMF, etc.).

Descriptive Methods

The network statistics available in NetMiner include methods to analyze the connection and neighborhood structure of the network (e.g., influence, structural holes) and subgraph configurations (dyad and triad census), to calculate centrality measures (e.g., closeness, betweenness), and to analyze subgroup structures (cliques, clans, cores). To show the integration of standard network methodology and visualization in NetMiner, the closeness centrality index was calculated for the dichotomized EIES acquaintanceship data (first observation). NetMiner, like Pajek, has the option to calculate the in- and out-closeness of directed graphs. UCINET only calculates closeness for undirected graphs.

Via the *Explore* menu, the in-closeness centrality was calculated. The output consists of two parts: a report containing the closeness indices (at actor and network level) and a graphic presentation of the calculated closeness, the so-called centrality map, presented in Figure 13.2.9. The figure shows the NetMiner user interface and the visual presentation of in-closeness statistics in the map frame, in which also the centralization index (the in-closeness for directed graphs) is given: 0.439. The out-closeness is given in the textual output (obtained by clicking the *Report* button): 0.156. For the second observation of the EIES data, the in- and out-closeness equal 0.686 and 0.537, respectively. The same values were found with UCINET and Pajek.

Figure 13.2.9 shows one of the interactive features of NetMiner: right-clicking a node opens a context-sensitive menu with which network properties of the node can be obtained (in-degree, out-degree, egonet size and density) or the neighborhood of the selected node can be drawn (in a new submap window). For actor 6, the network

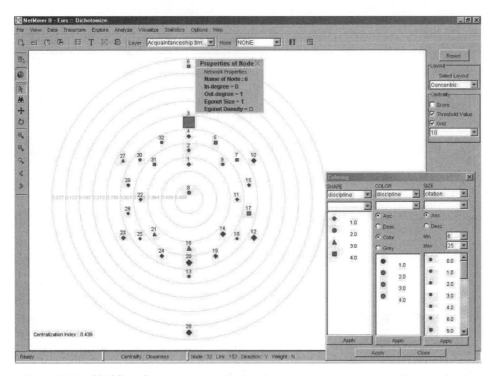

Figure 13.2.9. NetMiner II user interface showing the closeness index and centrality map for the EIES acquaintanceship data (first observation).

properties are presented (note that the egonet density cannot be calculated because node 6 is only connected to one other node).

Figure 13.2.10 displays the result of the analysis of cohesive subgroups: the visualization of cliques in the EIES data, dichotomized and symmetrized as before. It presents the cliques labeled G1 to G8 and its members. The cliques found by NetMiner are shown in Table 13.2.3, and are the same as those found by UCINET. In addition, NetMiner reports for each clique the cohesion index by Bock and Husain (1950). This index measures the degree to which strong ties are within rather than outside the clique. If the index is equal to 1, the strength of ties does not differ within the subgroup compared with outside the subgroup. If the ratio is larger than 1, the ties within the subgroup are more prevalent than the ties outside the subgroup.

Right-clicking a clique in the map opens a menu with which properties of the group, group member lists, or group networks can be obtained. In Figure 13.2.10, the member list of clique G7 is shown, as well as the group network of clique G3. Previous versions of NetMiner (Version 1.x) had the option to draw directly bipartite, comember, and overlap maps of the cliques. Unfortunately, in NetMiner these features can only be obtained indirectly. For example, the clique bipartite map can be obtained by adding the clique affiliation matrix to the data set (via the analysis report), selecting the affilition mode (in the *Transform* menu), and choosing the bipartite method. The node-clique bipartite graph for the EIES data is presented is Figure 13.2.11. The cliques are represented by yellow boxes labeled K1 to K8.

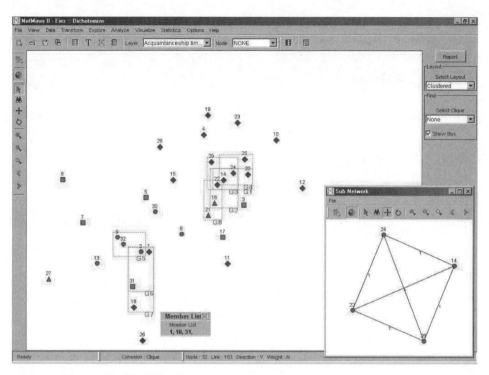

Figure 13.2.10. NetMiner II user interface showing the cliques (at least size 3) for the EIES acquaintanceship data (first observation).

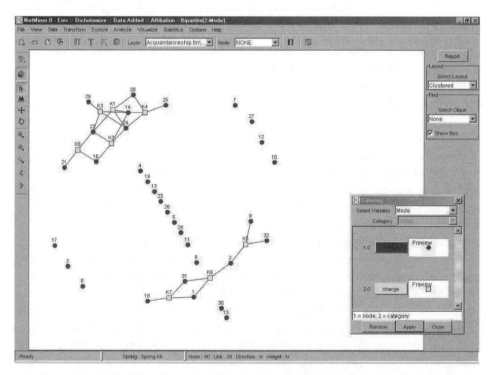

Figure 13.2.11. NetMiner II user interface showing the cliques bipartite map for the EIES acquaintanceship data (first observation).

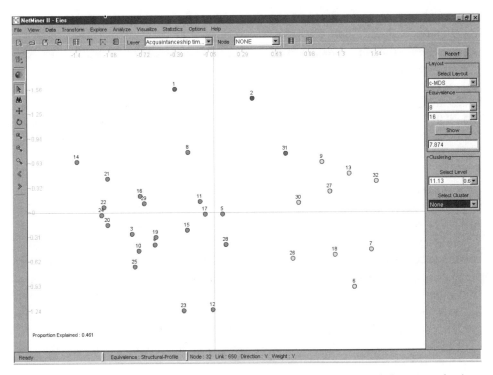

Figure 13.2.12. NetMiner II user interface showing the equivalence map and cluster map for the EIES acquaintanceship data (first observation).

Procedure-Based Analysis

NetMiner contains routines for multidimensional scaling, correspondence analysis, cluster analysis, and matrix decompositions (eigen, singular, spectral). These procedures are integrated in the *Explore/Analyze* submenus and are available as separate options in the *Statistics* menu. The program also contains some procedure-based routines to explore the role-set structure of a network (structural, role, and regular equivalence). Finally, blockmodel routines are available, including goodness-of-fit statistics and permutation tests of significance.

The structural equivalence procedure is used to analyze the first observation of the acquaintanceship network, based on the similarity of tie profiles among the actors. For all pairs of actors, the structural equivalence is computed using Euclidean distances (Burt 1976). The diagonal values are specified to be ignored. The mean distance between pairs is 11.75 (SD 2.39).

Subsequent hierarchical clustering of the equivalence matrix gives a cluster diagram and the possibility to show the different clusters in a map. NetMiner provides four possible cluster linkage methods (single, complete, average, and Ward), whereas UCINET provides three, and Pajek six. For the comparison of different linkage methods, a hierarchical cluster analysis with average linkage is performed. The equivalence map is presented in Figure 13.2.12. In this map, the different clusters are shown by giving them different colors (the number of clusters is chosen to be 4; the colors are assigned by the program). In the top of the map, actors 1 and 31 form one cluster, whereas actor

-2 constitutes a cluster by itself; on the right a cluster of nine actors is found, whereas on the left a cluster of twenty actors.

Comparing the cluster methods of the three packages UCINET, Pajek, and Net-Miner, similar results are found (given the different linkage methods). In all programs, the equivalence measure was based on Euclidean distances, and actors 12 and 23 were found to be most equivalent, and actor 1 least equivalent with these two actors (UCINET, Section 13.2(B)). Inspecting Figure 13.2.12 confirms this finding, where NetMiner locates actors 12 and 23 on one side and actor 1 on the other side of the map. The dendrogram presented by Pajek (Figure 13.2.7) shows a similar clustering.

Statistical Modeling

NetMiner supports a number of standard statistical routines: descriptive statistics, ANOVA, correlations, and regression. All these routines can be applied to both attribute vectors and (adjacency) matrices. The statistics are given with conventional significance tests (based on independence and normality, which may not always be appropriate) and random permutation tests. For adjacency matrices, QAP permutation is adopted (see Krackhardt 1987). Besides, NetMiner provides Markov chain Monte Carlo simulation tests for several network measures based on the on the $\mathcal{U} \mid X_{i+}, X_{+j}$ and $\mathcal{U} \mid X_{i+}, X_{+j}, M$ distributions (cf. the module ZO in StOCNET).

The QAP correlation found between the two time points of the acquaintanceship data is 0.809 (significant at $p = 0.001$ level, 1,000 simulations). This is the same result as found by UCINET, but, unlike UCINET, NetMiner provides no additional information on the test.

(E) STRUCTURE

STRUCTURE (Version 4.2; Burt 1991) is a program "providing sociometric indices, cliques, structural and role equivalence, density tables, contagion, autonomy, power and equilibria in multiple network systems" (Burt 1991, p. 1). It is a command-driven DOS program that needs an input file containing commands for data management and network analysis. After opening the input file, the program executes the required routines without the possibility of user interaction. The program can be downloaded free of charge together with a comprehensive manual including introductions to network analysis, network data, and network models.

STRUCTURE supports network models within five types of network analysis. These are autonomy (analysis of structural holes), cohesion (detection of cliques), contagion, equivalence (analysis of structural or role equivalence and blockmodeling), and power (analysis of network prominence and equilibrium). The programs UCINET, Pajek, and NetMiner contain procedures to perform analyses of one or more of these types. Most procedures in STRUCTURE, however, are unique and cannot be found in the other general programs. These procedures are discussed here.

Data Entry and Manipulation

STRUCTURE distinguishes four types of data: (1) direct measures of relations, (2) binary choice data (obtained with a name generator), (3) sociometric rank order data (where actors ranked their relations with others), and (4) (two-mode) joint involvement data (actors' involvement in the same events or affiliations with the same groups). The first three types have to be presented as adjacency matrices in ASCII data files with fixed positions. For the joint involvement data, networks are created by reading events in each network and aggregating the weight of events in which each pair of actors is involved. Actor attributes are entered as ASCII values. Output data files are written in ASCII fixed-column format (WRT).

The program has a few data manipulation options, which are only available for directed relations: using diagonal elements as measures of strength of self-relations, symmetrizing relations, and transforming relations (converting to row or column marginals, eliminating negative relations, making networks row and/or column stochastic). For joint involvement data, the weights can be defined in different ways.

Visualization Techniques
STRUCTURE has no procedures to visualize networks.

Descriptive Methods
The analysis of structural holes is the single descriptive method available.

Procedure-Based Analysis
The procedure-based analysis methods offered by STRUCTURE are hierarchical cluster analysis (detection of cliques, structural equivalence) and eigenvalue decomposition (to compute power measures). STRUCTURE can detect different kinds of cliques, depending on how relations are measured from the raw data and how cohesion is defined from the relations (Scott 1991). Detection of cliques by STRUCTURE is based on hierarchical clustering of the matrix of cohesion, and is therefore different from clique-finding procedures in UCINET, Pajek, and NetMiner.

In STRUCTURE, cohesion can be defined in several ways. If cohesion is defined by the weakest relation between actors (default) and if cohesion between clusters is defined by the minimum cohesion between the actors in the clusters (cliques), then the clustering procedure will merge clusters if the minimum cohesion within the clusters remains positive. Thus, cliques are found in which the actors are completely connected and have reciprocated relations. This also holds for cliques found by other programs, but the difference in STRUCTURE is that an actor can appear in only one clique. Other definitions of cohesion and other clustering methods result in different kinds of cliques (see Scott 1991).

Applying the algorithm to the acquaintanceship data (first observation) without dichotomizing and symmetrizing the network, results in the detection of seven cliques. These cliques are presented in the left part of Table 13.2.5, which also gives the minimum cohesion within the clusters, here equal to two for all cliques. As a result of the clustering procedure, there is no clique overlap. Applying the algorithm to the dichotomized and symmetrized (only reciprocated relations) EIES data again results in seven cliques, presented in the right part of Table 13.2.5. Comparing these results with the cliques in Table 13.2.3 shows that the solution is different, although cliques 5, 6, and 7 are found in both analyses.

Table 13.2.5. *Cliques in the EIES Acquaintanceship Data (First Observation)*
Obtained with **STRUCTURE**

Valued, Unsymmetrized			Dichotomous, Symmetrized		
Clique	Actors	Cohesion	Clique	Actors	Cohesion
1	11,16,21	2	1	4,19	1
2	10,20,23,25	2	2	10,23	1
3	3,14,18,26	2	3	21,25	1
4	4,19,22,24,28,29	2	4	13,27	1
5	8,13,27,30	2	5	14,22,24,29	1
6	1,2,15,17,31	2	6	1,18,31	1
7	5,9,32	2	7	2,9,32	1

Statistical Modeling

STRUCTURE contains two routines for statistical modeling of the network data: contagion analysis and analysis of network equilibrium. The analysis of contagion in **STRUCTURE** is based on the principle that the structure of the network is such that the behavior (attribute) of one actor is influenced by other actors. This means that attribute values of actors are correlated, due to the structure of the network. Stated otherwise, an attribute that is affected by contagion results in network correlation. In **STRUCTURE**, this is modeled with a regression equation in which the dependent variable is the attribute value of one actor (ego) and the independent variable is the weighted average of the values of the same attribute of the other actors (alters), where the weights reflect the structure of the network. This kind of contagion analysis is not directly available in the programs described earlier.

The program has two options to define the network weights: by equivalence (Euclidean distances) or by cohesion (relation values). Given these weights, the regression equation is estimated with ordinary least-squares (OLS). If the input data are a random sample from a population, OLS gives inconsistent and inefficient estimates, and other estimation procedures must be used (Ord 1975; Doreian 1980). If the data are population data, however, then OLS is accurate. This is typically the case in network analysis (Scott 1991). The significance of the contagion effect (the slope of the regression equation, i.e., the network correlation) is tested with a jackknife t-test. A contagion analysis was performed on the acquaintanceship data (first observation), with citation as the attribute affected by contagion and the weights defined by structural equivalence. The results are presented in Table 13.2.6.

The observed (ego) and expected (alters) citation rates are given together with the results on contagion. The network correlation of 0.323 is not significant according to the jackknife t-test (with $g - 1 = 31$ degrees of freedom), which indicates that structurally equivalent actors (researchers) do not tend to have the same citation rates.

The analysis of network equilibrium in **STRUCTURE** is based on the distribution of power, which is obtained with eigenprocedures (Katz 1953; Bonacich 1972). An actor is defined to be powerful if he or she receives many exclusive relations from powerful others. The scores range from 1 (most powerful) to 0 (weakest). Analysis of the first

Table 13.2.6. *STRUCTURE Output of the Contagion Analysis for the EIES Acquaintanceship Data (First Observation) with the Attribute Citation*

```
Observed responses                              mean:     22.906
                                                S.D.:     31.737

Expected responses                              mean:     24.088
from contagion                                  S.D.:      8.129

Contagion effect (32
observations)
                           regression intercept:         -7.426
                              regression slope:           1.259
                                   correlation:           0.323
                      jackknife t-test (31 df):           1.508
```

observation of the acquaintanceship data reveals that actor 1 is the most powerful (1.00) and actor 6 (0.05) is the weakest actor (see the graph of the network in Figures 13.2.4 or 13.2.8).

Network equilibrium is analyzed by predicting how relations in a network will change if powerful actors could initiate any relation they want. This prediction is based on a linear regression model that predicts the value of equilibrium relations from observed relations (Scott 1991). The equilibrium relations from actor i to j are defined by $z_{ij}(\frac{p_i}{p_j})$, where z_{ij} is the relation from i to j divided by the row sum (row stochastic adjacency matrix), and p_i is the power of actor i. The analysis of the first acquaintanceship network results in a regression equation that predicts 42.4% of the variation in the equilibrium relations (the correlation is 0.65). A high correlation means that equilibrium relations and observed relations are alike, which implies that the inclination to change relations is small.

The program gives a so-called turnover table to equilibrium (presented in Table 13.2.7), showing the association between observed relations and equilibrium relations. It is used to determine stability and locate unstable classes of relations. The relations are divided into four classes. From the table it follows that change is primarily zero

Table 13.2.7. *Turnover Table to Equilibrium in the EIES Acquaintanceship Data (First Observation) Obtained with STRUCTURE*

	Equilibrium				
Observed	None	Weak	More	Strong	Total
None ($z = 0$)	222	120	0	0	342
Weak ($z < 0.1$)	112	496	17	0	625
More	8	8	8	1	25
Strong ($z > 0.5$)	0	0	0	0	0
TOTAL	342	624	25	1	992

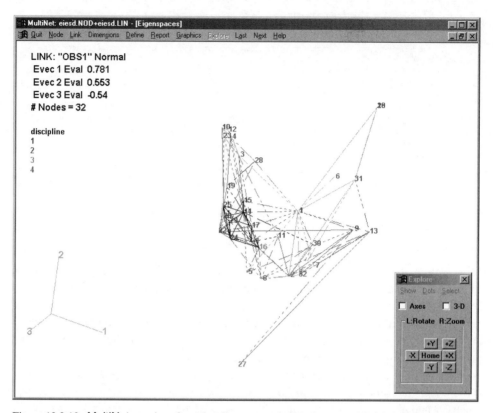

Figure 13.2.13. **MultiNet** user interface showing a normal eigendecomposition for the dichotomized EIES acquaintanceship data (first observation).

strength relations becoming weak and vice versa. This indicates that the network is relatively stable.

STRUCTURE provides an option for Monte Carlo network analyses. In such analyses, networks can be simulated according to the uniform, (nearly) normal, or lognormal probability distribution. With these simulated networks, studies of any of the network models in the program can be carried out.

(F) *MultiNet*

MultiNet (Version 4.38 for Windows; Richards and Seary 2003) is a program suitable for the analysis of large data sets and sparse network data. The program is designed for contextual analysis, that is, analyzing network data with nodal attributes. Besides network data, the program contains some methods to analyze attribute data (cross-tables, ANOVA, correlations). It is menu-driven, where higher level menus and extra menu items become available after the necessary options are specified. It has context sensitive-online help and, like **NetMiner**, gives both graphic representations of the results and textual output. An example of the **MultiNet** user interface (including an example of some graphic output) is presented in Figure 13.2.13.

The program is available from the authors. There is no complete user's manual, which makes it difficult to use and explore MultiNet to its full extent, but the authors provide useful information and some papers on MultiNet modules (Seary and Richards 2000; Seary 2003).

Some of the network analysis methods and procedures in MultiNet were originally contained in separate programs. FATCAT (Version 4.2, Richards and Seary 1993), for instance, performs the same type of categorical social network analysis and produces the accompanying contingency tables and panigrams as MultiNet. Although incorporated in MultiNet, FATCAT is still freely available as a stand-alone DOS program that runs under Windows. The program is interactive and menu-driven and it provides context-sensitive online help. Another program integrated in MultiNet is PSPAR (Seary 1999), which estimates the p^* model (Wasserman and Pattison 1996) for sparse matrices.

Data Entry and Manipulation

Because MultiNet is designed for the analysis of large networks, like Pajek it uses node and link lists as data input instead of adjacency matrices. The former is a list of all actors in the network together with the values of the available attributes; the latter is a list of the (existing) relations between the actors. There are three options to enter the data: (1) by opening a MultiNet system file (MNW), (2) by importing ASCII data from node (NOD) and link (LIN) files, or (3) by opening data in comma-delimited files (CSV). In the link file, nonexisting relations (e.g., the relations with value 0 in the acquaintanceship data) do not have to be specified. Multiple link variables, like the two observations of the EIES data, have to be included in one link file. Data are saved in MNW files or exported to ASCII NOD and LIN files. Distributed with the program are the two stand-alone utilities ADJ2NEG and FREEFIX to create node and link import files.

The program contains some data manipulation options (recoding, grouping variables together) and has a simple data manager. It is possible to specify a value for missing observations, which has to be the same for all network and attribute variables. There is also an option to treat missing links as zero values (no links) and vice versa.

Visualization Techniques

MultiNet contains procedures to provide graphic representations of almost all output generated by the analysis routines. It has graphic tools to draw histograms, cumulative distribution functions, and line diagrams. Networks are visualized using eigendecompositions (Figure 13.2.13). Cross-tables are visualized with so-called panigrams (Figure 13.2.14). Adjacency matrices can be presented visually (Figure 13.2.15), which can be useful to display large networks. To detect clustering, one can permute the adjacency matrix according to actor attribute.

All graphic representations are interactive, which means that the user can click on displays to inspect attribute values or probability levels, explore effects, permute displays, or find information on nodes and links. The program also has several options to improve the displays (rotation, translation, magnification). The graphs can be saved, either as postscript (PS) or bitmap (BTM) files.

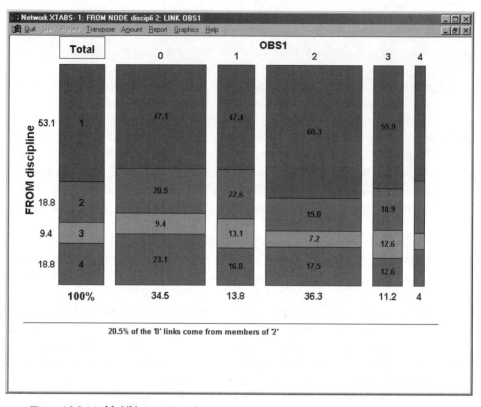

Figure 13.2.14. MultiNet user interface presenting the panigram of discipline and the first observation of the EIES acquaintanceship network (incoming links).

Descriptive Methods

For network data, the degree, betweenness, closeness, and components statistics can be computed, together with frequency distributions of these statistics. Frequency distributions and corresponding descriptives, like mean and standard deviation, of the network data (the links) and the attribute data (nodes) can also be obtained.

Procedure-Based Analysis

With MultiNet, one can analyze the structure of networks with several eigenspace methods. The methods create visual displays of the network such that the location of the actors reveals the structure of the relationships and their patterns (Richards and Seary 2000; Freeman 2004). Thus, the eigenmethods pursue the same goal as the spring-embedding algorithms (used in NetDraw, Pajek, and NetMiner) and the multidimensional scaling procedures (used in NetDraw and NetMiner). Pajek also contains some eigenmethods.

Eigenprocedures require dichotomized and symmetrized data. The result of an eigen-decomposition is an eigenspace that can be used to visualize the network structure (Seary 2003). In the visual displays, the coordinates of the nodes are based on the co-ordinates of the first two or three eigenvectors, yielding two-dimensional (2D) and 3D displays, respectively. Between the nodes, lines are drawn based on the link variable

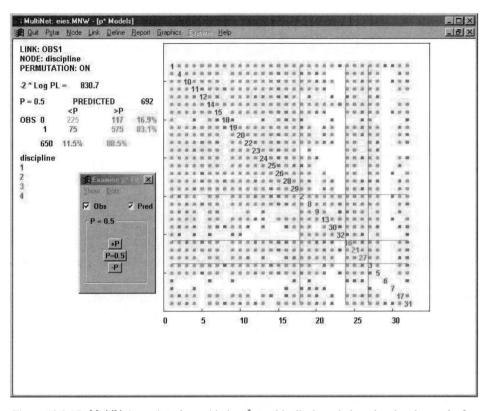

Figure 13.2.15. **MultiNet** user interface with the p^* graphic display window showing the results for the EIES acquaintanceship data (first observation).

(i.e., the dichotomized and symmetrized links in the original network). Associated with each dimension is a certain amount of variance in the original data, where the largest amount of variance is associated with the first dimension, and so on. A one-dimensional display of the network can also be generated, based on the first eigenvector. This is a so-called virtual adjacency matrix in which only the existing links are shown (using sparse methods; see Seary 2003).

The results can be rotated, resized, and rescaled to obtain a better presentation of the data. The eigenspace methods can also be used to partition the actors on the basis of the network structure. In Figure 13.2.13, the 3D normal eigendecomposition of the dichotomized EIES acquaintanceship data (first observation) is presented. The actors are colored according to their discipline (1–4: sociology–psychology). For every eigen-decomposition, a textual report is generated that includes details about the current eigenspace.

Statistical Modeling

MultiNet contains four statistical techniques to analyze network data, of which the first three can also be used for the standard analysis of actor attribute data: (1) cross-tables and χ^2-tests, (2) ANOVA, (3) correlations, and (4) the p^* exponential random graph model (Wasserman and Pattison 1996; Seary and Richards 2000).

Table 13.2.8. *ANOVA Results for the EIES Acquaintanceship*
Data (First Observation) Obtained with **MultiNet**

		Mean Citation of	
Relation	n	Receiver	Sender
Did not know	342	15.0	20.6
Had not met	137	29.8	23.2
Had met	360	27.8	23.5
Was friend	111	22.5	23.3
Was close friend	42	24.1	34.6
ANOVA: p-value		<0.01	>0.10

Cross-tables are visualized using panigrams. An example is presented in Figure 13.2.14. The tables and panigrams are used to explore the association within networks (out- and in-degrees, i.e., sender and receiver effects) or the association between networks and an attribute. In Figure 13.2.14, a panigram of discipline and incoming links (receiver effects) of the first observation of the acquaintanceship network is presented. The links can take the values 0 to 4 ("have not met" to "close friends"), discipline the values 1 to 4. Interactive help is available, explaining the meaning of the "cells." For example, 20.5% of the links with value 0 ("have not met") come from actors with discipline value 2 (anthropology) and 9.4% from members of discipline 3 (statistics). The χ^2-statistic equals 23.4 ($df = 12$, $p < 0.05$), which indicates a significant association between the variables (with sociologists receiving more friendship choices). The association between discipline and outgoing links (sender effects) of the first acquaintanceship network is also significant (results not reported here).

In Table 13.2.8, the results of two analyses of variance for the first observation of the acquaintanceship data are presented. The independent grouping variable is the nature of the relation between two actors (sender and receiver) at the first time point. The dependent variables are the mean citation rates of the senders and the receivers. A graphic display of the citations per relation group is also produced (not shown). From the table, it follows that there is a significant difference between the mean citation rates of receivers, but not between the senders. The means show that receivers are on average less often cited in the "did not know" relation group.

The analyses differ from those performed by **UCINET**, where only one row or column of the adjacency matrix is used in an ANOVA. By using all links in the analyses, **MultiNet** assumes independence between all relations, whereas **UCINET** assumes independence between actors. The former will generally not be the case, and the user should therefore be very cautious in interpreting the results.

MultiNet comprises **PSPAR**, an earlier program by Seary (1999), designed to fit p^* models to large networks by pseudolikelihood based on sparse methods. The method fits the model parameters to triad statistics selected by the user. Blockparameters can be obtained by fitting models of which the blockstructure is defined by one or more (categorical) actor attributes. Figure 13.2.15 shows the p^* graphic display window obtained for the EIES acquaintanceship data (first observation). The effects included in the model are density, reciprocity, transitivity, and the blockparameter "choice within

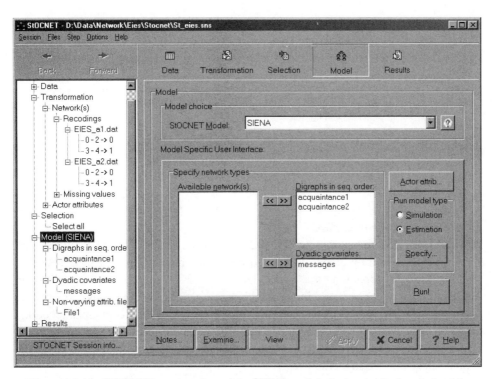

Figure 13.2.16. StOCNET user interface of the SIENA module for longitudinal analysis of the EIES acquaintanceship data.

blocks" with the blocks defined by the attribute discipline. All estimates were significant and are reported in Table 13.2.10 in Section 13.2(G) together with the estimates obtained in StOCNET. The p^* graphic display shows the adjacency matrix with correctly predicted links (green), the false negatives (blue), and false positives (red).

(G) *StOCNET*

StOCNET (Version 1.5. Boer et al. 2004) is an open software system, in a Windows environment, for advanced statistical analysis of social networks. It provides a platform to make available a number of statistical methods, presented in separate modules, and allows new routines to be easily implemented (Huisman and Van Duijn 2003). The program is freeware and can be downloaded from the StOCNET website. A user's manual describing the operation of the StOCNET system is available, as well as a programmer's manual, which describes the main procedures and functionalities of the system to facilitate the inclusion of new statistical methods. On the website, user's manuals of all modules and programmer's manuals together with source codes of some modules can be found.

Analyses take place within *sessions*. A session consists of (a cyclical process of) five steps: (1) data definition, (2) transformation, (3) selection, (4) model specification and analysis, and (5) inspection of results. A typical StOCNET window is presented in Figure 13.2.16 showing the user interface for the module SIENA for longitudinal network data (see Snijders 2004).

Table 13.2.9. *Estimated (Significant) Effects for the Evolution of the EIES Acquaintanceship Data Obtained with the* SIENA *Module in* StOCNET

Effect	Est.	SE
Constant change rate	2.47	
Density (out-degree)	−1.80	0.52
Reciprocity	2.06	0.39
Indirect relations	−0.27	0.13
Popularity	6.40	1.05

Data Entry and Manipulation

Network data have to be presented as adjacency matrices saved in ASCII format with the values separated by blanks. Actor attributes also have to be presented as ASCII files, with blanks separating the values. Data sets are saved as ASCII data files and StOCNET sessions are saved in session files (SNS). Export functions to MultiNet, NetMiner, Pajek, and STRUCTURE are available. StOCNET contains a recoding, symmetrizing, and selection option. Missing values can be specified, both for network data and attributes. The handling of missing observations depends on the statistical model selected in the modeling step.

Visualization Techniques

StOCNET does not contain procedures for the visualization of networks.

Descriptive Methods

In four of the five steps in a StOCNET session, descriptive analyses of the available data can be performed by clicking the *Examine* button. This button is available in the main windows of all steps (Figure 13.2.16), except in the last step (i.e., inspection of results). Degree variances, index of heterogeneity, dyad and triad census, degree of reciprocity and transitivity, and segmentation are some of the network statistics that are calculated for separate network data sets. For longitudinal analysis of networks, change statistics are calculated.

Procedure-Based Analysis

There are no procedure-based routines available in StOCNET.

Statistical Modeling

StOCNET contains six statistical modules: (1) BLOCKS, for stochastical blockmodeling (Nowicki and Snijders 2001); (2) ULTRAS, for estimating latent transitive structures using ultrametrics (Schweinberger and Snijders 2003); (3) P2, for fitting the exponential random graph model p_2 (Van Duijn, Snijders, and Zijlstra 2004); (4) SIENA, for the analysis of longitudinal network data (Snijders 2001, 2004); (5) ZO, for determining probability distributions of statistics of random graphs based on the $U \mid X_{i+}, X_{+j}$ and $U \mid X_{i+}, X_{+j}, M$ distributions (Snijders 1991; Molloy and Reed 1995) and (6) PACNET,

Table 13.2.10. *Pseudolikelihood Estimates Obtained with MultiNet and Markov Chain Monte Carlo Robbins Monro p*-estimates Obtained with StOCNET for the EIES Acquaintanceship Data (First Observation)*

	Pseudolikelihood		MCMC Robbins Monro Conditional on Ties			
Effect	Est.	SE	Est.	SE	Est.	SE
Density	−3.61	0.22				
Reciprocity	1.94	0.23	2.15	0.31	2.20	0.30
Transitivity	0.32	0.036	0.17	0.01	0.17	0.01
Dissimilarity discipline	0.55	0.22	0.25	3.32		

for constructing and fitting of structural models based on partial algebraic structures (Pattison and Wasserman 1995; Pattison, Wasserman, Robins, and Kanfer 2000). Other exponential random graph models can also be fitted in StOCNET: the p_1 model (Holland and Leinhard 1981) as *Examine* option in P2, and the $p*$ model (Wasserman and Pattison 1996) in SIENA where MCMC estimation with the Robbins-Monro algorithm is applied to a single network observation, instead of repeated observations (Snijders 2002; Snijders and Van Duijn 2002).

The results of applying modules SIENA and P2 to the EIES data are shown in Tables 13.2.9 through 13.2.11. Figure 13.2.16 shows the model-specific user interface for the SIENA module. Both time points of the acquaintanceship networks are analyzed with the dynamic actor-oriented model of Snijders (2001, 2004). The first observation of the network is analyzed with the p_2 model and with the $p*$ model. For all models, the dichotomized data were used.

The estimated effects of the SIENA model are presented in Table 13.2.9 (see also Snijders 2004, for a discussion on the interpretation of the parameters). The rate parameter shows that on average, the actors made about 2.5 relationship changes in the period between the observations. In the evolution of the acquaintanceship network, a clear reciprocity effect and a transitivity-type effect are present, the latter being specified as a tendency away from indirect relations. There is also a tendency for popular others (i.e., others who receive many choices). No significant attribute effects were found.[3]

In the SIENA module, MCMC estimation with the Robbins-Monro algorithm of $p*$ model is implemented. As Snijders (2002) noted, both the pseudolikelihood estimation (as implemented in MultiNet, but which can also be done with standard software for logistic regression), and MCMC estimation using the Geyer and Thompson (1992) method are unsatisfactory. The pseudolikelihood estimate is not a function of the complete statistic and has unknown properties. This leads in any case to underestimation of the standard errors of the estimates. MCMC estimation is not satisfactory either because the simulation of random graph distributions turns out to be a complicated matter due to bimodality and poor mixing properties of the Metropolis-Hastings and Gibbs algorithms, which leads to convergence problems. See Wasserman and Robins (2004) for

Table 13.2.11. p_2-estimates for the EIES Acquaintanceship Data (First Observation; Only Significant Effects) Obtained with **StOCNET**

Effect	Parameter	Est.	SE
Density	μ	−2.79	0.29
	Dissimilarity citation (abs. diff.)	−0.017	0.005
	Dissimilarity citation (diff.)	−0.013	0.003
	Similarity discipline	0.64	0.18
Reciprocity	ρ	2.36	0.32
Sender	Variance σ_A^2	1.01	0.24
	Citations	0.028	0.0082
Receiver	Variance σ_B^2	0.98	0.23
Sender–receiver	Covariance σ_{AB}	−0.40	0.18

an extended discussion of pseudolikelihood and MCMC estimation of p^* models. Snijders (2002) and Snijders and Van Duijn (2002) proposed several alternative simulation methods to improve convergence, based on single relations, dyads, and triplets, using Gibbs or Metropolis Hastings steps, making small or large updates (through inversion steps), and/or on conditional simulation (fixing the number of relations, or the in- and outdegrees and thus limiting the outcome space). More developments in this area are expected.

In Table 13.2.10, the results are given of fitting the p^* model to the first observation of the EIES data. Maximum pseudolikelihood estimates were obtained with **MultiNet** (see Section 13.2(F)). MCMC estimates with the Robbins-Monro algorithm were obtained with the **SIENA** model in **StOCNET**. It was not possible to estimate the p^* model unconditionally. As soon as the transitivity effect was added to the model, no convergence was obtained. It was possible to obtain estimates of the p^* model conditional on the number of ties, which means that no density effect is estimated. The convergence of the model with the dissimilarity (or block) effect of discipline was also unsatisfactory, which shows in the large standard error for this effect, given in Table 13.2.10. The convergence of the conditional model with only reciprocity and transitivity was acceptable. The estimates for reciprocity and even their standard errors are similar for pseudolikelihood and MCMC. The estimates for transitivity and the similarity (block) effect of discipline are quite different.

The p_2 model is a random effects model with the dyadic ties as the dependent variables (Van Duijn et al. 2004). The sender and receiver parameters, fixed in the p_1 model, are regressed on available – categorical or continuous – nodal attributes (*actor covariates*). If no attributes are available, the regression model reduces to random sender and receiver effects. Likewise, the density and reciprocity parameters can be linked to other available networks (*dyadic covariates*), without a random component. Dyadic covariates can also be computed from the nodal attributes, for instance, by taking their difference or absolute difference, which are both standard options in the **P2** module. Thus, dissimilarity matrices are created. If the nodal attribute is categorical, one can construct dichotomous (dis)similarity matrices, comparable to the blockparameters in **MultiNet**. Unlike the p^* model, the p_2 model does not contain network effects other than reciprocity.

Table 13.2.11 contains the parameter estimates for the fixed and random effects of the model. Dissimilarity with respect to citation has a significant negative effect on density, in two ways: expressed as the absolute difference of the actors' number of citations, and expressed as the simple difference of the actors' number of citations. The first effect implies that the probability of an acquaintance relation decreases the more actors differ with respect to their citations; the second indicates a directional effect that actors whose citations are high tend to choose less often actors whose citations are low. The second effect can be viewed as a refinement of the positive sender effect for citation, which indicates that the probability of an outgoing acquaintanceship relation (irrespective of the receiver attributes) increases with the number of citations. The positive effect of similarity with respect to discipline indicates that actors tend to choose more within their own discpline group, which effect was also found for $p*$ model in MultiNet. There is a general reciprocity effect, but this is not differentiated according to dyadic attributes.

Analysis of the first observation of the acquaintanceship data with the stochastic blockmodeling routine BLOCKS (results not shown here) reveals some classes of stochastically equivalent actors (i.e., they have the same probability distribution of their relations to other actors). The fit of the models, like the blockmodeling results obtained with Pajek, however, is not very good. The blocks found do not coincide with the partitions based on actor attributes.

ULTRAS, aimed at finding groups according to a latent structure based on ultra-metrics (i.e., triadic distances between actors), was also applied to the first network of the valued acquaintanceship network, using a Poisson distribution for the network ties. The groups can be presented as a tree, branching further with larger distances. The number of ultrametrics needs to be determined using a Bayesian model selection process. The analysis shows that a solution with less than three ultrametrics is certainly inferior to a model with at least four ultrametrics, whereas the distinction between four or more ultrametrics is less clear. The solution with four ultrametrics (not shown here) resembles to some extent the dendogram of the hierarchical cluster analysis found by Pajek (presented in Figure 13.2.7).

More examples of statistical analyses with the StOCNET modules are given by Huisman and Van Duijn (2003).

13.3 Social Network Software – Other Packages and Routines

In this section, other available software for social network analysis is briefly discussed, without illustrations. We distinguish general packages and five types of special pur-pose packages: for identification of subgroups, for knowledge networks, for hidden populations, for kinship networks, and for statistical testing. Only the most important features are mentioned. The final subsection treats routines and utilities for the analysis of social networks developed to be used in a general statistical software package or in a programming language.

(A) *General Packages*

In this section, seven general packages are mentioned (in alphabetical order). One of them, GRADAP, is well-known because it has been around for more than 15 years. We consider GRADAP, although outdated, worth mentioning because it contains routines and statistics not available in packages like UCINET or Pajek. The other programs are quite new and regularly updated. We distinguish two kinds of general programs: programs intended for data analysis that have visualization options (Agna and SNAFU), and programs intended for network visualization that feature analysis procedures (so-called visual exploration; InFlow, NetDraw, NetVis, and visone).

Agna (Version 2.1.1; Benta 2004): The platform-independent application Agna (Applied Graph & Network Analysis) is designed for social network analysis and sequential analysis. Sequential analysis deals with behavioral chains, which are modeled in order to find rules that govern the inner structure of behavior. This inner structure is represented by dyad transitions. Agna is designed to study communication relations in groups, kinship relations, and the structure of animal behavior. The analysis methods include general descriptives, shortest path analyses, and centrality and sociometric coefficients. The program has ample visualization options.

GRADAP (Version 2.0; Sprenger and Stokman 1989): The software package GRADAP (GRAph Definition and Analysis Package), an environment for analyzing graphs and networks, is an organized set of programs explicitly developed to analyze network data represented as graphs, and includes a wide range of cohesive subgroup and centrality methods, and models for the distribution of in- and out-degrees. It is only available as a DOS application and will not be updated to a Windows environment.

SNAFU–MacOS (Version 2.0; Hagen 2003): SNAFU (Social Network Analysis Functional Utility) is a general-purpose network analysis tool for MacOS systems, which is distributed "as-is" with no warranties or support beyond reasonable requests. It imports and exports to UCINET, InFlow, and some visualization programs, and is generally oriented toward connected graphs of a few hundred nodes. It includes network editing features, descriptive techniques, some matrix algebra, visualization tools, and multiple example data sets.

Visual Exploration

InFlow (Version 3.0; Krebs 2002): InFlow is a commercial software package for network mapping, especially aimed at organizational applications. It was originally developed for Macintosh, but has been updated to Windows. Interactively, it carries out network analysis and network visualization simultaneously (with ample graphic export options). Thus, it is possible to express changes in the network directly in terms of network measures. It features a number of descriptive and procedure-based routines, but no statistical methods.

NetDraw (Version 1.0; Borgatti 2002): NetDraw is a program for drawing networks. It is a free, stand-alone program, but is also distributed together with UCINET. This reflects its close relation with UCINET: it can be executed within UCINET and reads UCINET files natively without the need for import and export functions.

NetDraw uses several different algorithms for displaying nodes in a 2D space, using a circle layout or layouts obtained with multidimensional scaling or spring embedding. These layouts are based on geodesic distance (see Freeman 2004, and Sections 11.2(C) and 11.2(D)). It has tools for grouping and automatically recoloring, resizing, or re-shaping of nodes, ties, and labels to represent these groups. Graphs can be rotated, flipped, resized, and saved in several formats, among others, as BMP and JPEG files. Export functions to Mage and Pajek are available. NetDraw includes some analysis procedures, for example, identification of isolates, components, or *k*-cores, the results of which are displayed graphically.

NetVis (Version 2.0; Cummings 2003): With advances in open source software, so-cial network researchers have new opportunities for analyzing and visualizing network data. One such possibility is the NetVis module, a web-based tool to analyze and visual-ize social networks using data from CSV files, online surveys, and dispersed teams. It is available online, where data can be uploaded, analyzed, and output and (3D) graphs are generated, which can be downloaded. For all algorithms, the source code is available.

visone (Version 1.1; Brandes and Wagner 2003): The visone project team is de-veloping models and algorithms to integrate and advance the analysis and visualization of social networks. It facilitates the visual exploration of network data by experts and novices. Its origins lie in an interdisciplinary cooperation with researchers from math-ematics, computer and information science, and political science. visone is a research platform that is not intended to become a standard tool, and is in development and therefore subject to change.

visone contains several different algorithms for drawing graphs and representing results of analyses. It uses spring embedders, spectral layouts, layered layouts, and radial layouts to present networks. It has many options to improve the (layout of the) graphs and visualizations can be exported in SVG or postscript format. The analysis methods include local measures (degrees), distance measures (e.g., betweenness, closeness), and feedback measures (e.g., status, eigenvector, authority).

(B) *Special Purpose Packages*

In this section, we discuss nine packages, divided into five specific areas of social network analysis: identification of subgroups, knowledge networks, hidden populations, kinship networks, and statistical testing.

Identification of Subgroups

KliqFinder for Windows (Version 0.05; Frank 2003): KliqFinder is the Windows version of the FORTRAN and SAS-based program KliqueFinder (adapted for Windows by Richard Congdon). It is aimed at identifying cohesive subgroups and produces a so-called crystallized sociogram representing the subgroups and their relations within and between the clusters. The subgroups are identified in an iterative algorithm maximizing the log-odds of a tie within the group (Frank 1995, 1996). For the graphic representation of the subgroups, the program SAS is called from within KliqFinder.

NEGOPY (Version 4.30; Richards 1995): The main purpose of the DOS-based program NEGOPY is to find cohesive subgroups. To this end, it defines a number of role categories, such as groups, isolates, or participants on the basis of their linkage with other nodes, more or less similar to the *p*-cliques discussed in the section on Pajek. The reader is referred to the manual for exact definitions and how these definitions may be adapted, and short references in Wasserman and Faust (1994). The result is a discrete categorization of the nodes in the network. NEGOPY uses partial decomposition methods to approximate eigendecomposition methods unfeasible for large networks, whereas MultiNet calculates exact eigenpairs (see Richards and Seary 2000).

Knowledge Networks

Blanche (Version 4.6.5; Hyatt et al. 2004): Because knowledge of the knowledge network causes changes and further evolution of the knowledge network, the program Blanche was designed to create and simulate models of network dynamics. It uses a system of nodes and links, as well as (nonlinear difference) equations that describe how the strengths of links and the attributes of nodes change over time. It consists of three modules to create models, to create data, and to run the model and output the results, respectively.

Iknow (Contractor, O'Keefe, and Jones 1997): Iknow is specialized Java-based software that collects and presents data on communication and knowledge networks. In this kind of knowledge networks, the nodes are actors (individuals or organizations) and the links the knowledge or information they have about characteristics of the other actors. These characteristics typically concern knowledge of various domains. The software either collects interactively or automatically, from the web, information about the network actors and their links, and then presents this information in various ways.

Referral Web (Version 2.0; Kautz, Selman, and Shah 1997): This Java-based software was developed in the area of artificial intelligence. It is aimed at research communities and helps users, that is, researchers explore the social networks in which they participate (such that they can quickly find short referral chains between themselves and experts on arbitrary topics). It either shows the neighborhood of a specified researcher (the node), the path to some specified other node or to an unknown expert on a specified topic. The program operates by automatically generating representations of social networks based on evidence gathered from publicly available documents on the Internet. For instance, nodes who are found to be coauthors, are linked. The definition of association on which the linking is based may be difficult, and therefore the resulting networks may be incorrect and/or incomplete.

Hidden Populations

SNOWBALL (Snijders 1994): SNOWBALL is a DOS program for estimating the size of a hidden population from a one-wave snowball sample, implementing the estimates proposed by Frank and Snijders (1994). *Snowball sampling* is a term used for sampling procedures that allow the sampled units to provide information not only about themselves, but also about other units. This is advantageous when rare properties are of interest.

SocioMetrica LinkAlyzer (Version 2.1; MDLogix 2002): SocioMetrica Link-Alyzer is aimed at constructing a network from data obtained from (a sample from) a difficult or hidden population. The program was developed to investigate HIV links between drug users. The typical problem is that many actors in the network are difficult to identify because of their use of, possibly various, nicknames. To construct a network from the data that are usually collected as egocentric networks (by interviewers), it is necessary to find out which nominees are the same. The software tries to identify these actors by matching them on various possible attributes such as gender, age, appearance, location(s), and so on. Although the software is commercial (available in two versions for smaller and larger networks), a demo version can be downloaded from the web. It is possible to work with example data or with other data (containing not more than fifty actors) and thus to get an impression of the features of the program that also provides some standard network measures like centrality. It has import and export possibilities to common other packages such as UCINET, SPSS, and Excel.

Kinship Networks
PGRAPH (Version 2.7 for Windows; White and Skyhorse 1997): PGRAPH is software for kinship and marriage networks, where P stands for parent or parental. On the webpage, the authors call it a "toolkit for structural analysis of genealogical data and kinship and marriage data." The *p*-graph is a concept for a representation of networks in which the vertices are not individuals, but intersections between individuals (as in marriage), or between groups and individuals, where graph theoretic cycles and blocks are relevant units of analysis (see also Harary and White 2001). Networks can be analyzed using *p*-graphs with either the PGRAPH package, or with Pajek software in combination with some utility programs that preanalyze the data and convert it to Pajek input format (White, Batagelj, and Mrvar 1999).

Statistical Testing
PermNet (Version 0.94; Tsuji 1997): The program PermNet (PERMutation NETworks) contains a set of permutation tests for social network data. It provides symmetry tests, transitivity tests for real-valued data, and a triad census test for binary data (cf. NetMiner and the module ZO of the StOCNET software).

(C) *Utilities and Routines*

We mention five software toolkits with utilities available for programming, either in general software (Excel, Gauss, R/S) or in a common programming language (Java). The routines developed for Gauss and especially those developed for R are the most general and complete. The Excel routines are specifically aimed at ethological applications, and the Java-based libraries of procedures are largely aimed at visualization.

Next to these routines, some other data preparation utilities are available. Some of them (ADJ2NEG and FREEFIX) were already mentioned in Section 13.2(F). Another, PREPSTAR (Version 1.0; Crouch and Wasserman 1998) has been developed to perform $p*$ analyses in SPSS or SAS.

JUNG–Java Library (Version 1.4.3; White et al. 2004): The Java Universal Network/Graph (JUNG) framework is a software library that provides a common and extendible language for the modeling, analysis, and visualization of data that can be represented as a graph or network. JUNG supports a variety of representations of graphs (e.g., directed, undirected), and the current version includes algorithms for clustering, decomposition, random graph generation, statistical analysis, and calculating of network distances, flows, and importance measures. It also provides a visualization framework to construct tools for data exploration.

MatMan–Microsoft Excel (Version 1.1 for Windows; Noldus Information Technology, 2004): An add-in for Microsoft Excel, MatMan is aimed at performing specific matrix manipulations, common in ethologic research, for sociomatrices, behavioral profile data, and transition matrices. Furthermore, social dominance and correlation analyses can be performed.

SNA–R-routines for S (Version 0.44; Butts 2004): This collection of routines to be used in R or S ("Carter's archive"), contains many well-documented procedures for performing various kinds of social network analyses ranging from general analyses such as mutuality, betweenness, or centrality to specific analyses such as QAP and $p*$ analyses, or blockmodeling. It also contains visualization routines. The R routines can be called from the program Pajek (see Section 13.2(C)).

SNAP–GAUSS (Version 2.5; Friedkin 2001): Like SNA, a collection of network analysis routines that include procedures for calculating many graph theoretical properties of graphs and nodes, and for fitting social influence models.

yFiles–Java Library (Version 2.2.1; *y*Works 2004): The Java class package yFiles provides efficient and effective visualization algorithms. It is a class library for viewing, editing, optimizing, layouting, and animating graphs. Because it is written in Java, yFiles is fit for platform independent applications. It has a graph viewer and supports many functionalities, like labels for nodes and edges or multiple views of a graph. Furthermore, yFiles has some routines for exploration and descriptive analysis of networks (e.g., bipartitions, shortest paths, transitivity).

13.4   Recommendations

We conclude this section with a summary of the packages presented in Section 13.2. We scored the software at (1) functionality, using the earlier-defined categorization of procedures: data manipulation (data entry was found not to be a problem for any program), network visualization, descriptive methods, procedure-based methods, and

Table 13.4.12. *Scores for the Packages Presented in Section 13.2*

	Functionality					Support		User Friendliness
	Data	Visual.	Descr.	Proc.	Stat.	Manual	Help	
MultiNet	+−	+	+−	+	+−	+−	++	+
NetMiner	++	++	++	++	+−	+	+	++
Pajek	+	++	+	++	0	−	0	+−
StOCNET	+−	0	+−	0	++	+	+	+
STRUCTURE	−	0	+−	++	+	++	0	+−
UCINET	++	+[a]	++	++	+−	+	+	+

[a] The program NetDraw for network visualization is distributed with UCINET.

statistical methods; (2) support: the availability of a manual and a online help-function; and (3) user friendliness. The scores are given in Table 13.4.12. A + is used to indicate that it is good (or at least sufficient), ++ that it is very good or strong, a − that it has shortcomings, a 0 that it is lacking, and a +− that it is undecided (having both good and bad parts). We explain the scores, especially the negative ones, later in this section.

Obviously, we try to present an objective, substantiated view, but we admit that we cannot give a completely unbiased opinion. We also stress that it is impossible to make a fair comparison between the packages because their objectives are different, which leads to different functionalities. For instance, the aim of StOCNET is not to compete with but to be an addition to existing software, and therefore it contains no procedure-based methods. Likewise, STRUCTURE is too old to offer any visualization.

Therefore, we advise also reading the table vertically: for instance, if one is looking for a package with the primary aim to obtain many descriptive network measures, UCINET or NetMiner would be a good candidate. However, if network visualization is an important objective, Pajek and NetMiner are competing packages.

In two of the six programs, MultiNet and StOCNET, data manipulation obtained the score +− because they contain relatively few options. STRUCTURE received a negative score because it contains hardly any options for data manipulation.

The visualization aspect of UCINET is meager, but this is compensated by export possibilities to specialized network visualization software and the option to call Net-Draw within UCINET. StOCNET does not have any visualization options, but this is compensated via export possibilities to NetMiner and Pajek that score very well with respect to visualization.

The scores for the descriptive, procedure-based, and statistical methods, are indicative of the number of different features. The descriptive methods are rather sparse in MultiNet, StOCNET, and STRUCTURE. They are most comprehensive in NetMiner and UCINET. These programs also contain many procedure-based methods, whereas STRUCTURE has some unique procedures. StOCNET does not contain any procedure-based methods, but has many statistical methods, more, and more advanced, than the other programs. The statistical methods in Pajek are so limited that they score a 0 (although there is the possibility to call statistical routines in R). The statistical methods in STRUCTURE are also limited, but exclusive. The other three programs do contain a number of – sometimes exclusive – statistical methods, but they are presented uncritically, whereas some warning would definitely be warranted for the ANOVA procedures, estimation of the $p*$ model, and QAP regression.

In our opinion, the manual of STRUCTURE is the best because it contains both good practical information and a theoretical background. The completeness of the manual shows that it was developed in the pre-Internet era, and that it was – and still is – used for educational purposes. MultiNet's manual is, at the time of writing, incomplete, but the program has good, interactive, online help. Pajek's manual is so poorly instructive, that we scored it negatively. Without additional information, provided via the book by De Nooy et al. (2004), it is very difficult to use Pajek to its full extent. The fact that Pajek does not have an online help function is a further drawback.

We see some connection between the support offered in the various packages and their authors and development period. Except for NetMiner, the developers of all packages are or were rather active in the social network analysis community. Authors with a social science background (UCINET, STRUCTURE) are very able and experienced in communicating their methods and incorporating them in social theories. Packages with authors with a mixed background (both social and mathematical/computational; MultiNet, StOCNET) offer less social theory. The more mathematical orientation of the authors shows in Pajek, where the user is supposed to know what he or she wants. The most commercial – nonacademic – developers of NetMiner have been able to profit from the experience of previously developed software to join completeness and user friendliness.

The insufficient manual and lack of online help is the reason of the +− score for Pajek's user friendliness. STRUCTURE obtains a +− score because of its age. We find that it would be worthwhile to upgrade STRUCTURE or to incorporate it into one of the existing programs. The same applies to GRADAP. With respect to user friendliness, NetMiner stands out because of its interface where visualization, data, and procedures are integrated.

It remains, however, hard to compare the different packages, as we already pointed out at the beginning of this section. We leave it to the reader of this chapter to decide which software to use for the social network analysis he or she wants to do.

Acknowledgments

We thank Vladimir Batagelj, Ghi-Hoon Ghim, Andrej Mrvar, Bill Richards, and Andrew Seary for making their software available; Wouter de Nooy for his help with the documentation on Pajek; and the editors Peter Carrington, John Scott, and Stanley Wasserman, as well as Vladimir Batagelj, Steve Borgatti, Ron Burt, Ghi-Hoon Ghim, Andrej Mrvar, Andrew Seary, Michael Schweinberger, and Tom Snijders for their valuable comments and suggestions. This research was supported by the Social Science Research Council of the Netherlands Organization for Scientific Research (NWO), grant 400-20-020.

Table 13.4.13. *URLs of All Reviewed Programs and Software Toolkits*

Program	Ver.	URL
Agna	2.1.1	`http://www.geocities.com/imbenta/agna/index.htm`
Blanche	4.6.5	`http://www.spcomm.uiuc.edu/Projects/TECLAB/BLANCHE/`
FATCAT	4.2	`http://www.sfu.ca/~richards/Pages/fatcat.htm`
GRADAP	2.0	`http://www.assess.com/Software/GRADAP.htm`
Iknow	—	`http://www.spcomm.uiuc.edu/Projects/TECLAB/IKNOW/`
InFlow	3.0	`http://www.orgnet.com/`
KliqFinder	0.05	`http://www.msu.edu/~kenfrank/software.htm`
MultiNet	4.38	`http://www.sfu.ca/~richards/Multinet/Pages/multinet.htm`
NEGOPY	4.30	`http://www.sfu.ca/~richards/Pages/negopy4.html`
NetDraw	1.0	`http://www.analytictech.com/downloadnd.htm`
NetMiner II	2.4.0	`http://www.netminer.com/NetMiner/home01.jsp`
NetVis	2.0	`http://www.netvis.org/`
Pajek	1.00	`http://vlado.fmf.uni-lj.si/pub/networks/pajek/default.htm`
PermNet	0.94	`http://www.meijigakuin.ac.jp/~rtsuji/en/software.html`
PGRAPH	2.7	`http://eclectic.ss.uci.edu/~drwhite/pgraph/`
ReferralWeb	2.0	`http://www.cs.washington.edu/homes/kautz/referralweb/`
SM LinkAlyzer	2.1	`http://www.md-logic.com/id142.htm`
SNAFU	2.0	`http://innovationinsight.com/networks.html`
Snowball	—	`http://stat.gamma.rug.nl/snijders/socnet.htm`
StOCNET	1.5	`http://stat.gamma.rug.nl/stocnet/`
STRUCTURE	4.2	`http://gsbwww.uchicago.edu/fac/ronald.burt/teaching/`
UCINET	6.55	`http://www.analytictech.com/ucinet.htm`
visone	1.1	`http://www.visone.de/`
JUNG	1.4.3	`http://jung.sourceforge.net/index.html`
MatMan	1.1	`http://www.noldus.com/products/index.html?matman/index`
PREPSTAR	1.0	`http://kentucky.psych.uiuc.edu/pstar/index.html`
SNA	0.44	`http://legba.casos.ri.cmu.edu/R.stuff/`
SNAP	2.5	`http://www.soc.ucsb.edu/faculty/friedkin/Software/Software.htm`
yFiles	2.2.1	`http://www.yworks.com`
KrackPlot	3.0	`http://www.andrew.cmu.edu/~krack/`
Mage	2.1	`http://kinemage.biochem.duke.edu/kinemage/kinemage.html`

Endnotes

1. Except **FATCAT**.
2. A very helpful and well-written textbook by De Nooy, Mrvar, and Batagelj on using **Pajek** for exploratory network analysis is forthcoming.
3. Snijders and Van Duijn (1997) analyzed another dichotomization of the EIES data: not knowing/having met versus having met/being friends. They found different effects (especially effects of the attribute citation) influencing the evolution of the "meeting" network.

References

Table 13.4.13 provides the URLs of all reviewed programs and software toolkits. Most packages, or information on the software, can also be obtained via the software pages of the INSNA website at http://www.insna.org/INSNA/soft_inf.html.

Batagelj, V., and Mrvar, A. (1998). Pajek: A program for large network analysis. *Connections, 21,* 47–57.

Batagelj, V., and Mrvar, A. (2003). Pajek. Analysis and visualization of large networks. In Jünger, M., and Mutzel, P. (eds.), *Graph Drawing Software,* pages 77–144. New York: Springer.

Batagelj, V., and Mrvar, A. (2004). *Pajek: Package for Large Networks, Version 1.00.* Ljubljana: University of Ljubljana.

Benta, I. M. (2004). *Agna, Version 2.1.1.* Cork: University College Cork, Ireland.

Bock, R. D., and Husain, S. Z. (1950). An adaptation of Holzinger's B-coefficients for the analysis of sociometric data. *Sociometry, 13,* 146–153.

Boer, P., de Negro, R., Huisman, M., Snijders, T. A. B., Steglich, C.E.G., and Zeggelink, E. P. H. (2004). *StOCNET: An Open Software System for the Advanced Statistical Analysis of Social Networks, Version 1.5.* Groningen: ICS / Science Plus Group, University of Groningen.

Bonacich, P. (1972). Factoring and weighting approaches to status scores and clique identification. *Journal of Mathematical Sociology, 2,* 113–120.

Borgatti, S. P. (2002). *NetDraw 1.0: Network Visualization Software, Version 1.0.0.21.* Harvard: Analytic Technologies.

Borgatti, S. P., Everett, M. G., and Freeman, L. C. (2002). *UCINET 6 for Windows: Software for Social Network Analysis.* Harvard: Analytic Technologies.

Brandes, U., and Wagner, D. (2003). visone. Analysis and visualization of social networks. In Jünger, M., and Mutzel, P. (eds.), *Graph Drawing Software,* pages 321–340. New York: Springer.

Burt, R. S. (1976). Positions in networks. *Social Forces, 55,* 93–122.

Burt, R. S. (1991). *STRUCTURE, Version 4.2.* New York: Columbia University.

Butts, C. T. (2004). *Package SNA: Tools for Social Network Analysis, Version 0.44.* Irvine: University of California.

Contractor, N. S., O'Keefe, B. J., and Jones, P. M. (1997). *Iknow: Inquiring Knowledge Networks on the Web.* Urbana–Champaign: University of Illinois.

Crouch, B., and Wasserman, S. (1998). A practical guide to fitting $p*$ social network models. *Connections, 21,* 87–101.

Cummings, J. N. (2003). *NetVis Module – Dynamic Visualization of Social Networks.* Cambridge: Massachusetts Institute of Technology.

Cyram. (2004). *Cyram NetMiner II, Version 2.4.0.* Seoul: Cyram Co., Ltd.

De Nooy, W., Mrvar, A., and Batagelj, V. (2004). *Exploratory Social Network Analysis with Pajek.* Cambridge: Cambridge University Press.

Doreian, P. (1980). Linear models with spatially distributed data. *Sociological Methods & Research, 9,* 29–60.

Doreian, P., Batagelj, V., and Ferligoj, A. (2004). Positional analysis of sociometric data. In Carrington P. J., Scott, J., and Wasserman, S. (eds.), *Models and Methods in Social Network Analysis,* pages 77–97. Cambridge: Cambridge University Press.

Everett, M. G., and Borgatti, S. P. (2004). Extending centrality. In Carrington, P. J., Scott, J., and Wasserman, S. (eds.), *Models and Methods in Social Network Analysis,* pages 57–76. Cambridge: Cambridge University Press.

Everton, S. F. (2002). *A Guide for the Visually Perplexed: Visually Representing Social Networks.* Stanford: Stanford University. Available from: http://www.stanford.edu/group/esrg/siliconvalley/sivnap.html.

Frank, K. A. (1995). Identifying cohesive subgroups. *Social Networks, 17,* 27–56.

Frank, K. A. (1996). Mapping interactions within and between cohesive subgroups. *Social Networks, 18,* 93–119.

Frank, K. A. (2003). *KliqFinder for Windows, Version 0.05.* East Lansing: Michigan State University.

Frank, O., and Snijders., T. A. B. (1994). Estimating the size of hidden populations using snowball sampling. *Journal of Official Statistics, 10,* 53–67.

Freeman, L. C. (1979). Centrality in social networks: conceptual clarification. *Social Networks, 1,* 35–41.

Freeman, L. C. (2004). Graphical techniques for exploring social network data. In Carrington, P. J., Scott, J., and Wasserman, S. (eds.), *Models and Methods in Social Network Analysis*, pages 248–269. Cambridge: Cambridge University Press.

Freeman, S. C., and Freeman L. C. (1979). *The Networks Network: A Study of the Impact of a New Communications Medium on Sociometric Structure*. Social Science Research Reports No. 46. Irvine: University of California.

Friedkin, N. E. (2001). *SNAP: Social Network Analysis Procedures for GAUSS, Version 2.5*. Maple Valley, WA: Aptech Systems, Inc.

Geyer, C. J., and Thompson, E. A. (1992). Constrained Monte Carlo maximum likelihood for dependent data. *Journal of the Royal Statistical Society B*, *54*, 657–699.

Hagen, G. (2003). *Social Network Analysis Functional Utility (SNAFU), Version 2.0*. Wesley Chapel, FL: Innovation Insight.

Harary, F., and White, D. R. (2001). P-Systems: a structural model for kinship studies. *Connections*, *24*, 22–33.

Holland, P. W., and Leinhardt, S. (1981). An exponential family of probability distributions for directed graphs. *Journal of the American Statistical Association*, *76*, 33–50.

Huisman, M., and Van Duijn, M. A. J. (2003). StOCNET: Software for the statistical analysis of social networks. *Connections*, *25*, 7–26.

Hyatt, A., Contractor, N., Ferrone, T., Han, K. K., Hsu, F., Kochhar, S., Palazzo, E., Chunke, S., and Willard, B. (2004). *Blanche, Version 4.6.5*. Urbana–Champaign: University of Illinois.

Katz, L. (1953). A new status index derived from sociometric analysis. *Psychometrika*, *18*, 39–43.

Kautz, H., Selman, B., and Shah, M. (1997). The hidden web. *American Association for Artificial Intelligence Magazine*, *18*, 27–36.

Krackhardt, D. (1987). QAP partialling as a test of spuriousness. *Social Networks*, *9*, 171–186.

Krackhardt, D., Blythe, J., and McGrath, C. (1994). KrackPlot 3: An improved network drawing program. *Connections*, *17*, 53–55.

Krebs, V. E. (2002). *InFlow, Version 3.0*. Cleveland: Orgnet.com.

MDLogix. (2002). *SocioMetrica LinkAlyzer, Version 2.1*. Towson, MD: Medical Decision Logic, Inc.

Molloy, M., and Reed, B. (1995). A critical point for random graphs with a given degree sequence. *Random Structures and Algorithms*, *6*, 161–179.

Noldus Information Technology. (2004). *MatMan, Version 1.1 for Windows*. Wageningen: Noldus Information Technology bv.

Nowicki, K., and Snijders, T. A. B. (2001). Estimation and prediction for stochastic blockstructures. *Journal of the American Statistical Association*, *96*, 1077–1087.

Ord, K. (1975). Estimation methods for models of spatial interaction. *Journal of the American Statistical Association*, *70*, 120–126.

Pattison, P., and Wasserman, S. (1995). Constructing algebraic models for local social networks using statistical methods. *Journal of Mathematical Psychology*, *39*, 57–72.

Pattison, P., Wasserman, S., Robins, G., and Kanfer, A. (2000). Statistical evaluation of algebraic constraints for social networks. *Journal of Mathematical Psychology*, *44*, 536–568.

Richards, W. D. (1995). *NEGOPY, Version 4.30*. Burnaby: Simon Fraser University.

Richards, W. D., and Seary, A. J. (1993). *FATCAT, Version 4.2*. Burnaby: Simon Fraser University.

Richards, W. D., and Seary, A. J. (2000). Eigen analysis of networks. *Journal of Social Structure*, *1*. Available from: http://www2.heinz.cmu.edu/project/INSNA/joss/ean.html.

Richards, W. D., and Seary, A. J. (2003). *MultiNet, Version 4.38 for Windows*. Burnaby: Simon Fraser University.

Richardson, D. C. (2001). *Mage, Version 6.00*. Durham: Duke University.

Schweinberger, M., and Snijders, T. A. B. (2003). Settings in social networks: a measurement model. In Sobel, M. E. (ed.) *Sociological Methodology 2003*, pages 307–341. Boston: Basil Blackwell.

Scott, T. (1991). Network models. In Burt, R. S. (ed.), *STRUCTURE, Version 4.2 Reference Manual*. New York: Columbia University.

Seary, A. J. (1999). *PSPAR: Sparse Matrix Version of PSTAR*. Burnaby: Simon Fraser University.

Seary, A. J. (2003). *The MultiNet Eigenspaces Module*. Report for SAR 897–5. Burnaby: Simon Fraser University.

Seary, A. J., and Richards, W. D. (2000). Fitting to p^* models in MultiNet. *Connections*, *23*, 84–101.

Snijders, T. A. B. (1991). Enumeration and simulation models for 0–1 matrices with given marginals. *Psychometrika*, *56*, 397–417.

Snijders, T. A. B. (1994). *SNOWBALL*. Groningen: University of Groningen.

Snijders, T. A. B. (2001). The statistical evaluation of social network dynamics. In Sobel, M. E., and Becker, M. P. (eds.), *Sociological Methodology*, pages 361–395. London: Basil Blackwell.

Snijders, T. A. B. (2002). Markov chain Monte Carlo estimation of exponential random graph models. *Journal of Social Structure*, *3*. Available from: http://zeeb.library.cmu.edu:7850/JoSS/snijders/Mcpstar.pdf.

Snijders, T. A. B. (2004). Models for longitudinal network data. In Carrington, P. J., Scott, J., and Wasserman, S. (eds.), *Models and Methods in Social Network Analysis*, pages 215–247. Cambridge: Cambridge University Press.

Snijders, T. A. B., and Van Duijn, M. A. J. (1997). Simulation for statistical inference in dynamic network models. In Conte, R., Hegselmann, R., and Terna, P. (eds.), *Simulating Social Phenomena*, pages 493–512. Berlin: Springer.

Snijders, T. A. B., and Van Duijn, M. A. J. (2002). Conditional maximum likelihood estimation under various specifications of exponential random graph models. In Hagberg, J. (ed.), *Contributions to Social Network Analysis, Information Theory, and Other Topics in Statistics; A Festschrift in honour of Ove Frank*, pages 117–134. Stockholm: University of Stockholm, Department of Statistics.

Sprenger, C. J. A., and Stokman, F. N. (1989). *GRADAP: Graph Definition and Analysis Package, Version 2.0*. Groningen: iec. *Pro*GAMMA.

Tsuji, R. (1997). *PermNet, Version 0.94*. Sapporo: Hokkaido University.

Van Duijn, M. A. J., Snijders, T. A. B., and Zijlstra, B. J. H. (2004). p_2: a random effects model with covariates for directed graphs. *Statistica Neerlandica*, *58*, 234–254.

Wasserman, S., and Faust, K. (1994). *Social Network Analysis: Methods and Applications*, pages 148–161. Cambridge: Cambridge University Press.

Wasserman, S., and Pattison, P. (1996). Logit models and logistic regression for social networks: I. An introduction to Markov graphs and p^*. *Psychometrika*, *61*, 401–425.

Wasserman, S., and Robins, G. (2004). An introduction to random graphs, dependence graphs, and p^*. In Carrington, P. J., Scott, J., and Wasserman, S. (eds.), *Models and Methods in Social Network Analysis*, pages 148–161. Cambridge: Cambridge University Press.

White, D. R., Batagelj, V., and Mrvar, A. (1999). Analyzing large kinship and marriage networks with PGRAPH and Pajek. *Social Science Computer Review*, *17*, 245–274.

White, S., O'Madadhain, J., Fisher, D., and Boey, Y. B. (2004). *JUNG, Version 1.4.3*. Irvine: University of California.

White, D. R., and Skyhorse. (1997). *PGRAPH: Representation and Analytic Program for Kinship and Marriage Networks, Version 2.7 for Windows*. Irvine: University of California.

*y*Works. (2004). *yFiles, Version 2.2.1*. Tübingen, Germany: *y*Works, GmbH.

Index

Other books in the series (*continued from page iii*):